Western Mediterranean Europe

A Historical Geography of Italy, Spain and Southern France since the Neolithic

Western Mediterranean Europe

A Historical Geography of Italy, Spain and Southern France since the Neolithic

Catherine Delano Smith

Department of Geography,
University of Nottingham, England

1979

Academic Press

London   New York   Toronto   Sydney   San Francisco

A Subsidiary of Harcourt Brace Jovanovich, Publishers

ACADEMIC PRESS INC. (LONDON) LTD.
24/28 Oval Road,
London NW1

United States Edition published by
ACADEMIC PRESS INC.
111 Fifth Avenue
New York, New York 10003

British Library Cataloguing in Publication Data
Smith, Catherine Delano
   Western Mediterranean Europe.
   1. Europe, Southern - Historical geography
   I. Title
   911'.4   D974   78-73878

   ISBN 0-12-210450-1

PRINTED IN GREAT BRITAIN BY
WILLMER BROTHERS LTD.,
BIRKENHEAD

Preface

This is a book about the past in a certain part of Europe, seen through the eyes of a geographer. The selected area is western Mediterranean Europe, that is, Italy, Spain and the southern part of France, forming a small part only of the Mediterranean world as a whole. The time period in question is the last seven millennia. The period begins with the introduction of farming and permanent settlement into the western Mediterranean and merges into the historically known about half way through the first millennium B.C. This, therefore, is a historical geography which begins with the Neolithic.

The approach, however, is retrospective. One geographer, in speaking of ''the enduring qualities of the eternal present'' in Mediterranean lands (Houston, 1964, p. 135), has voiced the respect and affection of generations of scholars for what has been seen as the traditional way of life in these lands. The precise details of this way of life are generally left rather vague. Perhaps this has been because, to those well-versed in classical literature and art, scenes that were still common all over Mediterranean Europe in the second half of the nineteenth century, and which are by no means rare today, seem too familiar to question. A description of the tiny island of Ibiza, first written down in 1234 (and quoted in full in Cardona, 1976, p. 20), might as well apply to earlier as to later times in its portrayal of the essentials of the Mediterranean landscape and pattern of life. It refers to:

> . . . the castle and the township . . . saltpans . . . [their] ports and passages to the sea and over land, freshwater and brackish water, lagoons, trees, pastures, grazings, hills, plains, mountains, arable land and fallow, woodland, demesne and garrigue, ... fortresses, buildings . . .

Why, then, should it not be assumed that these words would serve also to summarize the landscape and life of Mediterranean Europe in prehistoric times, even in the Neolithic? This is the major thesis of the book.

Of course, there have been many changes throughout this long period, though change, it must be remembered, may be of form rather than of substance. Given that there has been but a limited range of ways of making a living from the land in western Mediterranean Europe, the range of potential life-styles has been correspondingly restricted. Moreover, change in this area, even since the Neolithic, has been not only in people's social, economic and technological activities, and associated patterns of settlement and land use, but also in the physical environment. It is probably true, as Marc Bloch pointed out (1932, p. xxv), that within each generation people as a rule notice their environment only when "change is afoot and the changes are sudden". Nevertheless, classical and modern authorities alike have recognized the essential continuity of the geomorphological processes that tend towards a final levelling of the earth's surface, through the wearing down of mountains and the filling up of the oceanic hollows; the dramatic and sudden, in fact, is comparatively rare. Translated into economic terms, however, even apparently modest physical changes may have had considerable local significance and, when aggregated, might have held far-reaching implications for society in general. In a historical geography of Mediterranean Europe since the Neolithic, therefore, physical change cannot be ignored.

It might be argued that a historical account should start at the beginning. It is precisely the beginning of the Mediterranean way of life, however, about which least is known. Fewer facts are available for the prehistoric period (which involves two-thirds of our timespan) than for the historic or even for the last hundred years, and their interpretation is liable to be correspondingly more subjective. It is doubly important, therefore, that the practices of recent times are closely studied and adequately understood. This means that a strictly chronological approach is less than satisfactory for a book of this nature. Instead, an attempt is made to observe, first of all, precisely how lives really were lived at all social levels in Mediterranean Europe during the historical period. Inevitably, the tenor is empirical. Interpretations are made, sometimes with deliberate provocation but usually with caution, bearing in mind the state of research into the many geographical aspects of the past in Mediterranean Europe.

In fact, it has to be admitted at the outset, this is a book destined soon to be rewritten. New information about many facets of this lengthy period is becoming available almost daily as the pace and the critical climate of historical and archaeological research quicken. The new evidence will lead to new thinking and to reassessment. Specialists will contribute to revisions. But there comes a time in the history of every subject when a total review is necessary, if only better to see the way forward. It is in this spirit of inter-disciplinary interest in the Mediterranean heritage of Europe that this book has been written.

July, 1979   C. DELANO SMITH

Contents

A*

List of Illustrations

Plates

Figures

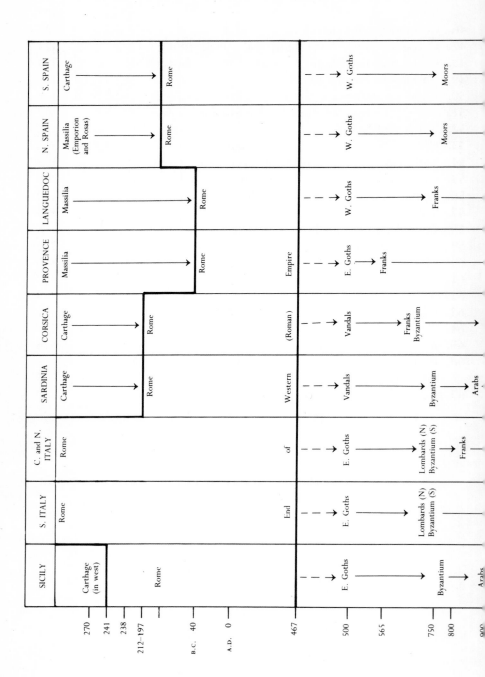

Date	SICILY	S. ITALY	C. and N. ITALY	SARDINIA	CORSICA	PROVENCE	LANGUEDOC	N. SPAIN	S. SPAIN
270	Carthage (in west)	Rome	Rome	Carthage	Carthage	Massilia	Massilia	Massilia (Emporion and Rosas)	Carthage
241									
238	Rome								
212–197				Rome	Rome				
B.C. 40						Rome	Rome	Rome	Rome
A.D. 0									
467		End	of	Western	(Roman)	Empire			
500	E. Goths	E. Goths	E. Goths	Vandals	Vandals	E. Goths	W. Goths	W. Goths	W. Goths
565						Franks			
750	Byzantium	Lombards (N) Byzantium (S)	Lombards (N) Byzantium (S)	Byzantium	Franks Byzantium	Franks	Franks	Moors	Moors
800			Franks	Arabs					
900	Arabs								

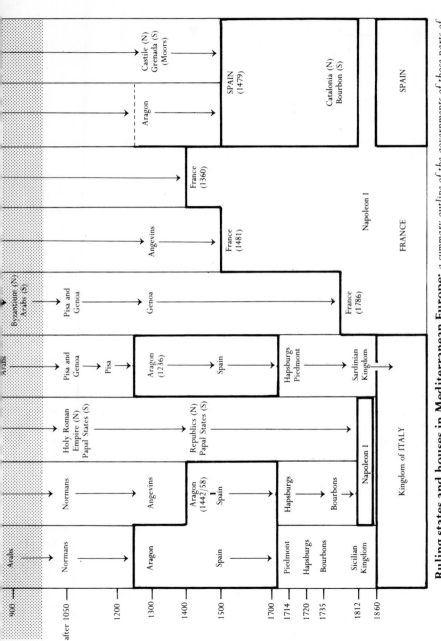

Ruling states and houses in Mediterranean Europe: *a summary outline of the governments of those parts of western Mediterranean Europe dealt with in this book.*

Acknowledgements

In the course of many years of research into various aspects of the historical geography of Mediterranean Europe, I have accumulated a very large debt of gratitude. I am grateful for practical and financial aid, academic help and advice, friendship and encouragement from so many in England and abroad that it is impossible to thank each one. The following acknowledgements record my debt only to those most directly involved in the production of this text.

Generous financial help towards the cost of fieldwork has come, in recent years, from the Aylwin Cotton Foundation (Rome); from my own Oxford college, Lady Margaret Hall, who elected me to the Susette Taylor Travelling Fellowship in 1976–1977; and from the British Academy and the British School at Rome. For help in the field, I should like to thank Dr F. Calvo (Murcia), Professor J. and Mrs L. Jehasse (Alèria), M. Liègeois (Sartène), Dr E. Llogbregat (Alicante), H. Prades (Lattes), C. Puxeddu (Mogoro) and Professor S. and Mrs F. Tinè (Genoa). Particularly, I owe my cousin, M. Raskolnikoff (C.N.R.S., Paris), thanks for many hours of sometimes tedious fieldwork. Dr M. Tizzoni (Milan) not only painstakingly translated an earlier book of mine into Italian, and several documents from late-medieval Latin into English, but has proved admirable in expediting many an urgently needed but elusive text. I should also like to thank Mrs Patience Bradford for permission to quote from Charles Singer's letters to her late husband, John Bradford, and for the use of her negatives in Plate 10.

In Nottingham I have received much help on the technical side. Mrs E. Pyper carried out the sediment analyses and Dr H. Fox programmed the results. The drawings have been done by K. Bowler, T. Murfin, C. Walter and the late M. Cutler. D. Jones has helped with the photographs, and R. Hudson and G. Hubbuck with the typing. Perhaps the biggest burden fell on Mrs E. O. Wigginton, who typed and retyped my drafts with predictable good humour, insight and skill and who provided timely encouragement. I am grateful, too, to Professor J. P. Cole and Dr P. T. Wheeler (Nottingham) for many useful discussions and to Dr R. Bradshaw (Nottingham) and Alan Griffiths (London) for help with references. Several people have commented on parts of the early drafts; Drs B. Hamilton (Nottingham), R. Whitehouse (Lancaster), G. Barker (Sheffield), P. T. Wheeler (Nottingham), Professor C. A. M. King (Nottingham) and Mr J. B. Ward-Perkins (late of British School at Rome). Dr Wheeler and Mr J. F. McCleary have kindly helped with the proofs. It has to be said, of course, that notwithstanding generous comment and criticism, without which I would be the poorer, the ultimate responsibility is my own.

There are, finally, four debts of a different order that I should like to put on record. My interest in Mediterranean Europe was nascent by the time I was an undergraduate, but I have always been grateful to my supervisor, Dr J. M. Houston, for fostering it. I have been grateful, too, to the late Professor Sir Ian Richmond for giving me the opportunity of becoming involved in the late John Bradford's Apulia project and to Sir Lawrence Kirwan, who once encouraged me not to give up. Above all else, however, it was my late mother's patience, understanding and selflessness over the years which made all possible.

C. DELANO SMITH

In grateful memory of my mother

Part I

People

Part I

People

1

The People of Mediterranean Europe

Like history, geography is in the final analysis about people. There are today about 97 million people in the three countries that constitute the Mediterranean Europe of this book: 55 million in Italy, 35 million in Spain, and over 7 million in southern France. This is more than double the population of 120 years ago. It is generally accepted, however, that this explosive demographic increase is peculiar to the nineteenth and twentieth centuries and that throughout the preceding 2000 years of historic and protohistoric times alone, the total number of people living in Mediterranean Europe would never have approached levels reached even in the middle of the nineteenth century.

Curiously, even though Mediterranean Europe has become relatively crowded during the last century or two, the way of life of most of the people has remained much the same as throughout the past in so far as it is essentially agricultural and largely rural. As late as the 1950s, nearly half (42%) of the Italian working population was agriculturally employed. So were 27% of those in Spain and 30% in southern France. In the past, the proportion directly and indirectly dependent on the land for their subsistence and livelihood would have been nearer 70 or 80%.

The form this dependence took was far more diverse than it is today. Some people were born, or arrived, high in the social scale and would scarcely visit their country estates let alone stoop to the plough or bend to the sickle. Others lived their entire lives ruled by the rising and setting of the sun and by the agricultural seasons. These people lived in a restricted world, composed of the fields they worked and bounded by the horizon of their village. A minority toiled in the fields for their livelihood but dwelt in towns with traders, merchants and artisans as neighbours. Viewing the three situations rather broadly, each one can be seen as concerning farming in one way or another. The people's food came from land they owned if not from land they themselves worked whole time or part time.

A threefold division of the people of Mediterranean Europe into landowners, peasants and urban farmers by no means does justice to the immense variety of ways in which people gained their livelihood from the land or were organized in their agricultural employment or to the subtlety of socio-economic distinctions. It is useful in the context of this book, though, in providing a simple framework for the identification of those individual social and economic features found in Mediterranean Europe in historic and prehistoric times which have been essential and permanent. In this respect, an elementary grouping of the varied sectors of population and of their ways of living or making a livelihood makes possible comparisons through time as well as across space. The question then arises, for example, as to whether the earliest Neolithic farmers of Mediterranean Europe can be described in precisely the same terms as those of Roman times, 5000 years later, or of more recent times, nearly 7000 years later.

Past Populations

The total population in Mediterranean Europe has doubled in the 120 years that have elapsed since 1850. It had also doubled during the preceding period, between the 1590s and the mid-nineteenth century (data for these dates cited by Braudel, 1972, p. 393ff). But it had twice as long to do so. The resultant demographic curve is of familiar outline: the astonishing upswing of the last century started in the late seventeenth century and accelerated in the nineteenth (Fig. 1a). Previously, throughout the historic period, the trend appears to have been more or less level. Few would disagree with McNiell's view that a persistent expansion of population like that of recent times is exceptional in the context of the entire human venture upon earth (McNiell, 1977, p. 103), though to us today, living in and part of this exceptional growth phase, the concept of a static level may demand not a little mental adjustment.

It is generally assumed that there were very many more people living in Mediterranean Europe in historic than in prehistoric times and that the Neolithic population would have been very small indeed compared with

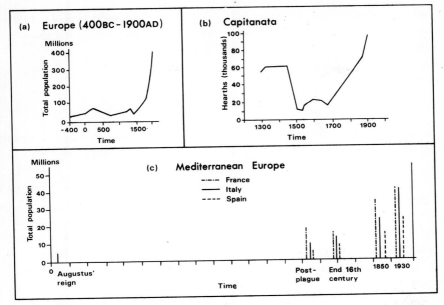

Fig. 1. *Aspects of the population curve.* Schlicher von Bath's graph (a) may be taken as representing the standard European curve for the historic period. The main Roman and late medieval peaks and the post-Roman and post-medieval troughs are clearly brought out. Not all regional trends, however, exactly conform to this generalized curve, as in the case of the province of Capitanata (now Foggia) (b). There, the post-medieval decline appears to start quite late while recovery was not completed until well into the nineteenth century. This protracted demographic "low" has to be associated with, above all else, local economic developments associated with the creation of institutionalized grazing, a view also expressed by Afan de Rivera in 1833. Of the 36 or so *villages* deserted in the province, the majority declined or were abandoned in this period. (The graph is based on data from Egidi 1920, Beloch 1961, and the censuses of 1861ff. In 1861, average family size in Capitanata was 4·45 persons, and this figure has been used to convert figures from Egidi and the census into hearths.) In (c) the total population in the later historic period of three countries considered in this book is set out for comparison.

that of the Middle Ages. It is also widely argued that the economic developments that contributed to the Neolithic (domestication of plants and animals, the emergence of mixed farming, and the concomitant creation of the permanent village) could not have failed to have led to a population explosion of an order comparable to that of modern times.

While the latter is an attractive idea, both it and the assumption of a steady upward momentum in the demographic curve from prehistoric times to the eighteenth century A.D. merit discussion.

The Demographic Curve in Historic Times

In the middle of the sixteenth century A.D., Italy was one of the most densely populated countries in the whole of Europe. Excluding the islands, the population has been estimated at 10 338 000 (Beloch, 1961, p. 349 ff). Fifteen-and-a-half centuries earlier, at the time of the census held during Augustus's reign, it was possibly about 7 000 000 (Brunt, 1971, p. 131). The net demographic gain, therefore, in Italy in the entire historic period up to the 1550s was less than 48%. That was slightly lower than the net gain estimated for the interval between 225 B.C. and the Augustan census in A.D. 14, when the Italian population may have grown from 5 to 7 million. The point to be emphasized in these paragraphs is that the ''steady state'' of the demographic curve throughout the historic period was in reality composed of a sequence of peaks and depressions and that it is essential to place correctly the population of a given region at any one moment in relation to these oscillations.

Roman census figures are impressive for the continuity and length of the run (at least 43 censuses were conducted between 508 B.C. and A.D. 47) and for the illusion of substance. So many uncertainties and problems however are associated with the extant figures that many would agree with Toynbee ''to discount their value as historical evidence'' (Toynbee, 1965, Vol. I, p. 440). [1] Because of the difficulties of separating urban and rural inhabitants from regional totals, Duncan-Jones, for instance, prefers to place greater reliance on epigraphic sources for an estimate of Roman urban populations than on the census data (1974, p. 272). This is not the view of Brunt who, after an exhaustive examination, concludes that ''to reject all the returns [on grounds of defectiveness] is a counsel of despair, which it needs stronger arguments to justify'' (1971, p. 83). Even so, the richest period for reliable historic demographic data in Mediterranean Europe starts not much earlier than the fourteenth century. There are earlier sources. The Arab administration in Spain carried out population counts in the eighth century and population lists were also often included in the *Repartimiento* (land distribution schedules) of the Reconquest (Mols, 1965, p. 45). But contemporary interest in population numbers in the medieval and post-medieval period was generally confined to the taxable element. The sources give details not of the total population but of *taxa boccarum* or *focularium* ("mouth" and hearth taxes, respectively) in Italy or of *vechinos* (tax-paying householders) in Spain. [2] These non-demographic entities have then to be converted into a total population figure by use of a multiplier representing what is thought to have been the average family or household size of the time. In the kingdom of Naples, tax figures for individual localities are not available until the eighteenth century. Prior to that, only the total amount of tax due from each district was recorded (Beloch, 1937, Vol. I, p. 169ff). Again, the problem is that of distinguishing the urban from the rural tax-payers (Mols, 1959, Vol. II, p. 26ff). Where these problems can be overcome, the results are often rewarding. For instance, the thirteenth-century *Liber Focorum* of Pistoia in Tuscany is described by Herlihy as part of "the oldest and possibly the richest series of population records which exists for any Italian countryside" (1967, p. 55).

One undoubted characteristic of the medieval and post-medieval population curve in Mediterranean Europe, as in Europe in general, is the pattern of alternating peaks and depressions. On a broad scale, these demographic oscillations form a generally applicable pattern, with four major phases between the eighth and seventeenth century. At the same time, a less publicized characteristic is the often extreme individuality of demographic history at local level. There is no conflict in these two characteristics. Authoritative detailed local studies are becoming increasingly available (see Cipolla, 1965) and these all confirm both the consistency of the general curve and the individual timing or severity of demographic trends at local level.

The medieval period is customarily divided into three main phases, with a "low" prior to the eighth century (on evidence increasingly questioned). Second is a phase of growth from the eight or ninth centuries, culminating in a peak by or about the start of the fourteenth century. Third, there is a phase of intermittent but usually catastrophic downward trend which lasts until about 1500. After this date population levels begin to pick up and in many districts the second half of the sixteenth century is associated with the major demographic expansion of the fourth phase. Pressure of population begins to be a problem again. In Valencia, for instance, population levels had remained fairly steady up to 1565 but in the second half of the sixteenth century there was an astonishing upsurge: in only four decades the total population of the kingdom increased by 50·9% (Lapeyre, 1959, p. 30). While in Valencia most of this rise can be accounted for by the Morisco (''new Christian'') element, and so was checked by their expulsion in 1609, similar trends are found in other regions of Spain as well as in southern France and Italy. This upward trend was usually maintained into the modern period and indeed to the present day. In certain areas, however, such as Apulia in general or Capitanata in particular, local circumstances are reflected in a late-seventeenth-century decline which left the region with no larger a total population at the start of the nineteenth century than it had at the beginning of the fourteenth century (Fig. 1b).

The post-medieval demographic ''low'' involved the pan-European epidemic generally known as the Black Death but certainly was not caused by it. It cannot be denied that some towns and their districts suffered catastrophically, losing a third or even a half of their population directly or indirectly because of the plague between 1347 and 1350. At Pistoia a combination of famine and plague in 1349–1350 carried off more than a quarter of the total population of both city and countryside (Herlihy, 1967, p. 104). However, the plague was neither the sole factor nor was it necessarily the prime factor accounting for the post-medieval ''low''. In many districts the decline was pronounced many years before the plague of 1347–1349. Forty years before the Black Death reached Millau (Languedoc), for example, the urban population had been reduced by one-sixth (Wolff, 1957, cited in Pounds, 1974, p. 154). After the plague it was reduced by another third. Nor was recovery from decimation by the plague necessarily immediate. The population of many Tuscan towns and cities continued to decline long after 1350 and whenever the nadir was reached it could be as low as a quarter of the pre-plague total (Fiume, 1962). In Catalonia and in Languedoc, the ''low'' reached by or after 1450 is thought to have had far greater economic consequence and a more dramatic effect on the agricultural landscape than had the Black Death a century earlier (Le Roy Ladurie, 1972, p. 15ff; Vicens-Vives, 1969, p. 179). In other districts, the post-medieval demographic slump was prolonged still further, as in Apulia. Early in the fourteenth century there were allegedly 300 000–400 000 people in Sardinia. By 1485 there may have been 160 000 (26 263 hearths are recorded). Due to another slump in the second half of the seventeenth century the early figure was not reached until after 1750. (Klapisch-Zuber and Day, 1965, p. 438).

Demographic evidence from Roman times shows that these oscillations were no less characteristic of the early as of the later historic period. It may well have been that the early demographic condition of Italy was unusual for the times. It is generally agreed that it was precisely the unusual strength of demographic levels in Roman Italy that made possible political expansion, conquest and colonization. And it may well be that the price was too great and that the very success of the Roman conquests, with its concomitant effects in the peninsula, may in the longer term have contributed to the late Roman decline. But in its details the Roman demographic curve appears to have had just the same ups and downs as were characteristic in succeeding centuries. One of the most striking of the oscillations is the slump in population levels in the third century B.C. The critical factor must have been the Second Punic War (Toynbee, 1965; Brunt, 1971). Analogy with the consequences of modern periods of war has led some to play down the post-Hannibalic demographic crisis (De Sanctis, 1907–1964, Vol. III; Thiel, 1954). The strain on Roman manpower, however, would have been far greater than on modern manpower, partly because production per person would have been lower in classical times than in the twentieth century and partly because of the longer duration of the war (Brunt, 1971, p. 67). In third-century Italy agricultural production almost certainly declined, not just because of a diminution of the labour force or through actual devastation in the areas of fighting or of marching but also because of epidemics and low levels of nourishment associated with famine. There was some recovery, of course, and Brunt notes that the population was "still growing" in the lifetime of Tiberius Gracchus before stabilizing at a high level by 144 B.C. Then there followed a period of fast natural increase at the close of the Republican era (80–28 B.C.). Some of the consequences of this, or some of the features associated with it, such as the continuing drift to Rome, are seen as proof of bad conditions in the countryside and this underlines some of the problems of identifying the demographic from the socio-economic factors in the early historic evidence.

Notwithstanding such problems, it may be seen that the behaviour of the demographic curve throughout the historic period (which is taken, *sensu largo*, from the second half of the last millenium B.C. to the present day) was consistent until the late eighteenth century. That is, the general level remained relatively steady with only a slight tendency to rise prior to the great upswing of the last two centuries, while accommodating a succession of peaks and depressions. In addition, individual depressions and peaks were of such proportion or duration as to merit singling out as of real significance in their economic, social, and perhaps political, implications. The post-Hannibalic War depression (third century B.C.) and the decline that started in the fourteenth century A.D. are the two cases in point.

It may be asked, then, that if this oscillatory behaviour of the demographic curve throughout the two millennia of the historic period is to be taken as the norm, should not a parallel situation be anticipated for the prehistoric period? On this basis it might be expected that, firstly, the overall level of prehistoric population increased during the four or five millennia in question but not dramatically. Secondly, it might be expected that this more or less "steady state" curve likewise contained a succession of peaks and depressions in population levels. Thirdly, it might be expected that a demographic event of singular order was no less possible in the prehistoric than in the historic period. There are problems, however. There is evidence for a major increase in the total population, at least in the Italian peninsula, prior to its Roman takeover. And there is the postulated Neolithic population explosion. Are these to be seen as instances of proto- and prehistoric demographic pressure similar to the crises of the late sixteenth and the eighteenth century A.D.? Or is the first at least so phenomenal and "unique" an event as to parallel in its relative enormity the population explosion of the nineteenth and twentieth centuries? It is in the light of such questions that the demographic evidence from the prehistoric period has to be reviewed.

Prehistoric Demography

It might as well be said at once that evidence on which to base a demographic curve for the prehistoric period is phantasmagoric. It is scarcely surprising that of the four contributions to the section headed "Population" in a collection of papers published for the Ninth International Conference of Prehistoric and Protohistoric Sciences (held at Nice in September, 1976), three are exclusively concerned with racial aspects and the fourth is medical. Obviously there is no demographic record in the usual sense for the prehistoric period. Demographic data from the prehistoric past can only be indirect and selective in their survival. There are skeletons (such as those on which the racial discussions referred to above were based) but these represent a mere handful of individuals from the untold millions who lived their lives in Mediterranean Europe between, say, 5500 and 500 B.C. Demographic

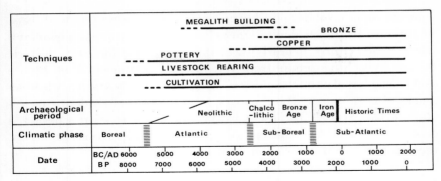

Fig. 2. *The time scale*, showing the major developments of the prehistoric period (from information in *La Préhistoire Française*, 1976).

growth has to be inferred not from remains of the people themselves but from archaeological evidence for the multiplication of their settlements and of their cemeteries or from the density of finds of their belongings. But simple expansion of a settlement or a cemetery is no sure index of an increase in population. There are no grounds for saying (as Potter (1976a, p. 319) did for Narce in the late Bronze Age) that a new suburb represents "sustained population growth" as opposed to the effects of rural-urban migration or of urban reorganization and replanning. As it happens, the countryside around Narce (Etruria) is remarkably well known, archaeologically speaking, and Potter may well be correct, but in other cases far too little is known about the region as a whole for such interpretations to be made.

There is not very much doubt that the significance of the Neolithic agricultural revolution lies in the fact that it provided the means by which population numbers could increase far beyond any level previously possible. On this basis, the commonly voiced idea of a population explosion during the Neolithic is an attractive one. The arguments for it are based on observations of the often remarkable density of Neolithic settlement evidence in regions practically devoid of signs of earlier occupation. In one 40-km^2 area alone in south-east Italy (Trinitapoli, Foggia), for instance, there are traces of no less than 24 settlement sites or possible settlement sites. Of southern France, Audibert wrote nearly two decades ago that the Chalcolithic (late Neolithic) saw a density of occupation never previously reached (Audibert, 1962, p. 55). On the other hand, it is also becoming clearer that the catalytic revolution was itself a very long drawn out series of processes of plant and animal domestication, involving possibly no less than four or five thousand years. The prehistoric past in Mediterranean Europe, as defined in this book, it is worth remembering, is nearly three times as long as the entire historic period. What may appear from this distance in time to have been a prehistoric population "explosion" is rather less convincing when set against that timespan. The demographic explosion of modern times is phenomenal precisely because it has taken place in so short a period, a century or two. The concept of a Neolithic population explosion, therefore, is one that has to be kept in perspective.

There is little more evidence to support the suggestion that a demographic curve for prehistoric times should have similar oscillations between "high" and "low" levels of population to those already observed as characteristic of historic times. In a brief review of the prehistoric anthropology of France, Riquet (1976) notes first a "veritable population explosion" (1976, p. 143) in the late Neolithic and then "a demographic slump, extraordinary because inexplicable . . ." (1976, p. 146) coming between the Chalcolithic and the (middle) Bronze Age. By the time he deals with the La Tène culture of the last millennium B.C. he is speaking in terms of "demographic pressure" (p. 149). In another region of Mediterranean Europe (northern Apulia) a similarly extraordinary hiatus closes the Neolithic and lasts until the late Bronze Age. The absence of recognizable settlement evidence has been taken by some as evidence of total desertion (Trump, 1966, p. 56; Tinè, 1975) but one should also refer to Delano Smith and Smith (1973) and Whitehouse (1974). These slumps involve several hundreds of years and, allowance being made for a slower rate of change, invite comparison with the effect of the Hannibalic War 2000 years later or with the Black Death and other factors in and after the fourteenth century A.D. Eventually it may indeed be possible to demonstrate that in prehistoric times, as in historic, the demographic curve was in reality composed of a sequence of rising and falling population levels, but a very great deal more evidence is needed before this can be established.

The Distribution of Population

The spatial distribution of people is normally conveyed in terms of average population density. In Italy today the average density is 184 inhabitants per square kilometre. In Spain it is 70 inhabitants. Earlier the spread was thinner. In 1861, it was 84 persons per square kilometre in Italy. At the end of the sixteenth century, the average for the whole Mediterranean world may have been nearer 17 inhabitants per square kilometre (Braudel, 1972, p. 397). Taken on such a scale, however, such figures have little real meaning. One of the outstanding and durable characteristics in Mediterranean Europe is that there is today, and appears to have always been, a very uneven distribution of population. On a population map, great wildernesses of emptiness, as Braudel has called them, are broken only by oases of sometimes very dense occupation.

It is perhaps surprising to find that even today there are districts in Mediterranean Europe almost devoid of inhabitants. But many of the less favourable hill and mountain areas are being deserted as backwaters of modern civilization. The nature of the terrain and the problem of accessibility is unsatisfactory for the modern style of living. Of hilly Provence it was said, not so very long ago, that ''man has a quarter of the land . . . and nature three quarters'' (Gachon, 1940, cited by Braudel, 1972, p. 399). In Languedoc, parts of the Garrigues of Montpellier are today a virtual desert. Communes such as Murles, Cazavieille and Argelliers contain two or three inhabitants per square kilometre even though they are less than 30 km from the rapidly growing city of Montpellier. Certain plains in Mediterranean Europe maintain a reputation for an emptiness that was understandable enough in the past when there was malaria or other problems but that is anomalous today. In 1961 the average population density of the Tavoliere of Foggia (Apulia) was 99 persons per square kilometre; in 1861 it was 38 persons. In the eighteenth and nineteenth centuries, this emptiness never failed to strike travellers: ''Puglia is truly a desert . . . without inhabitants'' wrote Galanti in 1788 (Vol. III, p. 125). Much the same is found in Spain, where on the steppelands of Aragon in the sixteenth century one could, it was said, ''walk for days on end without meeting a single inhabitant'' (Davity, 1617, cited by Braudel, 1972, p. 399).

Other parts of Mediterranean Europe became crowded early. The focal points were usually towns, particularly favoured plains, and intermontane basins. In 1595, when the average density of the Kingdom of Naples may have been 57 inhabitants per square kilometre, there were 160 inhabitants per square kilometre around Vesuvius (Beloch, 1937, Vol. I, p. 234). In 1600 the northern plain of Italy had, as now, exceptionally high densities, with 108 persons per square kilometre around Bergamo, 110 around Milan, and 117 around Cremona. The change since then has not always

B

been so great as might be expected. In 1861 Cremona had 184, though density in the province of Milan had already risen to over 500 persons per square kilometre. It was in the *huertas* of Spain that some of the most astonishing population densities were early reached. In 1587 the population of the *huerta* of Murcia numbered 3204 persons (Calvo, 1975). Since the area of irrigated land (*regadio*) totalled between 5844 hectares and 8210 hectares, the average density could not have been much below 400 inhabitants per square kilometre.

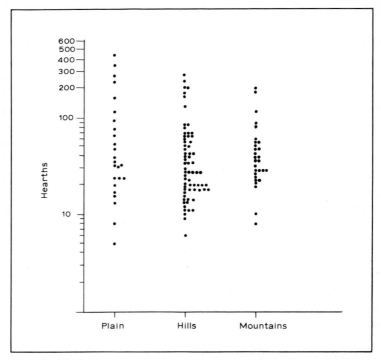

Fig. 3. *Population distribution and settlement.* The thirteenth century *Liber Focorum* (dated *c.* 1244) of Pistoia, Tuscany, shows that although the majority of the free commune's inhabitants lived in the hill regions, there was not a great difference in the size of hill, plain and mountain villages. The maximum range in settlement size was found on the plain, where there was Montemagno (431 hearths; subsequently deserted) at one extreme and the hamlet of Capraia (5 hearths) at the other (data from Herlihy, 1967). Herlihy's own graph of wealth at Pistoia shows that the inhabitants of the plain tended to be better off than those of the mountains and middle hills and that the city harboured the wealthiest of Pistoia's population, though sometimes only through immigration.

Evidence for similar concentrations in Mediterranean Europe is available for Roman times. According to the various estimates of the total population of Augustan Italy (summarized in Duncan-Jones, 1974, p. 274), an average density would have been between 24 and 40 persons per square kilometre if the slave population is excluded. Beloch allowed a density of 22 to 28 persons per square kilometre. This means an average density for Italy in Roman times similar to that of Sardinia, a country highly reputed in Roman times for its fertility and even populousness, at the time of the first modern census in 1861, when it was 28 persons per square kilometre. The spread of the Roman population was as uneven then as it has been more recently. There were complaints of *"solitudo Italiae"* (Brunt, 1971, p. 128) although this was as likely to have been a function then of the pattern of rural settlement and land holding as it was later, rather than of the low level of local population alone. As a result of the devastation of the Hannibalic War in Apulia and of its attendant socio-economic changes, the Tavoliere of Foggia may well have appeared lifeless (*"inanimissima pars Italia"* Cicero, *ad Atticus VIII* 3.4) compared with regions such as Campania, just across the Apennines. Many of these other districts that were densely populated by the Middle Ages were already so characterized in Roman times. This was particularly the case on the northern lowland of Italy, where Strabo referred, for example, to the Cispadane region with its "dense population, the size and wealth of its towns" (V.1.12).

The variable intensity of population distribution in Mediterranean Europe in the past has had interesting consequences. For one thing, the distribution was rarely static for long. Phases of demographic increase would occasion advances of the settlement frontier, clearance of wasteland and resettlement of the interiors, the coastlands or the forests. In addition to these temporal variations there were also spatial implications. For instance, the densely populated districts, particularly the urban ones, were the most liable to food shortage and periodic famines and this had bearing on trade in foodstuffs, particularly cereals. A bad year in the kingdom of Valencia could result in an increase of imported grain by over four times (as in 1435 and 1447) (Rausell Roizas *et al.*, 1974). The kingdom of Castile was normally an exporter of cereals during the mid-fifteenth century, when it was scantly populated, but by the end of the following century, having increased its own population, it had become an importing region (Braudel, 1972, p. 410). Another change associated with demographic pressure concerned land tenure and the organization of farming. For this reason, amongst others, the agrarian regime in Tuscany was completely transformed by the early fourteenth century (Jones, 1968). In reverse, economic stagnation could result from a permanently low density of population and from the absence of demographic pressure as in the case of the former frontier region of Castile (Spain) and of Capitanata (Italy).

The population of Mediterranean Europe, then, has varied in its size and in its distribution during the historic period and so far as can be judged from the evidence, this behaviour was paralleled throughout the prehistoric period. The major demographic event of the post-medieval period that affected most regions of Europe (the fourteenth-century slump) had a counterpart in certain districts at least in early Roman times (the Hannibalic War of the early third century B.C. for instance) and there may have been a parallel decline at the end of the Neolithic. Seven thousand years of human history is, after all, quite long enough for what may be regarded in the short-term view as ''unique'' to be recognized as a repeatable component when the timespan is reviewed in its entirety.

The Social Groups

Mere population numbers, however, are only the starting point. What is of greater consequence is the nature of the population, its economic behaviour and, fundamental to this, its social status. Throughout the historic period it is easy to see that social groupings have not only been complex and intricate but also, in one sense at least, fluid; each period had its parvenus and social climbers and, possibly, its eliminations and developments in the finer divisions. But the essential stratification of the population of Mediterranean Europe has been constant throughout the historic period. It is legitimate, therefore, to talk in terms of a peasantry at one extreme and an aristocracy or élite at the other so long as it is accepted that these are composite terms. It is not to be inferred that the intermediate rankings were unimportant or are to be ignored. On the contrary, much is lost if the internal subdivisions of the two classes used as a broad framework for discussion in this book are not kept always in view. If, for example, the peasant farmer is *sensu stricto* one who owns the land he depends on for his livelihood and who provides from his own family the labour to work it, it does not mean to say that the peasant class as a whole does not also include the landless and the less, as well as the more, successful of the peasant farmers. Those with inadequate land and those with none at all were equally obliged to seek additional or alternative sources of support or income, not necessarily always in agriculture. While some laboured for richer peasants or on the estates of the landowners, others were employed in domestic or rural industries, in textile working or in mining. Similarly, there were members of the élite whose position was not better than that of the most fortunate of the peasants but who were separated from them by a single element, normally of birth, translated into a difference in style rather than standard of living.

The peasant class, it may be said as another generalization, had a single aim; that of working only as much as was necessary to gain subsistence for the family unit. By subsistence is meant here not only all the basic necessities of life (food, clothing, shelter etc.) but also a sufficient surplus of production for the payment of rents, taxes and other dues, either in kind or, after conversion, in money. The landowners had a dual aim. No less than in the case of the peasantry, subsistence had to be assured—food, domestic requirements and money for payments—but in addition each family expected to produce a surplus that was available for disposal as a means to the acquisition of wealth. This wealth might be converted into still more land, be devoted to the patronage of the arts, be used in political manipulations, or remain as a liquid asset. Much less common a use of the landowners' wealth was for reinvestment in the agricultural, still less the non-agricultural, sectors of the economy. Obviously this varied from region to region and from period to period. There were large-scale silk producers, such as Antonia Rospigliosi in thirteenth-century Tuscany, or improvement-minded landlords, such as Bettino Ricasoli in the same region in the nineteenth century or the rice-growing landlords of the Po lowlands before then. But the use of local capital in the furtherance of either agriculture or industry has not been a widespread or durable characteristic of Mediterranean Europe to this day. On the other hand, it would also be overlooking reality to view even the medieval or feudal economies as wholly ''closed'' or ''natural''. As already pointed out, very few of the social groups were able to satisfy all their requirements and to make all payments owed directly and only from the resources of their own land. From both extremes of society, the majority were involved in external transactions of one sort or another, either to make up the shortfall in their own incomes or to dispose of a surplus. Whatever it is called (trade, exchange) and whatever its relative significance at each level of society, this attribute has existed since Neolithic times and in one way or another has been part of the way of life of rural societies in Mediterranean Europe throughout the past.

Peasants and Landowners Defined

As a class, a peasantry can only be found in an evolved society where there is division of social function. According to anthropologists, therefore, both peasants and landowners are by definition part of a single society (Fig. 4). It does not matter that the division of economic function by which a peasant is recognized might be rudimentary so long as it involves production for self (and family) in the first place. Production of a (usually small) surplus for sale or exchange or for payments in kind comes only in second place. More than that, it can be suggested that the peasant farmer specifically avoids being included in an exchange system. He has no wish to be concerned solely with production for a profit-yielding surplus. His chief object is to maintain a home and to support a family independently of the

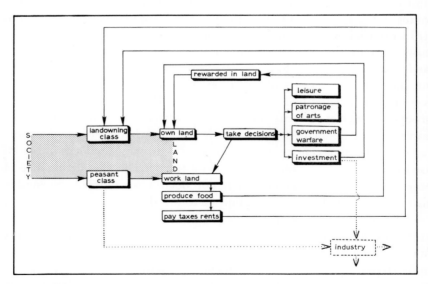

Fig. 4. *The population of Mediterranean Europe* represented as two major classes, with their major opportunities and obligations. In view of the lack of strong industrial development, particularly in recent centuries, this option is shown in "ghost" form.

external factors of an exchange system. Expressed in economic terms, the peasant farmer makes maximum use of his labour force (the members of his family) rather than attempts to make maximum profit from agricultural production. Seen on this scale, the peasant farm group constitutes a world of its own, an *oecumene* that is almost complete economically and certainly so socially.

In its narrowest definition a peasant is owner-occupier and farmer of his own land. More loosely, the peasant class is highly diverse. There can be rich peasants who own far more land than they themselves, with their families, are able to work. Rather than alter their farming system by hiring a labour force, that would have to be paid from a profit obtained by growing commercially viable crops, they lease surplus land to less fortunate neighbours in return for payment in cash, kind or for some informal service. These poor neighbours are also members of the peasant class. So too are those without any land at all, who offer their labour for hire for agricultural work. Those who have insufficient land of their own may be rented the land on which they depend on a cash or share-cropping basis. This was not necessarily an economic disadvantage though it may have been a social one. Jones found that by 1300 there was a system of perpetual tenancies in Tuscany that were little different from peasant properties and indeed often gave rise to them (Jones, 1968, p. 194). There were, too, opportunities for betterment. In periods of agricultural expansion, it was the peasantry who were often the main beneficiaries. Landowners found that the establishment of a peasantry on their estates was one of the most effective ways of colonizing or reclaiming land. Periods of labour shortage tended to result in the upgrading of tenants, since these gained from their security value, and in the reappearance of family farms (*podere*) (Jones, 1968; Osheim, 1977, p. 107ff).

The suggestion that "peasants form part of a larger, compound, society" (Wolf, 1966, p. 2) invites consideration of the other unit of that society. This would be what Wolf referred to as the "dominant group of rulers" composed of those who receive the surpluses produced by the peasant cultivators. A few years previously he had commented that "it is the crystallization of executive power which served to distinguish the primitive from the civilized . . . [and] it is only when a cultivator is integrated into a society with a state . . . that we can appropriately speak of peasantry" (Wolf, 1966, p. 11). The state, or its crown or imperial equivalent, turns out to have usually been the largest single landowner in the countries of Mediterranean Europe in Roman, medieval and post-medieval times. The holders of executive power were the leading families of the realm. Their status depended on the extent of land held. This in turn often depended on their relationship with the state. Office might be granted, or the post concerned went with, a specified extent of land. They might be rewarded with land for services to the state. Their subsistence and livelihood came from the land. Their wealth was determined primarily by the success of agricultural operations on their estates.

Most members of the landowning class did not themselves engage in farm work. The degree to which they took an interest in, or actively directed, agricultural activities was very variable. One impression gained, for instance, was that the majority of estate owners in Italy in Roman times were interested in their properties and in the means of production from them but that in the eighteenth and nineteenth centuries the degree of their uninterest was arguably scandalous (Mack Smith, 1965; Croce, 1970). Rostovotzeft (1926, p. 203) pointed out that very early in Roman times landowners had learnt that the way of getting a good income from land was not to cultivate it scientifically but to let it to tenant farmers. Toynbee (1965, p. 187) showed how a Roman's political career depended on the scale of income from his land. In this case the degree of interest taken in the new forms of agriculture might be expected to be strictly in relation to success in maintenance of the required scale.

If the landowning class was a class of consumers rather than producers, landowners could survive only so long as the class remained a minority. And so it generally was. According to the 1861 census of Italy, there were less than 2000 landowners in the province of Pavia but over 150 000 employed in agriculture, a ratio of 1:83. In Sardinia, where a much greater proportion of the land is uncultivatable and has to be used for grazing, the ratio was 1:25. Only in the province of Capitanata (modern Foggia) in the southern peninsula, where by the nineteenth century a substantial proportion of the land had been turned over to a highly organized and very exclusive ranching system, was the ratio astonishingly and unusually low, 1:8; the total population here had become exceptionally small for a potentially productive lowland region.

One of the differences between the landowning class and the peasantry was the degree to which an individual was free to choose what to do in his personal life. Another difference was the degree of responsibility towards others that he shouldered. For a landowner, the very fact of landownership opened up opportunities of involvement in government, warfare, in the church and in the arts that either brought its own rewards or entailed rewards in yet more land (Fig. 4). Involvement in agriculture itself was not considered a serious option. So Bettino Ricasoli's interest in his family's considerable Tuscan estates from 1830 to 1880 may be regarded as slightly non-conformist. Twice prime minister of unified Italy, Ricasoli nevertheless preferred to live on one of the poorest of his properties with the express intention of reorganizing it to increase the profit margin and to reduce the debts that had been incurred since his father's time. But this sort of attention made heavy demands on time and effort and was anyway largely unfashionable, particularly in the Italian south and in Sicily as well as in Spain. It was more common for landowners to attempt to counter the effect of falling prices or increased tax demands on their personal incomes through extending the area of their agricultural operations, instead of intensification of cropping and changes in farming techniques, still less through non-agricultural investment. In districts controlled by the Italian *Dogana* or the Spanish *Mesta* this meant yet more cereal land was turned over to grass as wool prices dropped in a vain attempt to mask financial losses by increasing output by enlarging the size of the flock. It also meant unfavourable conditions for the peasantry, even to the extent of the adverse pressures that contributed to the desertion of villages.

A landowner automatically acquired a responsibility to those who lived on his land. Neglect and lack of interest in the estate was usually positively harmful to his tenant farmers, as was the case in Sicily (Mack Smith, 1965). A major landowner (such as Melania, who had in the third century A.D. 62 hamlets on just one of her extensive estates, besides her own magnificent villa) might have control over the destiny and welfare of no fewer than 25 000–30 000 individuals (Jones, 1964, p. 782) Where share-cropping systems operated, it was for instance the landlord who decided the type of crops to be grown or the techniques to be used so it might in fact be to the tenant's advantage to have an absentee landowner if this ensured lack of interference. In theory, however, a landowner's decision, or lack of action, could determine the pattern of agricultural development over whole districts and the fortunes of a large number of peasants. Lapeyre has aptly summarized the role of the landowning class: "an appreciation of lordship is . . . one of the most important facts in the historical geography of a country" (1959, p. 18).

Peasant Farmers or Primitive Cultivators in the Neolithic?

One question that arises is whether the peasantry has always represented the lowest social group in the long history of Mediterranean Europe.

B*

Were the inhabitants of Mediterranean Europe already peasant farmers in the sixth millennium B.C. or were they what some economic anthropologists class as primitive cultivators? Not all authorities in fact agree that there is a real distinction between peasant farmers and primitive cultivators. Arguments against the distinction (e.g. Firth, 1970) focus on questions concerning the nature of economic transactions and the marketing principle rather than on social relationships. For Sahlins (1960), however, the definition of a primitive cultivator should involve the same criteria as that used to identify the peasantry. He pointed out that African societies generally accepted as primitive are not characterized by the prerequisite class and economic divisions. Each of these groups constitutes its own society and is not, like the peasantry, part of a wider society. A population of primitive cultivators is therefore basically an egalitarian society and one that is economically closed in comparison with the peasantry.

So far as early prehistoric societies are concerned it is this social distinction that alone might provide evidence as to the sort of society found in Mediterranean Europe at the beginning of the farming era. Since higher levels of production are associated with the development of higher social levels (Sahlins, 1960, p. 418), such a change in the organization of economic activity tends to be accompanied by the emergence of the sort of power that is invested in a chief. So archaeological evidence of chiefdomship or of well-developed social stratification in a prehistoric society in Mediterranean Europe is to be looked for as a possible indicator of the status of the earliest farmers and of the nature of their economic system. This is considered later in Chapter 8.

2
Peasant Farmers

The World of the Peasant Farmer

In his study of the modern peasant farmer in Europe, Franklin remarked that "the condition of the peasant . . . has changed considerably but the peasant economy survives." (1969, p. 4). This statement applies equally well to the past in Mediterranean Europe. There is increasing evidence that the condition of peasant life has altered from time to time. Sicilian and Languedocian peasants, for example, enjoyed better food between the late fourteenth and the late fifteenth centuries, when their diet contained wheat bread and an abundance of meat, than after the fifteenth century until recent years (Mandrou, 1961; Le Roy Ladurie, 1966, p. 184; Mack Smith, 1969, p. 179). On the other hand, the structure of the peasant economy has altered very little since classical times. Production of food for himself and his family has always been the peasant farmer's overriding preoccupation. Typically therefore he has lived his life and worked for his livelihood within a very constrained spatial world. His daily routine and the annual cycle of his affairs have been arranged for him by immutables such as the rising and setting sun and the changing seasons. Time and space for the peasant farmer have been equally clearly defined.

Time

Time for the peasant farmer is defined by the agricultural calendar. Almost every person in a village community is so affected. Out of a total of over 2600 individuals living in 1929 in a small, unmodernized village not far from Caltanisetta in Sicily (fictitiously named "Milocca") only 76 people (3%) were never out working in the fields (Chapman, 1973). The

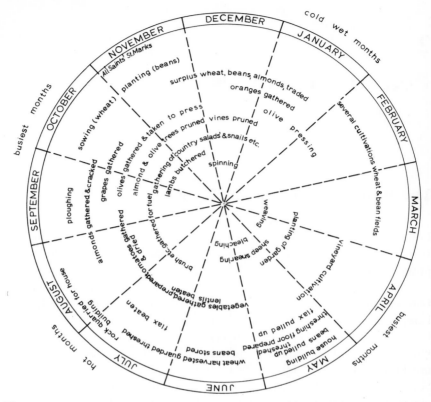

Fig. 5. *The temporal world of the peasants* as defined by the agricultural calendar (based on Chapman's account (1973) of a Sicilian village in 1929).

villagers grew nearly all their own food and the production and preparation of this occupied all the farmers together with a few "specialists" such as the millers. Agricultural work was also shared between the sexes. As fast as women hulled almonds, men skilled at the job cracked them. Women were responsible not for the planting but for the gathering of garden vegetables such as lentils and tomatoes and for the preparation of plants such as flax for hemp. The onus of harvesting was shared, if only symbolically, as the women cooked specially sustaining meals and took them out to the men in the fields or at the threshing floor. Again, while the men sheared, the women took the fleeces and during the rest of the year spun, wove, bleached and made the wool into clothes for the family.

The start of the farming year was marked by the first of the autumn ploughing, but, contrary to the popular un-Mediterranean view, the renewal of the cereal year scarcely followed a period of rest (Fig. 5). The villagers of "Milocca" had spent August gathering tomatoes, preparing and drying them for winter use, and gathering and preparing the almonds that were one of the few elements of export. As ploughing started and the arable fields had to be made ready for the seed on which next year's livelihood depended, the grape harvest was imminent, the olive harvest not far ahead, and the harvested almond trees needed pruning. There was pressure to complete both cereal sowing and bean planting by certain dates. According to the church calendar, beans were to be planted only after Souls' Day (2nd November) while by St. Martin's Day (11th November) all wine should be ready for testing. Then the Fascist government ordained, in the late 1920s, that all arable fields should have been prepared and sown by 15th December. And so the farming year progressed to a second period of crisis. By late Spring the pressure had once again built up.

If two parts of the year were undoubtedly the busiest, when labour shortage was acute and every able-bodied man, woman and child in the village had its allotted task, the other parts of the year were scarcely times of leisure. These were the seasons of unsuitable weather. January and February are cold, wet months in most of Mediterranean Europe when it is difficult to work the land, unpleasant to be out of doors, and when flood or snow impedes circulation. July and August are the hot months, the "dog-days" of the ancients, again months of enforced "idleness". Important to note, however, that this idleness is confined to the hours of sultry or scorching, dry, dusty heat. There are agricultural tasks that still have to be done. The essential chores of milking, cheesemaking, feeding the livestock, and necessary garden work, tend to be carried out in the cool of the early morning or late evening. Foreigners and northerners have to be blamed for the myth of the Mediterranean peasant's summer idleness. Evidently they travelled during the day and saw little of the activity that took place in the very early and very late hours of daylight.

The peasant farmer has little opportunity for leisure in the modern sense of the word. Periods of inactivity are treated as days of rest and recovery from other periods of intense and hurried toil. It is not time gained for personal enjoyment or for alternative activities. The peasant works in order to support himself and his family and to maintain a degree of independence. If he is hurried, it is only because of the amount of work that has to be fitted in according to the weather or into the agricultural season. Time off is for essential repose and for equally important socializing. There is little enthusiasm for changes that might increase pressure. In the peasant farmer's view, a move towards a more intense farming system would simply extend the existing pressure from certain periods to the entire year. It would also aggravate a labour problem already periodically acute because of the way effort is unevenly spread over the farming year.

The actual amount of time involved in peasant farming in Mediterranean Europe has been measured by a number of writers (Davis, 1973, app. VI; Brögger, 1971; Chisholm, 1968). Cereals, for instance, can be regarded as an all-year-round crop, so the modest total of 146 hours[3] is evenly distributed over the year. Olive cultivation involves a tremendous amount of work, mostly in December, harvest time; 105 hours of work per hectare by the men and 610 hours by the women. During the year the men spend another 162 hours pruning and ploughing the olive trees, bringing the total to 1592 hours of work per annum per hectare for olives. The pea crop involves more work for women than for men, though the season is fairly short (October to early April). The men contribute 40 hours of work, women 719 hours. Vineyards in contrast require attention throughout the year from both sexes. An average of 447 hours were worked by the men at Pisticci, 580 hours by women. October is the only month of the year in which there is no work in the vineyards.

The concept of underemployment hardly applies to a self-supporting peasant. His work load is defined by necessity, in respect of a supply of food for himself and his family, and of their other wants. A peasant's labour force is constituted by the members of his family. Whenever there is more work than he can handle alone, his wife and children are involved. But he cannot dismiss them as can the manager of an exploitation where labour is hired according to work demand. Unemployment however can exist. It affects labourers and tenant farmers rather than owner-occupiers amongst the peasantry. In historic times, as in the present day, it tended to reflect the fluctuating fortunes of the market in the major crops, particularly when this was arbitrarily influenced by government action. Any move that favoured extensive livestock rather than arable farming, for example, reduced the demand for labour. When, in 1535 in Sardinia, the Aragonese government closed the grain market in order to protect cereal prices, this eventually caused so much hardship and "so many were daily added to the trail of thieves and vagabonds" that by 1566 the order was rescinded (Sorgia, 1972, p. 156). Amongst the peasantry, pressure of work had no abstract merit. It could be something to be thankful for though since it was as near as anything could come to a guarantee of a livelihood for the peasant and his family.

Territory

The peasant's world is composed of a series of "territories", each of a different scale. Most immediately, there is the homely world of his house, his neighbourhood in his village and his fields. Then there is the village and the village territory more generally. Finally (in most cases) there is the wider world of the district or region, primarily composed of the neighbouring village or town with which the peasant might very occasionally have business or about which he hears more or less daily. It often included contiguous or distant lands that by some arrangement are also part of the extended village territory. Beyond these worlds, geographical scale had, in the days before radio and above all television, very little real meaning. In the minds of most "Miloccans", for example, there was little to choose between Naples, Milan or New York.

The peasant's view of his own fields and the village territory is usually represented as one composite, homely world. In reality it is a much more fragmentary world. A peasant farmer has neither time nor inclination to go much beyond the immediate locality with which he has business. Chapman found that "each person's knowledge of the region is bounded by his economic activities and his social relationships" (1973, p. 222). Considerable parts of the commune, or village territory, lie away from plots worked or paths walked and these parts remain outside the peasant's immediate focus and interest. For a peasant with an exceptionally small holding, or for a labourer who works largely in the neighbouring commune, first-hand or intimate acquaintance with his own village territory can easily be limited to a very small part. Another small part falls into the view scanned by the peasant from his house or his fields. As for the rest of the village territory, it would enter his consciousness only through the talk of associates, through the recollection of a childhood visit, or by a glimpse from the distance. For women, their immediate or first level world used to be still more restricted. "Milocca" in Sicily may be an unusually dispersed village but in the late 1920s there were adult women who had not personally visited all the seven neighbourhoods (robbe) into which the village was divided. So, taking an average-sized commune of

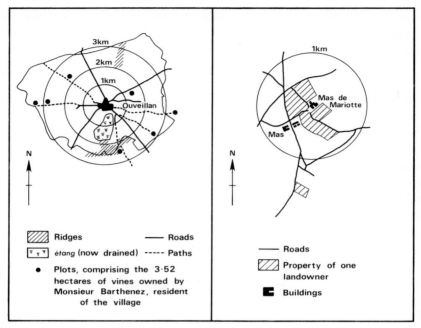

Fig. 6. *Farms.* The fragmented holding of a peasant farmer and a compact estate in Languedoc (from Galtier, 1960).

23 000 hectares, such as ''Milocca'' itself, measure can be taken of a hypothetical peasant farmer's ''world''. He is fortunate to have perhaps as much as 10 or 12 hectares of land that he can use. His home is in a neighbourhood containing eight to ten houses. Since each dwelling would be within hailing distance of another in even the most loosely grouped village, the total neighbourhood area of his home can be taken as adding up to perhaps half a hectare. Then there is the land bordering paths taken between house and fields, and the grazing visited. Briefly, the total measure of a peasant's ''world'' might amount to little more than 10% of the total village territory.

The greater part of a peasant's life in the past in Mediterranean Europe was therefore concentrated into an oddly shaped and somewhat disjointed world. Military service apart, there were occasions on which a peasant might leave his own village territory and enter into a second level of spatial consciousness. The most usual occasion for a visit to a neighbouring village was the annual *fiesta*. Only rarely might this be called a leisure activity (for the poorest or least adventurous newly married couples this might be all that was had by way of a bridal visit) since the object of the visit was usually the purchase or the sale of an animal. Only a few individuals found employment in a neighbouring commune. In the case of ''Milocca'', landless young men went regularly to work on the neighbouring territory of Campofranco, where there were several large estates requiring hired labour, but nobody travelled purely for pleasure except for the rare honeymoon, taken by a relatively wealthy couple.

One consequence of the self-containment of village life is that road communications between villages are often still very poor. Villagers do not normally travel. Where a major thoroughfare crosses their territory, it is irrelevant to their daily activities. Maraspina found this to be still the case in the Grichia district of the Salentino peninsula, where the road links two major centres just 50 km distant (1968, p. 58). The villagers of Ramosierra in Spain have little contact with their provincial capital, Soria, 40 km away. A road was built only in 1925 and even today they expect to be isolated by snow for up to 4 months each year (Kenny, 1961, p. 19 fn). The siting of each village worked against ease of external links anyway, particularly where these were older than the establishment of the village, because normally the village is as near as possible centrally situated in its own territory. In modern times there are other means of communication, radio, television and newspapers. However, at ''Milocca'', where eight newspapers were received daily in the village and were read by up to 30 persons, this ''informed'' section of the community comprised no more than 0·1% of the total population.

The spatial world of the peasantry is also defined by time. From ''Milocca'' to Campofranco is a straight-line distance of only 5 km. But this used to mean a walk of 2 hours over rough country, hardly an attractive option for peasants who are obliged to spend 5 hours each day travelling to and from their place of work within their own village territory, as did those who lived in the huge Apulian or Calabrian villages of southern Italy. Another limiting factor is lack of incentive. A peasant's requirements were, until recently, largely met from the resources of his own commune. What was not grown or produced there was imported by traders. Salt, salted fish, fresh fish and ironmongery were stocked in the village shops of ''Milocca'', for example. *Pasta* was brought in from other villages not because there was a shortage of local cereals (on the contrary, three-quarters of the annual harvest was exported) but because the type of wheat grown locally was not suitable.

The shape of the village territory, usually today transformed into the modern commune, reflects the advantage taken to gain not only as large an area as possible but also one that promised to satisfy the villagers' requirements as much as possible. In Sardinia, the size and shape of some of the communes in the mountains of the Gennargentu is such that summer and winter grazing can be found within the commune itself. The commune of Gairo, for instance, an inland village over 30 km from the sea at 900 m above sea level, has such an attenuated shape that the villagers have access to 8 km of coast (Fig. 7). Many other communes, however, are unable to keep their flocks within their own territories all the year around, however desirable this may be, for lack of space. They depend on other arrangements. Livestock belonging to the villages of Ovodda, for example, has to travel over 100 km to the mountains of the south-west (the Cixerri valley), or a shorter distance west to the coastal plain around Oristano, or about 60 km north-west to the Planargia plateau near the coast. The peasant's world is accordingly enlarged. He is rather alone within it, though, even when he is one of a group of shepherds, for he has left his village and its community behind. The life of a peasant is essentially a corporate existence. The majority of the peasantry do not move far away from the social bonds of community that also constitute the economic framework of their lives.

Aspects of Community

In a general way, most peasant farmers in Mediterranean Europe are very conscious of the antiquity of their land. This is hardly surprising for there are not many communes from which tangible evidence of past occupation has not been dug up in the course of farm work. In more precise terms though their sense of time is as vague as their concept of the outside world. In contrast, their feeling for their own world can be very strong indeed. It involves in part loyalty to the other members of their own community and in part loyalty to the land on which the community depends for its livelihood.

Modern *campanilismo* (as such local loyalty has been termed) is defined as a tendency to overstress village solidarity to the point of appearing hostile to outsiders and outside influences, notably urban ones. Even for the historic past, attitude is not something that can often be discerned in the documentary record. There are aspects of community life, however, which do in fact reflect local loyalties and which can be traced in the

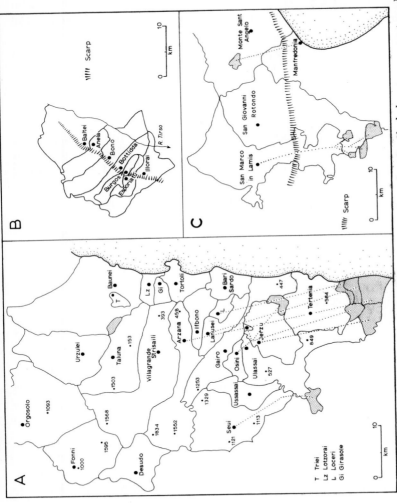

Fig. 7. *Commune boundaries and village territories in Sardinia (A and B) and Apulia (C). Shaded parts represent modern territorial exclaves. Heights are in metres. The granite and metamorphic Marghine and Goceano hills in the province of Sassari rise as much as 500 m above the Tirso valley (B). The limestone Gargano massif in northern Apulia (C) is lower but still a pronounced linearity is found in the older territories.*

archives. Two such aspects are codification of land use observances and of other matters of village affairs and the organization of the community's land. Peasants evaluate their land in pragmatic terms. A place is not judged according to the beauty of its landscape nor even by the agricultural convenience of its topography but by its fertility. This, to a peasant, is defined as productivity. To the "Miloccan" farmers, the "best" season was that which yielded most fruit and abundant harvest, namely the summer. The "best" land is where crops yield most prolifically and reliably. Measures taken to protect this land can be seen therefore as a practical expression of loyalty.

Village Codes

There were times in the past, the later Middle Ages for instance, when social and economic pressures were felt particularly intensely at local level. Since, as Chiva pointed out, "an important body of customary law goes with scarcity of goods and with economic activity whose simultaneous demands [may] conflict" (1963, p.100), attempts to protect village land from such pressures gave rise to regulations concerning land use and economic organization made by the community itself. These regulations were the village codes.

Some village codes in Mediterranean Europe survived into the twentieth century, albeit in attenuated or anachronistic form as in Corsica or Sardinia. Others have survived only in the archives, as in the case of the statutes of Laino in Calabria. Many more undoubtedly existed but were never written down, presumably because the old observed communal usages were overtaken and eradicated by the new feudalism before there was a need to have them formalized. It would seem therefore that Le Lannou was premature in regarding the Sardinian codes, still in use up to the last war, as a curious singularity amongst Mediterranean countries (1941, p. 114). Subsequent research has revealed the former existence of a number of local codes.

The surviving document of the Statutes of Laino in Calabria is dated 1470 but from the manner of phrasing it is evident that this was not the first time land use regulations had been written down at Laino (Cappelli, 1931). It is clear too that they were being not merely restated at this date but were receiving the overt approval of the feudal landlord, indicated by the word *placet* (it pleases). The earlier version is thought to have been drawn up about 1346, when the neighbouring community of Castrovillari

had likewise gained official assent for its statutes. The inference drawn by
Cappelli is that the earlier version was drawn up by the community itself,
through its *Universitas* or governing body, for its own members. This then
was a time when it was still possible for the community to decide the
conditions and norms under which all would live. Local problems would
have been economic ones, arising from community life or a function of
land shortage for example. By the fifteenth century, however, when feudal
control had become stronger than the local community, social or political
pressures had been added to the purely economic.

Presumably the 88 articles listed in the Statutes of Laino were intended
to cover every major aspect of contemporary village life. They deal with
taxation (head tax, rent for land, tax on animals); fines; enclosed land;
livestock; and industries and trades (for example, tallow manufacture and
butchering of meat). The large number (29 altogether) dealing with
livestock is not necessarily an index of pastoral bias but rather a reflection
of the potential nuisance value of uncontrolled livestock and dogs in a
mixed farming community. For example, certain village streets are named
as those along which livestock must be driven (article 54). Since Laino is
situated on the edge of the Sila mountains, with much of its land over
1200 m above sea level, the economic implications of such a location are
reflected in the Statutes. Chestnut forests are mentioned (articles 21 and
50) as well as vineyards and arable fields. Swine appear to have held as
important a place as cattle, sheep or goats.

Another aspect of community life is revealed in the decrees from the
Corsican village of Urtaca, a concern for the underprivileged members of
the community. For instance:

We decree as follows:
Art. 1. The gleaning of olives in the territories of Urtaca belongs exclusively
to the poor, the aged, the infirm, and the indigent of this commune.
Art. 2. The gleaners of olives may not engage therein until after we have made
it known that the harvest of olives is complete on this or the other section of
the territory.
Art. 3. No one may glean olives at the beginning or the end of the harvest,
before or after the setting of the sun and without carrying a certificate or ticket
from us attesting to their state of need.

Other customary rules at Urtaca (first written down in 1863) governed the
ownership of land and real estate; the regulation of cultivation;
agreements; transactions and contracts; and the local offices of assent and
arbitration (Chiva, 1969, p. 105).

The interesting thing about the Corsican decrees, and the light they shed on former community life, lies in the fact that Corsica has today a reputation for extreme individualism. Chiva's research into village decrees and customary law has shown that this individualism is a modern development and that the Corsican's reputation can be redeemed by "all that one [can] observe of a former village life which imposed everywhere its constraints, its disciplines and its communal usages" (1969, p. 98). He finds that a number of former estates still survive in the form of village properties, with anything from two to ten villages possessing the property jointly and indivisibly. This is a relict of the *pieve* organization, a federation of village communities and corporation of parishes creating an important socio-economic unit which officially disappeared more than a century and a half ago. He also finds that the "rates of collective labour, the managing of the organization of production such as irrigation, and the compulsory rotation of lands" continued at least to the last war within the modern commune, the old village territory. He finds clear implications that private ownership of land was a small and very strictly controlled element. Village life, in short, was governed above all by the operation of a vast extent of *collectively* held land.

Corsica is today an island with a reputation for the brutality of its individualism. The explanation for the general ignorance about the former strength of collective village life in Corsica lies in the fact that this is the only *département* in France whose customary law has hardly been recorded in spite of a law passed in 1928 aimed at the drawing up of collections of customary law in each *département* in France. It is also due to the fact that during the nineteenth century, Corsica embarked on a slow and uninterrupted social transformation that has gone a long way towards obliterating all signs of the old communal life. Village land has been appropriated by individuals. Modern commune organization stresses the powers and the functions of individuals rather than the older collectivity. As the island, after 1900, became increasingly "backward" in relation to neighbouring less-developed areas, so social and economic inequalities within or between villages have been created. The contrast is now between peasant farmers and the raised standards of living enjoyed by returned emigrants and by those who derive a living from tourism. These forces have now divorced Corsicans from the old subsistence style of life to such an extent that a recent and otherwise perceptive writer wrote that "Corsicans have not the characteristics of peasants in other countries—they have no real love of the soil" (Carrington, 1971, p. 64).

The writing down of village usages, as at Laino in the fifteenth century and in Corsica in the nineteenth, is symptomatic of a then new opposition between community and lord or state. The struggle was fundamentally social or political but it was inevitably translated into economic terms, given the importance of agriculture to almost every inhabitant of Mediterranean Europe. So questions of land use and land tenure became key issues. This is also seen in Spain, where confrontation between those who had rights to communal property and those with private property is illuminated by the sixteenth century *Relaciones Topographicas* of New Castile.

The *Relaciones* were replies to a survey carried out for Philip II between 1575 and 1580 (Saloman, 1964). There were two questionnaires; the first contained 57 questions, the second only 47. One of the points revealed by the *Relaciones* is that many villages were dissatisfied with what they regarded as erosion of their communal property by the nobility, ecclesiastics, townsfolk or rich peasants. Others were worried about loss of rights. [4] For example, in 1576 the inhabitants of Villaverde (Madrid) complained that they had lost the right to pasture their livestock in a certain wood because of its usurpation by noblemen from the city of Madrid. Others grumbled that the communal grazing (*dehesas boyale*) was no longer sufficient to support even their plough-teams and that they had to struggle against the nobility to remedy the situation. The municipality of Cazelegas (Toledo) had managed to buy, the year previously, several private plots for this purpose. But by the late sixteenth century, in Spain as elsewhere, communal property and village rights were being severely menaced by a gain in private ownership. The subsequent expansion of the bourgeoisie during the eighteenth and nineteenth centuries extinguished most communal practices and took over land once held in common. Even so, as late as 1881, the corporate spirit was still in evidence. Despite pressure for reforming legislation, new openfields were created at Cabeza del Buez (Badajoz) (Balabanian, 1975). In the old manner, stripfields were laid out and a 3-year rotation (fallow/cereal/fallow) introduced. Grazing on the fallow was auctioned to pastoralists (winter grass was traditionally sold to transhumants, summer and stubble grazing to large local herders) and the proceeds shared out amongst the villagers.

Openfields and the Community

In the case of Cabeza del Buez, the collective spirit was manifested in the nineteenth century in a temporary resurgence of openfield farming practice. There is evidence for openfield farming from other parts of Spain in earlier times. In Castile and Leon, for example, openfield traditions were once widespread (see map in Gil Crespo, 1975, p. 260; and Birot and Gabert, 1964, p. 315ff; Fernandez, 1965). It may be that not all of the four essential elements used to define farming in common in England (Thirsk, 1964, p. 3) were always present. But there was certainly an openfield landscape, a strip layout, and periodic redistribution of land. The latter, known as *sorteo de tierras*, has been traced back to the period of Moorish occupation. It also applied to newly cleared land in New Castile in the sixteenth century (Salomon, 1964, p. 150, citing also Costa, 1898, pp. 266ff and 332). There was grazing on fallow there in the openfields as in the closes (*deriota de mieses* or *abertura de heredas*) although no specific mention is made of cropping in common. It may have been that the practice was similar to that found in Sardinia where each member of the community was in theory free to crop as he pleased but in the event found that the constraints of an openfield system effectively enforced conformity (Le Lannou, 1947, p. 135). Nor is there any specific evidence in Spain for the prerequisite village assemblies. It is unlikely, however, that periodic redistribution of holdings and enforcement of rules governing pasturing in common could be maintained without something of that nature.

In Sardinia traces of openfield farming survived until very recently, as did the village statutes. Early writers and travellers described its working in some detail (e.g. Gemelli, 1776; La Marmora, 1839). Le Lannou (1947, p. 113ff) suggested that this system of farming, common in this century in southern Sardinia, was formerly widespread over the whole of the island and that it was extraordinarily close to that in the openfield regions of northern France and England. It went by the name of *vidazzoni*. There was the typical landscape with stripfields; obligatory crop rotation; collective work; and communal grazing herds. The open arable land was divided into two (or more) zones, for cereals and for fallow-with-grazing, and the annual allocation of land ensured each villager had land from each zone. Characteristic of the *vidazzoni* districts are the large rural agglomerations which housed all the farmers. One question of particular interest to Le Lannou was that of the origins of Sardinian openfield farming.

Vidazzoni and openfield farming in general bears little relation to the normal structure of farming in Roman times. This was based on a distinction between private and state land, on owner-occupation, and it involved various tenures. Accordingly, Le Lannou sought an origin for the

Sardinian system in the post-Roman period. Early village codes, such as the Statute of the Republic of Sassari of 1316, showed him that the practice can be traced back at least to the eleventh century through an institution known as *scolca*. This, deriving from the Italian *scolta*, refers to an overseeing authority and, by extension, to an oath which had to be taken by ''every inhabitant of Sassari aged between 14 and 70 years . . . to swear each year to cause no damage and to permit neither persons nor beasts to cause damage to any field or vineyard . . .'' (p. 128). It applied to a specified portion of village territory. Le Lannou was unable to document an earlier origin but since he believed the practice was unique to Sardinia, he was seeking reasons for what he supposed to be an indigenous development. These, he suggested, would have lain in what he described as a spontaneous reaction of the Sardes to the disappearance of Roman authority and administration but he also stressed the contribution of the island's physical characteristics and singular political history.

However, in Spain too researchers are looking to the same period for the origins of communal farming structures there, resisting the usual temptation to ascribe all singularities or novelties in the peninsula to that unique event, the Reconquest. There is no evidence, according to King (1972, p. 206ff), for legal compulsory regulation of arable under the Gothic administration. Few facts are available for Moorish agrarian arrangements but the Arab economic contribution is known to have been neither negligible nor negative. Relevant traditions of communal organization are strong in Africa, as well as in Iberia, where they pre-date Islamic legislation (Salomon, 1964, p. 138 fn). It is characteristic of usages that they do not normally need to be written down, unless challenged by external factors, as happened in Calabria for example. It is the need for a contract for private landholding arrangements, or for share-cropping tenancies, that ensures a relatively abundant, if unbalanced, documentary record. Undoubtedly, therefore, it is primarily a lack of evidence that masks the former extent of openfield farming in some, perhaps many, parts of Mediterranean Europe and that has disguised the earlier strength of community spirit even in the heart of the Romanized world.

Rural Settlement

Home for the majority of the peasantry of Mediterranean Europe (and not only in districts of former openfield farming) has tended to be in a nucleated rural settlement. To refer to these as villages may be convenient but it can also be misleading, since the nucleation might contain anything from a few hundred to 30 000 inhabitants. The latter phenomenon is best referred to as an agro-town. But dispersed settlement has also been more common in the past in Mediterranean Europe than is usually admitted in the textbooks. Certainly there have been periods when, for a variety of reasons, isolated steadings were rare or absent. The nineteenth and early part of the twentieth century was one of these. So many living writers and scholars have had personal experience of the pre-war emptiness of so much of southern Italy, Sicily, central and southern Spain, that it is understandable that they have tended to assume that this was also the case throughout the past. Settlement evidence, however, both archaeological and documentary, shows it to have been quite otherwise.

The Village

Little distinction is made even today in Mediterranean Europe between the agricultural small town and the village. The Spanish *pueblo*, the French *bourg* and the Italian *borgo* or *centro* are terms used to refer to nucleations that are overwhelmingly agricultural in function whatever the size of their populations and despite an often urban landscape. To cover the difficulty, geographers have coined the term agro-town. From the practical point of view, the only distinction needed by the administration is between the city (urban) and all other (rural) forms of nucleated settlement. In Spain, for example, the opposition is simply between the *cuidad* and the *pueblo* (Kenny, 1961, p. 8). The latter term serves to describe a very varied range of settlements.

Still more confusing is the variety of terms used in the past for these nucleated settlements. Sometimes what may seem to be inconsistency in fact reflects no more than regional differences. Even so, the modern student, accustomed to finding order in the ranking or description of settlement forms, is hard pressed to identify order in earlier times. For instance, most modern classifications are based on form and economic function but the latter criterion does not often apply in the past. In almost every nucleated settlement in Mediterranean Europe, except in the major cities and ports, the dominant occupation was agriculture. Yet a range of terminology is found to have applied to rural nucleations that to the modern mind could all be classified as villages. For example, medieval documents show that a village in Italy could be referred to as a *castra*, a *villa* or a *casalis*. In Romagna in the thirteenth and fourteenth centuries the larger and more important rural centres were always called *castra*. But this, according to Larner (1965, p. 114), was due primarily to the visual dominance of a castle. The smaller villages or hamlets were designated *villa* or *casalis*, as they were in the south. In eastern Spain in the thirteenth century, under the Moslems, there were *castillas* and *villas* (Fontavella, 1952, p. 309). In southern France at this time the terminology for rural settlements included *villa*, *castrum*, *mansus* and *locus* (Thomas, 1865; Maffre, 1872). Fasoli suggested (1959, p. 115, fn 138) that the designation *castrum* in the early Middle Ages was based primarily on territorial administration. Notwithstanding the size, economic status, aspect or townscape of a settlement, if it was designated an administrative centre, it was so referred to. If this was generally the case, the confusion of early terminology may be considerably resolved by the application of the single criterion of administration to the early ranking of rural settlements.

The word *villa* is Latin. In Roman times it applied to the big centralized farm complexes at the centre of an estate, the *villa rustica*, now known by a variety of designations (*masseria*, *cascina*) (see Varro, *r.r.* I. II. 14). How it came to be linked with a medieval village is less than clear. An obvious explanation would be that the one grew from the other. It is easy to see how this could have come about. They were centres of convergence for many interests and activities (Fasoli, 1959, p. 101). Rents would have been brought in by the free peasantry; workers lived there to maintain the buildings and fortifications and to supply local industrial needs; the lord held his tribunal and sent his orders out from there; possibly he resided there with his family and retainers; and the centre, particularly the lord's stronghold, would have been regarded as a place of refuge in times of troubles (an admirable if fictitious description of this is to be found in Manzoni's *I Promessi Sposi* (1872)). There is, moreover, growing archaeological support for such an evolution. At Coussergues, site of a Roman villa but a small fortified village (*castrum*) by the thirteenth century, the soil is "riddled with antique coins and broken pottery" (Le Roy Ladurie, 1972, p. 16). Work at Castel Porciano (Basilicata) convinced the excavators that there indeed had been continuity of settlement from the Roman *villa rustica* to an early medieval *fundus* which, given an increase in population and an increase in their mobility, was easily transformed into the bigger nucleation that eventually merited the designation *castellis* (Mallet and Whitehouse, 1967). An early medieval farm has been found near San Severo (Foggia) by a Roman road and with late Roman pottery on the same site. From this and from other finds in the area, Russi emphasizes that most medieval settlements in Capitanata were on Roman sites and ''probably represent continuity'' (1976, p. 41).

The list of such coincidences could be amplified. Adequate stratified evidence of settlement continuity, however, is less easily available. Today, in Sicily, Cadeli (Catania) is a *masseria* but it was a village or *casalis* in 1300 on the site of a Roman *villa*, the evidence for which are the mosaics. This mere spatial coincidence, Aymard and Bresc (1973, p. 963) point out, is hardly an adequate demonstration or proof of continual occupation over the intervening 800 or 900 years. The problem seems still more obscured in Languedoc by the use of the place-name element *villa* in the Middle Ages in localities for which there is not necessarily any evidence (to date) of occupation during the Roman period [e.g. *Villa Pratis* (A.D. 804) now Prades (Les Matelles, Hèrault)] as well as in localities that were settled then [e.g. *Villa Armantianius* now Aimargues, Gard; and *Villa Posiliaca*, now Pouzilhac, Gard (Blanchet, 1941, 1946)]. On the other hand, the idea of continuity has always had to be balanced against the observation that rural settlements, both large and small, can also be extremely fragile, a point emphasized for Sardinia by Day (1973). The phenomenon of the deserted village, in other words, belongs to all historic and, no doubt, prehistoric periods.

In appearance and arrangement, there is not much to differentiate Italian, Spanish or French villages today. In morphology they are remarkably similar and variations in layout or architecture are local or regional rather than national. Pitt-Rivers, in southern Spain, found that ''the villages are much alike at first sight'' (1954, p. 3). Here they are composed of houses clustered together on a knoll, ridge top or mountain flank but with the cemetery and its chapel, the *calvario*, some distance away. Documentary and archaeological evidence reveals that the typical medieval rural nucleation, however it was termed, was also compact. It may or may not have been walled, though the evidence is that most had become so by the later Middle Ages. There are many references to the punitive razing of walls, to their repair or reinstatement, or to requests for permission to construct them. The latter tended to come, as in the Garrigues of Languedoc, from areas of recent colonization. At Puèchabon, at Les Matelles (still a charming walled village) and at Combailleux, for instance, permission was sought in the twelfth or early thirteenth centuries (Casson and Meynial, 1902; Devic and Vaissette, 1872;

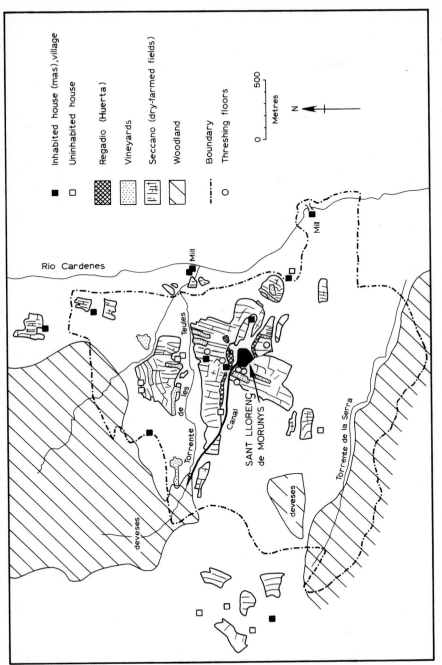

Fig. 8. *A village and its territory.* Sant Llorenç de Morunys (province of Lerida) in the fifteenth century (after Segret and Riu, 1969). The district is mountainous and the village is 925 m above sea level. A good deal of its land has to remain uncultivated. Each *devese* is common land, usually reserved for plough animals and where other rights may be strictly controlled.

Legend:

Inhabited house (mas), village ■

Uninhabited house □

Regadio (Huerta) ▨

Vineyards ⠢

Seccano (dry-farmed fields) ⊞

Woodland ▨

Boundary ─·─·─

Threshing floors ○

N

0   500
Metres

Rio Cardenes

Mill

Mill

Teules

de les

Torrente

Canal

SANT LLORENÇ
de MORUNYS

deveses

deveses

Torrente de la Serra

Thomas, 1865). In Sicily, not many villages remained unwalled by 1350 and each of those that remained open had a tower or castle as a precautionary measure (Cherubini and Francovich, 1973, p. 946). Foggia (capital of Capitanata), however, perhaps because of its late development, remained unwalled though its outermost houses were closely packed and inward facing.

One effect of the walls was to enhance the compactness of the settlement. There might have been some extra-mural development but this was evidently unpopular and at Sant Llorenç de Morunys (Lerida) in the fifteenth century, for example, only four houses lay outside the fortifications (Segret and Riu, 1969, p. 378) (Fig. 8). Unlike the big towns and cities, most villages could not afford either the time or the cost to enlarge their walled areas. The intra-mural area therefore could become very densely packed and villages tended to suffer much more from over-crowding than the towns of the period. In addition to the dwellings, which had also to accommodate the farmsteads, the walled area contained such major space-users as the church, the castle, and the public open space.

Of these three morphological dominants, it was undoubtedly the public open space (*piazza, place, plaza*) that had the most profound impact on the daily lives of the inhabitants, as part of the community's social bond. Pitt-Rivers observed that in the *pueblo* of "Alcala", "the distance of a house from [one of] these is something of a measure of its desirability" (1954, p. 5). This point was stressed in deeds of sale in documents concerning the now deserted settlement of Casalnuovo (Foggia); it was noted whether the house fronted the public square or overlooked the communal fountain (Camobreco, 1913, document 125 (1201) for instance). For the past, as for southern Apulia today, it can be said that "the piazza is an adjunct of village life . . . the heart of village life . . . vitally necessary to the village's social existence" (Maraspina, 1968, p. 59 ff). Because of its social importance the public open space also became an economic centre, to the extent that "the prosperity and status of a town or village can be estimated by the condition of the houses surrounding the piazza and adjoining it" (*ibid.*). Where there was no *piazza*, the main street took on its roles, as Lison-Tolosana found at "Belmonte de los Caballeros" (Zaragossa) (1966, pp. 95–97). An early reference to "*ipso platea maiore publica qui dicta Strata*" at Troia (Apulia) (Carabellese, 1924, document 2, dated 1034) shows that there were not less than two public squares at Troia (agglomerated population 6000 in 1861), but that one of these occupied a section of the street that used to be the great Roman highway, the Via

Traiana (built A.D. 109). In the same province, at Casalnuovo (a pre-Roman settlement), the public open space was known as the *platea publicis* (Camobreco, 1913, document 125) while at Lucera (a Roman colony) it was referred to as the *forum* (Egidi, 1917).

The morphological structure of a settlement is normally most conveniently described in terms of the relationship between house, house-plot and street (Conzen, 1962). In Mediterranean Europe, however, the first two elements are often coterminous and usually irregular in shape, especially in crowded hillside settlements. Occasionally, medieval house-plot measurements are given in cartularies and similar documents. One more regularly shaped plot at Casalnuovo was narrow but long: 24 × 48 *pedes* (about 8 × 16 m) (Camobreco, 1913, document 12). In other cases, the house layout could be complex, including outbuildings or a courtyard (*cum cortilio*) (document 286). Certainly there was a variety of status: some houses are specified in documents as *casalinum* and were evidently quite modest while others, referred to as *domum palatiatum* were much grander and belonged to the richer peasants or, more likely, to members of the nobility and the landowning class (documents 273 and 287, dated 1394 and 1430, respectively).

Not many archaeological descriptions of village houses from medieval sites in Mediterranean Europe are available as yet (though see Whitehouse, 1970; Mallet and Whitehouse, 1967; Steisdal, 1962). In Spain, Bazzana and Guichard (1974) have made two points concerning peasant dwellings in the deserted medieval villages they have investigated. First, they affirm that not all rural settlements were necessarily densely packed. At Monte Mollet (Castellon de la Plana), for instance, some of the rectangular cottages were found to be quite isolated from each other while others were only loosely grouped around some sort of court or square. Second, they classified village houses into two types, the elementary and the complex. At Torre Bufilla (Betera), the plan of the simplest houses was found to be most usually square (sometimes distorted to conform to irregularities of terrain), with walls of dry stone construction. Roman pottery was found in some of these, a find which supports the idea of continual occupation. The more complex houses were rectangular, measuring perhaps 4 × 8·1 m, and had the longhouse type of layout familiar from northern France and upland Britain. In the Spanish examples, though, there are separate entrances for humans and for animals.

There is little to suggest that the range of village houses in medieval times would not have been similar in the past to that found today in

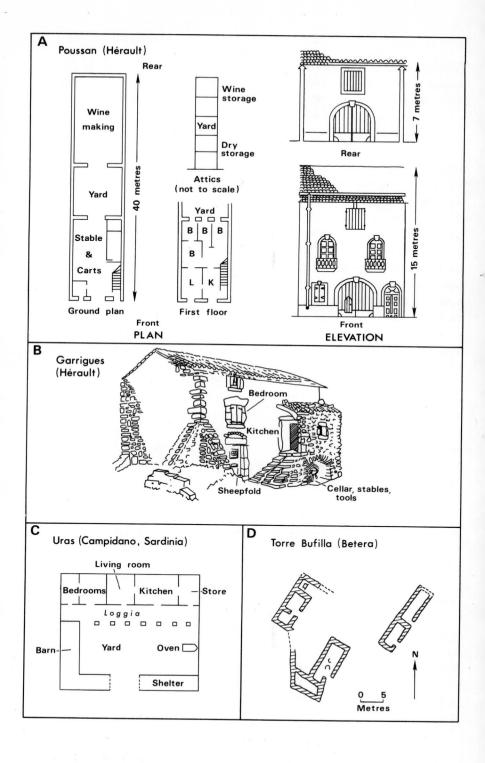

A Poussan (Hérault)

Rear

Wine making

Yard

Stable & Carts

Ground plan

Front

PLAN

Wine storage

Yard

Dry storage

Attics (not to scale)

Yard

B B B

B

L K

First floor

Rear

7 metres

15 metres

Front

ELEVATION

B Garrigues (Hérault)

Bedroom

Kitchen

Sheepfold

Cellar, stables, tools

C Uras (Campidano, Sardinia)

Living room

Bedrooms   Kitchen   Store

Loggia

Barn   Yard   Oven

Shelter

D Torre Bufilla (Betera)

N

0   5

Metres

Mediterranean Europe, just as some of the layouts may still be found (compare the plan of the Valencian *barreca* with the "long-houses" of Torre Bufilla). Pitt-Rivers commented on the variety of size and style of houses within the *pueblo* of "Alcala" in Spain. Here he found that the three-storeyed mansions with architectural pretensions were all close to the centre of the settlement. These houses date from the eighteenth century, a period of prosperity, and are associated with a particular social or economic group, in this case that of the relatively wealthy clothiers. He also found houses of two storeys, where the upper floor is in fact often little more than an attic. Finally there were the simplest houses, those inhabited by the poorest people, all of which were single-storey dwellings. Every house, however, had a yard at the rear, perhaps with a stable and an open veranda with its cooking area and a trellised vine. In Lison-Tolosana's village further north in Spain, all houses were found to have a yard around which are set stables and sheds. Over half the houses have two storeys but only the older ones have an attic-granary (now obsolete). As at "Alcala", the poorer ones were single storeyed. There were also a number of cave dwellings: 25 out of 33 caves were inhabited in the early 1960s.

The Sicilian village of "Milocca" was likewise composed mostly of two-room or one-room dwellings. Where there was a second room it had been built over the first and was reserved for the family, while the lower room served for storage and to house the domestic animals. The upper room was reached by an outside staircase, common to two closely adjoining houses. One difference between the Spanish and the Sicilian house was that a wealthy family in Sicily extended its house not vertically, as in the Spanish three-storey houses, but horizontally by taking over two or more units of two-storey dwellings and joining them by covered stairways. In the poorer single-room houses there was a manger near the

Fig. 9. *Peasant houses* in lowland villages can either develop vertically into the "tall houses" of Languedoc or spread horizontally into the courtyard type of the Campidano of southern Sardinia. The house at Poussan has the wrought-iron embellishments characteristic of early nineteenth century prosperity derived from viticulture. The house in (B) comes from the low limestone plateaux of the Montpellier Garrigues. Excavations at Torre Bufilla (province of Valencia), Spain, have revealed the ground plan of medieval village houses (Figs A and B from Nelli, 1958; Fig. C from Le Lannou, 1941; Fig. D from Bazzana and Guichard, 1974).

C

Plate 1. *Interior of a peasant's house.* This single, ground-floor room was photographed in Foggia, Italy, at the beginning of the twentieth century. The stable opens directly onto the street. The domestic portion, on a low platform at the rear, is orderly and almost homely (F. H. Jackson, *The Shores of the Adriatic: the Italian Side* (1906). Reproduced with permission from the Royal Geographical Society).

door for the livestock. Chapman related how the family's table and chairs, beds and chests would be set towards the back of the room and clothes hung from pegs in the walls. Plate 1 shows just such an interior on the mainland at the beginning of the twentieth century.

On the Campidano of Sardinia, the houses of richer peasant farmers are of the courtyard type (Le Lannou, 1947; Baldacci, 1952; Mosso, 1957). Access from the street is through a large, arched entrance which may have ornately carved or decorated doors (Fig. 9C). The courtyard is surrounded on all sides by buildings or high walls. The dwelling parts are always opposite the entrance. The entire unit is spacious, with apparent disregard for the area taken up. In Languedoc the typical village house for both plain and hill peasant farmers is today the tall house of three storeys (Nelli, 1958, p. 59). The ground floor houses the livestock; the two first-floor rooms (kitchen and dwelling room, respectively) are reached by an external staircase which terminates in a platform or simple verandah and the upper floor or attic used to be used as a hay-loft. Development of a tall rather than horizontal house is only up to a point connected with the availability of land. In lowland villages the oldest peasant houses are all two-storeyed, the three-storeyed ones having been built in the nineteenth century [5] when an increase in the family's income, through the profitability of viticulture, raised standards of living. In these villages, an occasional courtyard type (smaller and more compact than those of the Sardinian Campidano), turns out to have been the property of a noble landowner. Status and wealth, therefore, as well as availability of land and functional needs, have evidently been important factors in the style and layout of the houses of peasant farmers in the villages of Mediterranean Europe.

Village Site and Territory

A particular characteristic in Mediterranean Europe is the siting of villages in such a way that they overlook their own lands. The territory was an extension of the village itself not just economically but socially, administratively and politically. This is still the case. At "Alcala", Pitt-Rivers found that the village was "the social centre of a community stretching for eight miles around" (1954, p. 6). The local district (*termino*, *contado*, *pays*, *commune*) was used for the collection of taxes and for the numbering of hearths or heads of families.

In Corsica, parishes and villages were formerly organized into *pieve*,

Plate 2. *A village in the mountains*: the site and territory of Benifesa, Valencia. In 1735 the total population here was listed as 41 *vecinos,* much the same as today.

units that appear in most cases to have developed from the *civitates* of the Roman administration although some were new in the sixth century A.D. (Casta, 1974, p. 33). The *pieve* was officially an ecclesiastical unit, centring on a mother church, which contained a number of villages together with their territories. In a mountainous island such as Corsica, individual villages tend to be extremely isolated, each enclosed in its own part of the valley. The idea of the *pieve* was to foster, even to force, regular contacts between the several villages included within the *pieve. Pieve* boundaries were therefore designed to run along the crests. *Pieve* churches were sited not in the valleys or near an existing settlement but at the boundaries, particularly where several of these converged. Many of these churches are in Romanesque or Pisan style and survive as architectural gems in remote wildernesses of rock and forest.

The point of such a territorial arrangement was to ensure the economic advantages the enlarged territory could offer. But each village territory in Corsica can be supposed to have originated in the same way as any other in Mediterranean Europe, or elsewhere for that matter. The principles observed would have been those that ensured that each settlement would be permanently supplied with its essential resources. In the absence of large-scale industrial or commercial activity, the land has to be the sole basis of wealth and the five essential requirements of a rural community (water, arable land, grazing land, building material and fuel) would under normal circumstances be expected to be available from the community's own territory (Chisholm, 1968, p. 102ff). In England it has been noticed how many of the old ecclesiastical parishes appear to reflect earlier territories that, as the Orwins put it, had been "perfectly laid out for [the] purpose of . . . of giving sustenance to the village all the year around" (Orwin and Orwin, 1967, p. 26). There is no reason whatsoever to doubt that such principles also guided the initial selection of territory and of settlement site in Mediterranean Europe whenever this took place in historic or prehistoric times.

The relationship between a community and its territory is in the first place economic. Any threat to its extent or quality would have been jealously dealt with. Unless there was land to spare, any increase in population had to be sustained from an economic resource area whose boundaries were fixed. By the Middle Ages there cannot have been many communities in Mediterranean Europe who could afford to lose even a small part of what they regarded as their land. Hence the large number of boundary disputes recorded in the archives. One in Apulia, for example, dates from the first years of the eleventh century when the quarrel between Troia (ancient *Aecas*) and Vaccarezia (now a deserted site) in Capitanata was over grazing land in the vicinity of the river Vulgano which formed the common boundary. It was eventually settled by no less an authority than the Byzantine Catepan, Boianus (Trinchera, 1865).

Allowance has to be made for the physical nature of the land and for the shape of the territory but otherwise the initial selection of a site for the settlement would have been according to considerations that have been defined in the principles of central-place location (Christaller, 1933; Lösch, 1940, 1954). The inhabitants of a centrally placed settlement in a more or less compact territory enjoy the advantage of being able to reach all parts of their territory with equal ease. Such considerations are important since an agricultural settlement's permanency depends in the instance on the success of its economy. Other factors, such as defence, administrative convenience or political circumstance, are matters of secondary or even momentary consequence. A village is after all normally the home of a farming population. Yet the economic factor of central place has tended to be underplayed in discussions of early settlement patterns.

For instance, out of a score of papers dealing with mainly prehistoric settlement location at a recent conference, only five gave top emphasis to the economic factor (Ucko *et al.*, 1972; commented on by Willey, 1973).

The decision that one point or another within the central area was going to be the most suitable for the site of the houses and farmsteads that would eventually constitute the hamlet or village involved another set of factors. One might well be ease of defence but only if the period or area of colonization was politically unstable. Far more commonly, one suspects, the decision reflected considerations deemed convenient at that time by the majority of the inhabitants. Most villages and many farmsteads in Mediterranean Europe today occupy a rocky knoll or the crest of a slight undulation. In this sense they can be said to be "perched", though a distinction should be made between such sites and the more spectacular but on the whole less common "eyrie" sites. A raised site has many advantages in Mediterranean Europe. The village is healthily breezy in summer but safe above floods or temperature inversion in winter. Good arable land, all too often in short supply, is not lost under the built-up area. It is true that there is often little room and that the ridge-top can be over-crowded but the close-set buildings and narrow alleys create a welcome shade in summer and at all times foster the community spirit. With such a site, the need for defensive structure (walls) is minimized because the steep breaks of slope are themselves a deterrent to casual attack. Finally, but a matter of no small importance, was the advantage that the village overlooked its associated territory and was in sight or signalling distance of its neighbours.

Peasants on Estate Farms

Common though village residence has been throughout Mediterranean Europe in the historic period, it was by no means the only settlement form. A sort of pseudo-village community used to be found at the centre of an estate. Here lived, besides the landowner or members of his retinue, not peasant farmers *sensu stricto* but other members of the peasantry such as landless agricultural workers. There may also have been one or two share-cropping tenants, together with their families. The size of this estate community and the size and layout of farm complex depended on the extent and nature of the estate. A very large estate needed a vast labour force to work the fields and run the farm; 20 or 30 plough teams at work simultaneously in a single field would not have been uncommon in some districts. It meant too that the estate centre was usually at a considerable distance from neighbouring estate centres and from the villages of the district. The workers were therefore obliged to reside at the estate centre, at least during the week. In hill and mountain districts, the unevenness of the terrain might have acted against large-scale exploitation and the problem tended not to arise, but on lowlands and on the plains there were no such constraints to put a limit on the size of estates. These can be, and certainly were in the days before modern transport, little worlds in themselves, a nucleated centre isolated by great distances of private farmland.

There were no estates on the land of Chapman's Sicilian village "Milocca" but a few of the young men found employment on the *latifundia* of neighbouring communes. Many found it impossible to return home each night because of the distance and lodged instead in the large house provided at the centre of the estate for this purpose during the week. Some of them brought their families and established more or less permanent residence. In addition there was the landowner's representative, the bailiff and his family, together with those of specialist farm workers such as cattle men and shepherds. In such a manner, estate farmsteads could grow into a hamlet or take on the appearance of a village. Chapman found that with the considerable size of the community and the fact that "some of them have churches and shops of their own" they did indeed constitute small villages in effect (p.141). The Sicilian poet Verga (1883) had made a similar point in the previous century, when he referred to "a farmhouse as big as a village, with storebarns that look like churches . . . and a big well". The well used to provide the social focus for the estate community in precisely the same way as the communal fountain does in the villages. Architecturally, it is a conspicuous feature in the drier districts of Mediterranean Europe. Verga's church-like granary is found not only in Sicily but widely in Mediterranean Europe, particularly in the damper regions such as northwest Spain (Gutkind, 1967, p. 159). Then there were small industrial workshops, working particularly iron, wood and clay for domestic and agricultural needs. Finds of *scoriae* from sites of pre-Roman farms suggest that this was an early characteristic (Delano Smith, 1978, p. 163). On some of the wealthier and more exotic of the Roman estate centres, there were also gold, silver and copper craftsmen (Jones, 1964, p. 782). All these commodities could be exported when a surplus had accumulated and individual centres might gain a reputation for the quality or style of their products.

A variety of names, even within one country, is given to the estate centres but the only real difference is in the details of layout. In northern Italy, both *corte* and *cascine* are found on the Po lowlands whereas *fattoria* are common in Tuscany. The *corte* is again encountered in Campania but across the Apennines and in Sicily the same feature is called a *masseria*. In southern France, the *mas* or *mansio* is found both east and west of the Rhone. In Andalucia, Granada, Murcia and elsewhere in Spain the *cortijo* is a more common form except in Alentejo where it is the *monte*. Some of these words are known to derive from pre-medieval times. The words *masseria* and *mas* are said to come from a Low, or Lombardized, Latin word referring to the head of a family of servants or tenant slaves, the *massaro* being responsible for the running of the estate on behalf of the landowner (Fasoli, 1965; Drew, 1973). During the Moors' occupation of Spain, the Andalucian *cortijos* already existed as forms of settlement but were designated by the Arab word *madjshar* or *medshar* (derived from or related to the Moroccan *dshar*) (Lévi-Provençal, 1950, Vol. III, p. 265 fn 1). Further north, in Valencia there was the *quaryah*, ''a hamlet or number of farmhouses'' that has given rise to the modern *alqueria* (Imamuddin, 1965, p. 79).

The estate farmstead is recognizably the same settlement feature in modern and in medieval times. There are three defining characteristics. One is that it constitutes the central point of the demesne portion of an estate. Secondly, it is a multiple unit in terms of the functions and in physical layout. The third is that the number of people who live there are sufficient to comprise a hamlet or village community, which is how the modern Italian census classifies *masseria, fattoria* etc. Today, the number of workers employed by an Italian farmer is sometimes subject to government guidelines (Dumont, 1957, p. 233). The type of farming and soil fertility are taken into consideration so that there are regional variations, but in the Mantua district, for example, where the mandatory ratio is one labourer for every 19 hectares, a single modern *cascina* might easily employ 40 male labourers and house their families. Much depends on the average family size of the time. On the Ricasoli family's estates in Tuscany in the middle of the nineteenth century a tenant farmer's family is reported to have usually ten persons, including three or four men of working age (Biagiolo, 1970, p. 10 fn). Estate centres with a total population of several hundred, therefore, would not have been uncommon in the past, particularly in the southern districts of Spain and Italy where estates tended to be very large because of physical conditions.

In consequence of the size of the community and of the isolation of each complex, the estate farmstead in its heyday was a microcosm of the village. In many parts of Mediterranean Europe this is still the case. A zone of vegetable gardens and orchards surrounds the complex. Beyond this zone stretch the estate lands, possibly for several kilometres. In the arid districts of Andalucia or Apulia, where the countryside around a *cortijo* or a *masseria* is dry-farmed cereal land (*secano*), the intervening land is open, deserted and seemingly endless. Each centre stands out starkly in this naked landscape. In more humid or more fertile regions, as on the Po lowlands or the Languedocian plain or in Campania, estate centres are much closer and this, together with their characteristic courtyard layout, often gives an impression of almost cosy compactness.

Houston (1964, pp. 248–249) describes the Valencian *alqueria* as the "isolated house of a landed proprietor" and gives an illustration of a compact and comparatively small building. This is not surprising, considering the intensity of irrigated farming and the very high density of population in the *huertas* of Valencia and Murcia where "estates" also tend to be correspondingly small. In 1575, over a third of the holdings in the Murcian *huerta* were between 10 and 25 *taullas* (1 and 3 hectares), another quarter were between 25 and 45 *taullas* (3 and 5 hectares) and only 12% were over 200 *taullas* (10 hectares) (Calvo, 1975, p. 116). Moreover, few *alquerias* lay at any great distance from a town or village. The labour force therefore that had to be housed would have been small compared with that needed on the dry-farmed *cortijos* of the south.

The *alquerias* of Levantine Spain have had a varied history. Undoubtedly many of the earliest, Moorish or Christian, were originally built on land that at the time was *secano* and would have been laid out as for dry-farming. As the irrigation network was extended, so some were taken into the *huerta*, surving as rather over-large centres. This may help explain the association of the term "locality" with all but two of the 26 *alquerias* named as existing in the Gandia *huerta* in 1240 (Fontavella, 1952, p. 310). There were other changes too. In the fourteenth and fifteenth centuries there were several attempts at resettlement and large colonies of Catalonian peasants were brought into the Valencian *huerta* for instance (Vicens-Vives, 1961, Vol. II, p. 12 ff; Birot and Gabert, 1964, p. 295). These immigrants are recorded as having been housed in *alquerias* vacated by the Moors. The land of the former estate was subdivided and shared amongst the newcomers. Eventually the descendants of the colonists became hereditary tenants of increasingly small holdings. In recent years

C*

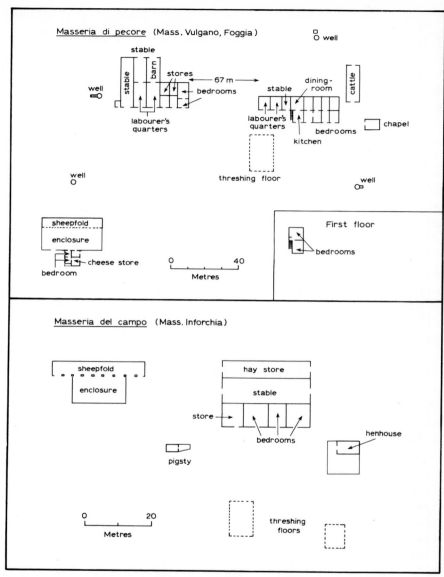

Fig. 10. *Estate centres* on the plain of Foggia, Apulia. Note the difference in scale; the *masseria di pecore*, a farmstead designed for large-scale livestock raising, is not only the more complex in layout but also occupies a much greater area than the predominantly arable *masseria del campo*. Note too that in neither case is the other branch of farming wholly absent. Sheep were kept at Mass. Inforchia for milk and manure and oxen for ploughing, while land at Mass. Vulgano was cultivated for animal and human foodstuffs (from Colamonico, 1970).

they have been able to buy their holdings, thus becoming peasant proprietors. In this way, many *alquerias* were transformed into villages as the population increased and remain so today.

The layout of an individual estate farmstead reflects the local cropping pattern. The livestock centres of Apulia (*masseria di pecore*) are composed of a number of buildings and rooms, each associated with a specific activity arising from large-scale livestock rearing (Fig. 10, upper). Altogether, the entire complex spreads over an area of 2 or 3 hectares. In contrast, centres on cereal estates (*masseria del campo*) are less complex and therefore more compact in layout even though they may house a greater number of people (Fig. 10, lower). In the rice-growing districts of the Po plain, the layout of the *cascinas* reflects the enormous amount of work involved in rice production as well as the importance of the estate. The buildings and intervening yards at Castel Merlino (Vercelli) occupy over 7 hectares (Dematteis, 1965). The estate, in 1960, added up to 300 hectares.

While many of the estate centres in Mediterranean Europe are of considerable antiquity, dating back to the early Middle Ages, their layout also reflects a periodic adaptation to agricultural change. Centres that are very complex and extensive today, like Castel Merlino, may not have started that way. The oldest units at Castel Merlino are those grouped around courtyard 1 (Fig. 11a). It was originally a cereal estate and the first buildings provided accommodation for the labourers, a block set aside for storage and for the stables, and the original two-storeyed house of the landowner. By the nineteenth century, rice growing had become so profitable that it accounted at Castel Merlino for a quarter of the arable area and had led to considerable expansion (courtyard 2). Modern technical changes are reflected in the addition of a third yard.

Similar adaptations to changing economic circumstances and to crop and land-use changes are seen in the layout of the *mas* in southern France. The original plan reflects land use before the descent of the vine and extensive viticulture on the lowlands and plains. The layout of the Languedoc *mas* is most commonly that of the closed courtyard type (*cour fermée, corte*), thought to be the oldest form and of direct descent from the Gallo-Roman *villa*. In a typical *mas*, three buildings define a yard closed on the fourth side by a high wall into which is set the imposing arched entrance. One of the blocks housed a variety of functions and included space for carts and wagons. There may have been silk-worm rearing here too. A second block housed the livestock, which was mostly sheep. The third was residential except for the vaulted ground floor which was used as

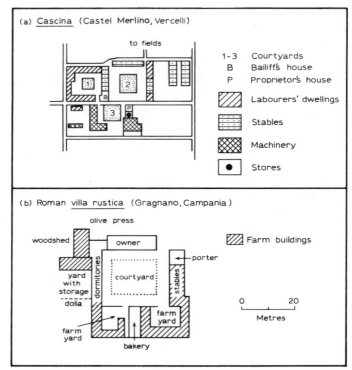

Fig. 11. *Estate centres.* A modern one from the Po plain and the excavated layout of a Roman one from Campania (adapted from Dematteis, 1965, and White, 1970).

a domestic wine-cellar and for the stables. In the residential block, an external staircase led to a spacious south-facing terrace which in turn opened in to an immense kitchen dominated along one side by the hearth. All domestic rooms communicated with the kitchen, as did the hayloft above. Towards the end of the eighteenth century, the increasing profitability of viticulture resulted in modifications at the *mas* in order to accommodate the new needs and new standards of production. A new house would be built for the landowner, usually a little apart from the main group and often in *chateau* style. Fewer animals are needed in the cultivation of vineyards than for arable farming but more space is needed for wine processing and storage. The former stables therefore became the wine cellars.

Growing conditions in central and southern Spain are amongst the most rigorous in Mediterranean Europe and the great size of individual estates reflects this. A greater proportion of land has to be left fallow each year in order to recoup its moisture content. Because of the extent of the low-yielding arable land, a greater labour force is required (Chisholm, 1968, p. 58). This has to be housed in the *cortijo* which becomes virtually a village in layout as well as in population size. There may be several rows of single-storey dwellings for the workers. There is a row of stables. Some *cortijos* have been walled or arranged in such a way as to form a single unit around a central courtyard. Each has its fringe of carefully watered and tended gardens for the fruit and vegetables consumed in the *cortijos*. Most of the buildings that are used today can be dated no further back than the seventeenth century but the feeling is that the site has been long occupied and that "undoubtedly they have replaced similar units of labour" (Houston, 1964, p. 250).

We are back therefore at the question of continual occupation of rural settlement, this time in the context of the estate farmsteads. There have been several detailed toponymic studies both in Languedoc (Thomas, 1865; Lognon, 1920; Hamlin, 1959) and in Spain (e.g. Caro Baroja, 1946, p. 235 ff). These usually concentrate on the relationship between a postulated Roman estate (*fundus*) with its steading (*villa*) and a documented medieval village. If little is known of this relationship, still less can be demonstrated about the continuity of estates *quae* estates.

In Languedoc, modern place-names ending in *-ac*, *-an* and *-argues* are thought to be derived from Latin forms indicating the proprietorship of a Gallo-Roman estate. In this way, the ending *-ac* comes from the adjective genitive *-acum*. The former *fundus* of one Florias becomes the name of the village Florensac [*Floriacus—Villa Floriachum* (in the Cartulary of the Abbey of Gellone in A.D. 804)—*Florensiacum villa* in A.D. 990]. Where the modern name ends in *-an*, the "c" has been replaced by "n" and the ending declines with the assumed word *fundus* (masculine, first order). So the estate belonging to Frontinus becomes *Frontinianum* and is now Frontignan. Names ending today in *-argues* have been formed from the word *ager* (arable land). The arable land belonging to Saturius (*Saturi ager*) is now Saturargues. However attractive such toponymic arguments may be, they are no substitute for stratified archaeological evidence. The postulated relationship between Roman estate and medieval estate or village needs the proof of evidence.

The interval between a Roman villa and a medieval *mas* could be as much as a thousand, often turbulent and certainly very changeable, years. Much more is known about Roman estate settlements than about anything in that interval. Archaeological activity has tended to centre on the remains of major villas. For instance, 36 Roman farm units on the slopes of Vesuvius were first excavated during the nineteenth century. Since then the technique of aerial photography has been developed by which the ground plan of villas long since vanished into the ground can be accurately discerned while descriptions of their former interiors and furnishings are found in the classical literature. Advice regarding their layout and management is contained in the major agricultural treatises. All these sources have contributed to a remarkably clear and authoritative picture of estate farmsteads during the Roman period.

Many of the early *villae rusticae* in Italy were unpretentious. It was only later, after the first century A.D., that a few became really luxurious. One of the early ones (second century B.C.) is the Villa Sambuco (Etruria). This was a farm run by a slave manager on behalf of the landowner and worked by slaves (White, 1970, p. 419). In due course increased wealth, status or aspiration resulted in increasingly complex and disparate villa layouts. At the Villa Sambuco the basic consideration had evidently been the need to group complementary activities in a single sector or wing. At first, villa layout therefore allowed space for stables in one of the wings and placed the manager's accommodation (office and sleeping quarters) near the main entrance so that he could keep a better check on all activities. Later, as the size of farm units tended to increase after the first century A.D., agricultural activities began to be separated from residential. The main building became increasingly luxurious while in ground plan the villa became similar to the village-like complexity of modern *masseria*. These developments were encouraged by agronomists as well as architects. Vitruvius (1.6.1) suggested that the kitchen and the cowhouse should be in the yard. A little later, Columella (1.6.21) advised the placing of the bakery and cornmill in separate units (partly to minimize the fire risk) and pointed out that two ponds should be provided in the yard. There was already space there for the compost and manure heaps, for the threshing floor and for the drying shed. In all major respects as well as in many details, therefore, the estate centres of Roman times were very similar to those of later centuries in layout and in function.

Isolated Settlement

A small proportion of the peasantry of Mediterranean Europe has lived not in village or even hamlet nucleations but in isolated farmsteads dispersed about the countryside. These farmsteads have not on the whole had the continuity of site occupation some of the villages may have had, and the proportion of the population living out in the countryside has always been in the minority. On the other hand, the isolated steading was undoubtedly a far more common pattern of settlement at least at certain times in the past in Mediterranean Europe than is generally realized.

The situation has been very different in the different regions of Mediterranean Europe and at different times. In the *huertas* of Spain isolated settlement was associated with the spread of irrigation and intensive cropping. In the drier cereal lands, where estates and other cereal farms predominated, the isolated farmstead was a rarity. According to the Italian census of 1861, hardly 4% of the total population of the province of Capitanata (now Foggia) lived in the *case sparse* of the plain.' Interestingly, although agrarian reforms carried out since the First World War and other factors have considerably altered the landscape and more than doubled the number of *case sparse*, the proportion has altered much less. Today only 6% of the total population live in isolated dwellings. The implication is clear enough. A home in one of the villages, or agro-towns, of the plain or in a *masseria* remains preferable in this region even in modern times. In contrast, on the vine-growing plains of Languedoc the move out from the villages to a permanent residence in the fields and vineyards was in active progress early in the nineteenth century. Improved security, drainage of lowlands and plains, eradication of malaria, changes in the social order and the demands of the new agriculture, were all contributory factors at one time or another.

The newness of the isolated farmsteads in many regions of Mediterranean Europe today has exaggerated the idea that dispersed settlement is only a modern development. But in other regions, or even in the same regions in earlier times, isolated farmsteads were to be found in considerable numbers. In Tuscany, by the turn of the fourteenth century, "detached farms already existed in numbers, some of them demesne buildings, with *turres* and *palatia*, others certainly the work of improving copy-holders" (Jones, 1968, p. 232). Even here, as Jones continues, "dispersed settlement was nothing new in Tuscany. It had Dark Age antecedents". In Liguria the pressure of growing economic demands in the twelfth and thirteenth centuries led to a substantial penetration of isolated settlement in the heavily forested mountains of Liguria to be followed by a second period of colonization (or re-colonization) in the sixteenth and seventeenth centuries (Moreno, 1973; Moreno and Maestri, 1975).

The most important incentive for the spread of settlement into the scarcely accessible mountains of Liguria was the forest. Timber was in heavy demand at Genoa and other ship-building localities along the coast below. Iron industries and glass industries, also in expansion, were heavy users of coppiced timber. In addition deforested or naturally open districts were becoming of major importance for sheep grazing as the wool industry of northern Italy gained in importance on the European scale. Exploitation of these forest resources led to permanent settlement not however in villages or hamlets but in isolated steadings. The process of settlement is recorded in the Statutes of Ovada.

The Statutes of Ovada were originally written in 1327 (Moreno and Maestri, 1975). They show that by 1585 there were 64 *case* (houses) scattered about the area and also a small number of *albergi de bosco*, *capsine* or *domi*. By the sixteenth century and the second major burst of colonization, circumstances had changed. In the medieval period the stimulus had been hope of gaining a profit from exploitation of forest resources. In the later period it was simply land hunger that drove people into the mountains.

In both periods colonization resulted in isolated settlements but the change in the circumstances was reflected in certain details. In the later period there are fewer references to *case* and the word *cassina* (not to be confused with the *cascina* of the Po lowlands) was being used instead. A *cassina* is strictly speaking a hayloft but since it was the addition of a hayloft (as well as stables) to the old *case* that was the distinguishing feature of the second phase of settlement dispersal, the word came to be applied to the steading as a whole. In this way, the 15 *cassine* of 1585 had increased to 177 by 1650 while the number of unmodified *case* dropped from 64 to 27. The new houses, with their haylofts and stables, were liable for an extra *decima* of taxation. The reason for the second wave of colonization in the Ligurian mountains, land hunger at lower altitudes, meant that wherever land was found that was at all suitable for cultivation (usually below 850 m) it was exploited by a peasant household for simple subsistence. The earlier colonizers, interested only in the export of forest resources, had had no need for the haylofts and stables now added to the old houses. The new colonists made a living with difficulty. Chestnuts were cultivated, which was always a bad sign. The emphasis on animal rearing was now subsistence. The forests were still exploited for timber, fuel and for the fruits and plants which could be gathered in them, but the products were for local consumption or for the external market only in a limited manner. Even with the addition of a *cassina* houses remained small and simple. They were stone built and apparently stone roofed and of simple rectangular plan. The ground floor was given over to animals, the first floor to residential quarters divided into a kitchen and a separate bedroom. Usually, because of the fall of the land in this mountainous region, the first floor was entered from ground floor level at the rear of the house. Otherwise an external stone staircase was provided. The attic contained the hayloft, capable of storing 25 to 30 *quintaux* of dried fodder.

Dispersed settlement had been as characteristic of some of the poorest or most difficult terrain in Mediterranean Europe such as the mountains of Liguria, as of some of the most unusually favoured, such as the regions of permanent irrigation, the *huertas*. The *huertas* of south-eastern Spain and their Sicilian counterpart were highly regarded by the Romans, well developed by the Arabs and subsequently maintained and extended. Today they are associated with some of the highest population densities and usually typified in textbooks as rare regions of dispersed settlement in Mediterranean Europe. Today in the *huertas* up to half the population lives in isolated farmsteads. After the expulsion of the Moriscos in 1600 the poorer coastal uplands of the Spanish Levant became more sparsely, and the rich lands became even more densely, settled. In 1857 there was an average density in the Valencian *huerta* of 283 persons per square kilometre; by 1950 this had increased to over 1005 persons (Houston, 1964, p. 189ff). In the nineteenth century a high proportion of these were housed in the isolated *barracas*. There were 3921 *barracas* in 1870 in the Valencian *huerta* in addition to 860 *alquerias* and 62 villages.

The *barracas* had increased in number during the eighteenth and nineteenth centuries, accompanying not only an overall population increase but also a dissemination of dispersed settlement. A *barraca* is an isolated dwelling with a single storey, a thatched roof and a timber frame with adobe walls. The rectangular plan is divided by ''a long corridor through which the peasants can move their farm carts'' (Admiralty, Spain, p. 111). A few can still be found isolated by the motorways on the outskirts of Valencia but most have been replaced by more substantial structures.

In documents from the first half of the thirteenth century there is no mention of the *barraca*. The 1252 *Repartimento* mentions only 44 *rahals* and 144 *alquerias*. There is evidence for the existence of isolated dwellings in

the *huertas*, however, at this date in the word *rahal* (*rafal, real*). This word
is of Moorish origin. Apparently in Murcia it originally applied not to a
building or a settlement but to a small holding or plot on permanently
irrigated land which was formed from the village or nearby town
(Fontavella Gonzalez, 1949). Two main lines of the subsequent
development of the *rahal* into a form of isolated settlement may be
suggested. First, it is known that where the plot or *rahal* belonged to the
Crown or to a particularly rich landowner, a pleasure house would
sometimes be erected on it. In this event the plot would be "completely
surrounded by walls or sheltered by a hedge or a big ditch [and] planted
with fruit trees—date palms, oranges, figs, apples, vines, etc."
(Fontavella, 1952, p. 312). It is possible therefore that in due course those
employed to tend these orchards started to live on the *rahal*, together with
their families.

The second line of development starts once again with the problem of
housing colonists drafted into the newly conquered districts from other
parts of Spain or from Languedoc. It is thought that up to 150 000
colonists, mainly Catalans and Aragonese, were eventually brought into
the Levantine *huertas* straight after the Reconquest and that no fewer than
333 *caballeros* and 2200 *peons* received shares of the Murcian *huerta*
(Vicens-Vives, 1961, Vol. II, pp. 43–47; Perez, 1958). Yet there is no
evidence that the period of Reconquest brought any major alteration to
the pre-existing distribution of population or changes to the agrarian
structure or irrigation systems. It has to be assumed that all the incomers
were accommodated in town houses vacated by their Moorish occupants
or on *alquerias* in the manner already described. What may now be
suggested is that at least some of the *rahal* plots were built on at this time
possibly by non-lordly colonists, in order to be lived in as farmsteads. It is
known that some of the *rahals* closest to the towns were built on as these
expanded (Fontavella Gonzales, 1949). It is also known that in some
districts (notably Valencia), James I of Aragon granted an unusual degree
of privately owned smallholdings and created a free peasantry on the
Roman model. What is not recorded is what land was involved. It is
unlikely that all new developments fitted into the newly sub-divided
alquerias and a certain number of colonists may have been obliged to settle
out in the *huerta* on their *rahal* plots. These arguments would help explain
why there were so many *rahals* in the Valencian *huerta* in 1252: If all had
been merely pleasure houses it would be surprising.

What is less conjectural is that some *rahals* became hamlets or villages in the same way as did the *alqueria*. Rafal (Alicante) had 74 houses in 1910 and 272 inhabitants and has given its name to a commune which, including four other groups of houses and a few scattered ones, contained a total of 568 inhabitants (*Enciclopedia Universal*, 1958). In 1735, or about then, the same settlement had 82 *vecinos*, giving a possible total population of about 369 (Mahiques, 1966, p. 66). In the Valencian district in the eighteenth century there was Rafelcofer (84 *vecinos*), Real de Gaudia (83 *vecinos*) and Rafol de Almunia (22 *vecinos*). The beginnings of such transformations are not clear. One notable period of demographic increase in eastern Spain started in the middle of the sixteenth century. In the Sicilian *huertas* however, some of the localities which have *rahal* place-name elements (e.g. *Rachaljohannis*, now Reggiovanni) were being referred to as *castelli* (fortified villages) as early as 1400 (Aymard and Bresc, 1973, p. 963).

Nor was isolated settlement confined to the medieval or later part of the historic period. It was by no means uncommon in Roman times, at least (it has to be stressed) in certain districts. The commonest and best documented form was the centuriation farmstead of the last centuries B.C. Extensive areas of both peninsular and continental Italy, parts of southern France and possibly extensive tracts of eastern Spain came under government control and were laid out in the manner of modern rural reform landscapes. Small steadings, 400–500 m apart, each isolated on its own small holding, were arranged on an accurately surveyed grid-iron pattern that was spread widely about the flat countryside. In Roman times, precisely as in the middle of the twentieth century, many of these steadings proved just too isolated for the liking of the new settlers and many were early abandoned (*see* p. 144).

Prehistoric Settlement

A geographical analysis of prehistoric settlement pattern remains a long way from completion. In most parts of Mediterranean Europe the record of settlement distribution is demonstrably incomplete or the dating of occupation at known sites is so broad as to mask the true contemporaneity of individual sites. An individual settlement may or may not have been occupied continuously during a period that was two, three or four hundred years long. Likewise, two neighbouring settlements even though occupied by people of the same culture need not necessarily have been exactly contemporary. Questions therefore concerning the evolution of prehistoric settlement region by region, or concerning its nucleated or dispersed pattern, generally remain unanswerable for the present.

During the middle and late Neolithic in southern France there was still a high proportion of cave dwelling. In eastern Languedoc (departments of Hérault, Gard, Ardèche), only a third of Chassey occupation sites and rather less than a quarter of those lived in by the subsequent Ferrières group were open-air sites (data quoted by Phillips, 1975, pp. 123–124). Of the nine best-known early Neolithic sites in the old provinces of Valencia, eight are in caves and this has led at least one archaeologist to comment that the preference for cave dwelling at this time is so marked as to suggest this was exclusively the habitation form of the period (Tarradell (ed.), 1965, p. 34; Savory, 1968, p. 79). Cave dwelling has been by no means the prerogative of prehistoric farmers. Doubtless it will be argued that it is the softness of the local limestones at Gravina, in the Apulian Murge, that has been the attractive factor there but inhabited caves are also common in the very much harder limestones of the Gargano a little further north (Calomonico, 1970, p. 21). In fact, troglodytic dwellers account for nearly 2% of the entire Italian population even today: over 3% of the population of the province of Bari and 7% of that of Taranto are living in caves or semi-cave houses (Baldacci, 1962, p. 183). In Spain, inhabited troglodytic settlements are still found in Andalucia, Aragon and La Mancha, and specifically at Chinchilla (Albacete) and Calatayud (Zaragoza) for instance (Gutkind, 1967, p. 160).

One attraction of early cave dwelling must have been that the cave offers a home more or less ready for occupation. In prehistoric times some caves or rock shelters seem to have been provided with extra features such as a wall or fence across the mouth to keep the worst of wind and water out (Pannoux, 1953) but the vast majority show few signs of having been significantly altered by their occupants. The major inconvenience of many of those inhabited in prehistoric times would have been that of inaccessibility. Even so caves were evidently an often popular form of dwelling. Despite precipitous slopes and the rockiness of the Verdon Gorge in Provence, at least 12 caves, in two 10-km sections of the gorge, were inhabited from the Neolithic to the Iron Age. Judging from the landscape shown in Plate 3, a major attraction may have been the sense of security that a cliff-side cave offered compared with the unprotectedness and relative flimsiness of a man-made structure set up on the plateau above surrounded by a forest that continuously threatened with its regrowth, its fauna and its concealed intruders.

Plate 3. *Prehistoric settlement in the mountains.* The cave of Fou de Bor, occupied during the Neolithic, is arrowed. It is in the upper valley of the Ségre, near the Franco-Spanish border. Despite inconvenience of access, in a similarly forested environment a cave-dwelling would afford its occupants a comfortable sense of security (photograph kindly supplied by D. Jordi Rovira I Port).

In the case of cave sites, the pattern of prehistoric settlement and its density is geologically determined. Certain limestone districts, such as the Causses or that of the Gorge of Verdon in southern France were relatively densely settled. Some early cave dwellers, however, must have found themselves living in what may be considered a form of isolated settlement. Not all caves are large enough to have housed more than one or two families, nor was every cave in a particular locality necessarily occupied simultaneously. In contrast with this, on lowlands and on plateau or wherever open-air settlement was the rule, the situation was very different. Here, the choice between nucleated or dispersed settlement would have been a function of social tradition, not .of geological constraints.

One of the richest records of prehistoric settlement in Mediterranean Europe comes from the great lowland of northern Apulia, Tavoliere of Foggia. This is an area whose archaeological interest has hardly yet been tapped. The distribution map of prehistoric settlement as known so far includes sites that would have been occupied at any time within a period not less than 2000 years long. It is virtually impossible therefore to make any useful analyses of the pattern of settlement. It can be suggested, however, that although the usual form of settlement during the Neolithic was the nucleated village or hamlet, there were also some isolated steadings.

Two aspects have to be taken into consideration in analysing a settlement pattern, the size of the individual nucleations or sites and the distance between them. On the Tavoliere, the average diameter of the ditched enclosures that surround each Neolithic settlement is about 200 m. This gives an internal area of 3 hectares which allows plenty of room within the enclosure not only for a small number (half a dozen) of domestic compounds but also for the open spaces thought to have been reserved for livestock (Bradford, 1947; Trump, 1966, p. 40; Tinè, 1975). One or two settlements were much larger. The settlement at La Panetteria (Lucera) included at least 14 domestic compounds with an average diameter of 22·5 m). At Motta della Regina (Foggia) there were 12 internal compounds. The only enclosed prehistoric village of the entire plain, La Lamia (Bovino), contains traces of at least 14 compounds each of over 20 m diameter (G. D. B. Jones in an unpublished report to the Society of Antiquaries). Another of the prehistoric settlement sites on the Tavoliere is unique but this time in respect of its sheer size and area. Passo di Corvo (Foggia) contains traces of over 100 domestic compounds within

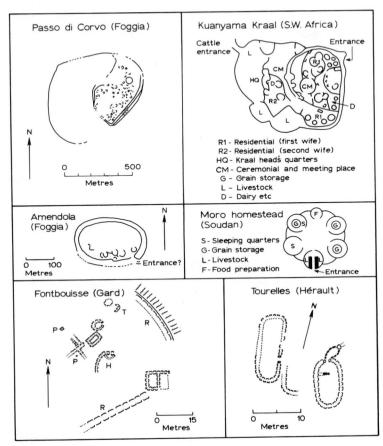

Fig. 12. *Prehistoric settlement.* The plans of Neolithic Passo di Corvo and Amendola have been traced from air photographs and confirmed by selective excavation. The African parallels show just how complicated the usage of such settlements can be but they also show that it tends to be low-density occupation, given the varied use of the individual huts (from Bradford, 1947; D. Fraser; Louis *et al.*, 1947; Audibert, 1962).

a total enclosure measuring 870 × 550 m and enclosing an area of some 40 hectares. In the view of one archaeologist, Passo di Corvo must surely from its size be considered a town (Trump, 1966, p. 41). However, only a third of the internal area was residential. The northern portion of the village area appears to have been left vacant and was presumably used as a livestock yard (Fig. 12). At the other extreme of the prehistoric settlement scale there were some very small settlements indeed. A number of sites on the Tavoliere of Foggia covers less than 200 m² (one or two are smaller still) and appear to have contained only a couple of domestic compounds. Where such sites lay at some distance from each other and certainly more than the 150 m of hailing distance that is used by geographers as a pragmatic measure of settlement isolation, they may be considered the prehistoric equivalent of the isolated steading (Fig. 13).

In France, on the limestone garrigues of Languedoc, it has been observed that on many late-Neolithic and Chalcolithic habitation sites "the huts are grouped in a circle around an empty space which bears a striking resemblance to the yard of a primitive farm" (Arnal, 1963, p. 127). The people of the Fontbouisse culture (third millennium B.C.) lived "generally in hamlets . . . not at any great distance from each other but in clearly separated clusters, each of 3 to 6 huts" (Guilaine and Roudil, 1976, p. 270). In Sardinia, the Bronze Age villages were so big in comparison with these earlier ones that they could be regarded as analogous to the modern agro-town. At least 160 hut foundations have been traced at the early Bronze Age (pre-Nuraghic) village of Puisteris Mogoro (Cagliari) but there is no doubt that there were originally a great many more, possibly double the number (Fig. 14). It is reported that most Sardinian villages in the Bronze Age also show some sort of spatial order in that there are recognizable clusters of dwellings and intervening open spaces (Lilliu, 1963, p. 43).

In some districts in Mediterranean Europe, Neolithic villages were enclosed. It is unlikely however that in any but the exceptional case the presence of an enclosing feature was intended to imply a defence in the strategic sense. There is scant evidence that the Neolithic was anything but a peaceful period of human history and the explanation of the enclosures would seem to lie in the nature of the local environment and in contemporary social and vernacular traditions. The Tavoliere settlements and those of the area around Matera, a little further to the south, were originally surrounded by the narrow, deep ditches, probably water-filled, that show up so clearly on the air photographs. The only unenclosed Neolithic village (La Lamia, Bovino) is also the westernmost village on the plain. This means it is one of the highest and even today it is in a comparatively well-wooded district. So it may be suggested that it too would have been enclosed, but with a timber fence or stockade instead of the more usual ditch. In the rockier districts of Mediterranean Europe,

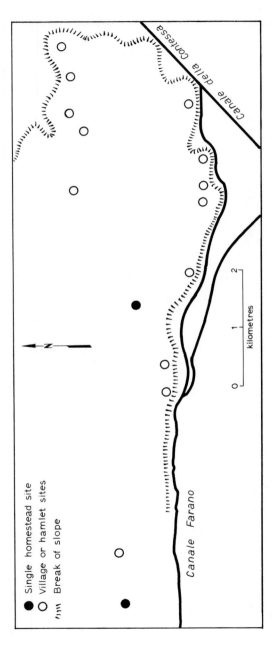

Fig. 13. *Prehistoric settlement.* Isolated and village forms near Amendola (Foggia). All the sites are clearly traceable on air photographs and nearly all have been checked on the ground. The two sites designated as isolated are so classified because of their small overall size, the small number of internal compounds evident or likely, and the substantial distance of each from its nearest neighbour, especially considering that 150 m ("hailing distance") is the pragmatic measure of isolation for rural settlement accepted by most modern geographers. There are no sites of any sort within 2 or 3 km west of the area shown on the map; much of the ground below the bluff around the eastern end of the Amendola terrace was occupied by the lagoons and marshes of Lago Salso.

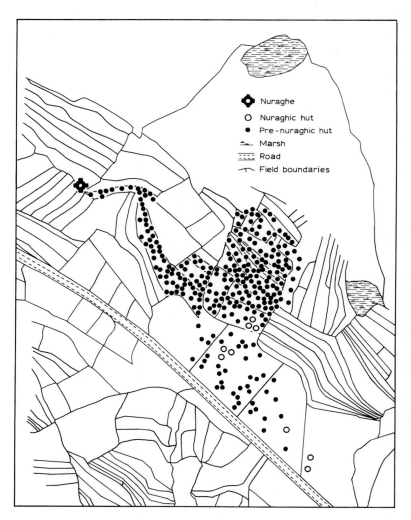

Fig. 14. *Puisteris de Mogoro, Sardinia.* Despite the obvious incompleteness of the evidence, the pre-nuraghic settlement must have been remarkably large. The distribution of the huts, however, reflects availability of archaeological evidence, as affected by present-day landownership and the pattern of archaeological discovery, rather than the original layout of the settlement (adapted from Puxeddu, 1975).

loose or easily quarried stone was taken for the construction of dry-stone walls. Many late-Neolithic and Chalcolithic sites in Languedoc and Provence are sited on a rocky ridge and in such cases a simple well across the neck of the spur was all that was needed to demarcate the village (Audibert, 1962). In fact, the wall might have been a later addition, as at Fontbouisse (Gard) (Louis et al., 1947). A truly fortified settlement at this time was a rarity. The Chalcolithic settlement of Lébous (Les Matelles, Hérault) would have been unique in the whole of the Neolithic Midi, being possibly even earlier in date than similar developments in Iberia at the Bronze Age site of Los Millares (Almeria) (Arnal et al., 1964).

With the exception of Lébous, the layout of villages in Mediterranean Europe remained simple and domestic throughout the Neolithic and Chalcolithic periods. The striking change came in the middle of the Bronze Age, the period of the *nuraghi* in Sardinia, of the *torre* in Corsica, and of the fortified hilltop villages of Spain. In Sardinia, the large villages of the period became markedly smaller. At Puisteris Mogoro, only nine of the 160 huts continued to be inhabited during the *nuraghic* period. Not far away, at Barumini, is the largest and best-preserved of all the Sardinian *nuraghi*. The village at its foot, however, was small compared with the earlier agglomeration at Puisteris Mogoro, accommodating perhaps 200, at most 300 people (Guido, 1963, p. 142). The *nuraghi* are unlikely to have been anything but defensive in function. The contrast between them and the usually modest settlement at their foot is the more marked for the magnificence and perfection of the architecture of the *nuraghe* itself. It is suggested that the rural population had by now moved out into the surrounding countryside (unless the smallness of the villages reflect a major demographic decline). In contrast, in Spain the fortified hill top settlements of the Bronze Age remained sizeable agricultural villages. At El Agar (Almeria), the settlement was spread over a hill top conveniently defined by natural drops to the broad valley below. The houses were occupied all the year around. They were distributed within the fortified area most irregularly but with plenty of open spaces between each group (Tarradell, 1975, p. 47ff).

A geographer would like to continue his review of prehistoric settlement with an analysis of house-type. However there are two problems. Usually little evidence is available about the superstructure of prehistoric huts and what there is tends to be heavily biased towards structures involving the most durable of the building materials, i.e. stone. Most of the available information therefore concerns the plan of the house, broadly classified as circular or rectangular. However, there are some remarkable groups of rock engravings which do show the elevation of early houses and these are of considerable interest.

The best-known and most numerous prehistoric rock engravings are those of Italian Alpine districts of Mont Bego (Tende) and of Val Camonica (Brescia). Some of these engravings are thought to date from the very late Neolithic (Anati, 1964). The majority were executed in the Bronze Age, a few early in the Iron Age. Altogether they portray a wealth of detail on contemporary life. On a single rock in the Val Camonica (the Naquane), 16 different buildings are depicted. From these it is possible to suggest that prehistoric houses in these Alpine valleys tended to be small and that they bear considerable resemblances to the timber-framed houses of modern times. Occasionally a house appears to have been supported by piles, presumably because it was on sloping ground. More commonly (or at an earlier date) the ground floor was used as a barn or granary and an outside stairway led to the living storey (*ibid.*, p. 241). A later stage of engraving shows that an outshot barn was sometimes added (in much the same way as the sixteenth-century-A.D. colonists added haylofts to existing *case* in Bosco di Ovada). It is the later period too that shows the most variety as regards house dimension and architecture and perhaps, by implication, status. As for building material, there can be little doubt that use was made of stone and rock, at least in the foundations or to create a level platform from sloping ground, but that timber was the preferred building material. Some engravings represent the building operation itself and "in one we see people lifting a beam onto a roof whose framework is not yet complete" (Anati, 1964, pp. 37–38) (Fig. 15).

Wood is perishable and the relative abundance or intactness of stone walls in the archaeological record gives the impression that stone was automatically preferred for house building in rocky districts. Against this however should be set the great number of prehistoric sites that contain evidence of post-holes, not to mention actual remains of wattle and daub or similar forms of wall panelling. It is clear that timber was used extensively even where stone was available. For example, in Chassey and Chalcolithic times in southern France, the common practice was to build a foundation and a low wall in dry-stone and then to add a superstructure and roof of timbers, branches and some sort of thatch. In south-eastern Spain, the round or oval huts investigated at El Garcel (Almeria) had excavated floors which were then similarly surrounded by a wattle and daub superstructure (Savory, 1967, p. 79). On the Tavoliere of Foggia, all huts

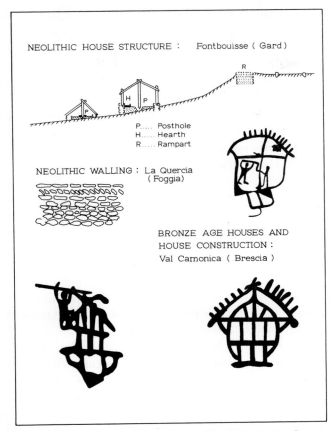

NEOLITHIC HOUSE STRUCTURE :   Fontbouisse (Gard)

P..... Posthole
H..... Hearth
R..... Rampart

NEOLITHIC WALLING : La Quercia
                        (Foggia)

BRONZE AGE HOUSES AND
HOUSE CONSTRUCTION :
Val Camonica (Brescia)

Fig. 15. *Prehistoric domestic architecture.* The sketch of Neolithic dry-stone walling does not do justice to the very fine techniques and skills of the early builders at La Quercia. The elevations at Fontbouisse, Languedoc, are reconstructions from excavated walls and post-holes and other archaeological evidence, but those from Val Camonica, in northern Italy, are thought to be contemporary representations, engraved on ice-smoothed rock-faces. The wall was sketched from a photograph taken by J. Bradford, now in the Pitt-Rivers Museum, Oxford. (Louis *et al.*, 1947; Anati, 1964).

were timber-framed, to judge from the post-hole evidence. Again, this could not have been because of a shortage of stone or because of ignorance of stone-building techniques. Stone walls were built in the Neolithic on the Tavoliere, and most elegantly for that matter, but they appear to have been used only as ditch revetments and for the enclosing wall surrounding the huts rather than for the huts themselves. An outstanding example of the high quality of Neolithic walling techniques on the Tavoliere was excavated by the late John Bradford at La Quercia. Standing less than a metre high and about 75–100 cm wide, the wall enclosed a cobble-floored domestic compound. It was built from blocks of calcrete, probably taken from the upcast material of the outer ditches (of which there are, most unusually and intriguingly, eight). Unprepared blocks were used for the lowest five courses. For the seventh course, these were set at an angle. The eighth and final course is a single row of neat, regular slabs laid flat to give a perfect finish to the whole wall (Fig. 15).

The selection of a site for a prehistoric village, fortified or otherwise, would have been governed by precisely the same sort of economic considerations that led to the choice of hillocks and hill tops as village sites throughout the historic period. There can be no proof that this was the case as no archaeological evidence can identify decision-making factors. But if the characteristics of each prehistoric settlement are reviewed in the light of the historic model, this conclusion is hard to avoid. For example, of the 70 prehistoric sites on the Tavoliere so analysed, only four were found to be over 2 km distant from a valley, and of these three were not on the interfluve but below the break of slope, suggesting that the normal process was to select a site at or near the contact between ecologically contrasting but economically complementary terrain. All other factors which might have bearing on site location (geology, soil class, aspect, depth of water table, altitude etc.) were also analysed for these 70 sites (Delano Smith, 1978, p. 105ff). In no way did these factors fail to support the impression that the primordial consideration in prehistoric site selection was to live as near as possible to the centre of a territory of varied economic resources. A similar conclusion has already been approached in the case of late Neolithic settlement in southern France, where it was noticed that almost every Chassey or Chalcolithic settlement site in the Montpellier district was found to be either at or very close to the contact between limestone (upland) and clay (valley) (Delano Smith, 1972). Similarly in Spain, Perona has noted that nearly all of the 23 Bronze Age sites found within an area of 186 km^2 between Pedralba and Bugarra (Valencia) are sited on ridges just above the broad valleys or *ramblas* (Martinez Perona, 1975).

Prehistoric settlement, its pattern, form and building styles, has been rather cursorily reviewed in this section, but sufficient may have been said to serve as a pointer towards an eventual settlement geography of the prehistoric period in Mediterranean Europe. The conclusion arrived at so far is that, allowing for changes in the physical environment (deforestation, soil erosion, sedimentation) and for changes in technique and building styles, the prehistoric village or prehistoric steading was in essentials the same as its historic counterpart. The range of house types parallels that of historic times and it would be hard to find a prehistoric village whose site also failed to conform to the constraints of village site selection that operated throughout the historic period. The suggestion that there was no discontinuity in these aspects of life in Mediterranean Europe from the Neolithic to modern times tends to be increasingly substantiated. In respect of settlement, at least, the traditional way of life in Mediterranean Europe can be said to date back to the Neolithic.

The Freedoms of a Peasant Farmer

The title of this section implies that a peasant farmer has effective freedom of action. This is a rather unreal proposition. It has been argued (Jones, 1968, pp. 195–196) that the stereotyped idea, which sees the late and post-medieval peasantry as being happily disenfranchised at the expense of landlords, themselves in increasing financial and social distress, is over simplified. There would have been times when there was a good deal of social mobility within the peasant class and an ambitious peasant could, and did, gain considerably from the new tenurial arrangements. But in practice the economic situation of the majority of the peasantry altered very little. If non-agricultural activities (silkworm rearing, weaving, for example) were taken up, this would have normally been less a real alternative for farming than a desperate attempt to find an additional means of livelihood to compensate for a deficiency in the output from the holding or for a total shortage of agricultural employment. No peasant at heart would have been really concerned with finding work of a different nature: as Lison-Tolosana (1966, p. 17) found in Spain, the desire is not to work at all! However, the ways in which members of the peasantry in Mediterranean Europe have made their livelihoods have been very diverse and it is to stress that point that the discussion is extended in this direction.

Social Rankings

In recent years, even a modest village community has contained an effective ranking of social groups within the peasantry. Each group is identified according to land or property ownership. So at "Milocca" there were the wealthy *burgisi* at one end of the scale and the landless agricultural labourers, the *viddani*, at the other. Not all the *burgisi* however were socially equal. The normal minimum requirement for *burgisi* standing was ownership of 1 or 2 hectares of land and a mule. A *burgisi* might rent land but only so long as it was on a cash, as opposed to a share-cropping, basis. Peasants who owned their own sheep were ranked with the *burgisi*, as were the bailiffs (*comperi*) who worked as overseers for large landowners. Swineherds and those who actually looked after the sheep and goats were ranked with the *viddani*, because they worked for hire. A peasant's place in his society was thus dependent on three factors: birth, wealth and occupation. Class consciousness, Chapman found, was acute amongst the peasantry. Within his class, however, each "knew his place". On the other hand, cooperation between the classes was close and willing, for the economy and livelihood of the entire community depended on it.

In Spain too, anthropologists have noted how ownership has been the fundamental criterion of social stratification amongst the peasants. This is the case whatever the type of activity engaged in and despite religious (rather than political) affiliations (Lison-Tolosana, 1966, p. 54ff). According to Lison-Tolosana, it is strictly speaking the amount of land worked by an individual that counts in determining his status, not just land legally owned. At Alfriden (Zaragoza) the lowest social group is a small one composed of landless *braceros*, men who have to offer their labour for hire for a living. Accounting for just under a third of the community's property owners, the second class is that of the *peons*, those who own less than a hectare of land. This is a sufficient acreage to ensure a vegetable supply and to allow the raising of poultry and a pig or two but it does not give the owner an adequate income and the *peon* has to work for another farmer or at a secondary occupation. The third class is that of the *proprietario*, the man who owns 1–3 hectares. This can be regarded as a minimum acreage. The highest peasant class, that of the *ricosricos* (ever-so-rich) is again a small group and includes those with more than 15 hectares of land. As in Sicily, the observance of social distinctions is traditionally very strict and much could depend on the ownership of an extra hectare or two of land.

The *Relaciones* reflect a similarly rigorous division in the peasantry of New Castile in the sixteenth century. Then the two basic groupings were that of the *journaleros* and *trobajadores* and that of the *labradores* (Salomon,

1964, p. 254ff). The first were the landless. Contemporary records leave little doubt that this was the most disadvantaged of all groups, particularly whenever there was unemployment. On the other hand, it was by no means a minority group. To judge from the *Relaciones*, over half the rural population in sixteenth-century New Castile fell into this class. A few individuals had been better off but had lost land and were obliged to turn to labouring for a livelihood. The depopulation of the territory of Manzaneque is attributed to the ruin of its villages through the acquisition of its land by wealthy Toledans and the lack of agricultural or other employment. Normally then the *journaleros* class was by far the largest, in the bigger villages at least. In contrast, the *labradores* class was always small and accounted for perhaps a quarter or a third of the village population. A *labradore* was distinguished by ownership of one or two plough teams, whether or not he owned any land. The *labradores* class was very heterogeneous. There were individuals who were exceptionally well-off and constituted the privileged *villanes ricos*. At Cobeja de la Sagra (Toledo), out of a total number of 108 hearths, there were 67 *labradores* (and only one *hidalgo*, member of the nobility) whose fortunes ranged from the poorest to considerable wealth. One widow's estate was valued at 13 000 ducats and two other people, Anton Rodriquez and Juan Martin, were the envy of the village for the abundance of their annual harvests. In a small *pueblo* there can be few secrets and such contrasts in fortune would have been obvious to all. If economically, all peasant classes were interdependent in the past, socially they could hardly have been more distinct.

Aspects of Land Tenure

Strictly defined, the peasant farmer is his own landowner. As already noted however the peasant class in the wider sense includes the landless and the tenant farmer. So far as an individual's freedom was concerned, there was often little to choose between the advantages of tenancy and the disadvantages of owner-occupation. Jones (1968) shows how after the Middle Ages, a situation arose in which there could be a complicated system of perpetual ownership. These tenancies differed in practice very little from peasant ownership. This was the case in Tuscany by 1500. In other regions, where the Roman tradition of individual proprietorship had survived most strongly or had escaped manorialization altogether, an owner-occupier peasant probably enjoyed little "freedom". As the total

D

economy developed, juridical servitude tended to be replaced by economic servitude and ties of bondage were replaced by ties of debt (*ibid.*, p. 196). The burden of production therefore could fall very heavily on owner-occupiers. In the eighteenth century in Sardinia there were approaching 40 000 owner-occupier farmers, 12 000 salaried labourers (*zappatori*) and a small number of share-croppers (Mondolfo, 1967, p. 433). Together these accounted for merely a quarter of the island's population. The remaining three-quarters was made up of shepherds, townsfolk and estate owners and their retinues. There was little industry and practically no commerce. It was the peasantry therefore, and in particular the owner-occupiers, who had the responsibility for the major proportion of the island's food supply.

One advantage a freeholding peasant might enjoy was the absence of an overlord. Tenant farmers were at risk from "the extravagant actions of those who are known to have larger prosperity" and who constantly oppress the poor, in the words of Rothar's Edict of the seventh century A.D. (Hodgkin, 1896, Vol. VI. p. 176). They were at the mercy of the individual personality of the landlord as well as of his personal fortunes. Hardship and the pressures felt by the latter were automatically passed on to the tenants and labourers on his land. In southern Italy in the sixteenth century, the peasant who happened to find himself a tenant on Crown land was generally more fortunate than his counterpart on baronial land. If the king was short of money he had only to press his barons for taxes and rents due, whereas the latter saw no alternative but to press their peasants for greater yields and larger shares. In Spain in the same period and no doubt for similar reasons, it was well known that the king was somewhat less oppressive than the lord (Vicens Vives, 1961, Vol. II, p. 246). One village, it was asserted, lost half its population (dropping from 800 to 400 hearths) because the king had sold it to a Seigneur and the inhabitants did not want to depend on a lay lord (Salomon, 1964, p. 47).

By far the commonest tenant contract in Mediterranean Europe has been some form of share-cropping. It is still to be found, notwithstanding official government disapproval and control. Formerly the method of division and the proportions deemed payable were decided by each landowner. He also decided other matters, such as the amount of money he might be expected to advance to his tenant and, naturally, the rate of interest. Share-cropping appears to be one of the oldest forms of tenant farming. In Mediterranean Europe the form it took varied from region to region, even landlord to landlord.

In its modern form, share-cropping in southern France dates from the beginning of the sixteenth century (George, 1935, p. 322ff). Contracts of *facherie* (or *faucherie*) could be collective or individual. At Vitrolles-les-Luberon, in Provence, a contract dated 1503 stated that the eight men named promised " . . . on behalf of themselves and their successors to come and inhabit and to reside continually with all their family in the locality of Vitrolles and [on] its territory in order that each one . . . cultivates the land . . . ".Clearly this was a newly founded settlement and it is possible that many of these collective contracts were the outcome of colonization. A similar development of the collective contract is also found in fourteenth century Spain. In Castile, as in other provinces of the Reconquest, the free peasant was the typical settler of the ninth and tenth centuries. But increasing financial difficulties and perhaps oppressive pressure from the upper social classes changed the status of the Castilian peasant owner for the worse (Smith, 1966, p. 434). By the fourteenth century over 600 villages "whose residents had individually or collectively accepted a lord's patronage . . . " were catalogued in the "Celebrated Book of the *Behetrias* of Castile".

On the whole, share-cropping contracts showed, at least up to the eighteenth century, a pragmatic flexibility. This took into consideration local physical factors as well as general economic ones. The difficulties of cropping new land were recognized. Payments during the first 5 or 6 years were relatively light and it could happen that the landowner received his first due only after the tenth year. On the other hand the assumption that a vineyard, once planted, involved less time and effort than arable land seems a sly way of raising the level of income on the basis of a fallacious argument. Payment demanded was heavier for grapes and for almonds and olives than for wheat and barley and the share payable by the peasant also varied from crop to crop. It was probably less onerous in the early medieval period than later, when a peasant might be paying out a third or even half his produce. Even on fertile land, half a harvest was scarcely sufficient to ensure the peasant's livelihood throughout the year. In the twelfth century, vineyards in Aragon were rented for a third of the wine produced. Elsewhere, rents of one-fifth seemed more usual (Smith, 1966, p. 435). When, in 1040, at Sant Cugat (Sardanoyola), the rent was a quarter of the general harvest and half the grape product, this was regarded as very expensive (Bonnassi, 1966). Under the Moorish system (which sometimes continued in Navarre and Aragon after the Reconquest), payments could be as little as one-tenth of the total crop.

However, often when rents appeared as low as this, other forms of income or service were expected by the landlords and the annual total payable by the tenant might be by no means so favourable as at first sight. For instance, the maximum boon service due was in theory a month but in non-Moorish Catalonia, serfs had usually to give only 6 days a year to work the demesne of the landowner, so it was not the length of the service that was critical so much as its timing. The peasant was obliged to render his service for his lord at the precise moment his own land and crops demanded urgent attention. Failure to give this in time jeopardized his own harvest, from which both his subsistence and landowner's rents were due. Under the Normans in southern Italy, the timing was specified; peasants having a pair of oxen owed 6 days of labour during harvest and 6 days during sowing (Chalandon, 1907, Vol. II, p. 498).

In Romagna, the Tuscan share-cropping system of *mezzadria* replaced older fixed rents during the second quarter of the fourteenth century (Herlihy, 1967). This seems to have been a response to population decline and to the resultant labour shortage. In this context the idea of sharing the harvest, rather than paying a rent, was seen as preferable and fair and the system was brought into disrepute only by later abuses. Otherwise the major advantage was flexibility; landlord and tenant alike shared the hardships of a bad year or rejoiced in a good harvest. An underlying motive in this favourable situation was the encouragement of new rentals and of maintaining cultivation. The monastery of Forcole, "fearful because of the plague that a piece of its property would remain uncultivated, converted the rent due from it from [the fixed one of] 12 *staia* of wheat to one half the produce" (*ibid.*, p. 136). Previously, when landlords had been experiencing little difficulty in finding tenants, rents had been as much as 40% higher than they were to be later on.

In Tuscany, from the twelfth to the fifteenth century, what Jones calls the "symmetry of manorial society" was giving way to fragmentation of holdings and to a land transfer (1968, p. 196). These changes benefited the emergent upper peasant class but also enlarged the lower, wage-labour class. New share-cropping contracts involved not only land (granted *ad medietatem*, hence *meytaderie, métayage, mezzadria* etc.) but also stock. The leases were designed so that landlord and tenant variously shared working costs and capital. At first they applied to holdings created from the demesne but gradually the distinction between demesne, *terra dominicatum* and the rest of the estate vanished entirely in the north of Italy (at much the same time, however, as the feudal system of the Normans was taking hold in southern Italy). Contracts were highly detailed and set out every aspect of the arrangements. In Tuscany share-rents came to be for thirds, quarters, even halves (*ad quartum, ad tertium, ad medium*). The conditions governing tenancy and farm work were detailed. The rotations, ploughing, dates of sowing and harvest etc. were elaborated and instructions given as to intensive cultivation by digging, green manuring, ditching, pruning, propagation of tree crops etc.

It is not difficult to associate the style of medieval share-cropping tenancies with those found in Italy under the Romans. Medieval share-cropping had come from Italy. *Facherie* had probably reached southern France from Italy (George, 1935, p. 328). Share-cropping in Spain was common under the Moors (Lévi-Provençal, 1950, Vol. III, pp. 266–268) but it was also reintroduced after the Reconquest with the reinstatement of Roman law. There was share-cropping in Roman Italy. In the second century A.D. for example, there were similar problems to those affecting landowners in Romagna and Tuscany in the fourteenth century and they elicited a similar response. What had happened in the second century was that a period of bad harvests and low prices (resulting from over-production) had led to a drastic reduction in the annual income of most landlords. Their tenants unfortunately were already heavily in debt. The reaction of Pliny the Younger was no doubt typical of many landlords. He turned from demanding fixed rents from his tenant farmers to a share-cropping system specifically in order "to deal with this growing evil and [to] find a remedy" (Letters IX, 37, 2–3). But share-cropping (*partiaro*) was no novelty even then; Cato, writing in the first century B.C. had suggestions about the terms (CXXXVI–CXXXVIII). In general, the Romans saw it as theoretically an equitable system but one in which the chief disadvantage was that there was little incentive for a peasant to improve his output. Any increase over and above what the peasant actually needed for his and his family's subsistence benefited only the landlord. Roman landlords were advised to send paid employees to oversee critical operations such as threshing and olive and grape pressing to ensure that if there was an advantage, it came to them. (White, 1970, p. 408). Favourable as the system at its best might be to tenant farmers, it did not endear itself to the landlords of Mediterranean Europe and it tended to be dropped whenever economic conditions swung to the landlord's advantage and money rents could be demanded.

Industrial   Opportunities

However much the peasant farmer's preoccupations may focus on the production of crops for food, each peasant farmer has need of a limited crop surplus to be used in, or to be converted into, cash. Slight though it is, it is this involvement with an external market which helps distinguish the peasant farmer from a primitive cultivator. An alternative source of cash for the peasants of Mediterranean Europe throughout the historic period has been from the industrial sector or from non-agricultural resources such as fish and salt.

The simplest approach was to gather and use or sell whatever resource was to hand locally. In southern Italy there are still individuals who live by the sale of salads and fauna gathered from waysides and wasteland (Dolci, 1959). In southern Spain, esparto grass grows wild on saline or semi-saline soils and Pitt-Rivers found at ''Alcala'' that it was usually those who could find no agricultural work or those who were really idiosyncratic about their independence who went out to pick, prepare and sometimes even work the esparto grass (1954, p. 45). In Roman times the Albacete plains were known as *Campus Spartarius* from the abundance of the grass there. Then as now it was used in the production of ''a kind of spart that is suitable for twisting into ropes . . . '' (Strabo, 3.4.9). Another product of these districts in Roman times was a rough haircord type of cloth made from the fibres of the European dwarf palm. This was common, according to Strabo (3.5.10), around Cartagena. In mountain or forest districts in Spain in the seventeenth century (and in the Sierras around ''Alcala'' (Cadiz) in the twentieth), charcoal burning was carried out by, once again, the poorest members of the community. At the hamlet of Hontanar (Toledo), officers collecting the *Relaciones* were told ''that the inhabitants of this village are poor people, who rely greatly on their charcoal'' (Salomon, 1964, p. 281).

Sometimes peasant farmers incorporated selected plants into their cropping system and grew them for their industrial value. This was particularly characteristic in southern France and northern Italy in the eighteenth century when farmers were being encouraged to vary their cropping patterns as a means of profiting from the otherwise obligatory 2-year fallow. Madder, a dye plant, made its appearance on the wettest soils of the Rhone valley in this way (George, 1935, p. 381). Teasels for wool carding were a speciality of other localities in the Rhone valley, all of which sent their produce to a single factory in Avignon. Hemp was less popular, although widely grown, since it demanded a good deal of time and large quantities of manure. Saffron, another dye plant, had long been grown.

In Mediterranean Europe at all times, the commonest agricultural "industry" was in some way associated with the textile industry. Ancillary needs, dye plants and teasels for example, were provided. Some peasants were involved in the production of thread, and more rarely, of the cloth itself, for an external market. In a strictly domestic context the women of the family had always been accustomed to spin, weave and make clothes from the fleeces of their own sheep, in prehistoric times as up to the twentieth century. Under special circumstances, though, individual peasants would take on extra work, in winter or when agricultural employment was lacking. Again, the sixteenth-century *Relaciones* of Castile reveal a variety of these semi-artisan peasants. Weaving of woollen cloth for sale in the national fairs was evidently very common in New Castile, particularly amongst the labouring class. At Iniesta (Cuenca) the peasants "worked wool which they had bought . . . and sold [the goods] at Ubeda, Baeza, Alcala, Tendilla . . ." (Salomon, 1964, p. 275). Involvement in textiles by no means precluded alternative activities for, in the same village, it was reported that "others lived from other work".

Wool was a commonplace textile. Silk was something special. The production of silk cloth in Mediterranean Europe goes back to the time of the Emperor Justinian when silk manufacture (as opposed to silk imports) was introduced into Byzantine Europe (Lopez, 1945). The Moors did much to advance the spread of techniques into the *huerta* regions of Spain and Sicily. Thereafter, individual rulers took an active interest, usually with a view to boosting the exchequer. Thus, for example, Frederick II decreed that trade in silk should be a royal monopoly (Mack Smith, 1969, p. 57). At the same time he tried to widen its area of production, attempting to introduce it into Apulia. Later, the centre of gravity of silk production shifted from Sicily and the southern peninsula to Tuscany and the Po valley, thence into the lower Rhone valley, and into Catalonia. By the end of the twelfth century, Tuscan and other northern centres were making cloth from thread imported from southern Italy and Sicily. Eventually, the production of silk thread was established locally. By the fourteenth century there were individual producers such as Antonia Rospigliosi, responsible for substantial transactions of raw silk that had been produced in Pistoia for sale in Florence, the major Tuscan centre for silk weaving (Herlihy, 1967, p. 177).

In France it may have been the presence of the exiled Papal court at Avignon that provided a stimulus to the market for luxury tissues and that initiated local interest in sericulture in the Rhone valley and in the neighbouring regions of Languedoc and Provence. Certainly by the fourteenth century Lyons was the main market with centres such as Nimes controlling local production of silk thread, semi-finished and even finished cloth. In Spain the traditional regions of silk production were the southern districts, Toledo, Seville, Granada and Murcia, as a result of Moorish encouragement. Each town was supplied with thread from its surrounding countryside. Before the Reconquest there may have been as many as 16 000 looms and 130 000 workers in the Sevillian industry alone (La Force, 1965, p. 8). But these figures give little indication of the vast numbers of peasant and estate producers of the raw silk. After the Reconquest it was Valencia, with its climate ''ideally suited for mulberry trees'' that rose to prominence. Eventually Catalonia took supremacy.

The rise of the silk industry was most commonly based on the peasant farmer's willingness to take advantage of all opportunities to increase his income provided little extra effort was involved. The mulberry is a tolerant tree, adaptable to a variety of Mediterranean conditions. This meant that the trees could be grown on spare land, on roadside verges, plot borders or around the house, where they provided shade. Accustomed to arboriculture, peasant farmers in Mediterranean Europe found no inconvenience in increasing the density of their productive trees. The resultant effect on the landscape, however, struck outsiders. By the eighteenth century there were so many mulberry trees in the Rhone valley that the countryside had acquired a *bocage* landscape and travellers from the north were commenting that the Midi was ''filled with trees as in Flanders'' (d'Hailly, 1790; cited by George, 1935, p. 398). The Spanish *huertas* were already areas of arboriculture and the periodic upsurges of sericulture merely intensified a long established *bocage* aspect. In the middle of the eighteenth century, 73% of the Murcia *huerta* was planted with mulberry trees. There were some zones specializing in silk worm production (La Nora, Aljucer) but more generally, mulberries were grown in association with other forms of arboriculture (Calvo, 1975, p. 85) and the scale of local silk production was very much smaller. Altogether in the Murcian *huerta* sericulture supported something approaching 100 000 persons. It also contributed to a dispersal of settlement and to the construction of a vast number of *barracas*.

The secret of success of sericulture amongst the peasants lay in the fact that it fitted so effortlessly into any farming routine. Silkworms demand close attention during only one-and-a-half months each year. The work was best done by the women and the younger members of the family, who had patience, time and nimble fingers. Sometimes estate farms shared the interest in sericulture. In many *mas* in southern France there was a special room (*la magnaneri*) for the silk worms and residence for the extra labourers needed for large-scale production. The room had to be heated in winter. In Tuscany certain estate owners chose to specialize in the production of eggs for sale to peasant silkworm cultivators, as did Ricasoli for instance in the early nineteenth century (Biagioli, 1970).

Production of silk cloth over the centuries in Mediterranean Europe was one of the most jealously guarded and monopolized of all industrial activities. Production of silk thread, however, was a more informal affair in which a major role was taken by peasant farmers. From the peasant farmer's point of view sericulture could provide, for little capital investment and very little extra effort during the year, a broader basis from which to derive his livelihood and to support his family.

3

Landowners

Like the peasantry, the elite was ranked internally. The basic grouping was threefold. There was the king himself, the single most important landowner. There were landowners who were senior members of the church. And, thirdly there were the landowners belonging to the nobility. The last group was the most heterogeneous. In Spain, for instance, the *hidalgo* represented the lowest category in the nobility but not even all *hidalgos* had identical characteristics. Reconquest Spain was a country of unparalleled social opportunism. For those who had no true blue blood, there was the chance of a land grant. For those lacking land there were the merino sheep; Lopez (1953, p. 168) talks of the "élitism of wool-raisers". In Castile, after the Reconquest, there was a complex hierarchy of stockmen, ranking from the military orders, with great herds and flocks and extensive estates, to the middle or small-sized ranchers, whose real wealth was in livestock rather than in land, but who took their place socially amongst landowners of similar standing (Bishko, 1963, p. 55). The social order was never static. Even in the sixteenth century, to judge from the *Relaciones*, some individuals were still searching for prestige while others were the tardy representatives of a medieval class well advanced in the process of disappearance (Solomon, 1964, p. 289). In general, therefore, the landowning class was also sharply divided between the more and the less successful, especially with regard to manners and wealth.

Peasants are usually destined to remain anonymous. Landowners, on the other hand, whether members of the church or of the nobility, have the chance to achieve political, cultural or intellectual fame and their names may become as well known as that of their kings or emperors and their personalities and actions form the substance of history books. Here, however, they are viewed as owners of land and of entire settlements and therefore as (willing or unwilling) directors of economic affairs, notably of agriculture.

Constraints on Landowners

It is not an altogether exaggerated view to suggest that the majority of landowners in the past in Mediterranean Europe, as elsewhere, have not inevitably been in a position to enjoy as much comfort or freedom of action as is popularly supposed. To make too much of their hardships, for example during the later Middle Ages when the advantage was to the peasantry, would be inappropriate. But the lives of most of the nobility, lay or ecclesiastical, were constrained by the need to conform to the ethics of their class, by financial problems, and by economic pressures from both national and local interests. At worst, they were middlemen. Pressed from above, they in turn were liable to weigh down the very peasants on whose cooperation and economic well-being their own position usually depended. With or without feudalistic elements in the social structure, there would be little liberty for the average landowner so long as the economy remained narrowly based and almost exclusively agricultural.

Feudalism in Mediterranean Europe

Most of the constraints felt by individual landowners in medieval times derived from what is rather loosely referred to as the feudal structure of society. In some respects, few status-defining systems can have been so clearly set out as the feudal. On the other hand, feudalism in Mediterranean Europe as elsewhere, was far from uniform in its attributes or static in its arrangements.

The concept of a feudalistic system may have had common origins in certain institutions of the late Roman Empire and of early Germanic kingdoms but it appeared in different parts of Mediterranean Europe at different times and from quite different directions (Fig. 16). This diversity of origin alone goes a long way to explain how there was little in common between Spain, Italy and southern France in, for instance, the obligations of landowners to their overlord or in the security of their tenure. Similarly, feudal practices disappeared or were abolished at various times in the different parts of Mediterranean Europe. In southern Italy official

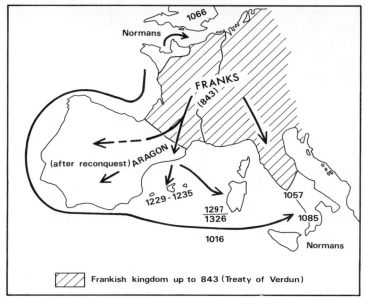

Fig. 16. *The spread of medieval feudalism* in Mediterranean Europe from the eighth-century Frankish Kingdom. Two dates are given for Sardinia; the earlier one represents the granting of the island to James II of Aragon, as a fief, by Pope Boniface VIII. The second represents the effective implementation of the feudal system with the Aragonese Conquest.

abolition of tenurial matters came only with the nineteenth century but in northern Italy the manorial aspect of feudalism was already eclipsed by the fourteenth or fifteenth centuries.

In Merovingian France royal grants of land were made in full ownership, but Charles Martel, as an emergency measure in the face of the Saracen threat in the south and because of the urgent need to raise and equip an army, granted land in tenure only. This enabled him to grant out church lands for military purposes without technically alienating them from the pious uses. His successors saw the advantages of this system, which reserved ownership of fiefs to the crown, and came to apply it to all grants of crown land for military purposes. In this way, the Roman concept of absolute ownership (*dominium*) was replaced by a concept of relative ownership.

Southern Italy in early times illustrates these two concepts. So long as the southern peninsula (and the Exarchate of Ravenna) was administered by Byzantium, the state considered itself absolute proprietor of the entire empire (Guillou, 1966, p. 452). For the Normans in southern Italy, as in England, the feudal system was an instrument of centralizing authority. When the Norman administration was established in the eleventh century, however, the crown at first regarded itself as no more than a major landholder while the land belonged to the nation and was administered on the nation's behalf by the ruler (Evoli, 1931, p. 193). With this in mind, fiefs and other benefices were granted by Norman rulers to individuals subject to the proviso that all the inhabitants on the land in question had rights which applied to all categories of land. Unfortunately, this purist view failed to survive the test of experience. Fiefs became inheritable and land began to be alienated from common usage. The change came about in the Norman kingdom of Italy not because of any external threat, as provided by the Saracens in France, but through internal abuse by individual landholders. Attempts were made to reverse the process. Frederick II tried, at Melfi in 1231, to restrict baronial privilege. His Angevin successors allowed common usages (*usi civici*) to be regarded as privileges that could be granted or withheld at pleasure rather than as rights due to every member of society. This created the real break with the original concept so far as southern Italy was concerned.

In Spain it was the frontier situation, prevailing from the Moslem invasion in 711 to the conquest of Granada in 1492, that explains the individuality of the feudalism developed in the Iberian peninsula (Mackay, 1977, p. 2). Elsewhere, feudalism offered a structure for the organization of life under relatively stable conditions and its military aspects were meant to apply only to a small group of nobles and knights. In the event, this particular attribute of feudalism was not usually particularly long-lived. But in Spain, it was inevitable that the military element was paramount and that it, and the consequences of an ever-changing frontier, affected nearly all the population and led to a more pragmatic and military form of feudalism. Only regions that escaped the full force of the Reconquest, such as Catalonia, were ''properly'' feudal in the twelfth century. Even in Castile the title of Count was not at first hereditary. But as organizer of the Reconquest, the king had to be the central figure and all lordless land belonged to him to dispose of as he deemed suitable. Blending relics of Roman, Visigothic and Moorish law with local custom law, it was the king who saw to the drawing up and the granting of the *fuero* (charter) to each town together with its district as it was reconquered (Kleffens, 1968, p. 158). Not until the middle of the thirteenth century was there a single law code for all the reconquered lands, the *Siete Partidas* (dated about 1265). It was in the *Siete Partidas* that social divisions were clearly specified and the personal status of individuals set out, as were the laws that concerned the granting and holding of fiefs.

The end of feudalism came variously in the different parts of Mediterranean Europe. The French were the first to abolish it both *de jure* and *de facto*. In the night of 4th August 1785 the National Assembly agreed its abolition and in 1793 the Convention annulled all dues arising from feudal titles and ordered the destruction of all feudal deeds. Neither Italy nor Spain escaped the influence of the French Revolution or the edicts of their Napoleonic administrations. In northern Italy, the Cisalpine republic suppressed feudal authority in 1796. In southern Italy suppression was initiated by Joseph Buonaparte. It proceeded slowly, on the mainland as in Sicily, under the restored Bourbons. In the event it was only in 1832 that the surviving elements of feudalism were finally abolished on the mainland and in Sicily and Sardinia. In Spain, the New Plan of the Bourbons (1716) had heralded certain changes. The constitution of the Revolutionary French administration in Madrid, headed by Joseph Buonaparte, provided for the total abolition of seigneurial privileges (but only in 1812). Even so, the Bourbons, supported by strong military and religious institutions with vested interests in the maintenance of a feudal order, delayed progress for some time.

There were aspects in the feudal landholding system that discouraged landowners from investing effort and expense in their land in much the same way as the share-cropping tenant was reluctant to raise yields for the benefit of his landlord rather than himself and his family. In the early days of feudalism, in France and Italy at least, insecurity of tenure could be as real a fear for the fief holder as for tenant farmers. Periodic redistribution of estates was scarcely amenable to improvement in farming. Another, more permanent, problem was estate sub-division. Inheritance practices could lead to the fragmentation of fiefs into estates eventually becoming too small to be viable. Such inheritance procedures were checked by individual monarchs, such as Frederick II, but probably not so much because of the economic inconvenience of small estates as because they prevented the impoverished baronage from fulfilling its military obligations to the state. There were other reasons why estates did not necessarily remain intact for long. Periods of labour shortage or of falling prices could also lead to fragmentation. One such period started in the fourteenth century A.D. In Provence, for example, the estates of the commanderie of the Knights Hospitallers had been once sufficiently extensive to support a household of 24 knights and eight servants, but by 1411 the estates had been almost wholly leased out and the household was reduced to six individuals who worked the remnant demesne themselves (Duby, 1968, p. 322).

The fostering of non-agricultural interests did little to encourage or support a landowner in his agricultural obligations. In Reconquest Spain, many of the new landowners were little more than adventurers who happen to have been rewarded with grants of land. Not surprisingly, many of them found the discipline of estate life irksome and the minutiae of agriculture intolerably dull. In Norman Italy the military obligations of fiefholders were nowhere near so heavy as in Spain but observance of personal service to the ruler in early days resulted in the firm idea that court and capital were more attractive than life on a provincial estate. In this way arose the traditional view that landowners abandoned their properties to the care of managers and to the labour of peasants while they themselves "surrendered most readily to the attractions of the capital" (Luzzatto, 1961, p. 165). So, in 1595 it could be reported that "in the Roman Campagna it is not the inhabitants who plough the land, for the region is empty of people. The majority of the land belongs to Roman barons who are in the habit of letting them to '*marchands*': people who are rich and of considerable influence in this profession which they call *l'arte del camp* . . ." (Paruta, 1595, cited by Delumeau, 1957, p. 571). In the Pyrenees more recently, large estate owners prefer to rent unoccupied waste to outsiders rather than take on themselves the risks of pastoral exploitation (Chevallier, 1956, p. 293). Yet absentee landlordism has never been either a successful or a profitable way of running an estate.

Social Divisions in the Landowning Class

For nearly 2000 years most of the land of Mediterranean Europe has been in the hands of either the crown (or state), the church or the nobility. The same period has also seen a more or less active three-cornered rivalry between the three groups of landowners. The irony lies in the fact that it was the imperial state that gave the church (orthodox and Roman) the very land and privileges that were to become the bases for challenging social force and political power. The balance of power between the three groups was rarely even and never stable. Except in the Papal States, there was probably less land in the hands of the church in most regions of Mediterranean Europe than in the other two groups, either singly or combined. In twelfth-century Sicily the crown may have held up to 30% of the land (Galasso, 1969, quoted in Abalufia, 1977, p. 39 fn 21). The church had to share the remaining two-thirds not only with baronial landowners but also with the village municipalities. For this was still a time when the southern kingdom in general could be described as a land "which belongs to the municipality (*universitas*) . . . and whose use is shared amongst the citizens" (Evoli, 1931, p. 190). Very much later, for example in 1860 when the Sicilian government confiscated half-a-million acres of church land, ecclesiastical property accounted for no more than a tenth of the island (Mack Smith, 1965, p. 102). According to Galanti's figures (1970, Vol. III, p. 22ff) the crown held 22% of the land in the Kingdom of Naples in 1788, the barons 74%, and the church an insignificant 4%. These proportions were more or less constant in all the provinces except in Terra di Bari, where the church had 8% of the land where there was a better balance between crown and baronial property (42 and 49% respectively).

The traditional view of the late medieval church as rich, privileged and powerful is not always a fair reflection of the situation. Hated by both crown and nobility, the ecclesiastical sector was more often than not the losing side. When the Reconquest came to an end in Castile and Leon (in 1248), the church there was found to be far from rich (Hillgarth, 1976, p. 107). It had been obliged to finance the Andalucian campaigns and a third of its tithe income had already been alienated to the crown, never to be recovered. The rural monasteries were in the weakest position, for their worst enemies were at hand in the local nobility. Rents were made hard to collect and the monks were subjected to political pressure, to seizure, theft and even violence. Elsewhere, anti-clerical hostility could mean wholesale confiscation of land and properties, especially in the "Ages of Enlightenment". In November 1768, the lands and houses of Jesuits throughout the Kingdom of Naples were confiscated by royal officials (Acton, 1956, Vol. I, p. 118). Their extensive estates passed to the crown. In France, in the same century, the *Vente des Biens Nationaux* (1789–1802) saw the alienation of virtually all church property. This meant that in certain districts up to 20% of the land changed hands, particularly in northern France (Picardy, Artois). In provinces such as Burgundy or districts such as Berry it was a smaller but still an important proposition. In southern France, the proportion of land held by the church

by the late eighteenth century was generally much smaller. Only 2% of
the mountainous lands of the south-east changed hands, although around
Montpellier the former churchlands had amounted to 6% of the total area
(Soboul, 1958, p. 96).

Like the peasantry, the landowner class had its own groupings. Unlike
the peasantry, however, rivalry between the different groups was usually
bitter and often violent. The underlying problem was economic. The lack
both of agricultural intensification almost everywhere and of industrial
investment meant that an increase in income for all groups could only be
obtained through increasing the amount of land held. In the final analysis,
it could be said that land shortage was the fundamental cause of rivalry
between the landowning groups. State exchequers tended to be short of
revenue, particularly as political activity after the Middle Ages and the
value of money fell. A king would press for dues owed to him by the
barons. In their search for additional income the barons could attempt to
augment their estates through the acquisition of peasant holdings or village
lands or by trying to usurp or buy out royal land, measures which made
them unpopular in all directions. Another way in which baronial
landowners attempted to raise the output from their lands was to convert
as much as possible to grass and to increase the size of their flocks and herds
while wool and meat prices were high. But the extra number of animals
meant extra land and while this move may have helped baronial graziers of
Capitanata in the sixteenth and seventeenth centuries, it only added to the
pressure put onto the peasantry to release land they themselves needed for
food production. While villages in Capitanata declined and were
abandoned, their territories being taken into crown demesne, King
Ferdinand was writing to his agent at Foggia pleading his own hardship and
begging his agent to hasten with delivery of the rents due from the barons
and other landowners for hire of grazing on crown lands (Spola, 1953,
p. 133 fn 4). Of Sicily it came to be said that "the poorer the nobles, the
greater the frauds they committed" (quoted by Mack Smith, 1968,
p. 292) and it cannot be denied that many of the landowners were relatively
badly off by the seventeenth and eighteenth centuries. As Mack Smith has
pointed out, too many visitors to the island saw only the great grainlands,
the irrigated orchards, the rich clothes of the nobles and failed to observe
either the personal debts or the very real precariousness of the island's
economy in general. Only Colonna, writing in 1578, recognized that
after a bad harvest "there are few kingdoms poorer than this one".
In such circumstances, landowners and peasants suffered alike as rents

remained unpaid and debts accumulated beyond the hope of redemption.

The nobility was very varied. In 1558 in the Kingdom of Naples there were 139 dukes, marquises or counts and another 800 barons (Braudel, 1973, p. 717). Proliferation of the lesser nobility was a result of the break up of the great "states" of older noble families, such as those of the Princes of Salerno and Taranto or of the Duke of Bari who had suffered a series of family tragedies. In the sixteenth century, the high nobility of Castile may have consisted of a hundred individuals out of a total number of 130 000 nobles. Whatever the size of their estates Spanish nobles were liable to catastrophic debts, overwhelming mortgages and a struggle for existence, albeit on a scale far removed from that of the peasants. Wealth could be apparent rather than real. Certain nobles were really privileged. The Duke of Medina Sidonia had a fortune of 150 000 ducats per annum at the end of the sixteenth century and 22 other dukes, 47 counts and 36 marquises between them disposed of an annual income of three million ducats (Alberi, 1839, cited by Braudel, 1972, p. 714). Yet at precisely the same time as these few individuals were secure in their wealth, other marquises and counts and members of the Spanish nobility were begging loans at interest from Venetian bankers (*ibid.*). In Spain as in southern Italy, the answer to impoverishment was seen to lie in the acquisition of more land. The process of "seigneurialization" of the land, at the expense chiefly of the peasantry but also of the crown, started in the sixteenth century, as the *Relaciones* record.

If the crown was the major landholder in the kingdom of Sicily in the twelfth century, this was far from the case by the end of the sixteenth century. Already at the beginning of Frederick II's reign there had been signs of this regal displacement. One of the young emperor's first acts (1220) was a series of measures designed to seize back some of the royal *demanium*, usurped by Sicilian barons during his minority, and to depress baronial power (Kantorowicz, 1931, p. 35). All grants, gifts, donations, privileges, confirmation of titles etc. made during the previous 30 years would be subject to re-examination in the imperial chancery and all castles that had been newly constructed during the same period were to be surrendered to the crown or razed. At Celano (Molise) on the mainland, one of the most powerful of the baronial strongholds, that is apparently just what happened. The castle was destroyed, the inhabitants of the township at first scattered, then were reassembled and deported to Sicily, ultimately returning to their renamed village (Caesarea) (Kantorowicz, 1931, p. 11f). After Frederick's death, however, the balance of power swung in favour of the barons. Four barons had been appointed as "vicars" and left in charge of administration in Sicily by Frederick. They now began to annexe royal land "almost at will" (Mack Smith, 1969, p. 87). By 1579 the barons, together with the church, had come to hold 1563 villages or towns in the Neapolitan kingdom as against 53 held by the crown (Braudel, 1972, p. 708). In addition the majority of new villages were being created by baronial landowners and the disproportion was increased. In 1586 the figures were 1904 and 69 respectively. A similar history of the changing fortunes of church, nobility and crown as landholders is also seen in Spain operating within a single century. In New Castile, the *Relaciones* show that in the early part of the sixteenth century the crown was still in the position to make grants to favoured nobles and to confiscate land from those who had offended or defaulted. Accordingly, 11 confiscations to 5 grants were made in the first quarter of the century (Salomon, 1964, p. 206ff). By the middle of the century, however, only one estate had been added to the royal demesne, scarcely compensation for the loss of nearly 30 villages and their territories, mostly alienated as a result of sales. By the third quarter of the century, under Philip II, the demesne was still losing to the barons (another 24 villages) but had gained as much (24 villages) from the church.

Land, the Basis of Wealth and Status

All through the historic period, the fact of land ownership has had to serve many purposes. It was not only a source of food or a measure of an individual's wealth, it was used as a currency for reward or bribery, as a form of investment, and as an index of social acceptability. It could also be sold for immediate cash.

In the Spanish conquest of Sicily in the latter part of the fourteenth century, the Spanish general Cabrera had to sell his Catalonian estates to raise money with which to equip his soldiers (Mack Smith, 1968, p. 88). When Palermo surrendered to him in 1392 and the defeated Sicilian leader, Chiaramonte, was beheaded, Chiaramonte's vast estate, which included eight fiefs, was bestowed on him. The estates of other Sicilian barons were confiscated and used as bribes to encourage defection to the Spanish cause. Land was also granted to Spaniards who came as adventurous knights. These "impoverished malcontents" eventually rose to become the aristocrats of the Sicilian and Neapolitan kingdoms. A century earlier, Charles I of Anjou had done just the same thing on the mainland. A total of 160 estates had been handed out to companions and followers, mostly of French origin (Croce, 1970, p. 70). Earlier still, the process had been similar in Roman times. Sufficient evidence points to a number of "bad" Roman emperors as having secured the condemnation of wealthy senators for treason in order to be able to confiscate their estates (Jones, 1974, p. 189). Nero, Domitian, Septimius Severus and Caracalla are all quoted as having operated on such a scale that the formerly small department of *res privata* was built up into a huge ministry.

Wealthy or poor, the landowning class has at all times derived its income primarily from the land. There was usually no conceivable alternative to the land as a source of revenue and everything in the last resort related back to agriculture. Royal wealth depended on agriculture both directly and indirectly. Grants of *demanium* involved the holding of land in return for part of the produce or for a *census* or tithe payable in grain, and much of the other income was in kind. In 1375 Frederick IV of Sicily, for instance, received supplies of wheat, barley, wine must, cotton, cows and mares, wax, honey, flax, hides and sows from just his Maltese estates (Bresc, 1973). When, 2 years previously, he had intervened in the island to suppress a rebellion, 13 out of the 32 documents he issued during what was essentially a political manoeuvre in fact concerned grants of land. Another aspect of the widespread interest in land as an investment is illustrated by the celebrated goldsmith Benvenuto Cellini who in 1560 bought a small estate near Florence expressly as a security against his approaching old age (Braudel, 1972, p. 527). With rising prices and economic uncertainty, Cellini's relentless pursuit of land and titles "would have been a farseeing policy, a prudent and responsible course of action."

The same had been true earlier on. In late Roman times, involvement in commerce was regarded as an unseemly activity for senators and public service was the usual way of making money outside income from land (Jones, 1964, p. 115). Even so, the salaries for these public services came from the land and its resources. Loans made by private citizens to the state were redeemed in land taken from *ager publicus*. Fortunately the state was well off, at least during the Republic. Between 200 and 157 B.C. rents from these public lands and from provincial tithes (paid usually in grain) together accounted for nearly a third of the total state income (figures in Frank, 1933, Vol. I, p. 141).

All landowners, whatever category they belonged to, were like the peasantry in their dependence on the land for subsistence. Unlike the peasantry though, landowners were free to attend to other interests and most took advantage of this. When it came to the actual running of an estate, an all too common tendency amongst landowners was to engage a bailiff and then ignore even its supervision. This attitude may have been more typical of the Middle Ages and later, when members of the same family preferred to combine a wide range of occupations such as commerce, banking, learning, the law and professional or part-time administration or soldiering (Hyde, 1973, p. 7) rather than show an interest in their land. In the later Roman empire the tradition was quite different. Senators had to be landowners of some substance, and most were only too pleased with their ability to live well from the resources of their own estates. These men were prepared to hold only the minimum number of posts deemed necessary "to achieve the illustrious rank which they regarded as due to family pride", while some amongst them "thought even the highest office beneath them" (Jones, 1964, p. 558).

Roman landowners were equally at at home in the countryside and in the town and this was a long-lasting tradition. Because of the involvement of landowners with active politics, the strength of local landowners' interest in local affairs has been seen by Sismondi as the foundation of Italian medieval history (Hyde, 1973, p. 3). In more recent centuries, however, the failure of the landowning class as a whole in Mediterranean Europe has been its lack of interest in mercantile and above all in industrial activities. This weakness in the non-agricultural sectors of the economy can be attributed in part to the rigid cast of society and to the nobility's "natural reluctance to seek wealth outside the traditional military-social framework" (Callahan, 1972, p. 3). By the sixteenth and seventeenth centuries, a concept of "honour" had emerged that rigorously excluded any possibility of enlarging the social class by the inclusion of merchants and artisans, so automatically these activities were disdained by its own members. A new deep fissure emerged, "opening up gulfs which nothing would ever bridge" (Braudel, 1972, p. 755). The victim was national economic development.

Estates

The paramount importance of land and agriculture in 'Roman, medieval and later Mediterranean Europe has meant that one aspect of the history of the landowning class has been the continuous struggle to maintain a minimum size of estate. Three factors operated against this: fragmentation by inheritance; periodic lack of labour; and the rivalry between the different groups of the landowning class, a rivalry quite unparalleled in the peasantry.

From Roman times to the present day, the question of very large estates has aroused a good deal of emotive comment. Less attention has been paid to the smaller estates, estates which had often been painstakingly built up over two or three generations (Fig. 18). Yet it might be argued that such "acquisition by degrees" is a normal tendency in a free society, the healthy goal of an individual's working life, while "estates of the moment" are those which come into being as a consequence of a highly unusual combination of circumstances. Amongst such events of political change affecting Mediterranean Europe so profoundly as to leave a permanent mark on almost all levels of social or economic organization must be numbered the Reconquest of Spain in the Middle Ages and the defeat of Hannibal by Rome in southern Italy in the third century B.C.

Latifundia

The term *latifundia*, as used in later Roman times, was associated with large landed properties. In modernized forms, the word is still so used (*latifondo*, Italy; *latifundios*, Spain). It appeared, however, only in the first century A.D. and was used always in the plural (White, 1967, p. 63). Confusingly, classical writers used it to refer to estates of very different size. Cato for instance was advising on a vine-growing property of a 100 *iugera* (about 25 hectares) which by some has been regarded as a "large-scale" farm, by others as a "medium-sized" unit. Clearly in this sort of assessment much depends on the category of land use. A livestock ranch, a dry-farmed cereal estate and a vine-growing estate all have different labour requirements and what is large in the case of the latter might be extremely modest were it to be turned over wholly to the production of livestock. It has also to be remembered that a large estate is not necessarily held as a single bloc of land. On the contrary, it was probably more usual to find that the apparently vast acreages cited as belonging to a single person in the Roman period were usually made up of a number of discrete units, whose individual parts were widely spaced not so much within one region but over the entire country, even abroad (Jones, 1964, p. 781; White, 1967, p. 74; Duncan-Jones, 1974, p. 323).

The most famous examples of the later Roman estates were almost without doubt the result of five or more centuries of "acquisition by degrees", albeit on a particularly expansive scale. A judiciously contracted marriage was an important factor in this process (Jones, 1964, p. 555). One lady landowner, Melania, was supposed to have had an annual income of 1600 *lbs* of gold from estates in Italy (Campania and Apulia), Sicily, Spain and Africa, yet she was described as a landowner from the middle ranges. Another individual, also of medium wealth, had 12 villas in various parts of Italy (including Samnium and Apulia) as well as in Sicily and Mauritania. Pliny the Younger was by no means amongst the richest of the senators of the Early Empire but he owned and maintained at least six houses in Italy (Duncan Jones, 1974, p. 17). He had substantial estates around his native town of Como, a second bloc of property in Umbria near Tifernum Tiberium, and his favourite house for relaxation at *Laurentum*, near Ostia. These several properties assured him of sufficient income for him to be one of the most munificent benefactors of his time. On the other hand, while the richest amongst the Roman senators must have owned several thousand square kilometres, there were others who were quite inadequately supported by a single farm.

That there were estates in existence before the first century A.D., whatever they were called, is clear from the literature of the time. The case of C. Caecillius Isidorus would have been as spectacular to his contemporaries as it is today. He is reported to have owned 7200 (plough) oxen, 4116 slaves, and 257 000 herd animals (Pliny 33.135). Cogent arguments show that this estate could not have been a single bloc of land since none of the figures are consistent with contemporary slave/plough or oxen/arable ratios (Duncan-Jones, 1974, p. 324). Two estates of 1000 *iugera* each (approximately 250 hectares), located near Rome, were mentioned by Cicero (*Att.* 13.31) and Varro (2.3.10) but never termed *latifundia*. It is rare that actual acreages are given by early writers and the acreage of an estate has to be arrived at rather obliquely. For instance, it is recorded that 32 farmers in Sicily had altogether an area under wheat of 30 000 *iugera* (Cicero, *Verres* 2.3.113, 116 and 120). Allowing for fallow, this gives each estate a total acreage of 1900 *iugera* (475 hectares) (Duncan-Jones, 1974, p. 325).

Adopting Dohr's classification, White has suggested that as a general guide anything over 500 *iugera* (125 hectares) should be taken as falling into the *latifundia* (large estate) class (White, 1967, p. 64; Dohr, 1965). For comparison, a vine-growing estate in the Camargue of southern France is today classified as large if it is over 100 hectares (Dugrand, 1963a, p. 108). The average size of over 1200 estates in Bas-Languedoc works out at 610 hectares. By no means do all the estates in the Roman period for which the size is known come into this class, however. There was a senator's 200-*iugera* (50 hectare) estate at Recite, for example (Varro, 3.2.15). It is clear that, in Roman times as later on, *latifundia*, smaller estates and other forms of land holding were not necessarily mutually exclusive within a single district. Despite an established view that the southern part of the Italian peninsula was early abandoned to the evils of what are seen as excessively large estates, it is now accepted that not only were there several categories of large estates within the *latifundia* class, but that these could, and did, co-exist with other much smaller units (White, 1967, p. 74). Moreover, far from being most numerous in the south, the majority of Roman *latifundia* for which a location can be identified were in northern or central Italy.

Occasionally in history there have been events that have had a significance far outlasting the actual moment. Their effect has not been truly catastrophic, resulting in a total break with what went before, but catalytic in that the result was a new and lasting pattern of social and economic arrangements. Two such "events" were the Hannibalic Wars in Italy and the Christian Reconquest of Moorish Spain. The first lasted precisely 17 years (218–210 B.C.). The second was drawn out over a more indefinitely defined five-and-a-half centuries (ninth century to 1260 A.D.). In the process of each the opportunity arose for the granting to, or the acquisition by, individuals of *latifundia*, estates "of the moment".

The presence of Hannibal and his troops in southern Italy from 216 to 204 B.C. had two immediate consequences. The first was the devastation caused by the demands of the army, more or less limited "to a broad swathe along their line of march" (Sherwin White, 1966, p. 449). The second was the harsh punishments effected by victorious Rome such as the razing of up to 400 villages and the expropriation of their land and land from Italian cities which had, at one time or another, helped Hannibal. The total area of land expropriated is unknown, but if the area of the *Ager Romanus* was about 24 000 km^2 before the war, it is thought that confiscations from Samnium, Lucania, Bruttium and Apulia may have brought this figure up to 37 000 km^2 (estimated from Beloch, quoted by Frank, 1933, p. 124). What is known is that the standard scale of penalty in south-eastern Italy was sometimes a quarter, sometimes a third, of the city's pre-war territory (Toynbee, 1965, Vol. pp. 119–121).

After the war the Roman government found itself responsible for what eventually became a politically embarassing quantity of *ager publicus*. At that time, demographic levels were low and a sufficient number of colonists for the new land were hard to find even though most of it was of good agricultural quality. Eighty years later most of it remained untouched except for some squatters and trespassers who had in the interval provided the government with a respectable income from fines imposed (Frank, 1933, 113; Livy, 33.42.10 and 35.10.12). Some of the land had been made available as large leaseholds to anybody who was in a position to take them up. What, as Toynbee has expressed it, "was a burden . . . for the Roman government was a gold-mine for Roman private capitalists, because these had the means of developing it" (1965, Vol. II, p. 242). The post-war years had brought a revival of cereal production in certain areas (in the *Ager Capenas* for example), or a partial rehabilitation of the peasant economy (Samnium), or some form of short-term measures (Bruttium). But in the south (Apulia and Lucania) the new *ager publicus* was left largely to private enterprise simply, it is presumed, because of a shortage of labour. Writing retrospectively, the historian Appian described how "those who were willing to work it might do so for a toll of the yearly crops, a tenth of the grain and a fifth of the fruit. From those who kept flocks was required a toll of the animals, both oxen and small cattle . . . " (Civil War, 1.7).

Under such circumstances, it was inevitable that a few individuals were in a position to benefit. Appian goes on to speak quite plainly on this point: "for the rich, getting possession of the greater part of the undisturbed lands . . . came to cultivate vast tracts instead of single estates, using slaves as labourers and herdsmen, lest free labourers should be drawn from agriculture into the army". What was tolerated as an interim measure, however, eventually became permanent. It would have been difficult to usurp the owners of the new *latifundia*, especially if, as Frank believed (1933, p. 112) it was some of the most influential Romans who had taken a large proportion of the leases. This last point was substantiated by Livy (42.1.6) who, 30 years after the end of the war, described how private landowners were able to encroach on the public land in Campania through a stealthy boundary extension.

On the identity of these individuals or as to the initial or eventual size of their estates there is next to no information. By the middle of the first century B.C. there was a certain Domitius at Corfinum (Samnium) who evidently had an estate of not less than 16 000 *iugera* (4000 hectares)

(Caesar, Civil War, 1.17). But although by the first century A.D. references to exceptionally large estates are commonplace in the literature, only a few are specified as being in the south. Seneca, a very rich man and owner of large properties, gives one hint when he scorns those who define a man as rich "just because his gold plate goes with him even on his travels, because he farms land in all the provinces, because he unrolls a large account book, *because he owns estates near the city so great that men would grudge his holding them in the wastelands of Apulia*" (Letters 87.7; my italics). On circumstantial evidence, however, it is reasonable to link the origins of at least some of the later *latifundia* with the unusual opportunities for land acquisition available in post-Hannibalic southern Italy.

The Reconquest of Spain brought into existence a similar problem, that of how to settle and farm vast and empty or emptied territories. There was a policy for repopulation, particularly in the major Andalucian cities and in the Levantine states, but the work was achieved in several phases and often after several revisions. In Murcia, for instance, there were no less than five *Repartimiento* phases, the first under James I of Aragon, the others under the Castilian crown. The ethos was of a "whirlwind of liberty", and this gave unique opportunities for social mobility and new conditions for social stratification even within the context of feudalism (Mackay, 1977, p. 40).

The process of Reconquest took place in three major phases. Only the last resulted in the development of large estates. At first, in the ninth and tenth centuries, the Christian kingdoms of Castile and Leon managed to advance and expand into what is today Old Castile (Malefakis, 1970, p. 50ff). This area had been intentionally depopulated by Alfonso VI in an attempt to create an uninhabited buffer zone between Christian and Moslem Spain. So the first task was to repopulate the area. Small settlers, free or freed peasant owner-occupiers, were attracted by the right of free possession (*presura*) that was applied to the newly occupied land. A few large estates were created for important individuals or taken by religious foundations but these were limited by the general shortage of labour. The result, therefore, of this first stage of Reconquest was a zone of numerous and small holdings, *behetria* settlements and a strong tradition of peasant independence and freedom (Sanchez-Albornoz, 1963). This contrasted greatly with the feudal estates existing in Catalonia and in Galicia.

As the frontier moved south, beyond the Tagus, with the second and third stages of Reconquest (1020–1030s and late eleventh century

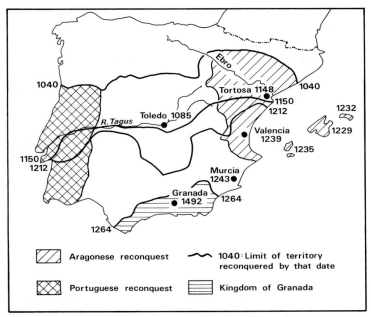

Fig. 17. *The Reconquest and the "frontiers" of Spain.*

onwards), changes took place in the old buffer zone (Fig. 17). The small and independent landholding system was replaced by one of lordships. The process of colonization of the new frontier zones also reflected new circumstances. From the start of the twelfth century there was almost continuous warfare and a warrior caste, "whose collaboration had to be rewarded", developed (Malefakis, 1970, p. 54). Liberties were imposed by the crown in the form of quasi-feudal lordships granted to towns, nobles and military orders. The acquisition in 1148 of Tortosa, for instance, just upstream from Ebro delta, resulted in a single lordship that covered the town and its territory but that had to be shared between the Order of the Temple and the house of Moncada (Mackay, 1977, p. 42).

The fall of Toledo in 1085 heralded the sudden opening up of an immense area of the peninsula. Over 155 000 square miles were gained between 1212 and 1250. It was the sheer magnitude of this period of the conquest that so deeply affected the social reorganization that followed. The spatial immensity of central-southern Spain was exaggerated by the sparseness of the existing population. Regions such as Estramaduro and La Mancha had been losing population since Roman times. Around Toledo itself the Moorish settlement pattern had been one of *alquerias*, estate centres isolated by the empty countryside. [5] An expansion of sheep ranching after 1085 along the new frontier had done little to remedy this seemingly endless, dry, emptiness. There was very little else that could be done with this sort of district under the circumstances other than to establish a system of extensive livestock ranching. For this the circumstances were ideal; there was plenty of room for extensive grazing estates and the labour demand in a ranching system is minimal. As it so happened, these ventures turned out to be highly successful economically. The price of wool in Europe began the steady upward trend characteristic of the second half of the Middle Ages. The number of ranches multiplied and livestock numbers increased. Transhumance to moister summer pastures was the answer to the problem of a shortage of summer pasture locally. Once again, what had been a matter of expediency became a permanent economic attraction.

The Reconquest cannot be held responsible for every Spanish *latifundia*. Some had survived in Andalucia since the later Roman Empire though nothing is known about their number or size (Malefakis, 1970, p. 57 fn 39). Others were created through the amalgamation of smaller holdings over the generations. This was true of ecclesiastical as well as of lay property (Fig. 18).

In general, in the emergence of *latifundia*, physical conditions are of small consequence. An extensive system of agriculture, whether involving dry-farmed cereals or livestock ranching with transhumance, and a problem of low yields (which in Spain could be four or five times lower than in the rest of Europe), may reinforce the survival of an estate economy. Physical conditions do not dictate the initial establishment of *latifundia* which, as it can be seen from the experience of Spain in the Middle Ages and Italy in the Roman period, had more to do with socio-economic factors and with the peculiar circumstances of the moment. This means that it is unrealistic to attempt to predict the sort of farming system likely to be found in any part of Mediterranean Europe at any time simply on the basis of physical conditions. If one single factor was the most important in the development of *latifundia* in Italy and Spain, it was a shortage of people, owners and labourers in the relevant districts.

Labour Shortages

In fact, the availability or otherwise of sufficient labour to work estates in the preferred manner has been recognized as a key factor in agrarian

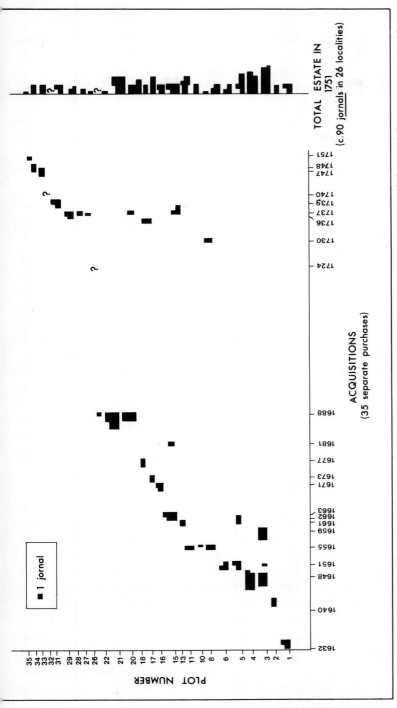

Fig. 18. *Piecemeal acquisition of an estate*, huerta of Tarraga (Barcelona). A modest property of about 40 hectares (one *jornal* equalled approximately 0·43 hectares) belonging in the mid-eighteenth century to Francisco Anton de Capons was the result of a series of painstaking, small acquisitions by his father, grandfather and great-uncle since 1632. The family were lawyers by profession. By 1761 the ennobled owner was no longer using his professional title and resided in the capital as a "don". The graph shows the year by year gains of small plots, usually in quite different places. Where the purchases included adjacent plots, the second plot number has been omitted from the left-hand scale for the sake of clarity (from data in Vilar, 1967).

change. Two periods of labour shortage in Mediterranean Europe in the historic period stand out. The first was from the fourth to the sixth centuries A.D.; the second from the fourteenth to the fifteenth centuries.

In the late Roman Empire, landowners of great, middle and small-sized estates suffered alike. Privately held land was hived-off as tenant farms, including a good deal of the imperial estate or *res privata*. One element in the labour shortage was a decline in the slave population, which was noticeable by the middle of the second century A.D. Columella, despite himself, had to take account of this need for tenant farmers: "we should take pains to hang on to tenants who are country-bred . . . when we are not in a position to till the land ourselves, or when it is not feasible to cultivate it with our own staff" (1.7.4). This shortage meant that so long as landowners were anxious to keep tenants (*coloni*) on their land, conditions remained very much to the tenant farmer's advantage. If he disliked one landlord, the tenant was secure in the knowledge that if he moved another landowner would welcome him. This mobility however, was abruptly curtailed by Diocletian, perhaps not specifically as a remedy for the problem of agricultural labour but as a means of fiscal reform (Jones, 1974, p. 299). In the event the labour shortage of late Roman times resulted in the loss of a great deal of land from cultivation. Over 14 000 hectares in Campania alone were reported derelict (*agri deserti*) by the end of the fourth century A.D. (Stevens, 1966, p. 118). The greatest inconvenience to landowners and government alike of the growing *agri deserti* was loss of income. By the fourth century the government was encouraging anybody who would to cultivate deserted land by offering it for sale by auction and by granting tax-free periods of clearance. At the same time, landowners who accepted *coloni* who had run away from abandoned estates were fined.

Demographic decline and shortage of rural labour were not the only factors accounting for the phenomenon of *agri deserti* in the later Roman Empire and early Middle Ages. There was the very real problem of security in times troubled by invaders from central and eastern Europe, and raiders from North Africa. So it was not until the tenth and eleventh centuries that the *agri deserti* were the scene of a vast series of pioneer movements from southern France to northern Italy. Recolonization, reclamation and resettlement transformed these old established and formerly well-settled provinces into frontier regions of rather a different nature from those being created in Spain at the same time. Yet by the second decade of the fourteenth century demographic disaster had set in once more and a similar tale of famines and plagues by 1450 was imprinting the landscape of these same regions with the characteristic traits of depopulation: deserted farms, deserted villages, retreat of arable land, extension of fallow and uncultivated areas, of forest and secondary vegetation, of marshland and malaria.

This second period of labour shortage coincides with the Black Death but was not necessarily caused by it since demographic decline had been typical of many districts for three or four decades previously. When it did come though, the effect of the Black Death could be dramatic. In Languedoc it hit the already declining and impoverished populations particularly hard. Marsillargues, on the plain near the Vidourle, lost 50% of its population. In the hills behind, losses were even greater. Ganges counted 132 heads of households in 1366 but by 1433 there were only 89. The downward trend continued after 1348, helped by new outbreaks, well into the first third of the fifteenth century to stabilize at a dismally low point only after 1480 or, in some cases, not until 1500. Dereliction marked the landscape. By 1401 the town ditches of Montpellier, "once planted with gardens, orchards and vines", had become "filled with briars and thorns, snakes and lizards" (cited by Le Roy Ladurie, 1972, p. 15). The acreage under vines shrank the most. Near Bèziers in 1353, there had been 40 vineyards to every 100 arable fields but by the end of the fifteenth century there were no more than 6 vineyards to each 100 fields. The usual practice had been to plant vines on marginal land so it is not surprising that these were the crops most severely affected by abandonment. Another factor in the retraction of viticulture was that vines are very labour intensive. In such circumstances, the quality of the land becomes a matter of paramount importance. Landlords with good alluvial soils managed to maintain as good a profit even from sales of wine in 1393 as in 1236, while profits from cereals definitely dropped. In Lodève, vine-growers refused to work all but the best land. Cereal land also suffered a general decline but again all in marginal areas. Particularly hit were the zones of heavy, wet soils such as those near the coast and the lagoons, where rising salt, increased marshiness and a new persistence of "bad air" accompanied the abandonment of land and the desertion of villages.

The demographic crisis and the period of labour shortage in the fourteenth and fifteenth centuries led to changes in estate management and to the re-emergence of share-cropping. It also resulted in a considerable reshuffling of landholdings. In this the chief gainers were the major landowners, though in the sixteenth century there was a great rise in the number of rich peasants. The process of acquisition is well documented. In Languedoc, for instance, the village of Coussergues had been a lagoonside walled *castrum*, with 24 heads of family recorded in 1317. By 1496 its site was deserted and the entire territory of the former village had been bought by one noble Pierre de Sarret, who thus laid the foundations of a vast landed fortune which survived the next four centuries (Le Roy Ladurie, 1972, p. 17). In one village in Hérault (Lespignan), where in 1492 there had been no more than five relatively large holdings (over 110 *sétérées*), by 1607 there were 12 in this category (Le Roy Ladurie, 1972, p. 86).* The increase in the larger properties was at the expense of the holders of medium-sized estates (20–100 *sétérées*). At the other end of the scale, the smallest often untaxable holdings were also greatly increased in number. In part this was due to the creation of tiny plots out of the marsh edges or wasteland fringes. At Saint-Thibery, there were 33 of these holdings in 1460 (each a tenth or less of a *sétérée*) but 132 by 1690.

In northern Italy the shortage of labour led to the development of some relatively favourable leases. In 1448 the commune of Imola leased 60 *tornatura* (1·2 hectares) of waste, scrub and woodland in the Po valley to a single individual rent-free for 29 years on condition that the land be made fertile. The lease, cited by Larner (1965, p. 125), explains the circumstances:

> In the territory and land of Imola in the farm of Barignano . . . there are many possessions and lands, once in past times cultivated and ploughed; which . . . are now shrub, gravel, wood, and pond, useless uncultivated and fruitless. It has long been so, through lack of men and people, and on account of the troubles of war and floods. Wherefore our . . . Lord Taddeo . . . desires the same places to be brought to fertility . . .

In the very same area, a fever of land reclamation in the early thirteenth century had been the result of land shortage. At that time there was no lack of potential colonists. For example, 87 families from the commune of Imola had agreed to live together at the new settlement of Massa San Paolo and to bring 1 *tornatura* (about 20 hectares) of wooded land into cultivation each year. The old style of family holdings (*mansi*) had been destroyed by population growth and by repeated sub-division and the movement onto newly reclaimed land led to the creation of larger agricultural units, *poderi* (Jones, 1968; Osheim, 1977, p. 107ff).

---

* Le Roy Ladurie gives no metric equivalent for a *sétérée* in Hérault. This unit of land measurement could vary considerably; there were *sétérées* of 33 ares, 54 ares and 81 ares, for example. From another source it looks as though the Hérault *sétérée* might have been no more than 20 ares.

The Church as Landowner

In Spain, the Reconquest gave particular advantage to the ecclesiastical orders. There seem to have been other factors explaining their initial involvement in what was otherwise a military operation besides the obvious one, a crusading interest. An important factor in the success of the ecclesiastical bodies as landowners was undoubtedly the efficiency of their internal organization and the literacy of their members. The Cistercian order was much admired by Frederick II, a ruler who had little time for the church which eventually excommunicated him, because of the monks' practical as well as theoretical knowledge of farming and husbandry (Masson, 1973, p. 168). Another factor was the readiness of many orders to live in solitude, a preference which made them ideal colonists in the frontier regions of Spain and the districts of *agri deserti* in southern France and northern Italy.

In Spain six military orders rose to prominence during the twelfth century Reconquest: Knights Templar, Knights Hospitaller, Calatrava, Alacantra, and the two branches of the order of Santiago. Their patrimonies tended to be so broad as to constitute veritable palatine lordships, falling outside the law and jurisdiction of the king and his officers (Bishko, 1963, p. 52). Out of the new Castilian conquests of the thirteenth century, 22% (totalling about seven-and-a-half million hectares) fell to the church. The nobility did better with 60% but the ecclesiastical orders had ascendancy over the crown, which gained a mere foothold with 18% of the land. In La Mancha and Estramadura the church had jurisdiction over 31% and 34% of the territory respectively (Malefakis, 1970, p. 59). The Knights Hospitaller had received pre-grants as an inducement and they became the most formidable of the ecclesiastical landowners, acquiring castles, whole towns and villages, the homes and the estates of Moslem leaders. Their major acquisitions included, for example, two villages (Benirrage, in 1233, and Benyaz), the castle and township of Gervera, the castles and towns of Torrente, Silla, Sueca and the village of Alcudia de Silla (by the Albufera lagoon) together with its 30 fishing boats (Burns, 1967, p. 185).

The Cistercians were also major landowners. They had two great abbeys in the kingdom of Valencia, Benifesa and Valldigna. In 1229 James I had confirmed a grant for the erection of the monastery of Benifesa. The land belonging to the Benifesa eventually included a generous sweep of the

E

Plate 4. *The church as landowner* was not always richly endowed. The monastery of Benifesa, on the northern frontier of the medieval kingdom of Valencia, was given an extensive grant by James I of Aragon in 1229. The territory, however, was mostly mountainous and soon after its foundation the monks were reported to be struggling for survival. They cultivated land in the immediate vicinity of the monastery and lay brothers were responsible for farming the rest from distant granges. After lying in ruins, the monastery has been restored in the last few years to its former use. The neighbouring village is shown in Plate 2.

countryside around it, together with ''the castle and valley . . . of Malagraner, the castle of Fredes, the place and the whole country of Bojar with its valley and plains and districts, and the whole country of Rossell and Castell de Cabres, and the castle of Bel with its districts, each and every castle and place'' (cited by Burns, 1967, p. 216). The monastery was also permitted to guarantee itself an income from tithes. A full half of each tithe could be taken by the monks. The other half went to the bishop of Tortosa in whose diocese the new monastery lay. The monks also gained the tithes payable on ''first fruits, all mills and half the ovens''. Additions to the acreage of free grazing were made a few years later (in 1237) when further grants were made of rights to crown land in the kingdom of Valencia.

By 1250 there were 43 monks at Benifesa. Their estate was typical of

Cistercian estates in that it was contained in a single bloc of land. It was cultivated for arable both in the immediate vicinity of the monastery and further away, when the land was worked from a number of granges inhabited by lay brothers. Further gifts and privileges accrued, such as tax exemption for sheep. But life in this mountain district was not easy. The monastery was in debt by 1260 and in 1272 it was reported that the monks were living at a bare subsistence level. Their struggle for survival took the form not only of hard farm work but also of litigation, as they attempted to gain more land and to preserve what was already held. Between 1258 and 128ᵏ there were at least nine clashes between the monks of Benifesa and their Valencian neighbours over boundary disputes, rights of wool-gathering, grazing privileges, rents and other rights. The monastery survived and eventually gained some sort of economic stability but it was never to rank amongst the wealthy.

This question of ecclesiastical poverty has another aspect. The shortage of manpower in medieval Spain was chronic and acute to a degree untypical of the other countries of Mediterranean Europe, or indeed Europe in general. The frontier situation had placed a great strain on the arable economy of the demesne in districts well to the north. The monastery of San Millan de la Cogolla (Longrono), for instance, had formerly had an area of demesne that was worked in the classic manner by peasants owing services (Segret and Rui, 1969). By the later years of the eleventh century the monks felt obliged to change from direct demesne exploitation to a labour attractive system of rents, tenanted farms and seigneurial dues, anticipating changes in northern Italy by a century or so. The decline of the manor was precocious in northern Spain because of the frontier situation. Mackay sees the timing of the changes at San Millan de la Cogolla as significant in coming so soon after the fall of Toledo. With the opening of the frontier further south, manpower gained in premium as would-be colonists migrated south (Mackay, 1977, p. 71). But evidence from another monastery, also north of the old frontier, shows that the process of fragmentation and agrarian change had started earlier still. Since the ninth century at Santo Toribio de Liebuna (Santander) there had been no single bloc of land that merited the designation of a big holding, let alone an estate (Gautier Dalché, 1962). The monastery's property was no more than a wide scatter of small plots.

The cartulary of Santo Toribio nicely reflects the usual manner in which ecclesiastical properties were gradually built up over the centuries. By far the most important source of land was the bequests. The bulk of these at

Santo Toribio were made between the beginning of the ninth and the beginning of the fourteenth centuries. Only 13 contracts (out of 83) mention purchases made by the monastery and only seven exchanges were embarked on, all before the fourteenth century. The property involved was varied: arable plots, vineyards, apple or cherry orchards, grazing meadow, a pair of oxen, a few cows, a horse, houses and churches, mills, barns, a wine vat (in 1036), a close and so on. Each acquisition was small and it was usually fragmented. As part of a single bequest made in 1051, one vineyard was located at Mus, one arable plot at Ortelia and another at Arzellero.

In Italy by the thirteenth and fourteenth centuries, the church was wielding its power in a different way. It had its own consolidated kingdom, the Papal State, in which it had absolute (if not undisputed) sovereignty. The Papal State by this time accounted for perhaps a third of peninsular Italy. Right up to Unification, it prevented polarization between the states of the northern plain, Lombardy and the Po valley, and the Kingdom of Naples. Its origins lay in eighth and ninth century donations from Pippin and Charlemagne to the papacy which complemented land remaining in papal hands since Roman times. The huge estates of the Roman church had been amongst the largest concentrations of landed property in Italy but a good deal was lost in the north during the reign of Pope Gregory, when Lombards seized church land in Liguria and Slavs and Avars took land in Dalmatia (Partner, 1972, p. 70). In the south, church property remained relatively intact. In 731 the Byzantine emperor Leo III confiscated the papal patrimony in Sicily and annexed it to the Byzantine fisc (Ostrogovsky, 1956, p. 146). The Byzantine reconquest of the tenth century largely left the existing Lombard system alone. The Lombards themselves took less from the church here than they did further north.

In late Roman times the most extensive blocs of church land had been in the south in general and around Rome in particular. Under the later Empire, church estates had been organized into aggregates of individual estates each known as *domusculta*, "a large holding of mixed agriculture administered by the Pope and generically parallel to the *latifundia* of the late Empire" (D. Whitehouse, 1973, p. 862). Size was the striking characteristic of the *domuscultae* (Partner, 1967). The bloc of estates which formed the *domuscultae* of Crepacorum (Etruria) for instance may have measured 9 × 24 km; that of Caleria, which stretched from the Via Clodia to the Via Portuense, would have been some 20 km in breadth. Although the *domuscultae* disappeared during the troubled times of the

Arab invasions (late ninth and tenth centuries) much land remained in ecclesiastical hands or was later restituted to the papacy through donations to churches and to monasteries.

Not all the land held by the church in Mediterranean Europe was profitable land. Estates in Corsica and Sardinia were notoriously difficult to exploit. It was from the northern peninsula of Italy that the basic requirements of the papacy were best supplied. Here by the thirteenth century the papacy had evolved its own administrative system, though the episcopal bureaucracy remained small in comparison with the communal (Osheim, 1977, p. 86). There was a rector in charge of each province and a treasurer who controlled the finances gathered in from hearth taxes (*focaticum*) from subsidies payable by the clergy (*decima*), and from various sources such as road taxes, mills, fines etc. (Larner, 1965). In its turn, each bishopric had to make payments to support the Roman see, to meet the costs of warfare and to support itself.

The burden of supporting the ecclesiastical sector was a heavy one. In 1291 the diocese of Faenza was responsible for one bishop, resident in the city of Faenza with ten canons and one chaplain; four monasteries in the countryside; and at least 20 religious houses in or near the city. There were houses of the Augustinian, Dominican and Franciscan friars, and the particularly wealthy canons of San Marco at Mantua. The Camoldi had three houses, the Fonte Avellana and the Vallambrosi one house each. There were two military orders; four convents for women; and at least six hospices and hospitals. There were 30 rectors in the town and 154 churches in the territory of Faenza. As in Spain, by no means were all of these religious institutions rich; 62 of the country rectors in the diocese of Faenza were too poor to be taxed and the Knights Templar paid only under protest a *decima* levied on their annual income of £1335 (in comparison, the canon of San Marco had a taxable revenue of £13 350).

From the point of view of the peasantry, papal control was little different from control by the crown or by the nobility except that financial pressures may have been worse. Certainly the church was more unpopular as landowner in districts such as Romagna. The local population found that taxation tended to be heavier on church land. Like the crown, and for the same reasons, the church was prone to indulge in speculation and would pocket outstanding profits from marketing cereals in times of famine and high prices. The reign of individual popes, on principle elected to office only at an advanced age, tended to be short and every change of pope brought the threat of a change of policy. Even more than in the case of the baronial landowners, finance was at the root of troubles of the papacy and of ecclesiastical landowners in general. To make matters worse, there were lay landowners within the area administered as the Papal State. Their estates were not necessarily large and their status correspondingly modest. In Romagna there were scores of small feudatories, such as Cione who held Certairo (Macerata), a stronghold of no more than 34 hearths in 1371, but their presence served only to underline what the local population felt was an unfair hardship, being a tenant farmer on church land.

Villas, Castles and New Villages

By the later Middle Ages, in Italy in particular, many landowners seem to have become townsmen at heart, a characteristic which greatly developed in later centuries. Barons living in Sicily in the eighteenth century were probably the most outstanding in their lack of interest in their agricultural estates. It was a sad and economically disastrous fact that was reported by the Professor of Agriculture at Palermo in 1800: ''hardly one of our large landowners . . . is an active farmer'' and ''there is hardly another country in Europe where so much land is owned in large farms by so few and where landowners have so little desire to live in or even visit their estates'' (Balsamo, 1800. pp. 78, 95–96, quoted by Mack Smith, 1965, p. 89). Some landowners resided in mainland cities and died, it was asserted, without ever having set foot on their estates. In contrast the impression gained for the Roman period is of a much higher and genuine degree of interest in agriculture amongst landowners. Even so, major landowners in the later Roman Empire were no less appreciative of urban comforts than their later counterparts and when they resided in the country or visited one of their estates, it was an urban standard of comfort they expected and created there. Permanent country residence entailed isolation from political and cultural interests and was therefore not popular, except where these interests were poorly developed, as in medieval Spain.

The Roman *Villa Urbana*

The residences of landowners in Roman times showed considerable variety in the manner of their association with agricultural functions. There was the *villa rustica*, wholly agricultural and similar to the medieval or modern *mas* or *masseria* in that most of the complex comprised rooms or buildings needed in the exploitation of the estate. The landowner's residence, whether occupied by him or not, took up a relatively small proportion of the buildings. Then there were two forms of *villa urbana*. In one type, the complex contained a set of rooms or buildings for agricultural functions (including residential apartments for the bailiff and for the hired labourers and slaves) and another set of rooms or buildings which contained the landowner's residence. The balance between the two sectors, residential and agricultural, varied. Secondly, there was the out-of-town villa which had no agricultural quarters at all. Often these were by the coast or on the shores of a lake. Many were originally simple, agricultural villas transformed stage by stage as increased opulence or ambition led to the addition of architecturally stylish wings, marbled and mosaic floors, *piscinas* and other embellishments.

The provision of urban standards of comfort in country residence reached an advanced stage in the later Roman period when life on the estate was deliberately made as remote as possible from the farming activities that supported it and that were carried on all around. The *villa urbana* of Casa del Menandro is unusual probably only in the sequence of developments by which it was transformed from a town house in one of the most fashionable quarters of the city of Pompeii into an extensive but highly operational farming unit. It would not have been unusual for the way in which care had been taken over the new layout, which ensured that "the owners could have their land worked for them without any inconvenience to their position as prominent members of the city bourgeoisie" (White, 1970, p. 435). It was only the landowner with more than one estate who could afford to run another establishment with no agricultural wing or attached farming activities. As in the case of Pliny's Ostian villa, these were supplied with food, wine and other necessities from the often distant agricultural units of the estate.

The age for the great, luxurious establishments, the reputation of which has passed into posterity as one of the wonders of Roman times, was the fourth century A.D. While Italian wall paintings, African mosaics and surviving literature provide an immense amount of detail, archaeological excavation also reveals the astonishing spatial extent of many a *villa urbana*. The Villa d'Arianne (Capua) was a modest establishment with 13 rooms but the Villa dei Misteri at Pompeii, strictly a town establishment, has at least 50 rooms in just that part of the complex that has so far been excavated. In the countryside not far away, at Gragnano, another villa has over 30 rooms occupying at least 200 m^2. Pliny's villa at Laurentum (Ostia), by all accounts an opulent establishment overlooking the dunes and the sea, was only one of a number of *villae urbanae* along this stretched coast. Their roofs, Pliny tells us, "now in unbroken line, now scattered, resemble a number of towns and add colour to the coastline with their charming irregularity" (Letters, ii, 17,27). The attraction to landowners of this particular coast lay in the fact that it was only 17 miles from Rome and was thus considered accessible after a day's work in the city (Duncan-Jones, 1974, p. 22; Columella, I. 1.18). Around the Bay of Naples were villas designed to take full visual advantage of the natural surroundings (D'Arms, 1970, p. 126). Their peristyle design was based on that of Hellenistic royal palaces. There was a large central court with the residential apartments on three or all four sides. There were no agricultural preoccupations. Equally luxurious, and much favoured in these coastal areas, was the portico design, where long colonades fronted directly on the sea. This was a common arrangement in the elegant *villae maritimae*, villas built right on the shore itself and even jutting out over the water on artificial terracing. At Astura one such villa had its own private port, two piers projecting to the south-east from a fishery connected to the villa (Schmeidt, 1964, p. 32). In those days the villa was on a small island connected to the mainland by a long bridge but since then a sandy isthmus has formed to join the island and the shore.

By the fifth century many of these bases of wealth and splendour had to be fortified against brigands and raiders (Stevens, 1966, p. 112). In this adaptation may lie, as has already been discussed, the origin of many of the medieval fortified villages, *casale* or *castra*. The complex and extensive layout of a villa would have lent itself to multiple occupancy. Their compactness lent itself to easy enclosure and fortification. There may have been a regular market (Fasoli, 1959, p. 101).

Castles

The early part of the medieval period was characterized by the predominance of nucleated forms of settlement. Landowners therefore had to find room within the villages and townships for their residences or else find security for their castles at considerable topographic inconvenience. Many of the nobility, particularly first generation nobles, would have been living in crude conditions. There was little scope for elegance or even comfort in many baronial strongholds. Not all castles, however, were necessarily placed as is La Rocquette (Montpellier). First mentioned in 1123, now in ruins, the castle occupied the end of a knife-edge ridge near Pic St. Loup. It could only have been reached (in the manner of the Meteora monasteries in Greece) by ropes (Fabrège, 1894, Vol. I, p. xxiv). It is true that these baronial homes were intended to be strongholds. In Romagna there were strongholds such as Montebello ''on a very high rock on an impregnable mountain . . . [a] . . . rocca''; Castiglioncho, with an inner wall, an outer wall, a keep with a portcullis and inaccessible rocks to the south-west; and Verghetto, where the Abbot held ''a tower, very strong and very apt for war, which dominates the surrounding district'' (Larner, 1965, p. 113). The domestic quarters in the majority of these castles would have been wooden buildings, scarcely a luxurious form of baronial mansion. It was the outer aspect that mattered, a symbol of lordship, rather than personal comfort. In other cases, it is clear that the fortress was never intended as a residence. Only a small permanent garrison, which could be brought up to strength should the occasion arise, was stationed within.

A rather less uncomfortable way of demonstrating status was for a landlord to fortify his estate farmstead. Moated farmsteads became widespread, particularly on the plains and lowlands. In 1419, Torre di Gualde (Rimini) comprised a moated site (enclosing two buildings); a large farm building where the labourers lived; six other houses close by; and, a little apart from these and fronting onto the road itself stood the *hospitium*, residence of the lord. Here there was a garden, a well, an oven for baking and stabling for perhaps as many as 40 horses (Larner, 1965, p. 112). Also on the Po plain is Malpaga (Bergamo) a rare survivor of just such a fortified estate steading. It has been described by Morton:

> The farm buildings occupy an immense square like a Roman camp, in the centre of which stands the castle with its fishtail battlements rising above a dry moat. The old soldier [of the *condottori* Colleoni family] designed it as if it would have to endure a siege . . . The farm buildings are two storeys in height, and in the lower are the barns and storehouses, the granaries and cow-byres, and above are the dwellings of the farm labourers (1964 p. 155).

Most of the castles built for Frederick II in southern Italy and Sicily in the thirteenth century would have served well as fortifications but some cannot have been more than mere symbols of power. The beautiful octagon of Castel del Monte in Apulia, for example, while it is an

E*

architectural gem and inspiration, also serves through its domination of the Apulian countryside for a radius of 50 or 60 km as an effective reminder of the ruler's authority. Similarly, in Tuscany in the same century, the tall, towered houses of the newly arrived merchant families were built on the site of old manors not as effective fortifications but as *case de signore* "part villa, part farm, part estate centre" (Jones, 1968, p. 234 and fn 2).

Occasionally it suited an individual noble to remain on his estate rather than dance attendance on the king or at court. Long after the victory of the Normans at Civitate, in Apulia, the new Norman Count of Lesina persisted in dating his letters according to the old Byzantine calendar (Gay, 1904, p. 543). In Spain in the sixteenth century, the nobility tried to avoid the strong rule of Philip II by hiding on their estates. Deprived of their urban comforts, they created splendid country palaces. Many of these remain, incongruous in their poor, dusty, villages with their renaissance windows, broad staircases, moulded ceilings, exposed beams and huge fireplaces (Braudel, 1972, p. 712). Only when the crown's hold weakened, under Philip III, did the Spanish nobility venture back into Madrid, tempted by offers of major government posts. Their town houses were at first a dismal contrast to their country palaces and in 1597 the visiting Cardinal Borghese found them far inferior to those of the Italian nobility.

Landowners and their New Villages

There were several factors (apart from the Reconquest in Spain) which contributed to make the creation of new villages an attractive proposition for landowners, lay or ecclesiastical. One was the financial advantage. Where land was more plentiful than labour, tracts of uncultivated land could be let to peasants willing to clear it and convert it into arable for which rents would in due course be charged. Because of the scarcity of population in such districts the landowner had to be prepared to create the entire village. Another was the prestige that the foundation of entire new settlements conferred on the landowner, together with what Mack Smith has called "the illusion or reality of power" (1968, p. 196). Yet another was political. In Sicily, for example, the creation of a new village of not less than 80 families entitled the landowner to a seat in parliament. For this reason alone the number of parliamentary barons in Sicily rose sharply from 72 in 1556 to 277 by 1810. Another aspect of the financial incentive was that the provision of the essential rural services—corn mills, olive presses and bakehouses—often compulsorily used, was a highly profitable extra source of income for the landowner even where an alternative existed. The main disadvantage of founding a new settlement was that these longed-for returns tended to be far from immediate. The landowner had to grant an initial rent-free and tax-free period. He had to allow certain unchargeable rights for the use of water and of wood (for fuel or for the construction of ploughs) etc. It was not always the case that a sufficient number of inhabitants were speedily attracted to the new venture. The new village of Castelvetrano (Trapani) in Sicily had very few settlers when it was started in the early sixteenth century. It was only when leases were reorganized a century later that the number of inhabitants had increased to 576. Things could be easier. At Casteltermini (Agrigento) it took only two decades to reach a total population of over 2000 by 1629.

In all, nine villages were created in Sicily by baronial landowners during the fifteenth century and a further 150 over the following two centuries. The new residents were of either local or immigrant origin. Local colonizers came in particular from areas where baronial courts were unduly exigent or from royal demesne as a means of avoiding repayment of debts. Some came from the towns. [6] A major stimulus in the creation of new villages in southern Italy and Sicily was the influx of Greek and Albanian refugees from the Turkish occupation of the Balkans. They were warmly welcomed during times of labour shortage. Half-a-dozen Greek or Albanian settlements were established in Sicily alone between the end of the fifteenth and the seventeenth centuries [Mack Smith (1969, p. 195) says "seven main villages"; Rother (1968, p. 4) names five; Aymard and Bresc (1973, p. 968) mention six]. On the mainland, the church created 20 in Calabria between 1570 and 1707 (Rother, 1968, p. 18). Eventually the total rose to 70 new villages populated by Greek and Albanian refugees in the southern part of the peninsula. Many existing settlements also received groups of the new arrivals. Some of these new settlements have remained Greek or Slav-speaking to this day. Near Lecce there is a district appropriately enough known as La Grichia, where Greek is still spoken in nine of the original 29 villages settled by the immigrants (Maraspina, 1968, p. 12).

There were other foreign immigrants for the new villages. Frederick II transplanted 16 000 Moslems from Sicily, in order to give peace to that island, to Lucera in Capitanata (Kantorowicz, 1931, p. 130). The duty of the new inhabitants of this ancient town, whose new minarets and mosques were "visible afar across the levels of Apulia", was to cultivate neglected land and to pay special taxes imposed on them for tolerance of their faith. Frederick, in short, needed labour on his extensive Apulian estates (as well as the advantage of a fiercely loyal bodyguard) but his gain was the Sicilian landowners' loss. These had to employ some of the exiles from Celano and others from Lombardy in place of their Saracen labourers and tenants. Later, having destroyed the Saracen colony at Lucera, Charles of Anjou had to bring in Frenchmen in an attempt to remedy the labour shortage and to swing local loyalty on to his side. Two new villages in the Apennine foothills in northern Apulia, Celle and Faeto, were built for them. The names of 140 colonists transported in 1273 directly from Anjou and Provence are known and reveal the status of the immigrants, who turn out to have been mainly artisans, peasants and members of the *petit bourgeois* class (Durrieu, 1886, p. 246; Leonard, 1954, p. 58ff). Each family was given land in proportion to the number of its members and the allocation included arable, vines, a vegetable garden and a pair of oxen, as well as a small amount of cash to pay for basic farming equipment (Papon, 1777, p. 58). Wood rights were granted, and pasture land with running water was available. Advances of grain for food and seed were included, there was tax exemption for the first 10 years, and the houses were built at government expense. "One would think that one was reading the prospectus of an agent for the colonists" remarked Leonard (1954, p. 79), but the truth was that Charles was desperate to repopulate the territory of Lucera (Apulia) devastated by his siege of its Saracen garrison. In the first modern census (1861) it is recorded that a Provençal dialect was still being spoken in these two villages.

In Provence itself, charters relating to new settlements were numerous after 1450. Here the movement was largely one of relocation or reorganization of older population groupings rather than the establishment of foreign immigrants or of colonists drawn from a wide area (Livet, 1962, p. 147). Nevertheless the settlements reflected their newness in their geometric morphology, usually a sure index of systematic laying out and of planning. Some of the Provençal villages date from the beginning of the sixteenth century (Vallauris, Mouans-Sartoux, Valbonne), others from the eighteenth. In some cases the landowner and organizer was ecclesiastical, in others lay. In lower Provence, the village of La Roque d'Anthèron (Bouches du Rhone) was founded in 1514 by Jean de Forbin, a local landowner. He settled 25 families on land which was "shared and divided into proportional parts among all the newcomers" (article 5, cited by Livet, p. 148). However, all were not so lucky. The Bishop of Gap purchased two granges at Chateaurenard, one of which had about 600 hectares of land attached, but neither developed into villages. Sometimes there was more than one phase of reorganization. In the Durance valley the village of Charleval was first established in 1540 when there were only a few farmsteads on the entire territory. It was reorganized in 1741, when a grid-plan layout was imposed and uniformity of architecture insisted upon. Each farmstead was to be low; to front onto a broad street; and to have a large gateway that gave onto a small yard, around which were the stables and the shed for carts and ploughs.

Much of the activity of ecclesiastical landlords in southern France led to the establishment of isolated forms of settlement or perhaps of a hamlet associated with a monastery. The monastery of St. Victor at Marseilles used to own an agricultural estate on the plateau of Cengle. It had been acquired in the middle of the tenth century and by 1064 was recorded as the *castrum quod nominant Baiao* (Livet, 1972, p. 152). In 1143 members of the order of the Knights Templar were installed there. Two centuries later there was still no major nucleation; two priests and 13 laymen ran an estate that was big enough to need 16 plough oxen and to carry over 300 sheep and 450 goats. West of the Rhone the Benedictine foundation of Gellone, at the southern end of the Hérault gorge, was from its earliest days associated with a village, now St. Guilhem du Desert. This had grown out of a settlement originally established as housing for the worker force employed in the building and the furnishing of the monastery (Casson, 1907, p. 220). A high proportion of modern village names in the Garrigues of Montpellier incorporate the name of the saint to whom the first church was dedicated. For instance *villa sancti Bricii* (first documented in the ninth century) was known as St. Brès by 1625 while the reference to *Villa Rhoas ecclesia sancti Andr. . . .* (in 804–806 A.D.) is to modern St. André de Buèges (Thomas, 1865). To what extent these place names reflect merely the fashion of the period in which many of the villages originated (eleventh to the fourteenth century) rather than the active involvement of local monasteries and churches is not clear but it is generally accepted that the church did have a major role in the medieval resettlement of the Garrigues of Languedoc.

By the late eighteenth century circumstances for the creation of new settlements had changed. Reform was now the chief motive. In Spain, the Reconquest had absorbed all energy and all available population for new settlements in the frontier districts. Later on after 1610 the expulsion of the Moriscos and the attraction of the New World led to the desertion of settlements rather than to opportunities for new foundations. But in the eighteenth century the township of Nuovo Baztan (Madrid) was established, carefully laid out and designed by an architect (Gutkind, 1967, p. 274). It was at the centre of life on the estate of a wealthy banking family and the new settlement had long, low buildings, neatly laid out in pairs or rows, not far distant from the old seigneurial residence. There were others. Passing La Carlotta, in the province of Cordoba in 1776, Henry Swinburne described this village, established by the king for German settlers about 8 years previously. Each settler had been given 20–30 acres as an allotment from which to support his family, the king supplying his seed corn, and was under an obligation to remain there 10 years before leaving or electing to remain as owner-occupier. Meanwhile, the ''parish church, inn, director's house, some shops and dwelling houses for handicraft men, form a very neat village on an eminence''. (1779, p. 275). Another of Carlos III's creations was La Carolina, carved out of the forests of the same province. The original immigrant Germans had not stayed long. Even so, Swinburne reported that ''they talk of ten thousand families already being settled here [and supported from an area of arable hardly three leagues square] but I do not see how it is possible''. A novelty of rather a different nature was the model farm, Campo Flamenco, at Villamejor (Aranjuez) ''lately taken in by the marquis Grimaldi, and laid out on a grand scale'' (p. 341).

In southern Italy, first Carlos III and then King Ferdinand IV of Bourbon showed altruism in their motives. Between the late eighteenth century and the present day, 38 entirely new rural nucleations have been created in the province of Foggia. Of these, 10 were the direct result of Ferdinand's reforms. Another 175 years were to pass before the theme of reform was taken up again after the First World War. King Ferdinand himself was responsible for eight of the new settlements. The other two (Zapponeta and Poggio Imperiale) were established by private landowners inspired by his example (Ciasca, 1928, p. 67ff). Near Bari, Poggio Orsini was also a private establishment. For some of his villages Ferdinand assigned a total of 5000 *versura*, expropriated a few years previously from the Jesuits, to 500 peasants in *quote* of 10 *versura* each (12·5 hectares). Five agricultural colonies were set up: Orta, with 105 families; Ordona (deserted since the late Middle Ages) with 93 families; Stornara with 83; Stornarella with 73; and Carapelle with 56 families. In the traditional manner, each colonist family was issued with a pair of plough oxen, mules and tools. A church was built at each centre and there were rows or blocks of single-storey, two-roomed houses. There were many adversities; the inadequacies of the colonists themselves, drawn from the poorest population in the locality; shortages of water and of fuel; unfavourable legislation and taxes; and the hostility of successive landlords. But Ferdinand's well-intentioned colonies have survived. By 1806 when Stornarella sought and gained municipal autonomy, there were 227 families and a total population of 876. Today its population is over 3600. Ordona, with less than 1500 inhabitants is today the smallest of the original five; Orta (Nova) is the largest with over 11 000 inhabitants. Nowhere else in the southern kingdom did Ferdinand and his followers succeed on such a scale in offering so many of the poorer or less fortunate peasantry a new opportunity.

Taxes and Dues

Like the peasant, the landowner had a single overwhelming preoccupation. In his case, however, it was with money rather than with crops. Whatever the status of the landowner, his financial problems were as likely as not to be acute. At the head of society and with the best of intentions, the crown found that ambitions for the general good were costly. Rulers such as Frederick II involved themselves in an increasingly expensive form of government and learnt from usually uncomfortable experience that "to coordinate expenditure with available resources was not easy" (Mack Smith, 1975, p. 57). Their income from crown lands and from customs duties was just insufficient. In order to maintain the law and order that was essential for an efficient economy, the proceeds of taxation needed to be increased. The *collecta* started as an occasional emergency measure, imposed only on landowners early in Frederick's reign. From his last years onwards it became a permanent and general property tax. At the same time, its revenue was inadequate and alternative sources of income were also sought. The royal monopoly on mines and minerals was reasserted and a royal licence was decreed necessary for the selling of commodities such as iron, steel, pitch, hemp, silk and wheat. The dyeing industry became a royal monopoly.

By the late fifteenth century in the kingdom of Sicily, the problems of finance affected all levels of society and everyone complained of taxation.

By the 1620s even the government of the island of Sicily was borrowing annually in order to meet normal expenditure, let alone extraordinary outgoings. Licences were introduced for hunting and the holding of firearms, and the silk export tax was yet again increased. The peasantry were involved. They also had to pay the basic taxes and it was they who suffered first and most acutely from the inadequacies of administration such as food shortage, high prices and banditry. For Sardinia, Putzulu said that feudalism meant ''in each village a tyrant'' (1967, p. 150). The tyrant referred to was not so much the personality of the landowner as the fiscal pressures he represented. Agriculture was the basis of the economy, and inevitably taxation fell most heavily on the land and on its traded products.

By the sixteenth century, another contentious aspect to the problem of money was political. There was a tendency for money raised locally to be spent elsewhere. For instance, southern Italy and Sicily in particular were menaced by the Turkish presence in the Balkans and by increasing raids from Moslem pirates. So long as expenditure was on military and naval operations associated with the defence of the Neapolitan kingdom there was little complaint. However, from 1571 to 1577 the Sicilian government spent more than $1\frac{1}{2}$ million *scudi* not only on the defence of Sicily but also on grain and armaments, supplied to Spain, for the whole Spanish armada (Koeningsberger, 1951, p. 55).

Koeningsberger has aptly illuminated the complexity and effects of taxation and empire finance in Sicily. Money was the key to the strength or weakness of Spanish dominion in Sicily. Military and naval expenses amounted to over 90% of the island's budget in 1580 while local civil administration cost only 6% (or 60 000 *scudi*) a year. To meet these changes, the government had three sources of revenue. Parliamentary grants were based on the *donativi* which had been fixed in the fifteenth century but which could be superseded by extraordinary grants voted for definite periods. The burden of this taxation was allocated in fixed proportions amongst the population. The clergy were responsible for one-sixth, the nobility and the towns together for the remainder. Baronial and crown communes were then allotted their share according to the censused population. A second source of revenue came from crown property and crown rights. These might be tolls, fines imposed by the courts, feudal dues, payments for grazing or forestry rights. A third and more arbitrary source were taxes imposed by the government without the consent of Parliament when government revenues were inadequate to meet normal demands (which included road and bridge building, the upkeep of royal palaces, crown pensions and charitable contributions, and interest on government debts). But there was no denying the Turkish threat and expense on defence contributed to the ruination of the export trade and so had an indirect effect on agriculture. When the harvest failed (as in the plague year of 1576/1577) the Sicilian government budgetary deficit was frightening.

The financial story in Roman times was not very different. There was the same reliance on agriculture and on the products of the land as a source of money and Roman governments had very similar budgetary struggles, the army being likewise the single greatest expense. Fiscal pressure similarly passed from government to nobility to rest with the peasantry, to whom economic hardship meant shortage of daily food, insecurity of tenancies, and perennial and ever-increasing indebtedness rather than just shortage of cash. But it was the Roman period that saw the greatest change in the concept of taxation. Prior to Diocletian, the fiscal system of all ancient states had been remarkably rigid (Jones, 1974, p. 177). For something like six centuries, the rate at which Roman provincial customs were levied remained at a fixed 2–2½%. Diocletian, however, introduced a flexible budget and the new idea that the rate of taxation could be varied according to need. Subsequent governments discovered how easy it was to vary the rate of tax and taxation went up year by year to double over the 40-year period between A.D. 324 and 364. It was true that each increase had to be justified to the population, but the government was no longer really trying to keep expenditure within its budgetary level.

The main direct tax of both empire and republican Rome applied to agriculture. According to Cicero, there were two main forms of taxation, the *stipendium* and the tithe. The former was a provincial tax often payable in kind. Corsica and especially Sardinia paid in grain which contributed significantly to army needs and which perhaps influenced the pattern of land use in the lowlands of those islands. The tithe was associated with a pasture tax on numbers of cattle grazed. By Diocletian's reign there was also the *anona*, the chief tax in kind, levied on land of all kinds except houses and gardens. A *capatio* (a money poll tax) was taken for farm animals and for the rural population. So important was agriculture to the economy that it was only later that the urban population was also taxed.

The financial affairs of the nobility were those of the crown and of governments in miniature. The nobility needed some money to pay to agents they employed to run their estates though their main financial commitment was usually to the maintenance of a comfortable, luxurious or even ostentatious, style of living. This was just what was noticed in 1594 when a foreign envoy in Naples remarked on the way the income of the baronial class was absorbed in the maintenance of huge palaces, large numbers of servants, extra-marital relationships and costly standards of living (Croce, 1970, p. 115). Not all landowners spent their money in this way. Some spent it in the benefaction of great artists, the patronage of men of letters or of music, or on the collection of works of art, and posterity has reason to be grateful to them.

The church had its financial power and its financial problems. In Romagna "finance" summed up the intense unpopularity of the papacy. By the thirteenth and fourteenth centuries the papal government, like the crown, had three chief sources of revenue: the hearth tax (*fumentaria*); the tallage (*tallia militum*); and the monopoly of salt (*salaria*) (Larner, 1965, p. 43). These were collected by the communes on behalf of the *Curia*. At first the *fumentaria* was relatively light but as the exiled papacy struggled in the fourteenth century with its enemies in central Italy, taxation became heavy. The amount expected from each commune may not have been changed but since there had often been considerable losses as a result of the Black Death, the *per capita* share for the remaining population had effectively increased. The tithe was initially a universal income tax, the first attempt on a large scale "to tap all incomes at source . . . and to make this tax proportionate to the prosperity or decline of the land" (Boyd, 1972, p. vii). It was introduced for the first time in southern Italy in 1097 as a compulsory tax by Roger I. Only later did it come to be closely associated with the church, as rulers made gifts to bishops, the chief administrators, of the right to collect tithes for the benefit of the church.

Peasant farmers also had to pay taxes. An idea of the combined effect of these contributions emerges clearly from Salomon's study of the sixteenth century *Relaciones* of New Castile. Reviewing these, Salomon (1964) remarked "the peasant farmer of those times is a marvellous beast of burden. He carried on his back the Nobility, the Church, the State, urban Landowners, Merchants, Financiers . . . the splendour of the 'Golden Century' rested on him". Salomon went on to point out that not all the wealth and splendour of the period can be explained by incoming American gold and Indian treasures; much was torn from the soil of Spain by the peasant farmer and made available through taxation (p. 213). Probably over 50% of the harvest went in one way or another to support the non-peasant class and on the remainder the peasant and his family were meant to survive.

The heaviest tax burden in sixteenth-century Castile was the ecclesiastical *diezmos* or tenth. By now the proliferation of tenths had reached staggering proportions. The tenth itself generally conformed to the 1/10th of its nomenclature but there were as many as seven different tenths, all payable by each village in the provinces of New Castile. The seven were for "bread", for wine, for livestock, fowl, olive oil, for "other things", and for a "general" purpose. Payments to the church could in total be 10 to 20 times heavier than those due to a lay landowner. Payments to the crown were five to ten times less than the tenths but still three or four times more than seigneurial dues. While the tenths were accepted as a long-established tradition, the burden of crown dues appeared as much resented novelties in the late sixteenth century. They were in the form of a simple due (*pechos*) and a *servicio ordinario*. The latter had originated as an extraordinary levy. In 1590 the Spanish parliament granted the king a third source of levied income, the *milliones*. Then a second *milliones* was granted in 1597, followed by a third in 1600. As in the case of the Italian *collecta*, the *milliones* was becoming a regular payment. Taxes paid to the landowning nobility were the lightest. For instance, the lord of Cuerva received, between 1575 and 1580, a total of 400 hens, 450 *fanegas* of barley, 160 *fanegas* of wheat and 12 000 *maravedis*. The village of Cuerva, however, was relatively large, with 300 hearths so the annual burden for each family amounted to no more than one (or more) hen (levied on *huerta* plots), 1½ *fanegas* of wheat (levied for arable land) and 40 *maravedis* for vineyards and houses.

It was not though the lay landowner who was enjoying the benefit of these payments. Most of it would be passed on by the landowner to the crown. As the value of money fell during the fourteenth and fifteenth centuries in Spain, it was the landowners, in the middle position, who were the hardest hit of all. The peasant of New Castile owed taxes in three directions: to the nobility (the local lord); to the church; and to the crown. Taking all these dues into consideration, Salomon (1964) has worked out that an individual peasant in sixteenth-century Castile might have been paying, each year, as head of a family:

a maximum of 40–50 *maravedis* to the lord
a minimum of 446 *maravedis* plus $\left. \begin{array}{l} \\ 7 \text{ } \textit{fanegas} \text{ of grain} \end{array} \right\}$ as a "tenth" to the church
a total of 472 *maravedis* to the crown.

But landowners too were liable for all these taxes except the *pechos*. More often than not, their peasant tenants were in debt, unable to pay the dues on which the landowners counted to pay their own taxes. Small wonder perhaps that despite their responsibilities and opportunities the majority of lesser landowners have tended to be less than actively interested in agricultural innovation and economic development in the medieval and, above all, in the post-medieval period in Mediterranean Europe.

4

The Urban Farmer

The distinction between rural and urban has had little meaning in most of Mediterranean Europe in the past. On the surface, this seems to have given rise to some ambivalence. On the one hand, a leading historian talks of the entire Mediterranean world as a single urban region in the sixteenth century (Braudel, 1972, p. 278). Others have singled out the self-governing town as the most characteristic phenomenon of the Middle Ages (Previté-Orton, 1926, p.208) or, as recently, have asserted that "It is well known that Italian civilization is essentially urban" (Mannoni and Poleggi, 1977, p. 120). To an architect, too, the Roman civilization comes across as "assertively urban" (Rykwert, 1976, p. 25). On the other hand, it is suggested that the demographic data show that the majority of the population would have been rural, in a plausible ratio of 3:1 (figures in Russell, 1972, p. 46).

Undoubtedly Mediterranean Europe, and Italy in particular, has had a very strong tradition of urban development since Roman (and pre-Roman) times. So much, however, depends on what is understood by the words "town", "city" and "urban" and it is this problem that is at the root of the ambivalence. There is little obviously in common between a fully-fledged modern town, a medieval town and a Roman town, still less between any of these and a pre-Roman town. Moreover, the degree to which Mediterranean Europe was in the past urbanized tends to be easily exaggerated. For all its city republics and the strength of city politics in late medieval Italy, most of the population was rural. In the fourteenth century the urban district of Imola had 1624 hearths (*fumantes*) while its territory or *contado* was nearly twice as populous, with 2881 hearths (Larner, 1965, p. 211). Pistoia had a taxable population in 1344 of nearly 20 000 in the countryside compared with rather more than 6000 in the city[7] (Herlihy, 1967, p. 75 and Appendix 1). Florence may have had

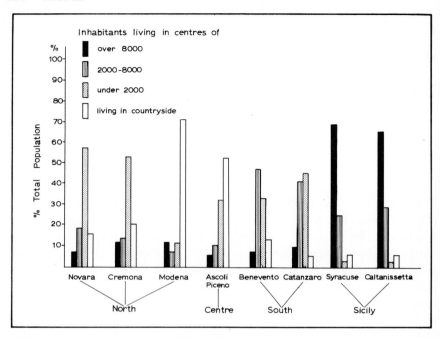

Fig. 19. *Town size in Italy* at the time of the 1871 census. The proportion of the total population living in the countryside (also shown) is everywhere in the minority except in provinces in the Apennines (Ascoli Piceno) or in provinces with a good deal of Apennine terrain (Modena). What is interesting is the very small size of centres classified by the census as urban in all regions except in Sicily. Even there, truly a land of empty countrysides, the "big cities" start at 8000 inhabitants!

96 000 in the city alone as against 120 000 in the countryside (Russell, 1972, p. 40ff). The situation was similar in Roman times (Duncan-Jones, 1974, p. 2ff). But it is not merely a question of how many people lived in the towns and how many more lived in the countryside. The very nature of the towns needs more accurate identification. The majority of urban centres in Mediterranean Europe, particularly the smaller, provincial towns, were often very little more than villages in function and even landscape. They were towns only because they were called towns and because they were given a particular status. The links were two-way links. It is possible to think in terms of the urbanized countryside (which is presumably what Braudel had in mind) as well as of the countrified town.

The divorce between town and countryside that is typical of modern times is, according to Mumford, a product of the late eighteenth century (1961, p. 549).

The Countrified City

For every medieval or renaissance town that might accurately be described as overcrowded, with dwellings packed within the walled area, there were undoubtedly many more in which the intramural area contained not only the spacious gardens and orchards of the rich but a fair extent of the fields and common lands of the urban peasants. Centres such as Avignon, hugely successful economic centres such as Milan and Barcelona, even hill towns such as Arezzo and Siena, and plain towns such as Forli, Padua, Pisa and Zaragoza—all could have up to a quarter, a third, or even a half of their intramural area as fields (Fig. 20). This was not accidental. The inclusion of agricultural land within a town's walls was intentional. It was a safeguard in times of siege or when food supply was in difficulties for other reasons. The open land was a recreational asset at all times. It is difficult to avoid the conclusion that maintenance of a certain amount of agricultural land and open space within the town was deliberate policy. A town would have been judged overcrowded not when every plot of land within the intramural area actually had a house on it but when there was no longer sufficient land for building. When this happened, or in anticipation of it, the authorities organized an extension to the walled area. At Barcelona, for example, a huge 90-hectare expanse of land lying south of the river was enclosed in 1350 (Gutkind, 1967). This land remained largely open and agricultural throughout the fifteenth century. In Valencia, land that had been enclosed by new walls in the fifteenth century remained relatively thinly occupied nearly two centuries later (see Vicent Tosca's plan in Tarradell (ed.), 1975, p. 224). Gardens and fields were included within the walled area of most medieval and many post-medieval towns as a matter of course.

These fields and gardens were intensively cultivated, richly manured from city waste, and often watered. Within the town there was also space for the processing of crops gathered from these plots and those brought into the town from suburban fields. So the town became the scene of important farming operations at certain times of the year. There were

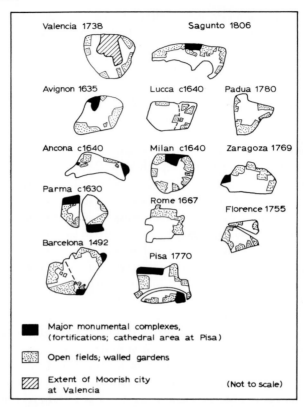

Fig. 20. *Open space in the walled towns and cities of Mediterranean Europe.* Except for Valencia (shading), Barcelona and Lucca (broken line), the older walled areas are not shown. The open spaces included unenclosed fields, enclosed fields and orchards, and enclosed gardens only if the latter were of noteworthy extent. Based on published maps, many of which are adequately reproduced in Hiorns (1956).

threshing floors in thirteenth-century Prato (Origo, 1957, p. 244). There were wine-making areas at Prato and, in Languedoc, at Béziers and Montpellier (where they could be still found earlier this century). Crops were brought into the towns for storage and livestock herded in each evening. The hay harvest in 1509 must have been a good one around Padua, for ''every day much hay was harvested and . . . the loads were so great that they almost had to be forced through a gateway'' (Pierre du Terrail, seigneur de Bayard, cited by Braudel, 1972, p. 325). On the same plain, the town of Imola was still largely interspersed with fields, gardens and orchards in the fifteenth century, according to Larner (1965, p. 128), who also points out that a ''town house'' for agricultural labourers was no more than a cottage which, being mostly timber-built, presented a high fire risk unless isolated by vineyards and plots, another good reason for deliberately maintaining low densities in towns.

There was fruit production within the walls of almost every town in Sicily (Abulafia, 1977, p. 38). In Sassari, second city in Sardinia, there were not only the usual markets for straw, hay and wood in the central *piazza* in the thirteenth century but also the pound for unreclaimed livestock (Brigalia, 1976, p. 10). In Rome itself, as Samuel Rogers noted in the early nineteenth century, the Piazza di Spagna was unpaved and uneven (Hale, 1956, pp. 68 and 88). Early in the morning flocks of goats or one or two cows were led around the *piazza*, stopping from door to door, to supply the inhabitants with milk. The forum was used by local farmers for herds of these animals. The most cogent summary of the ruralness of the late medieval townscape is Petrarch's. He lived in Parma early in the fourteenth century and in a letter to a friend wrote: ''I have a country house in the middle of the town and a town house in the middle of the fields'' (cited in Hiorns, 1956, p. 107).

In view of the presence of these fields and farming activities within the walled area it is to be expected that not a few of the townsfolk were farmers or agricultural employees. But a much larger proportion of urban farmers worked land outside the walls and often at quite a distance. This was the case even very recently. In Sicily in the 1950s, only 11% of the total population was living in the countryside, ''a quaint phenomenon for a state subsisting in the main on agriculture'', as Bolkenstein put it (1958, p. 21). More remarkable perhaps is the high proportion of agricultural workers in the smaller towns of northern Italy. According to the census, those in agricultural employment in 1951 accounted for 5% of the active population of the densely packed urban commune of Pavia (over 1000 inhabitants per square kilometre). At Cremona, nearly as densely built up, the proportion was nearer 9%; at Vercelli, it was 12%.[8]

The importance of the agriculturally employed in urban centres was still greater in the past. From a study of the 1751 *compoix* (tax) lists for Montpellier ''the striking fact that emerges is without doubt the existence of a truly urban peasantry'' (Soboul, 1958, p. 28). At Montpellier, nearly half of the urban territory was worked by 1223 agricultural labourers, journeymen and gardeners, the majority of whom were the owners of their intramural and suburban plots. Nearly 400 members of the artisan class were cultivating another 354 hectares. In towns large and small, the situation was much the same; not far away from Montpellier, in the bourgs of Mauguio and Vendargues, Soboul found that viticulture was "essentially the responsibility of citizens whether large or small landowners" (1958, p. 77).

There were many reasons for the average citizen's sentiment for the land and for his involvement in agriculture. One was that most of the medieval and post-medieval urban population was of immigrant origin and came directly or indirectly from peasant stock. In particular the eleventh and twelfth centuries constituted a period of major country–town migration. In Tuscany, feudal landlords replaced direct management of their estates by tenants (under the *mezzadria* system) as a result of labour shortage, and took to living in towered town houses. Up to a point, the shortage of rural labour can be accounted for by the increasing urban population. Where adequate data exist this drift to the town is remarkably demonstrated. In Pisa in *c.* 1272–1274, over 50% of the parishioners of San Christofano (quarter of Kinsica) were new arrivals to the town and many of them can be traced to their villages of origin (Herlihy, 1958a, pp. 35ff and 188ff). In 1293, 65 out of 98 notaries operating in the same quarter were probably all recent immigrants from the surrounding countryside. The walled area of Pisa had to be extended after 1150, to accommodate this swelling urban population. The new walls enclosed not 50 hectares as before but 114 hectares.

In the case of Pisa, country–town migration developed early, perhaps due to the commercial attraction of the port, but the same thing in due course happened elsewhere. Florence's new walls (projected in 1284 to enclose a total of 630 hectares), included an urban area seven times greater than the twelfth-century precinct. Lucca began a second circle of walls in about A.D. 1200, completed them by 1265 (when the total enclosed area was 75 hectares), and did not extend them again until late in the sixteenth century. These growing towns were also in the process of becoming major employment centres on quite a new scale. The major industries of the day, above all the cloth-making industry, were urban located. Peasants accordingly moved into the towns attracted by the supposed economic opportunities. Some individuals made good fortunes as craftsmen or as guild workers, and their first instinct would have been to put their small savings back into the land, at first leasing then perhaps buying a suburban vineyard or orchard. Others came from families who had never released their property in their villages of origin. Modern parallels to this phenomenon of "relict landownership" are easily found. In the 1950s in the Cevennol village of Saumane (Hérault), for example, only 63 of those who owned land there (out of a total of 142) were actually resident in the district (Dugrand, 1963a, p. 91). In such ways, the agricultural interests of the urban population were maintained throughout the centuries until modern economic developments have all but eradicated the countrified city.

The Urbanized Countryside

The hold of the towns over the rural areas took a variety of forms. The most obvious town–country link at any time was the fact that agriculture was dictated by and directed towards the towns. The growing demands of city populations for food was a key factor in agricultural changes not only in the suburban and local area but also much further afield. Through such things as market demand, land ownership, settlement schemes and capital and technical investment, the urban centres spread their influence over the Mediterranean countryside. Where agriculture "failed" for one reason or another, so did urban development. This was because agriculture contributed so largely to a trade which was, as Braudel put it, the first of three stages in the development of a town's economic life (the second being industry and the third the banking which guarantees the town's economic adaptability and survival) (1972, Vol. I, p. 319). It is the agricultural crisis of the mid-fifteenth century, which came at a time when southern Italy's trade was wholly in the hands of foreigners (Catalans, Venetians, Florentines, Genoese, Ragusans), that is held to explain the lack of urban and commercial tradition in the south today (Grohman, 1969, p. 7).

After the Reconquest in Spain, integration of town and country was a deliberate policy designed to hold the new territories. The major centres of New Castile (Madrid, Toledo, Talavera de la Reina, Guadalajara and Henares) each had a sometimes large number of dependent villages (*aldeas*), settlements which were not autonomous, as were the *villas*, but whose municipal bodies were subject to control from the city (Salomon, 1964, p. 23 fn 3 and p. 201ff). Then there was a more direct and practical link. In Castile again, colonists of all social classes, knights and peasants, received an allotment which included a town lot and a portion of arable land (Bishko, 1964, p. 53). The same happened in Valencia, where the average city man, Burns has established, was also a small-scale farmer (1967, p. 151). Clearance and resettlement of *agri deserti* in Languedoc and Provence, like the colonization of newly claimed land in the Po Valley, also led to the establishment of urban loyalties in rural areas, either through the creation of new towns or because the initiative and capital was provided by families or by religious houses from older urban centres.

Some land in the countryside was acquired by urban dwellers specifically as an investment. Very largely this reflected a conviction, still running deep in the emotions of many Europeans, that the only real riches and the only true security lies in land. But there could also be the attraction of real gain. During the early fifteenth century in the Venetian hinterland, for example, landed estates were producing profits of up to 20% for their owners (Longworth, 1974, p. 220). These estates were at that time becoming a more tempting investment than trade, which had to run risks in the increasingly threatened Levant. By the late sixteenth century, capital was even being withdrawn from commerce in order to be placed in land and land improvement. Whereas in the 1550s about a third of the Venetian mainland was waste, only three decades later most of it had been reclaimed and farming with the new crops (maize and rice) successfully introduced.

Much the same thing was happening in Languedoc. There, a certain number of estates on the coastal lowland may or may not have descended more or less intact from the Gallo-Roman period, as Dugrand suggests (1963a, p. 344) but most modern estates originated in periods of land reclamation or of land investment. Le Roy Ladurie (1957) has shown how the process could unfold. Not far from the city of Montpellier was the declining Roman port-city of Lattes (Hérault). Its decline had led to the neglect and abandonment of a large extent of its former territory. At the beginning of the sixteenth century only a small village was left. The inhabitants farmed a much-reduced area, in total a thousand hectares of arable meadow and vineyards. During the sixteenth century, the former village lands at Lattes were being "bought out" by families resident in Montpellier. By 1547, already over half the land was said to belong "to those in Montpellier". There were some peasant owners still; the potter, baker, stone-mason and wool-carder for instance, but the other landowners at Lattes were members of the nobility who lived in the city and who had recently acquired land at Lattes. Not that their estates were yet very large: few held more than 40 hectares each. Their efforts, however, eventually led to an increase in the arable acreage. By 1607 the cultivatable area at Lattes had been increased by nearly half again, largely as a result of land reclamation and of drainage near the lagoon and along the lower courses of the Lez. The *compoix* records of 1677 reveal clearly the source of both incentive and capital. There were by now fewer landowners, only 11 altogether, in fact. Not one was a peasant, artisan or trader. All were new and all belonged to the higher professional classes of magistrates, tax collectors and finance officers or to the nobility, lay or ecclesiastical, in general. All were resident in Montpellier.

At about the end of the fourteenth century, the bourgeoisie in Spain embarked on a similar process of investment in the countryside. According to Vicens-Vives (1969, pp. 188–189), acquisition of rural property by city dwellers proceeded in three stages. The first was marked by the development of pleasure retreats in the countryside near to the cities. In the second stage, land was acquired as a safe investment in the early phases of business crisis. Only in the third stage did the landowner become really interested in the manner in which the profits came from his rural property. One consequence of the interest of the urban bourgeoisie in agriculture was a certain amount of technical and agricultural improvement of the land. Another, more widespread, consequence was a social change and the creation of what Vicens-Vives called a ''second-class nobility.''

In Italy the townsman's interest in the countryside was evidenced still earlier but there were other factors involved. In the fourteenth century, the merchant Dantini worked steadily towards the possession of about 120 hectares of land in the countryside of Prato (Origo, 1957, p. 244ff). Although he already possessed 20 town houses, all with land or agricultural facilities, that was evidently not the point. Astute as he was, Dantini would hardly have acquired his country holdings for their economic value, for this was very small compared with his annual investment in trade. His country holding comprised a number of small orchard farms in the hills near Prato, each of 5–10 hectares. Clearly Dantini hoped to gain something other than mere financial profit from his investment in the countryside.

The enhancement of personal status, in other words, must have been an important motive at all times in the past. In Languedoc, reclamation of the coastal plain could be a pretty direct means of ennoblement, resulting in the emergence of a new class of aristocracy, similar to Vicens-Vives' ''second-class nobility'' in Spain. To the older *noblesse de l'épée* was added the new *noblesse de la robe*, derived from the bourgoisie and distinguished by a very untraditional interest in capital investment and in commerce (Soboul, 1958). In four villages east of Montpellier there were 23 landowning families of the old nobility against 15 of the new in 1751. The latter however were individually better off, having between them 697 hectares in contrast to the 721 hectares shared by the old nobility.

In some of the less healthy districts or where summer tended to bring an unpleasant and sultry heat, the more fortunate of the townsfolk were able to leave their urban homes for a country residence. Last century it was noted how the inhabitants of Grosseto, in the Tuscan Maremma, left for 2 to 3 months each year (Young, 1886, p. 131). A retreat from the city was also a common reaction in times of epidemics. In the great plague of 1630 in Milan the majority of those who had not died were reported as "departed", i.e. to the country (Ripamonti, 1630, cited by Manzoni, Chapter XXXI). A rather happier benefit the urban farmer derived from his country holdings was a high degree of domestic self-sufficiency. Dantini relied on his farms to supply him and his household with all the wheat, wine, olive oil, capons, ducks, pigs, eggs and vegetables needed for his table whether he was in Prato, Florence or Pisa. Only surpluses were sold, though these could be substantial. While the family was in Bologna in 1401, Dantini sent to his farms for 1138 *lbs* of olive oil, of which he kept only sufficient for family use. It is much the same today, when the modern urban farmer living in a town like Montpellier can assure himself and his family of a generous all-year-round supply of wine (about 600 litres per urban family) from his own vineyards. Dugrand has found that in Montpellier such urban farmers increase their monthly salary by between one and eight times from the sale of surplus produce. In the 1950s, one in every 12 families was so benefiting (1963, pp. 94–95).

Economic interest, capital investment, political motive and status-seeking apart, there may have been still another aspect to the townsman's interest in the countryside. It is manifest in Dantini of Prato's *desire* to have a country estate and in his patent enjoyment of it. It was observed by Leandro Alberti of Bologna that "there is a vast deal of satisfaction in a convenient retreat near the town, where a man is at liberty to do just as he pleases" and he goes on to insist that "I, for my part, am not for having a [villa] in a place of such resort that I must never appear at my door without being completely dressed" (1550, cited by Mumford, 1961, p. 485). It was the privilege of a minority to be able to find pleasure in the countryside that for the vast majority was no more than an often toilsome means to a livelihood.

Whatever the reasons in individual cases, by the thirteenth century a 5 km zone around Florence was already occupied by rich estates with costly mansions. Venetian families sought land on the *terra firma*, preferably along the valleys of the Brenta where Palladio built them luxurious villas. There were the *rahals* of the Spanish *huerta*. The pattern can be observed operating on a local scale and around quite small townships. In Capitanata in 1432, a certain Martinus Silanus, resident of San Severo (and property owner in the declining Casalnuovo) was also the owner of a rather grand house (*domum unum palaciatum*) in the countryside (Camobreco, 1913, document 289). Pleasure, in short, was undoubtedly a contributory factor in the maintenance of extra-urban property. For those who had sufficient wealth to ensure nobility as well as time for leisure, country life retained its magnetism. For them it was but town life recreated in an attractive and private setting, *urbs in rure*.

Roman Times and Earlier

The phenomenon of the urban farmer was not confined to the medieval and post-medieval periods. Livy described how, in 211 B.C., the city of Capua was spared by the Romans so "that the tillers of land might have some abode" (XXVI, 7). Not without pride, the Romans pointed out that the founding fathers of the Eternal City were tillers of the field first and foremost and men of State only when the affairs of the Senate demanded it (*ibid.*, preface 18). Even Italian towns in the Roman period were populated largely by peasants (Brunt, 1971, p. 345). Yet it is easy to see why the Roman civilization, like the Greek before it, is regarded so widely as "essentially urban". Belloch counted 434 towns in Roman Italy (1880, Chapter I). To the Roman mind, the town was an administrative centre, capital of a *civitas* (a self-governing tribal area) or a provincial capital (Février, 1977, p. 317). A hierarchy of designated cities was the means of territorial administration throughout the Roman world and (as in the case of the medieval centres) whatever their size, economic status or architectural aspect, they were intended as the "tangible point of contact between ruler and ruled" (Ward Perkins, 1974, p. 8). This world, 2000 years ago, was both inspired and held together by a doctrine, that of *Romanitas* (Mazzolani, 1970, p. 201) which idealized not a whole national territory as fatherland but (in early days at least) a single urban centre. It was an urban centre which happened to have imposed its own prescription for organizing the business of living widely about Europe and eventually over the entire Mediterranean world.

Urban Interest in the Countryside

Rome's overriding interest in the countryside that stretched beyond the city gates and surrounding suburbs concerned the city's food supply. Being close to Rome, the rich alluvial soils around Ostia were intensively farmed for the production of fruit and vegetables expressly for the Roman market. According to Pliny, Ostian leeks competed favourably with those from *Aricia* (XIX. 110). Figs and mulberries, possibly also melons, also grew well around the lower Tiber. Market gardening would have been the most profitable form of agriculture for Ostian farmers although there were also a number of large and highly profitable estates in the district (Meiggs, 1973, p. 266). To the south of the town the plain was crossed by a network of "fine parallel public roads that . . . helped no doubt preserve the pattern of small holdings" and to speed the fresh produce to the Roman market. There were also pigs and poultry at Ostia and at least one poultry specialist, M. Serius, who seems to have been a business-like, rather dour man. He ran his estate strictly on business lines with little place for needless ornamentation, concentrating on the raising of bees (for honey), poultry and, for the luxury market, peacocks (Varro, Vol. III, 2, 7–14; 6, 3–5).

Regions far distant from Rome also became involved with the market. After the Hannibalic War, the new estate proprietors (for whom Cato's book *On Agriculture* was largely written) took advantage of the extraordinary market Rome offered. Apparently distances of 200, 300 or even 400 km and the convenience of a nearer market in local urban centres did not matter (Toynbee, 1965, Vol. II, p. 299). Cato was unequivocal in his advice to these landowners: "if you ask me what is the best kind of farm, I should say: a 100 *iugera* of land, comprising all sorts of soils, and in a good situation; a vineyard comes first . . .; second, a watered garden" (I. 7). In this way, reflecting the influence of the urban market at Rome over much of central and central-southern Italy, the old pattern of peasant subsistence farmer was replaced by a new form of land use, an intensive, plantation system of agriculture, producing expressly for the growing urban markets and particularly for the Roman one. The success of these economic ventures was undoubted and in turn benefited even "the smaller towns in the south-central lowlands [which] were now being adorned with buildings and with works of art" (Toynbee, *ibid.*).

Urban-owned settlement in the countryside was also as characteristic of the Roman period as of later times. By the second century B.C. it had become a measure of a rising standard of living to have a dual style of life, and "to have an estate near the city which even the busy man may easily visit every day after his business in the forum is over" (Columella, I. 1.19). As in later centuries, the agricultural products of the Roman estate were desptached to the home of the landowner in the capital city or to another *villa urbana* or *villa maritima*. Pliny the Younger had an elaborate house near *Tifernum Tiberinum* (in the upper reaches of the Metauro river) in Umbria. The Tiber provided a convenient means of transport of produce from his estate to Rome or to his seaside villa at Ostia. Some landowners on the other hand, professed to have little interest in the agricultural aspects of their rural properties. Horace seemed less concerned with cold economic matters than with the charms of his famous Sabine estate when he was writing to Quinctius: "Lest you, my good Quinctius, should have to ask me about my farm, whether it supports its master with plough-land, or makes him rich with olives, whether with apples or vine-clad elms, I will describe for you in rambling style the nature and the lie of the land" (Epistles, I, 16). It was its beautiful surroundings, amongst a continuous chain of hills, "broken only by a shady valley, but lying in such a way that the rising sun lights up the right side and, when it sinks, with its vanishing train, heats the left side", which gave him most satisfaction. Part of a villa complex has recently been brought to light in the Licenzo valley which is thought to have been Horace's.

Despite the agrarian basis of the Roman economy, the majority of the most troublesome domestic political problems in Roman times tended to focus on urban matters. Even so they greatly concerned the countryside. For example, whatever additional motives can be attributed to Tiberius' and Caius Gracchus' land reform laws (133–123 B.C.), colonization of long-deserted *ager publicus* with veteran soldiers and urban overspill would have been one way out of a pressing and embarrassing problem in the city of Rome. For nearly a century Rome had been an outstandingly attractive economic centre, resulting in a spectacular increase of the urban population from the strong and persistent migratory current to the capital. No more Latin colonies had been founded after 187 B.C. and no Roman ones between 157 and 122 B.C., so in the second century B.C.

F

Rome was absorbing most of the peninsula's restless or homeless population. Several crises punctuated the passing of the second century B.C. but that of an urban grain shortage was always by far the most urgent. In part the adequacy of a cereal supply had been reduced by the development of market gardening in the central part of the peninsula. Besides the development of market gardening, the new plantation farming system had replaced cereals with vines and olives so that Rome was now more dependent than ever on imported grain which came from Sicily (above all), North Africa and Sardinia. In view of this problem alone, any reduction in the urban population, or at least of its pauper element, would be a benefit. The Gracchan land reforms were no doubt motivated by several considerations but some advantage must have been expected by the authorities from the settling of the overspill population in the countryside. Indeed, it would have been an attractive proposition, since there was no problem in finding suitable agricultural land for such allotments: the *ager publicus* that had been so much augmented as a consequence of the Hannibalic war had scarcely been touched and was proving something of an embarrassment to the government.

The Gracchan reforms were not the only ones to result in the Roman land distribution system known as centuriation. There had been earlier resettlement schemes, such as that resulting in the unusual layout of a very early system at Lucera (Foggia). [8] Centuriation became common over much of Mediterranean Europe and North Africa by the second century B.C.

The hallmarks of centuriation are similar to those of modern land reform; a geometric sub-division of the land and a regular distribution of small, isolated steadings on modest allotments. The outline land divisions have often survived, or at least can be traced, in the modern field patterns, as on the Po lowlands or in Istria (Bradford, 1957). But little was known from archaeological evidence of the internal arrangements until air photograph evidence became available during the last war for the Tavoliere of Foggia. This has resulted in evidence of extraordinary detail and precision (Bradford, 1949, 1950, 1957). It is difficult to suggest how much of the Tavoliere may have been covered by centuriation at any one moment (Fig. 21). Sometimes only fragments of a system can be traced (approx. 13 km^2 between Troia and Lucera), while at other times it appears that a 40 km^2 layout might account for its entirety (east of Lucera, perhaps). In yet other instances, the 35 to 40 km^2 that are traceable quite obviously represent only part of the original whole (the southern portion of the main system at Troia). At Ascoli Satriano there

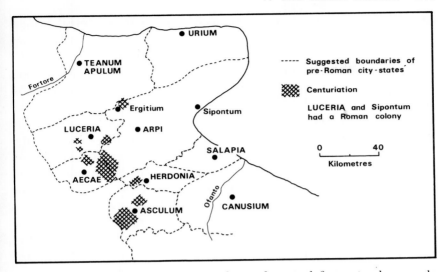

Fig. 21. *Centuriation* in northern Apulia as discerned from air photographs. Superimposed grids, as at Ascoli Satriano (*Asculum*) are not differentiated. (Information concerning the grids is from G. D. B. Jones; the suggested boundaries of the pre-Roman city states are taken from Toynbee's maps in *Hannibal's Legacy*.)

were several re-orientations of the system, on sometimes quite different axes.

Examining the spacing of individual farmsteads on one of the systems as revealed by excavation or the air photographs, Professor G. D. B. Jones estimated that each farm could have been about 20 *iugera* (5 hectares) in size.[9] Four neighbouring farmsteads have been discovered recently at Posta Crusta (Ordona) in a zone containing evidence of centuriation and of at least 12 other similar steadings. The distance between them is about 500 m (de Boe, 1975). From the cropmarks recorded by the air photographs it is possible to discern which land was used for vines, which for olives and which for cereal (Bradford, 1949). Professor Jones's study of these marks and excavation of the trenches which produce them confirm that in size, spacing and layout, there is an exact correspondence between the Apulian ones and what was recommended by the Roman agronomists in their texts. The evidence from the Tavoliere has led Professor Jones to suggest that from 60 to 65% of each holding would have been planted or inter-planted with tree crops. There can be little doubt, therefore, that each holding was laid out as a family farm and was intended to provide subsistence for the holder and his family from polyculture (cereals, vines, olives, fruit and vegetables and a small number of yard animals). They were planned peasant farms, in short.

The fact that the life of each centuriation system was not always very long is not surprising, especially bearing in mind the experience of twentieth-century land reform schemes in southern Italy and Sicily. One reason for the abandonment of individual steadings in the first and second centuries B.C., as in recent times, was discontent with agricultural life. The Tavoliere of Foggia in particular is a scenically dull and environmentally stark lowland and would have seemed even more so after the excitement of the army or the city. Another was changes in the economy in general. The archaeological record shows what happened to the Apulian centuriation systems. As some of the small holdings became vacant, they were taken over by neighbours or other landowners. After amalgamation, the old farmstead might have become an outbuilding. One near Masseria Nocelli (Lucera), excavated by Professor Jones, was deserted by 23–22 B.C. and was then used to house olive-oil settling tanks belonging to an increasingly prosperous neighbour. This individual would have in turn altered his own life-style to match the changes in the size and organization of his farm. So, at Posta Crusta, excavation has shown how the first small and simple colonial steading (dated to the third or second century B.C.) was replaced by a more stylish villa. The villa eventually went through nine phases of alteration and embellishment before it was abandoned at the end of the fourth century. As at Masseria Nocelli, the alterations made at Posta Crusta involved not only the farmstead and the cropping pattern but even the farming system. Subsistence mixed farming was replaced first by large-scale olive production then (in the fourth century) by cereals.

The field and air photograph evidence for centuriation that comes from the Tavoliere of Foggia is of particular interest because of the unusual amount of information that can be made available regarding crops and farming system. But many other country districts were similarly laid out and, one may suppose, farmed in similar fashion. In many cases, the centuriated land was laid out simultaneously with the establishment of a colony and remained closely under urban control. This was the case on the northern Italian plain and other frontier regions (Bradford, 1957; Dilke, 1971). In southern France too there was centuriation wherever the terrain was suitable in the vicinity of the new colonies of the Rhone Valley, at Orange for instance, where at least eight different systems have been traced (some superimposed on each other) and at Valence. There was centuriation on the Languedoc plain near Narbonne (Dilke, 1971, p. 159ff and bibliography p. 244). In comparison, little is known of centuriation in Spain. A contemporary document gives the measurements of the grid (120 × 40 actus) on which a system at Merida was based (Bradford, 1957, p. 76 fn 3). Recently a series of studies has been published (U.A.M., 1974) which argue (rather than in each case produce evidence) for the former existence of no less than 13 areas of centuriation in south-eastern Spain and one in Mallorca. Of these, one of the most convincing concerns the Jumilla and Yecla districts in Murcia. The appropriate and regular spacing of present field boundaries, traceable on air photographs, can be associated with a number of Roman villas or occupation sites. The suggested system would have covered over 4000 hectares and could have involved up to 300 families. Each allotment would have been about a dozen hectares, and would have included irrigable land. Another well-documented instance of

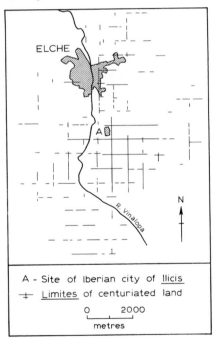

Fig. 22. *Centuriation and the town*: the street plan of Elche (Alicante) (not shown here in detail) appears to have been strongly influenced by what can only be supposed to be the ancient centuriation network of routes and trackways (simplified from Gozalvez Perez, 1974).

centuriation is at Elche, also in Murcia. This is of particular interest since the axes of the field system were aligned on the former Iberian town of *Ilici*. The modern town of Elche grew up under the Arabs in the Middle Ages but its early street pattern closely observed the structure of the fields it was built over (Fig. 22). Here, possibly, is a case of Roman centuriation influencing the morphology of a medieval town.

Under the Romans most of the countryside of Mediterranean Europe belonged to the territory of one city or another. This was true of Italy to such an extent that in censuses taken during the Empire, no clear distinction is made between urban and rural population (Duncan-Jones, 1974, p. 259). In the strictly legal sense therefore, even a quite ordinary peasant farmer could describe himself as a citizen of such and such a town. The prime function of the Roman provincial town was the administration of its territories. The smaller towns would have been distinguished from large villages by little else besides this administrative function.

Country Elements Within a Town

Not surprisingly, therefore, the majority of less important Roman towns would have had the same sort of rural air as most of the medieval and later provincial towns. Similarly, they would have housed agricultural functions within the built-up area or administrative urban district. Archaeological excavation on the sites of Roman towns or the architectural survivors in modern cities tends to create an exaggerated importance of architecture and urban planning. The concentration is on the formal areas of the town centre and it is sometimes difficult to find out anything about the backstreets or about the detailed structure of urban living. What is thought of as typical of Roman towns—an orderly townscape, compact layout, careful planning, attention to details such as drains and road surfaces, and magnificent or even extravagant architecture for visual dominants such as the temples and the forum—is more likely to have been confined to a relatively few major cities of the Roman world. In secondary centres such characteristics would have been found on a smaller or more modest scale and of restricted extent. In the great majority of provincial towns and so-called urban centres, such characteristics are more likely to have been noticeable largely for their absence.

As in medieval towns, in other words, there would have been quarters away from the forum and from the fashionable commercial axes where such agricultural features as threshing floors and wine presses could be found and where housing comprised the cottages and huts of farming peasants. There is little evidence as yet for this. At Pompeii, the Villa dei Misteri was a farmstead. It is appropriately situated in the suburbs close to the Herculanean Gate (White, 1970, p. 438). In the same city, however, a much more splendid complex, that of Caso del Menandro to which farm buildings were added in the middle of the first century A.D., fronted one of the most fashionable streets in the heart of the city. Recent excavation at Pompeii has revealed a large vineyard within the city walls, abutting onto one of the arterial roads, and other large open spaces (Raper, 1977, p. 200). At Rome itself, in the second century B.C., there was still a belt of enclosed plots and of gardens (*hortuli*) immediately outside the city walls (Grimal, 1969). Each of these gardens, Pliny informs us, "was in itself a poor man's farm; the lower classes got their market supplied from their gardens" (XIX, 52). Many had a little shelter or storehouse (*taberna*).

The early Roman garden tradition had little to do with the pleasure gardens for which the capital city later became renowned. Initially the garden was so fundamental to the pattern of daily living as to be incorporated into the Law of the Twelve Tables. The *hortus* itself was a private enclosure but the word for it is thought to have derived from *heredium*, the allotment that was once every male Roman's birthright (*ibid.*). The *hortus*, in being "reserved for the intensive production of everyday food", was thus ranked as more important than the house which stood on it but which is never itself mentioned in the Twelve Tables. As the city expanded, however, these once crucial fields were engulfed by buildings and dwellings. The suburban garden zone was eventually pushed so far out as to become beyond the range of daily accessibility and the peasant urban farmer disappeared just as the need for his produce became still more urgent. The new town houses had gardens but these were the ornamental ones depicted in the frescoes and mosaics of Pompeii and elsewhere. At most there was an orchard. Instead, production of fruit and vegetables (and flowers) became the prerogative of specialized farms well beyond the city, the *fundus surburbanus*, and in more distant districts.

These features, the urban or intramural fields and open spaces and the presence of farms even at the heart of the city, show that the Roman town was countrified in the same way as were many of the medieval towns and their successors. [10] In view of this, it should be anticipated that evidence for agricultural land use will be encountered in a pre-modern town in Mediterranean Europe and that this should be regarded as normal. There appears to be only one major difference between the Roman and the medieval town that would have affected its townscape, and that concerns socio-economic status. Evidence so far suggests that the earlier towns were less socially differentiated than the later, at least within the intramural zones. In the case of Pompeii, one of the few places for which this sort of study has been embarked on, Raper found himself admitting first that "The residential areas . . . show marked similarity in the large sizes of the *atria*, proliferation of murals and frescoes, increased occurrence of private baths and many other variables of wealth value" (p. 192), and then, in summary, that " . . . the dwellings of all classes were remarkably similar . . . " (p. 208). A similar observation was made for Sagunto in Spain. Here it was found that whatever the class differences may have been amongst the inhabitants, according to archaeological evidence their standard of living did not vary very much at least as far as housing within the walls was concerned (Tarradell, 1975, p. 128). Most citizens at Sagunto would have lived comfortably even if not all lived palatially. These observations would suggest that the greatest contrasts in Roman townscape are more likely to have been not between sectors within the walls but between the intra- and extra-mural areas as a whole. In the process of Romanization of native towns, the deliberate creation of a new or even a separate walled town was a critical step, and one that may well have created just such intra- and extra-mural contrasts.

Native Townscapes

To judge from the archaeological evidence, the relationship between the new Roman administration and the pre-existing urban centres would not always have been a happy one. Not many pre-Roman towns escaped abandonment or drastic re-planning when they came under Roman rule.

Some pre-Roman towns developed from the union of a number of prehistoric villages. Rome itself developed from a scatter of hillside settlements. In other cases, the urban nucleus was a settlement occupied since prehistoric times to which successive generations had added urban elements. At Pompeii there was first the Oscan settlement then the Greek. At Elche (Alicante) the Iberian towns of *Ilici* had been developed from late Neolithic settlement. At Narce (Etruria), Potter has found evidence of continuous occupation from Bronze Age times (1976a, p. 36). There was a pre-Roman settlement at Bologna, and Avignon was occupied at least since the Chalcolithic (Février, 1977, p. 323).

The urban layout of these pre-Roman towns was very unstable. At Ordona (Apulia), Mertens has demonstrated how land use in a given quarter would change radically over a few centuries; in one quarter he excavated, the sequence went from residential to necropolis, back to residential and once more to necropolis (1976, p. 24). At Narce a similar sequence was observed (Potter, 1976a, p. 319). So little is known of the morphological details of pre-Roman cities in Mediterranean Europe that Mertens excavated outside the Roman walls at Ordona in the express hope of discovering something about the native town. He found not only the succession of land use just mentioned but also a succession of building styles. The sequence started with wooden huts, dating from the eighth century B.C. which were then replaced by rectangular houses ''well-constructed from river cobs and unbaked bricks; the [new] houses comprised in general two rooms; their floors were of beaten earth, the internal walls were sometimes concealed with a lime or marl wash'' (1976, p. 24). There was a recognizable order in the orientation and disposition of these houses which was maintained even when ashlar replaced the traditional building materials in the Roman period.

Density of occupation in pre-Roman Ordona was very low and it was not until the late sixth century B.C. that this part of the Daunian city could be described as built up. Even so, when the Romans took over in the third century B.C., Ordona was a rich and prosperous centre, importing costly goods and fine pottery, supporting itself by agriculture from the surrounding countryside, and with a complex urban fabric of stone houses set about a well-defined street network. The Romans however ordered the digging of a town ditch. Apparently no regard was paid to the existing layout and the new ditch was cut across the Daunian town. The upcast material was simply deposited on top of nearby houses and streets in order to build up an external *agger*. When it was completed, the rampart brutally divided the old city. Part fell into the new intra-muros area and was liable to replanning according to the Roman prescription. The surviving part continued as a native extramural suburb, apparently subject to none of the replanning or architectural transformations that were effected within the walls.

Merten's excavations at Ordona have shed light on what may have been the common process of Romanization of native towns. Many of the native cities of southern Italy were huge. That is to say, they occupied a considerable area although housing can only have been of relatively low

F*

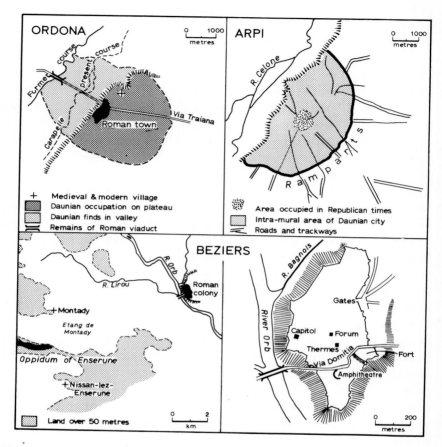

Fig. 23. *Relationships between the Roman town and the existing, native towns.* In cases such as Ordona and Arpi, southern Italy, the new and sometimes drastic Roman developments were confined to comparatively small areas of the original urban centre. In cases exemplified here by Béziers, in southern France, the Roman administration created an entirely separate settlement, usually a colony, often at considerable distance from the native town. The advantages of Enserune's site, a narrow but sharply defined calcareous ridge dominating the plain by some 120 m, was of no interest in the context of a Roman province. While nothing was done to Enserune, it was destined to lose population and to be abandoned eventually in the face of changed circumstances and competition from the walled colony of *Baeterrae* (Ordona from Mertens, 1976; Arpi from air photograph; colony of Béziers from Grenier, 1958).

density. There must also have been a good deal of agricultural land within the ramparts, garden plots, stabling, sheds and storage facilities. Daunian Arpi, one of the most important cities in northern Apulia at the time of the Hannibalic war, was spread over nearly 10 km ^{2}. The *agger* surrounding it was over 13 km in length and is still a prominent feature on the ground. The area occupied in early Roman times, however, was scarcely 600 m in diameter. It too was enclosed so the construction of its rampart and ditch in the heart of the old town must have been carried out in much the same way, and with similar consequences, as at Ordona. Further north in the Italian peninsula, the Etrurian town of Alba Fucens was likewise "replanned" by the new Roman administration. Together with 40 other *oppida*, Alba Fucens was taken by Rome in 304 B.C. (Mertens, 1969). It was lucky though to be one of the few to escape burning or razing to the ground. On the contrary, in the following year a Roman military colony, destined to become one of the most important, was planted at Alba Fucens. The old town was "restyled" along new axes, and the *cardo* and *decumanus* of a centuriation system was established in the surrounding countryside.

Such simple words as "restyling" or "replanning", however, mask, to judge from the experience at Ordona, what was at the time a drastic event. Not all new Roman colonies or settlements were laid out within the native centre. Many were adjacent to, some at some distance from, the existing town. At *Emporion* (Ampurias) in Spain the new town abutted the Greek port-city of Neapolis, separated from it by little more than a wall (see Fig. 64). Where the native city had occupied a hilltop, as was often the case in Languedoc (*Narbonensis*), the old town may have become inconveniently crowded and constricted. The new Roman settlement was accordingly laid out on lower ground. So Roman *Baeterrae* (Béziers) replaced the native settlement of Enserune in *Narbonensis* (Grenier, 1958; McKendrick, 1971, pp. 16–18) (Fig. 23). At Barcelona, the pre-Roman occupation area seems to have been on the hills of Montjuich and El Putxet. The inhabitants moved down to the Roman colony and it was from this nucleus that the medieval town developed (Duran I Sanpore, 1973). In Apulia, the native town *Salapia* (Foggia) covered nearly as large an area (200 hectares) as did Ordona but before the Romans had time to replan it it was decided to establish an entirely new urban area just 4 miles to the east (Vitruvius, 1.4.12; Tinè and Tinè, 1969; Delano Smith, 1978, p. 157). In such cases, archaeological social area analysis of the settlement in Roman times should not be attempted without evidence from both native and new towns. Until the former were wholly abandoned, they should be counted as part of the urban settlement pattern despite the spatial discontinuities. Archaeological research, therefore, has to be designed to cover intra- and extra-mural areas and both Romanized and native sectors.

Finally, the native, or pre-Roman towns of Mediterranean Europe were also associated with a rural territory. In Etruria, the former *pagi* of the native cities are quite well known and Potter has been able to suggest a sequence for the development of city territories in the Tiberina district before the fifth century B.C. (1976), p. 26; see also Ward Perkins, 1962, 1972). Early writers such as Strabo and Pliny make it clear that the quality even more than the extent of the territory was of vital importance. The Greek colony of *Massilia* (Marseilles) for instance, was poorly endowed in this respect, but later, the Massiliotes were able, by their valour as Strabo put it, to take in some of the surrounding plains (4.1.5). *Nemansus* (Nimes) was perhaps unusual in having no fewer than 24 subject villages, together with their territories, for this was carefully emphasized by Strabo (4.1.12). It meant that the total population of Nimes was greater than that of Narbonne. In northern Apulia there were seven or eight native (Daunian) cities on the Foggia plain. Each one could have had, on average, a territory of 500 to 600 km^2, not an unreasonable size for an urban commune to judge from some of the modern ones. In fact not all of the Daunian cities were of equal size. While Arpi and Ordona were outstanding for their large size, others (such as *Ergitium* at Casalnuovo near San Severo) were very small. A town whose built-up or intramural area covers no more than 20 or 30 hectares, as compared with one covering 200 hectares, may well have commanded a correspondingly smaller territory.

Town–country links in Mediterranean Europe, then, have taken a variety of forms. All forms can be traced back to Roman times and some documented for pre-Roman times too. The urban farmer is still a small part of the urban scene, as at Montpellier. Agriculture has been an important if not always the major economic element of the smaller towns in the past. At the beginning of the last millennium B.C. it would have been all-important. Recognizable urban centres were still in the process of emerging from growing and coalescing villages. For most of the past in Mediterranean Europe, a truly "urban" city—that is densely built up and primarily industrial or administrative in function—would have been the exception. Port-cities and a few of the major inland centres would have stood apart from the majority in this respect. Agricultural interests bound the rest, however, very closely to the rural scene. Urban or rural, the farmers of Mediterranean Europe have shared a common preoccupation, that of coaxing a living from the land and its organic resources.

Part II

Land and Land Use

5
The Land

The land of Mediterranean Europe evokes a conflict in the minds of many northerners. It is at once familiar and strange. It is familiar in its geological structure, with Hercynian foundations and abutting, folded Alpine massifs. It is familiar in its seasonal rhythm and in the reassuring presence of cool temperate vegetation in the valleys and along the water courses, or on higher, cooler slopes. It is strange, however, in the way geological outcrops are starkly outlined and relief is uncompromisingly sharp and in the way some elements of the vegetation seem exotic, even tropical. A landscape to look at or to travel in, though, is one matter; the same land has also to provide an environment to live in. The land of Mediterranean Europe has had to be a source of livelihood for a long succession of farming generations. As an *oekumene* it has often been misunderstood by indigenes as well as by outsiders. Too often the distinction between the real land and the perceived has been blurred and it is the myth that has tended to be the more durable over time.

The Reputation of the Land

Modern peasants, it has already been noted, evaluate their land according to its productivity. So it was in the past. In Sardinia, particularly in south-central districts, it is still the custom to base all land measurements on the *moi*, a measure equivalent to 40 ares or to about 40 kg of its dry weight yield (Angioni, 1976, p. 65). In Corsica, the traditional land measure is the decalitre, also a dry weight measure. Throughout southern Italy, the *tomolo* is equivalent both to about half a hectare and to 45 kg (Davis, 1973, p. 188). The use of these measures is entirely logical since it is the total yield that matters, not so much the actual measurements of a plot, since a small plot of highly fertile soil can yield as much as a larger one of less fertile soil. Yet there is nothing absolute about productivity either, for so much depends on the total outlay of cost, time and effort. The island of Corsica can be described as "poor in all respects" (Renucci, 1974, p. 64), but only in the sense that its soil is made to yield sufficient to support a predominantly peasant population only after long hours of toil. In fact, a good system of agriculture can be defined as one which produces as much food as possible, for humans or for farm stock, from the land *at reasonable cost* and without impairing its fertility. This has always been recognized. In Castile in the sixteenth century villagers believed that their community had grown in size "because of the fertility of the soil and good husbandry and [because of] the healthiness of the land" (quoted in Salomon, 1964, p. 235).

By newcomers, however, the fertility of a region might be over-optimistically assessed simply because it compared favourably with their experience elsewhere. To the Arabs in Iberia the harshness of much of southern Spain was nothing after the deserts of North Africa (Lévi-Provençal, 1950, p. 262). In Sicily and southern Italy the Normans found "a land of milk and honey", according to Amato of Monte Cassini (cited by Abulafia, 1977, p. 34 fn 6). In comparison with these, a Greek coming to the Western Mediterranean might be expected to be more objective. Yet Strabo rarely found cause for adverse criticism and in his commentary on Iberia, southern France and Italy, region after region is praised for its fertility, rich soils or bountiful and diverse production. Even where the land was undeniably disadvantageous in some respects, Strabo would note how the inhabitants had found a way of farming to their advantage. He could not disguise the fact that the soil of Paestum (Calabria) was thin and the entire district marshy and unhealthy but took care to point out that the inhabitants had developed a specialized garden economy, producing flowers for the Capuan perfume trade (6.1.1; 5.4.13).

So there are two aspects to the question of land evaluation. There is the responsibility of individual writers, classical and modern, for portraying a "country of the mind" rather than the real world, and for recording for posterity sometimes hasty judgements rather than careful observation or considered opinion. And there is the very real possibility, discussed in the third and final part of this book, that the quality of the land may indeed have changed through time. So strong is the power of the pen, however, that a geography of the past cannot safely be based on documents alone when it comes to the reputation of the land, and the soil itself has to be investigated wherever possible.

Were Strabo to have reconsidered his text in the eighteenth century it is doubtful that he, or his informants, would have found nearly so many regions deserving praise as they did in the third century B.C. Environmental conditions had indeed changed, or they were thought to have changed, or the basis of assessment had changed: certainly, something was different. The rich territories of *Graeca Magna* were already taking form as the Poor South of modern Italy. Locri, which had been called by Plato the flower of Italy, had become "a deserted place" by the eighteenth century and the Tavoliere of Foggia was also described by Galanti as a "true desert, almost without production and deserted of inhabitants" (1788, pp. 124–125). In the sixteenth century, Camile Porzio had listed the factors for this plain's economic insignificance; it was "poorly inhabited, lacking in good air, deprived of trees and timber, most poor in water. In summer, infested by a very great heat, innumerable mosquitoes, and a great number of serpents . . . " (1595–1597, p. 361). Yet in pre-Roman times it supported no less than eight highly prosperous cities and their territories.

Amongst eighteenth and early nineteenth century commentators there were individuals who recognized that the poverty of certain parts of the Neapolitan kingdom was not primarily due to any inherent fault in the land or to a failing in natural conditions but to human failures. Many sensible and even prophetic things were being said in the economic debates of the late eighteenth and early nineteenth centuries. In 1790 the Abbot Longano insisted in the foreword to his book that the Tavoliere of Foggia could become one of the most prosperous provinces of the Neapolitan kingdom instead of remaining the most miserable. A few years later Afan de Rivera asserted that the same region was in fact rich in physical endowments and that all it was needing was that humans should "organise themselves to take advantage of these instead of inducing ruin and devastation" (1832, p. 185). Such views had unpopular implications. More explicit was Giovanni's view that the deplorable sparseness of population in Roman Campagna was due to the prevailing attitude of the landowners and not at all to physical conditions (1848, pp. 14–15). Another way of putting it was to say that the Roman Campagna is "incapable of being mediocre; it is either very rich or very poor *according to the amount of effort put in*" (Vidal la Blache and Gallios, 1927, Vol. VII, p. 342, my italics). Sardinia, an island praised by the ancients as highly fertile and richly endowed, as famous for its fruitful fields as was Sicily (Fara, 1580), was in a precarious situation in the sixteenth century when Philip II of Aragon insisted that the economic crisis derived not so much from the sterility of the soil but *"per non exercitarse la gent en la terra"* (through the people not working hard on the land) (quoted by Sorgia, 1972), p. 158).

A good deal of the myth of sterility and environmental adversity in certain districts of Mediterranean Europe can be traced back to the classical poets and writers. The poet Horace was a proud native of Apulia but has much to answer for in promoting the unfavourable reputation of his homeland. He personally may have found the heat of the dog-days quite unbearable (Epode, Vol. III, pp. 15–16) but it may also have been that he was simply looking for a simile or a suitable turn of phrase. In this way the aridity of northern Apulia [*pauper aquae Daunus (Carminium,* 30.11; *Satire,* I, 88–91)] and the fierceness of rivers in flood [*violens obstrepit Aufidus (Carminium,* III, 30.10)] could easily become exaggerated. On the other hand, Horace's readers are not without blame either for the selectivity with which they retain only the catch phrases. The longer-winded panegyrics go unobserved, such as a fond boast that "the produce of all the acres the sturdy Apulian ploughs" and that "my stream of water, my woodland of a few acres, and sure trust in my crop of corn bring me more blessing than the lot of the dazzling lord of fertile Africa" (Book III, ode 16). Unfortunately for posterity not all readers, let alone travellers, have been like Goethe who travelled in Italy trying "to keep my eyes open all the time . . . and not to judge more than I can help . . . " and to consider the soil "in its reality" and not to "approach it fancifully" (1786; 1962 edition, p. 112).

Sometimes the basis of the ill-founded reputation is factual ignorance rather than poetic licence or subsequent misinterpretation. Trees for instance may have a special significance for most Europeans who, accustomed to the fertility of formerly forested land, see them as so direct a token of the soil's fertility that an absence of woodland is taken as an adverse reflection on its worth (Wreford Watson, 1969). The treelessness of central Spain still tends to be regarded as a result of poor physical conditions (especially climate). Modern authors have tried to stress the role of medieval and later deforestation (Bishko, 1963, p. 49). Despite this, the abundance of references in the early documents to grassland is quoted in support of the view of a naturally treeless interior. The fact is that the bulk of these documents issued from the business of a grazing or a grass-needing economy (not the same things) and are bound to be concerned mainly with open land. Very much the same thing has happened to the reputation of southern Italy. Nearly every modern traveller, and all the standard textbooks, comment disparagingly on the treelessness of the Tavoliere of Foggia. A few early writers, such as Cagnazzi, were careless in their choice of words and wrote that the nature of the subsoil rendered the plain *"unsuitable* for the growth of trees" (1832, my italics). From then on the region was described as having a subsoil "impenetrable to the roots of trees" and was assessed as "useless for orchards and vineyards" (Semple, 1932, p. 326). Yet there have been orchards and vineyards on this plain since Roman times, planted in trenches cut into the offending subsoil calcrete (and revealed with astonishing clarity on air photographs). The treelessness of this region as of so many others is of recent origin, a result of commercial ranching and of associated official policies. Similarly, the barren limestones of the Murge tablelands and similar areas are all that are left today of a formerly wooded landscape with a sometimes thick soil cover (Evans, 1972, Fig. 102, for instance).

The Real Condition of the Land

There is no denying that certain aspects of the land of Mediterranean Europe do present the farmer with difficulties. Relief can be high and slopes very steep. One of the commonest rock types is limestone, a formation which weathers slowly, producing little soil to replace that which is lost and offering a harsh, rocky surface. The climate has distinct thermal advantages but the pattern and nature of rainfall means that growing conditions can be exacting. To farm successfully in Mediterranean Europe and to make a livelihood from the land there, man has had to be cunning and careful, adaptable and watchful. Only then may he be able to sit back and marvel at the "diversity of fruitfulness" that can result.

Plains, Mountains and Hills

In Mediterranean Europe the contrast between upland and lowland is usually sharply defined and more often than not corresponds to an underlying geological contrast. In textbooks, much has been made of the so-called, and much extolled, symbiosis of mountain and lowland. It is held, for instance, to *account for* certain systems of livestock farming, notably those involving transhumance. However, it needs to be recognized that what applies on one scale does not necessarily hold good on another. For instance, on the largest scale, the inclusion of the Pyrenees and the southern Alps, even the Apennines and the Iberian ranges, in Mediterranean Europe, lies outside the consciousness of the majority of the region's inhabitants. For farmers who did not travel and for peasants whose horizons were limited by illiteracy and lack of education, the alleged interrelationship of these distant mountains with their own district was an academic point. Their lives would have been passed wholly within one of the three major environments of Mediterranean Europe; their homes were either in the hills, or on the plains, or in the mountains. Only on a smaller, more intimate, scale can it be suggested that the contrast between the local *monte* and the lower, flatter land of a village territory has been of relevance in the villagers' use and arrangement of their land. Even so there are other factors to be considered in attempting an understanding of land and land use relationships in Mediterranean Europe.

The threefold classification of the land of Mediterranean Europe dates from Roman times at least. Classical agronomists, like the *Istituto Centrale di Statistica* in Italy today, thought in terms of the "three simple types of land—plain, hill and mountain" as Varro put it (1.6.2). In Italy today the hills start officially at 300 m above sea level, in Spain at 200 m. Less than a quarter of Italy lies below 300 m or can be described as plain. Only 11 % of the whole of Spain and just 15 % of Provence is so classifiable. Major units of lowland are therefore unusual in Mediterranean Europe and they tend to have acquired a special significance that has not always been to the advantage of their inhabitants. The northern plain of Italy, the Po lowland, has been described as the most fought over in all Europe. The Tavoliere of Foggia, which with its 7000 km^2 is the largest plain in the peninsula, has had a similarly embattled history. Only insularity and isolation has spared the Campidano of Sardinia from a similar fate. Although representing only 14% of the island's total area, this lowland stretches for nearly 100 km from coast to coast across the south-east of the island. In Spain, where the dichotomy between plain and mountain coincides with that between coast and interior, the division has had, in Mira's view, "profound sociological repercussions which have been translated into political and institutional conflict" in the Kingdom of Valencia (1971, p. 106). For these reasons and for many others, associated in part with the physical instability of low-lying and lagoon-fringed coasts and perhaps political insecurity and in part with the individual combination of factors that make each region's history unique, the lowlands and plains of Mediterranean Europe have often been troubled regions despite their immense and obvious attraction in a land of so much rock and mountain.

By and large, therefore, it seems to have been the intervening hill districts that have been regarded as terrain of predilection in the historic period. However, these regions can be as physically unstable as the riverine or coastal lowlands. Whether of hard rock, most commonly limestone, or of soft, yielding, sediments (clays, sands, marls), the hills have presented the farmers of Mediterranean Europe with many environmental problems. Limestone is often spoken of as epitomizing southern Europe and the Mediterranean in general but this is largely due to deforestation and soil erosion which have laid bare the underlying rock. Even on the relatively level surfaces of the plateaux, there is no doubt that the soil cover is thinner and very much less continuous than it would have been in earlier times. What is left is a misleadingly craggy, stony surface where lithological differences in the limestone strata are clearly exposed (Plate 5).

If the terrain of many of the hills and plateaux of Mediterranean Europe is rough and rocky, the softer-rocked hills are not necessarily without disadvantages of a different nature. Attractive though the gently rounded landscape may look, it contains not a few hazards. Landslipping and pernicious gully erosion pose a very real threat to those to whom the soil is the source of their livelihood. The Tertiary strata that compose so much of the hills of Mediterranean Europe are typically of very mixed rocks, most of which are shallow-bedded, and all of which have been tectonically warped. The frequent juxtaposition of strata of contrasting geological properties, where pervious sandstone or shallow limestone overlie impervious shale or clay, leads to situations where the uppermost strata tend to slip down a lubricated contact plane, especially where the dip is steep. In the Italian peninsula, the occurrence of landslips (*frane*) is highly characteristic of the Apennine foothills. Most slips are local but some have been spectacular. Near Potenza (Lucania) on 10th February 1884, 10 km² of hillside started to move as sandstones, clay and shale, 40–50 m thick, slipped downhill (Admiralty, Italy Vol. I, p. 493). Sometimes it is exceptionally heavy rainfall or the jolt of an earthquake that provides the impulse. Between the 5th February and the 10th April 1783, no less than

Plate 5. *The texture of the land.* Even the limestone districts of Mediterranean Europe are far from homogeneous. The upper photographs show (left) Upper Valanginian limestone on the Hortus plateau (Hérault) and (right) Tithonic limestone on a neighbouring plateau. In Neolithic times, the inhabitants of the Montpellier Garrigues used slabs of Valanginian limestone for their tombs. Dolmen de la Coste (lower photograph) is nearly 20 km away from the nearest outcrop of this facies.

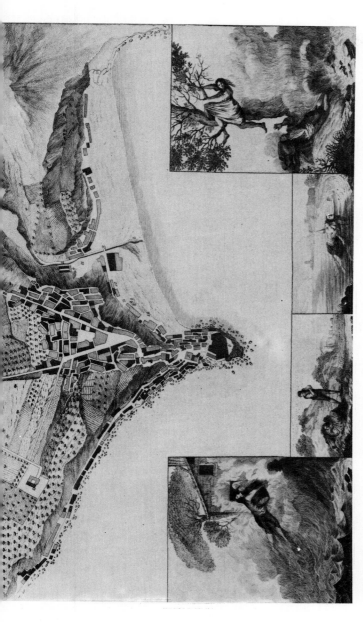

Plate 6. *A coastal disaster* of major proportions occurred in the series of earthquakes that devastated Calabria and much of southern Italy and Sicily in 1783. A *tsunami* resulted from the first of the seven major sets of tremors on the 5th February. At Torre di Faro there were 26 victims and waves swept up to $\frac{1}{2}$ km inland, drowning crops and vineyards and burying them under sand and mud. Scilla (above) suffered particularly badly. The buildings shown in black survived, those in the lighter shading were ruined. Reporters despatched by the Royal Academy of Sciences at Naples to these regions nicely caught some of the most dramatic (and more fortunate) personal experiences of the inhabitants of Scilla (reproduced with permission from The British Library).

Plate 7. *Hazards in the hill regions.* The soft-rocked hill districts of Mediterranean Europe do not necessarily provide an easy life. To the perennial threat from *frane* and *balze* are added the not-so-infrequent earthquakes. Towns and villages situated, like Mileto, (upper plate) ''on the back of a group of mountains'' were particularly susceptible to the earthquakes of 1783. Mileto was ''horribly flagellated'' by the first of the earthquakes and razed completely by the second, 2 days later. In the upper plate (1) marks the church of the Royal quarter, (2) the city itself and (3) the cathedral and ecclesiastical quarter. At Polistina (lower plate), as at Mileto, the task of reconstruction was evidently promptly and efficiently carried out, houses for the survivors being provided on new land (reproduced with permission from The British Library).

seven tremors devastated Calabria (Reale Academia di Napoli, 1784). Lakes were opened up, roads split, rivers flooded or dammed. At Polistina (Reggio di Calabria), the amphitheatre all but vanished into the *balze*. At Mileto (Catenzaro), unfortunately situated ''on the back of a group of mountains,'' the first two tremors resulted in a horrifying mud flow (*creta argillacea*). Coastal districts were liable to flooding and to *tsunami* (Plates 6 and 7). The *balze (barrancos* in Murcia and Almeria) result where soft sediments, capped by more resistant strata, are undercut by streams and eroded from the base into vertical cliffs. The monastery of San Salvatore at Volterra is even today threatened. Two other churches have already been lost here, one in 1140 and the other in the seventeenth century. Entire villages may eventually become vulnerable as the cliff is eaten back, as described so vividly by Levi (1948).

Another hazard in the soft-rocked hill regions of Mediterranean Europe is gully erosion. Steep slopes, soft sediments, downslope ploughing and the torrential nature of much of the rainfall are all factors in the development and encroachment of badlands, the *calanche* of Italy, the *malas tierras* of Spain. Over 2000 km² of Italy are reported affected to the point that roads and railways are threatened. No national figure is available for the area of farmland so ruined but regional estimates can be made. Nearly half of the province of Lucania, for example, is affected by soil erosion of one sort or another (data in Kayser, 1961). In Andalucia and other southern provinces in Spain, Miocene clays and marls rest on softer Triassic conglomerates, clays and gravels. During the long dry summers, the surface of the ground is baked into a hard crust. When the rains eventually arrive the water collects at first in puddles and then pours off the surface in the form of flash floods. These cause ravines and undermine river banks. Debris eroded by the floodwater is later deposited, particularly where a steeply graded hill stream emerges onto the plains or meets the flat bed of a *rambla*. In such ways, therefore, large parts of the hill regions of Mediterranean Europe have been rendered useless or spoilt as farmland simply as a result of geomorphological processes, irrespective of man's contribution through vegetation degradation or soil exposure.

Land and Land Use: *Ager, Saltus, Silva*

The ancients' threefold topographical division of Mediterranean Europe was paralleled by an economic classification of land into arable, grazing and woodland (*ager, saltus* and *silva*). Some modern writers see a direct correlation between the topographical and the economic categories. Carrère and Dugrand, for example, wrote concerning Mediterranean France that "to the trilogy of the natural landscape corresponds that of human activity: *ager, saltus* and *silva*" (1960, p. 160). In a very general sense indeed this may be true, but it would be a mistake to see in the land-use arrangements of a village community or the crop location of an individual farmer the effect of physical factors only.

The designations *ager*, *saltus* and *silva* are Latin words that were standard in the vocabulary of the Roman agronomists. They have come to be used, particularly by French geographers and botanists, as the components of what is seen as an agro-sylvo-pastoral equilibrium (explained by Kuhnholtz-Lordat in a seminal publication in 1938 (rewritten in 1958)). The term *ager* refers to all cultivated land, *saltus* includes all land that is grazed irrespective of its botanical composition or ecological status, and *silva* all natural arborescent vegetation (planted woods, such as poplar groves, being counted with orchards as a tree-crop on arable land). According to these original definitions, it is recognized that these are essentially categories of land *use* and not, as many have come to assume, classes of land *potential*. The actual spatial extent of each category is as variable as its nature, hence the concept of a delicately poised agro-sylvo-pastoral equilibrium at local level (and even at national and world levels). A change in the area of one category has repercussions on the others. Arable and grazing tend to be extended at the expense of woodland, a point also stressed by Nougier when he suggested that "the humanised landscape dates from activities of Neolithic Man" (1959, p. 29). Grazing may be extended over arable (on fallow or on abandoned fields) as easily as into degraded forest vegetation. According to Kuhnholtz-Lordat the *vocation pastoral* of a tract is determined by the quality of its grass. It is, therefore, strictly a shepherd's or grazier's assessment. But this term, too, has come to be taken far too generally. It is clear from his writings that Kuhnholtz-Lordat never intended to suggest that the physical nature of the land under the grass would necessarily determine its land use or even its economic potential. Yet this is how the idea of a *vocation pastoral* or a *vocation agricole* tends to be used today. In many writings it is assumed that thin-soiled, scrub-covered limestone terrain has, and always had, a pastoral "vocation" and that it is fit for no other use despite the fact that, even today, after millennia of degradation, there are patches of cultivation on these very same hills and plateaux, wherever there remains some soil. Likewise, it is assumed that the plains and alluvial lands are, or have become, arable land *par excellence*. This is true as far as it goes, but there are plenty of instances where even these "best" soils were at one time or another quite intentionally not cultivated (as on the Tavoliere of Foggia in the fifteenth and sixteenth centuries and later). Indeed, were it not for the effects of cultivation or grazing, these lands would carry some of the heaviest woodland in Mediterranean Europe. Two distinctions, therefore, are important. One is that between land use and the geological or ecological nature of the land. The other concerns this nature in the past as opposed to the present.

The foregoing argument is not made to suggest that an individual farmer, in early or later historic times, ignored the geological condition of his land or disregarded its relief. But when it comes to the planting and growing of crops, the aspect that matters most is that of soil texture. The nature of the underlying bedrock may have bearing on this but otherwise it is of secondary consequence. Early literature and practice as well as that of recent times reflect this bias in a farmer's appraisal of the physical condition of his land. The Roman agronomists made it quite clear that the texture of the soil was to be the prime consideration in deciding the use to which it was to be put, which crops were to be grown on it and which varieties of a particular crop were best suited. Cato started his chapter (VI) by giving a rule "as to what you should plant in what places". He goes on to specify: "In heavy, warm soil plant olives—those for pickling . . . the Sallentine, the *orcites*, the *posea*, the Sergian . . . Plant the Licinian olive in colder and thinner soil". For grapes it was the same: "Choose soil for laying out a vineyard by the following rules." For the most suitable land, he suggested the small Aminnion, the double *eugeneum*, and the small part-coloured varieties, but on a soil that is heavy "plant the large Aminnion, the Apicion, and the Lucanian". Varro too urged his readers to consider the topography of their land and then concentrate on "the type of soil of which the farm is composed" (I. VII. 5.) He even went as far as to attempt to classify soil texture, eventually listing 15 different textural states (I. II. 3–7). According to him, soils could be described as fat or lean, heavy or light, dense and sticky, compact or loose, friable, gravelly, rocky, chalky, sandy, loamy, clayey. Columella used much the same terms in describing "six species of soil—fat or lean, loose or compact, moist or dry" (II. II. 2), giving the time-honoured field test for soil texture: . . . "a clod is sprinkled with a little water and kneaded in the hand, and if it is viscous and cohesive when firmed with the slightest touch and, [here he quoted from Virgil] in the manner of pitch is shaped to the fingers in handling, . . . and does not crumble when dashed to the ground, this test informs us that there is in such earth a natural moistness and fatness'' (II. II. 18). To all the ancient agronomists the colour of the soil was also an index of its quality. By the nineteenth century, the basis of description had become more scientific and by 1880 Molinari was accounting for the soils of the Neapolitan kingdom under the three modern soil type headings: siliceous, calcareous and clayey (*cretosi*) soils. The essential preoccupation, however, had not changed and soil texture remains the critical factor even today.

The classification of a soil as light or heavy is subjective. It depends on the techniques of cultivation employed and above all on the type of plough used. Established assessments of ''best'' land are therefore liable to be radically challenged as these techniques change. The ancients recognized this too. Palladio (1. 43. 1) stated that ''Ploughs are either simple or, if the open nature of the country permits, eared . . . to counteract the high water table in winter'' (cited by White, 1967b, p. 123). From literary and other evidence it is clear that by Roman times there was in Western Europe both the ard (*arrare*) plough and the mouldboard (*carruca*) types of plough. It is also fairly clear that both types of plough could be provided with wheels, in order to reduce the drag of a heavy instrument or in heavy soils (Fig. 24).

The relationship between soil texture, plough type and soil ''fertility'' is extremely close. Recent experience in Apulia illustrates how technological changes can lead to reassessment of soil fertility. In the past, Apulia was renowned for the quality of its cereal output and for the reliability of its surpluses. Prior to the modern post-war period, these cereals were grown on the broad flat interfluves of the northern plain, never on the heavy soils of its alluvial bottomlands. On the interfluves, soils are relatively light and on the whole well-drained, even where there is a sub-soil calcrete. Cereals are shallow-rooting plants and neither their growth nor ploughing was in any way impeded by the calcrete. Since the Second World War, however, tractor-drawn ploughs have been introduced. Amongst other things, this has meant that heavy, moist soils on alluvium now not only can be used for arable but are sometimes ranked as the ''best'' soils. However, it should be noted that not all alluvial soils are equally fertile according to these new standards. On a seven-point scale, only some of the alluvial soils are placed in the top category (Consorzio). The others come in second or third place, together with the soils of the interfluves. In third place, for instance, is the heaviest alluvial

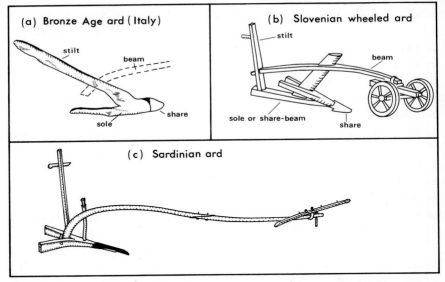

Fig. 24. *Ard ploughs.* Although there is considerable variation in detail, even within a single region, the essential form of *ard* ploughs has been remarkably constant throughout the period and Mediterranean Europe in general. The archaeological evidence for the earliest ploughs is scant and this crook-plough from Ledro in northern Italy must be, despite the loss of its beam, one of the best examples. The plough in (a) is drawn from photograph in Barfield (1971); (b) is from Haudricourt and Delamarre (1955); and (c) is from Angioni (1976).

soil, that developed from the most recently deposited alluvium. These are so sticky (for reasons given on p. 357) that caterpillar-tracked machines are needed to draw the modern ploughs; texturally this is a distinctly unfavourable soil.

Only in very special circumstances it may be that other factors have to be given overriding consideration. Such a case is found in the high mountains of Mediterranean Europe where orientation or aspect is the governing factor in the location of arable land. In the central Pyrenees the ''best'' land is that of the *soulane* (Chevalier, 1956, p. 103). Generally speaking, a *soulane* is a south-facing aspect, but in practice it is that slope which receives the maximum direct sunlight according to the disposition of the peaks around. The advantage is greatest in deepest winter, when the duration of sunlight may be as little as an hour a day. If the *soulane* coincides with a favourably textured soil, so much the better, but soil texture is not here the prime concern. In fact, Chevalier has shown how the entire process of settlement at those high altitudes reflects the availability of land of suitable aspect. The shady *bac*, the side where snow lies longest, has almost always been avoided for permanent occupation. In the upper valley of the Ariège, for example, only 12% of the total population appeared to reside on the shady side. Closer examination showed that even this proportion in fact came from small hamlets on secondary *soulanes* in lateral valleys. There had once been two villages on the shady side (Sortadel and Leucate) but both had been late established, no doubt under population pressure, and early deserted. In the central Pyrenees, wherever hamlets are found on the *bac*, all prove to be of recent origin, surrounded by pasture land rather than arable or dependent on the relatively novel crop of potatoes rather than cereals.

Polyculture is the key to a peasant farmer's subsistence and for this a variety of terrain and of soil is necessary. The villages of the coastal lowlands of eastern Spain illustrate this point. In the eighteenth and nineteenth centuries, each village territory contained four categories of land (Houston, 1949, p. 204). Each territory had been so laid out that it ran from dry upland across first the plain and then the irrigated *huerta* to the coast. The dry *terra alta* was on the sandstone hills of the interior. It was used mainly for grazing and was left as open pasture or under woodland. Lower down came a more discontinuous zone of *terra rodina*, warm, well-drained, stony soil on the screes and dejection cones that are found at the point of emergence of each gorge from the hills. This sort of soil is ideal for vines. Along the margins of the plain the soil becomes heavier and colder and passes into *terra archila* (clayland). Although this is sometimes used with or without irrigation it more commonly forms a zone of grain land. Finally, out towards the centre of the plain, near the coast or in the flood plains of major rivers, is the *terra chopet*. This includes soils that are heavy and moist but also rich in humus, subject too to regular irrigation.

Village territories in Mediterranean France were likewise laid out so as to include as many different conditions or types of land as possible. Traditionally, the highest, rockiest slopes were given over to olives and almonds, the screes at their foot were used for viticulture, and the "best" soils of the valley or plain reserved for cereals.[11] Only with the arrival of cheap bulk imports of grain from the Black Sea or North America, at the end of the eighteenth century, did each village no longer feel the need for self-sufficiency and the pattern was altered completely with the "*descente de la vigne*". Stimulated by a fortuitous series of failures of the grape harvest in northern France at the same time, vineyards began to replace the traditional cereal fields on the lowlands. Viticulture henceforth became a commercial undertaking, with vines cultivated on an extensive basis and for an external wine market and no longer the prerogative of the polyculture of the peasantry (Galtier, 1960, Vol. I, p. 112ff).

While the question of soil fertility is resolved rather simply by many a peasant farmer, who knows that if he is fortunate enough to hold "good" land he needs to work less hard for his livelihood than if he holds only "poor" land, the history of land use in such regions shows that it is rare to find a district in Mediterranean Europe in which the required variety of terrain type cannot easily be found within reasonable distance of the farming community. Such is the effect of the fragmented nature of the relief in Mediterranean Europe and of its geological contrasts. However, other non-physical factors have to be taken into account in attempting to understand the land-use pattern of any district. These include the farmers' idea of convenience, their cropping priorities, which are not inevitably what might be expected, and of course the number of people dependent on the produce of the land at any one time.

Land Use Zonation

Within constraints set by the physical condition of the land, the pattern of land use in its details results above all from what might best be termed "factors of convenience". The critical point concerns the distance between the plot and the farmstead. It arises from the fact that different crops and farm stock not only have specific needs in respect of soil and water etc. but are also variously demanding on the farmer's time and energy. If, for example, the annual labour requirement in Mediterranean Europe of wheat and barley is represented as a base index of 100 man-days per hectare, cultivation of irrigated vegetables is found to amount to as much as 10 to 20 times as much, vines three to four times, and olives just less than twice as much (Chisholm, 1968, p. 59). Chisholm's figures are derived from Italian experiences in the later 1950s. In the arid and difficult growing conditions of central Spain, he found that cereals demand far more time and that they may take up an even greater proportion of the farmer's time than do vines and olives. Differences in methods of cultivation and in plant strains are additional factors.

The result of these differences in the demands of the basic subsistence crops of Mediterranean Europe is the characteristic agrarian landscape of three or, more rarely, four zones of land use surrounding each town, village, hamlet or farmstead. The first zone is the closed (*chiuse*) zone of walled, fenced or hedged gardens and plots, mostly privately owned. They are cultivated by spade or hoe and irrigated whenever possible. Then comes the second zone of open fields and dry cereal farming. The third zone comprises uncultivated but by no means unproductive land. In Italy and southern France, vineyards and olives are usually found in the enclosures of the first zone. In fact, early in the seventeenth century, an enclosure was defined not according to the nature of its boundary but as a field that had "at least five olives per *modiolo*" (just under 25 ares; quoted by Desplanques, 1959, p. 97). The three zones form as concentric a series as the nature of the locality permits but the order in which each occurs can vary from one part of Mediterranean Europe to another. In the Sierras of southern Spain, at "Alcala" for instance (a village of just over 2000 inhabitants), Pitt-Rivers found the settlement to be surrounded by "a great number of plots of land . . . some eight hundred of under two hectares whose average size is half a hectare" (1954, p. 42). Most of these plots lay within a radius of 3 km of the village. In La Mancha, however, the sequence is inverted. Outside the enormous villages lie the open cereal fields. Vineyards and olives are at some distance, "generally not nearer than 3 or 4 kilometres" (Birot and Gabert, 1964, p. 218). Beyond this orchard periphery is the uncleared land. This inversion is explained by the fact that, given the total agricultural conditions of this part of Spain, it is the most logical arrangement. For here it is cereal cultivation rather than that of olives or vines that tends to demand most of the farmers' time in these excessively dry districts.

Normally, then, it is the crop with the maximum labour-demands that is put nearest to the village or farmstead. The resultant pattern in Sardinia was described by Le Lannou:

> From whichever side one leaves a village, one is struck by the rigorous disposition of the various elements of the country-side into concentric zones. Around the village . . . there is a first zone in which the view is restricted, where the parcels are small and bounded by hedges of prickly pear, growing vegetables, olives, almonds and vines. But this pleasant labyrinth constitutes only a narrow belt, and suddenly there opens out a landscape which is flat and bare . . . the arable lands (1941, p. 188).

Until recently most of the Tavoliere of Foggia could be described as "an

G

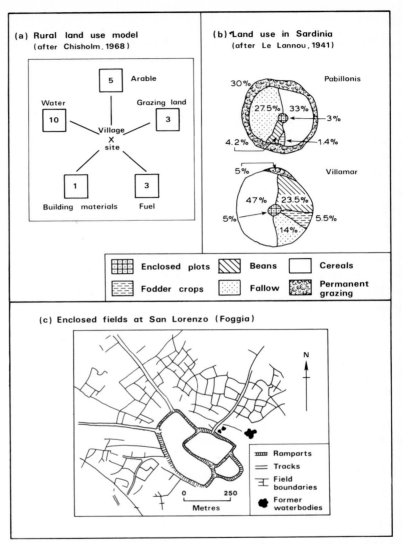

(a) Rural land use model (after Chisholm, 1968)

5 Arable

Water
10

Grazing land
3

Village
X
site

1
Building materials

3
Fuel

(b) Land use in Sardinia (after Le Lannou, 1941)

30% — Pabillonis

27.5% 33% — 3%

4.2% — 1.4%

5% — Villamar

47% 23.5%

5% — 5.5%

14%

Enclosed plots
Fodder crops
Beans
Fallow
Cereals
Permanent grazing

(c) Enclosed fields at San Lorenzo (Foggia)

N

Ramparts
Tracks
Field boundaries
Former waterbodies

0   250
Metres

Fig. 25. *Land use patterns.* The suggested weightings, or rankings, of the five essentials (a) that have to be taken into account in rural settlement location also provide the key to land use zonation in Mediterranean Europe (b). Aerial photographs show (c) that medieval villages on the lowlands of Apulia were surrounded first by the predictable inner zone of intensive cultivation, normally in enclosed plots, and then by an outer zone of open and very much larger cereal fields. San Lorenzo was a taxable settlement, with rich palaces favoured by Frederick II and Charles I of Anjou, at the beginning of the fourteenth century but had completely vanished by the mid-seventeenth century (first published in Delano Smith, 1975).

immense pasture from which rose, like oases, the cities and the *borgate*, [each] surrounded by a zone of cultivation'' (Labadessa, 1932). It seems to have been a less common arrangement to have four zones but up to the early part of the present century in Corsica (an island usually presented as ''exclusively pastoral''), the arable was sub-divided into a sort of infield/outfield arrangement (Ravis-Giordani, 1974). First, close to the village, came the almost inevitable zone of small plots (*orti*). Then came the *campi*, the dry-farmed open fields. Half of these were cultivated, half left fallow each year in the normal manner. Then came the ''outfield'', a zone of *maquis* and other secondary vegetation which was occasionally cleared and cultivated but which was allowed to revert to scrub whenever pressure on the land slackened. Finally came the zone of permanent grazing, land which was never cultivated and which was often uncultivatable, being too distant, too steep or at too high an altitude for use as arable even though the soil might be good.

The zonation in Sardinia described by Le Lannou can be dated back to at least the fourteenth century through documentation (Le Lannou, 1941, p. 127ff). Using air photographs together with the archive evidence, the innermost enclosed zones around now-deserted settlements on the Apulian lowland can be dated back to at least the thirteenth century. The photographs reveal clear traces of the former ditches defining each plot in a belt a kilometre or two wide around the former village (Fig. 25). Measurements are available not only from the air photographs but, more directly, from contemporary records. The Cartulary of San Leonardo of Siponto, for example, contains a large number of documents recording the sale or transfer of such plots at Casalnuovo, and other localities in Capitanata, giving in nearly every case precise measurements and a description of land use (Camobreco, 1913). Generally the size of arable plots went up to over 2 hectares or even over but those used for vines or vegetables tended to be smaller; one of the smaller vineyards was less than 500 m^2 (document 42, dated 1156).

In the Sardinian villages studied by Le Lannou, the enclosed plots accounted for not more than 5% of the village's total territory (Fig. 25). The open cereal land accounted for between 67 and 90%. The remainder was permanent grazing. Obviously the proportion was not a fixed one, and much depended on local circumstances, both physical and demographic. In a study of contemporary peasant farming on the Greek island of Melos, carried out to try to understand the peasant farmer's attitude to distance, the question was asked: ''how much time do you think it is worth spending in walking to a field in order to work it?'' (Wagstaff, 1976, p. 18ff). It was clear from the replies that expressed in this way the question meant little to the peasant farmers. What they gave by way of an answer was simply a statement of the actual time spent. This varied from 0·15 hours to 6·0 hours, with a mean of 2·4 hours per day. Wagstaff concluded that travel time and field labour are fixed factors in a peasant production system and that once acquired, land would be worked at almost any distance from the farm so long as its produce was needed. The concept of economic marginality is therefore not relevant to a peasant farmer. Disposal of land that yields poorly in relation to the amount of effort put into its cultivation cannot be contemplated so long as it is needed to help assure his and his family's livelihood.

Another characteristic of Mediterranean land use is that land can be used in different ways according to the time of year. It can even fall into two categories simultaneously (Karman, 1964; Delano Smith, 1968). For instance, while arable land lies fallow, it may still be productive in terms of food (wild salads and small game), fuel, fodder, and an often vital supply of grazing. Another case is where there is inter-cropping. An olive grove can be classified as an orchard, as arable or as grazing according to the season. The Roman agronomists recognized the inherent flexibility of Mediterranean land use. They talked of a summer as opposed to winter *saltus*, for example (Pliny, XXXIII. 135). Kuhnholtz-Lordat made allowances for this in distinguishing between temporary *saltus* (stubble or fallow), artificial *saltus* (land cleared of forest, or, conversely, arable abandoned to secondary vegetation), natural *saltus* (where grassland is the climax vegetation for climatic or edaphic reasons, and aerial *saltus* (where tree leaves are gathered to feed livestock) (1958, p. 55ff).

So although the standard land-use model, as outlined by Chisholm for instance, is an invaluable guide to an understanding of land-use patterns in Mediterranean Europe in the past, it cannot be used to predict or affirm past patterns of land use where there is inadequate or incomplete evidence. The physical nature of the land does involve one set of the factors that have to be taken into consideration, but only one. Moreover, its present condition is no certain guide as to its past potentiality. The other factors contribute to what has been termed the farmer's ''total operating environment'' (Chapman, 1974, p. 72). There are almost always major deficiencies of data for these even from the historic past, and still more so from the prehistoric past.

Extending the Cultivatable Land

The ancients were on the whole content with their land, to judge from the general tone of classical literature. Certainly there were complaints but these tended to be about spoilation through deforestation and erosion. As already noted, more often than not it was a question of praise for its productivity. However, from time to time, or from region to region, pressure from an increasing total population, from growing towns, and from the rising expectations of at least the higher social classes meant that this productivity had to be increased. The introduction of irrigation is one way of increasing output per hectare, as it normally leads to a more intense farming or cropping system. The construction of terraces and the drainage of waterlogged land actually extends the total area of land available for cultivation and that is another way of increasing total productivity. In all these forms of agricultural improvement, the ancients as well as their medieval and modern successors were greatly interested.

Irrigation

Rainfall in Mediterranean Europe is unlikely to fall in the quantity or at the precise moment convenient from the farmer's point of view. In the present day, watering of crops in periods of dry weather serves three main purposes. The growing season can be extended to continue throughout the summer, so vegetables that can normally grow only in the moister months may be produced throughout the year. Then, the range of crops can be extended to include those that normally would not survive the relatively dry Mediterranean climate although thermal conditions are satisfactory. Finally, the yield of certain Mediterranean xerophytes, such as the vine, can be improved with regard to quality even if quantity is less affected through watering. An additional bonus is that land regularly irrigated also tends to be the most highly fertilized, since the more intense forms of cropping would otherwise soon exhaust the soil. In modern irrigated farming, watering is no longer confined to garden plots (*hortus*) or to the main *huerta* areas. It is applied now to entire fields. Field irrigation may not have been unknown in Roman times but on the whole irrigation in Mediterranean Europe in the past was strictly controlled by the availability of water for technical reasons and tended to be reserved for garden crops and for orchards. For all their engineering skills, neither

Roman nor Arab engineers were able to reach the aquifers or to build the dams of the size that today assure Mediterranean Europe's water supply.

So only in one respect can irrigation be regarded as an almost primeval reaction of the Mediterranean farmer and that is where it concerns garden crops. Accordingly, some of the prehistoric rock engravings in the Val Camonica (Brescia) have been interpreted as showing that irrigation was practised in this Alpine valley at least by the end of the second millennium B.C. (Anati, 1964, p. 113; Blumer, 1964). But no doubt in the past as today, it would not have been every farmer who was anxious to extend his irrigation to land beyond the one or two gardens used to supply him and his family with fruits and vegetables. The difference in outlook between one peasant farmer who is content to water only these garden crops and another who takes on the relentless routine of an irrigated farm is almost as sharp as the landscape contrast itself between dry and irrigated land. In modern Pisticci (Basilicata), Davis found that peasant farmers viewed the introduction of irrigation as an unwelcome invitation to modernize not only their farming system but also their entire way of life (1973, p. 97ff). Agriculture that responds to such external pressures is no longer primarily concerned with subsistence or self-sufficiency but is on the way to becoming commercial cropping.

The pressures on land use and farming systems come from the urban centres. Today, few farmers in Mediterranean Europe are insulated from the pressures of urban markets both local and distant and from the effects of a fully developed exchange economy. In the sixteenth century the extension of irrigation was, in Braudel's view, a form of agricultural improvement directly stimulated by the pressures or attractions of demand from the urban markets (1972, p. 69). The influence might be quite local. In Castile, in the same century, only 16 out of 81 communes in one part of the Toledo province, 24 out of 145 in the whole of Guadalajara, and 13 out of 90 communes in the Madrid province, had *tierras de regadío* (irrigated vegetable gardens and orchards) (Salomon, 1964, p. 87ff). But all the Madrid villages having this form of intensive farming were located on the periphery of that city and it is difficult not to agree with Salomon when he suggested (p. 82) that "it is evident that the development of market gardening in these localities was not unrelated to the growth of the city and its alimentary needs". The situation was much the same in northern Italy. By the end of the century, Braudel pointed out (p. 70), population was increasing in such a way that towns were impelled to improve their food resources either by taking more land into cultivation or by intensifying agriculture through irrigation. It was not always a straightforward matter. In 1534 the authorities of Brescia hesitated; "we should achieve a good supply of water by diverting the Oglio but it would lead us into endless litigation with the people of Cremona . . .". A little later, in 1593, the people of Verona and Mantua failed to avoid just that sort of confrontation. Milan, however, was already well supplied with water for its suburban gardens. One canal, bringing water from the Ticino 50 km away, had been completed by 1257 and a second one was built in 1456 to bring water from the Adda. Frederick II was a great admirer of the Cistercians in Lombardy who, like the Benedictine houses in the twelfth century, had developed an extensive system of channels, often overhead, fed by the *fontanelli* of the upper plain. These spread water over low-lying meadows, increasing the quantity and frequency of the hay yield and enabling cattle to be fed on green crops for all but 2 months of the year (Masson, 1973, p. 168). One of the great attractions of the newly introduced rice, for which field irrigation was being extended by the fifteenth century, was that it was an alternative cereal for land that was anyway liable to flood.

In southern France, the first irrigation canals were possibly those constructed in the lower Rhone valley by the Romans. Many fell into disrepair during the early Middle Ages and it was only during the eleventh and twelfth centuries that interest in irrigation was revived here on any scale (Georges, 1939, p. 441). The first known, or surviving, record of permission to take river water for irrigation is dated 1104. By 1235 the bishop of Cavaillon was granting to the townsfolk "the full and total power to water their *ferrages*, meadows, gardens, vineyards and other possessions that they would like to water from the leat of our mill." Early in the thirteenth century, 1000 hectares of land around the town of Avignon could be irrigated with water from the Canal de l'Hôpital. More water was brought to the southern and eastern suburbs from a canal that became known as the Durançole. In the lower Rhone in general, irrigation took on an impressive grandeur of scale after the fifteenth century. Adam de Craponne was concerned mostly with drainage schemes but a number of these incorporated canals for irrigation. One of his achievements was the Alpilles canal. This still carries water from the Durance near Salon along the contours of the northern footslopes of the Alpilles ridge towards Arles and the Rhone. Since 1784 it has had a flow of 8000 litres per sec. The increase in the scale of irrigation schemes brought problems of water shortage. The area being irrigated in the eighteenth century included not only old arable land but land recently brought into cultivation after successful drainage. Yet the lower Rhone was not unduly well endowed with springs. Nor was there any systematic rationing to prevent water shortages. On the contrary, because of the danger of overflowing (from the Alpilles canal, for instance) there was every reason to draw on the supply, whether the land needed irrigation or not, in order to keep the level in the canal sufficiently low.

Irrigation on the plains of the lower Durance and Rhone supported an aureole of market gardening around each of the small towns that served as the market and as the centre of distribution. But market gardening in southern France was on an extremely modest scale compared with that of the *huertas* of Levantine Spain. The Spanish *huerta* towns were already of considerable size and importance by the Middle Ages and the irrigated area supporting each one could be extensive. The *huerta* of Valencia, for example, covered 50 km². But each of these major districts of permanent irrigation, it should be recalled, was the result of centuries of piecemeal accretion. The *huerta* of Valencia in fact comprises five distinct units: Castellon (La Plana, watered by the Mijares); Sagunto (watered by the Sogorb); Valencia (watered by the Guadalavier, now the Turia); Cullera (watered by the Jucar); and finally Gandia (watered by the Serpis) (Glick, 1970, p. 11ff). The bonds between each town and its own *huerta* were several and close. Most of the irrigated land in fact fell within the municipal boundaries and the cultivators of the *huerta* districts were therefore numbered amongst the townsmen. Then, many of the truly urban dwellers owned farms in the *huerta*. Another form of link was that the same irrigation channels supplied both the town and the countryside and both urban and agricultural needs. Finally, the products of the *huerta* included industrial materials as well as food, all marketed in the town. Changes in urban demand could determine the rate and extent of expansion of the irrigated farmland.

Two types of irrigated land can be distinguished in the Spanish *huertas* (F. Calvo, personal communication). There was a relatively constricted area of true *huerta* or *rahal* land, where irrigation was permanently and regularly supplied. And there was the more extensive *regadio alfayt* which was irrigated only when an abundance of water allowed, such as under flood conditions. Expansion of irrigated land was governed first and foremost by the availability of water or of capital to invest in the dams and canals needed to provide it. The modern period of major *huerta* extension in eastern Spain started in the seventeenth century. In Murcia, the area of permanently irrigated land had amounted to 4000 hectares in the thirteenth and fourteenth centuries but by 1621 it had been doubled and today it covers over 21 500 hectares (Calvo, 1975, p. 69). The Arabs had earlier constructed numerous dams and reservoirs and a network of master canals (*acequias*) as an attempt to regulate the very unpredictable supply from rivers and to distribute irrigation water at least intermittently over a wider area than could be supplied permanently from wells. As one result of their efforts, 28 *acequias* divert water from a single masonry weir on the Turia river to what has become the Valencian *huerta*.

Almost as important as the canals themselves were the increasingly complex system of rights and privileges over "old" and "new" water that developed. Differences in scale of irrigation between Arab and non-Arab parts of Mediterranean Europe are partly at least a reflection of two quite different concepts regarding the ownership of water. In Christian France and Italy in the Middle Ages water was regarded as private property. It became public only under exceptional circumstances. The special nature of the Venetian territory had led to "nationalization" of all water in 1556. Much later, when water shortages through excessive demand became commonplace or when land reclamation was undertaken on a major or official scale (as in Tuscany in 1782), water and major watercourses might be declared "waters of public interest" (F.A.O., 1953). Extension of irrigation could be limited also by the scope of individual landowners for action. In this way, the Levantine coastlands of Spain benefited from the Moslem view that water is the property of the community and given a supply, development of irrigation could advance on a relatively grand scale for the profit of the greatest number of people (Admiralty, Spain, Vol. III, p. 190). The grander the scale, however, the more necessary that the use of the water was controlled by institutions such as the *Tribunal de las Aguas de la Vega de Valencia* which continues to meet before noon, every Thursday (the Moslem Saturday), in the porch of the Cathedral at Valencia (Boira, 1953). It is thought that the present structure of the Tribunal dates from the reorganization, in A.D. 960 of an older body, although it is also quite possible that it originated under the Romans. Despite the difficulties of assigning a date of construction to a canal and to simple hydraulic structures, there can be little doubt that at least parts of the Spanish *huertas* were in existence during the Roman period if not earlier still. The *regadio* of Elche (Alicante) is one case in point (Gozalvez Perez, 1974) and that of Castellan de la Plana (Valencia) may be another (Lopez Gomes, 1957, p. 333).

G*

Cropping in the *huerta* used to be far less specialized than it has now become. The major transformations took place in the nineteenth century when the tendency was to break down the old polyculture, orientated as much to the needs of the peasant farmers themselves as to the urban market, with the introduction of two market crops. In the Murcian *huerta* nearly half the land is now under citrus while only 8 % remains for cereals, whereas as late as the beginning of the nineteenth century, a quarter of the land was being used for cereals and over a third for alfalfa and fodder grain (data in Calvo, 1975, Fig. 22). Another third was under tree crops (including mulberry), which left room for vegetables (3 %), vines (1 %) and a few textile plants (such as hemp). The last, together with the vines, have now totally disappeared and the vegetables, today occupying 16 % of the land, are now destined as much for the export market as for the local urban centres or for domestic use. Under such an intensive cropping system, only careful rotation with as much manuring as possible, helps preserve soil fertility. Houston (1949, p. 130) gave as a typical eighteenth-century rotation in the *huerta* of Valencia the following sequence of crops:

Hemp	March to mid-July
Beans	July to end August
Maize	August to October
Wheat	November to July.

There were thus four harvests a year and the land could be free for ploughing any time between November and March. In districts to the south of Valencia, sugar cane was certainly being grown from 1400 onwards (though possibly much earlier too under the Arabs). The Valencian monasteries introduced American plants such as cotton, aloes and capsicum into the *huerta* rotation (Houston, 1959, p. 177).

Roman farming practice with irrigation does not appear to have been any different from that typical of later centuries. In Roman times, as later, irrigated farming was concerned with the production of fruits and vegetables for an urban market. As later too, a perennial problem was the shortage of feed for stall cattle and horses so pasture land might be irrigated in order to provide as many cuts of hay as possible. Alternatively, fodder crops, such as lucerne, may have been watered in order to stimulate growth and to ensure at least four cuts a season (Columella, II. 10.25). Field crops such as beans and even cereals might receive water under exceptional circumstances, according to Pliny's evidence, in an attempt to save the harvest from total failure for example (Pliny, XVII, 250; White, 1970, p. 155). The main emphasis was undoubtedly on vegetables. Cato, in his advice to the investment-conscious new farmers of the second century A.D., ranked an irrigated vegetable garden (*hortus irriguus*) as second only to a vineyard in profitability (I. 7).

The availability of water for irrigation is one advantage of the mountainous relief and the geological contrasts of Mediterranean Europe as a whole. The disadvantageous aspect is that the total area of lowland is everywhere relatively small and each plain, mountainous or coastal, tends to be of limited extent and hemmed in by steep or rocky slopes. Intensification of production therefore sooner or later involves either literally the construction of terraces on the slopes or the drainage of low-lying areas along the coast and major rivers.

Terracing

It may be that the construction of a terrace is one of the oldest ways of creating new arable land. This sort of structure, however, is virtually impossible to date. Classical writers and agronomists are silent in the matter, certainly as regards the western Mediterranean world. Varro has a reference to the construction of boundary walls (I. XIV) but makes no mention of the problems of terrace maintenance, an essential preoccupation. Homer makes Odysseus find his father Laertes "on the vineyard terrace" and mentions "terraced Ithome", in the mountains of Thessaly, though it is by no means clear whether this was to describe the appearance of the settlement or of its agricultural land. There are indeed, as Semple pointed out (1932, p. 440), ancient retaining walls on the steep slopes that fall to the Argive plain around Mycenae, but there is no mention of evidence demonstrating their contemporaneity with the inhabitants of that city nearly 3000 years ago. It does seem reasonable to assume, however, that if the mountainous islands of Cos and Lemnos in the Aegean were as "well-peopled" as Homer stated (XIV, 255–256; XXI, 39), this must have been due to extensive terracing if only because there would otherwise have been insufficient crop land. The documentary silence on terraces is not confined to the classical period. A careful and detailed analysis of post-medieval Liguria is illustrated by several seventeenth- and eighteenth-century views that show terraced fields very clearly (Quaini, 1973). Yet nowhere does the fact that they were terraced receive attention.

The conclusion that comes to mind is that a retaining wall has been so commonplace a feature in the hillier or mountainous regions of Mediterranean Europe and so fundamental a fact of agricultural life, that to writers, comment simply seemed superfluous. Where there are steep slopes, it could be said, a "field" would by definition be an area of soil contained artificially. When it comes to the silence in the documentary record of more recent centuries, a relevant fact is that the construction of a terrace is normally the responsibility of an individual. In Provence, Livet noted (1962, p. 301) that each terraced unit identifiable in the landscape is not necessarily recorded on the cadastral plan because the tillage unit (the terraced field) is not necessarily the same thing as the tenurial unit (the *parcelle* or plot). What happens, in the case of a relatively large *parcelle* on a steep slope, is that the proprietor finds himself obliged to sub-divide the plot into several units, separated by terrace walls for greater ease of cultivation.

The presence of a retaining wall has several advantages. It is a means of extending the cultivatable land by the literal creation of new land within the walls, the soil often being carried up by the basket-load from elsewhere. It serves to hold soil in danger of being lost by soil wash. And, very important in drier districts, it is a means also of conserving moisture through the reduction of the downward movement of both sub-soil and surface moisture. Finally, by terracing and allowing or creating a build-up of soil, the degree of slope can be reduced which helps with ploughing, and the plot is in this way also contoured for irrigation by gravity flow. Arab agronomists writing in early medieval Spain left detailed instructions for the surveying and levelling of hilly or irregular terrain for the creation of fields which could be watered in this way (Imamuddin, 1965, p. 24).

Most commonly, retaining walls are of dry-stone construction and are perhaps only a couple of metres long. The plot contained therein may be little wider than the wall is high in the most extreme cases but on lower gradients terraced fields can be spacious and gently sloping. In rocky districts exceptionally large boulders which cannot be moved are usually left in the new fields. This is no great inconvenience to cultivation where hoes or ard ploughs are in use but they do reduce the area available for planting and can affect the growth of crops immediately around them. Not all terraces can be watered even if the farmer wished; the newest and highest may be above the source of the water supply. Not all terraces have to be contained by walling. At lower altitudes where gradients are more subdued or on soft-rocked hills where the contours are rounded, it may be sufficient to create a stepped profile and to leave the banks under grass, the latter providing an extra source of grazing or fodder. [12]

It is, not surprisingly, the highest terraced plots that are taken out of cultivation at the earliest opportunity. Their construction in the first place reflects the severity of demographic or other pressures that from time to time result in the transformation of seemingly impossible, often rocky, slopes into minute scraps of arable soil. Such abandoned terraced hillsides have become a familiar sight in Mediterranean Europe. In Corsica, terraces covering entire mountain sides are today discovered only when a forest fire clears the vegetation and reveals the surviving walls (Renucci, 1974, p. 173). Yet scarcely more than a century ago these same plots were being used to grow olives and vines and even for arable. Some were sheltered by a screen of growing cypresses which created an exceptionally favourable micro-climate which, to the peasant farmer, compensated for the other inconveniences of the terraced plot.

Drainage

The creation of new arable land through terrace building tended to be the result of individual effort or of community operations on a comparatively modest scale. This was not generally the case where the cultivatable land was extended through drainage and land reclamation. With drainage as with terracing, though, it is the landscape rather than the archives that bears witness to periods of acute land hunger. The landscape also reveals that a fair amount of piecemeal reclamation did go on, particularly around the marshy edges of lakes and lagoons (Fig. 26). In Spain between 1912 and 1947, for instance, some 900 hectares of the Albufera of Valencia were reclaimed illegally in this way and it is possible that not a few of the tiny saltpans sold or given to the monastery of San Leonardo di Sipontum (Foggia, Italy) in the twelfth and thirteenth centuries had similar origins (Camobreco, 1913, e.g. documents 25 and 26). It would seem too that the existing network of drainage channels (*roubines*) on the lower Rhone flood plain owed much to the efforts of individual landowners between the tenth and thirteenth centuries (Georges, 1935, p. 312).

Drainage channels need an efficient outflow and successful reclamation therefore depends on successful disposal of the surplus water. Reclamation of quite small areas was sometimes long delayed because of the problems of finding a suitable outlet. Moreover, effective maintenance of the drainage system as a whole is as essential as the provision of a suitable outlet in the

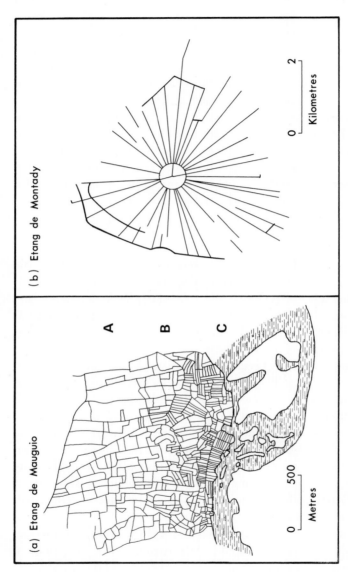

Fig. 26. *Piecemeal and organized drainage in the landscape.* Contrasts in field size and shape not far from the village of Mauguio (Hérault) coincide with the slope of the land (3-4 m above sea level at A) and phases of peasant enterprise in post-medieval reclamation (zones B and C) (traced from air photographs). Fields in the former Etang de Montady, near Béziers, retain almost intact the radial pattern imposed by the drainage of the lake in the thirteenth century under the direction of ecclesiastical authorities.

first place if the reclaimed land is to stay in good condition. Different plants have different rooting depths. For modern cereals the optimum on the best soils is as much as 90 cm but the older forms would probably have needed less. For all but specially adapted crops, such as rice, roots should be able to grow freely in unsaturated soil to about 10–20 cm above the water table (More, 1969). [13] In thinner-soiled areas, therefore, or wherever the water table is close to the surface, even quite small variations in the level of the water table could stunt the plants' growth and hence the yield.

The history of drainage has shown that there are few short-cuts to the completion of a successful programme of land reclamation and still fewer to the maintenance on which the survival of the system depends. Major investment is inevitable, be it financial or in costed terms of time, effort or organization; hence the importance of high-placed individuals and local authorities. These have had the major role in initiating, coordinating and supporting major land drainage schemes. The more modest the authority, the more difficult it could be to achieve the necessary cooperation. For instance, protection against flooding along the lower reaches of the Rhone in the Middle Ages used to be organized by each *Viguerie* and carried out by *lévadiers* or *robiniers*. The latter were local men who had been charged with the task of inspecting and repairing dykes and ditches (*roubines*) and of manning them whenever flood threatened (Dienne, 1891, pp. 262 and 538). The *lévadiers* of Beaucaire, on the west bank, had been organized in this way since before 1265; an Act of this date speaks of the *re*construction of the dykes protecting their territory from the Rhone and there were treaties between them and the *lévadiers* of neighbouring Fourques (Eyssettes, 1884). Inadequate equipment and perhaps also lack of close supervision accounted for not wholly successful work but there may also have been an element of careless planning. By the fifteenth century the inhabitants of Arles were sueing those of Tarascon for allowing water from their drainage ditches to flood low-lying land in the *Viguerie* of Arles and the first task that confronted the engineer Adam de Craponne a century later was to reconcile the two communities (Dienne, 1891, p. 267).

Some of the best-documented drainage work tends to be that carried out for a local authority, whether rural (such as the *vigueries* of Provence) or urban. The urban municipality of Pistoia (Tuscany) was obliged to keep the city and suburbs free of water and this charge had been written into the city's Statutes in about A.D. 1200 (Herlihy, 1967, p. 50). Three whole sections in these Statutes were devoted to the troublesome Stella (tributary of the Ombrone). In the Papal States, it was generally an

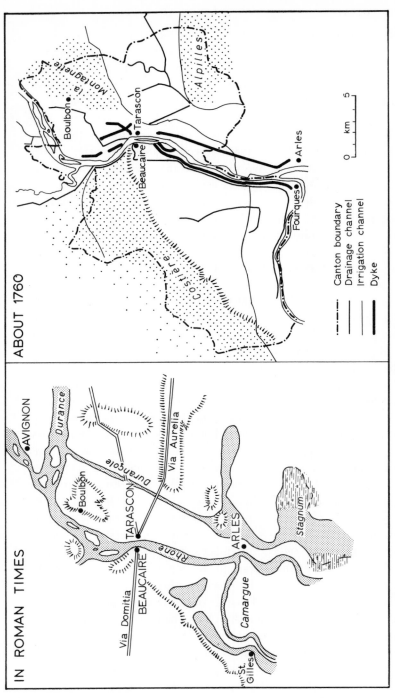

Fig. 27. *The lower Rhone flood plain.* It is thought that the Rhone (or one of its branches) passed to the east of the limestone *butte* of La Montagnette until relatively late in prehistoric times. It would be the abandoned course of such a branch that was marked in Roman times and up to the early Middle Ages by the canalized Durançole. The *Fossae Marinae* offered an improved navigation channel along the east bank of the Rhone through lagoons and marshes (*stagnum*), past Arles and up to the point where the southern branch of the *Via Aurelia* crossed the Durançole. The rather generalized view of the area in Roman times is provided

ecclesiastic who would have to present the case for some local drainage scheme. In 1371 Cardinal Grimoard was writing from Romagna that:

> the territory is low and the waters do not hold the course they should, nor are there any ditches or dykes . . . Now from day to day villages are submerged and the land is returning to marsh. In time, little by little, the greater part of this area will be under water (quoted by Larner, 1965, p. 7).

In some instances, it was the engineer in charge of improvements who was answerable to the funding authority who has left the most detailed records. This has been the case with the drainage of Lago Salpi (Apulia) in the early nineteenth century. The Neapolitan government had become interested in the lagoon only because of heavy losses to the national exchequer through illicit salt production and smuggling. It is because of Afan de Rivera's reports to them in 1838 and 1845 that very much more is known of the processes of attempted improvement and eventual partial drainage of Lago Salpi than of any of the other neighbouring lagoons and marshes (Delano Smith, 1978, p. 66ff).

The Romans were interested in land drainage from a number of angles. Agronomists urged that good field drainage was part of good agriculture (Pliny, XVIII. 47). Cato (CLV) said that ''land ought to be drained during the winter and the drainage ditches (*fossas inciles*) . . . kept clean.'' He went on to suggest that when the rains began ''the whole household must turn out with shovels and hoes, open the ditches, turn the water onto the roads . . . and see that it flows off''. The point has already been made that there were in Roman times as in later centuries periods of population increase, when demographic pressure must have at least sometimes meant land hunger. At such times the deep, rich soils and level land of recently drained lakes and marshes were easily seen to repay the cost and effort of their reclamation. Characteristically practical, Roman engineers tried wherever possible to provide dual-purpose channels. In southern France, for example, the *Fossae Marinae* was a series of ditches and channels between the inlets and marshes of the lower course of the Rhone constructed in 103 and 102 B.C. Its route was very much the same as the modern canal which runs from Arles to Port de Bouc (Russell, 1942, p. 193ff). By means of the *Fossae Marinae* quite large ships could pass along the left bank of the Rhone as far as the Alpilles, where the Roman army was then stationed (Plutarch, *Marius*, 15). Some of the Roman engineers' drainage or flood prevention works have been judged technologically superior to those of modern times (Lanciani, 1897, p. 13). At Rome, the early engineers gave the Tiber channel a carefully designed stepped profile. This meant that there were in effect three different channel widths: the narrowest (66·5 m wide) served in times of drought; the second (97·5 m wide) in conditions of moderate flow; and the third (135 m wide) was for extraordinary flow or flood. The advantage of this stepped section was that adequate stream velocity could be maintained even at low water so that the rate at which silt and mud were deposited in the river channel was considerably slowed down. Modern engineers, however, have given the Tiber at Rome a uniform bed, 100 m wide, for both drought and flood flow.

The reclamation of over 750 km of marshy coastal plain south of Rome was first tackled in 160 B.C. Livy records that ''the Pontine marshes were drained by the Consul C. Cethegus . . . and cultivatable land was formed from them'' (Book 46 *Epitome*). A master ditch ran parallel to the Via Appia. How much land was so reclaimed or how many colonists were settled is not known but evidently there were good results, for there is a dense scatter of Roman villa sites, water cisterns and tombs (Tomassetti, 1910). Not all the area was dried out, parts remained sufficiently wet to harbour the frogs and mosquitoes which troubled Horace's sleep so much (*Satires*, 1.5. 14–15). After the Roman period, however, neglect led to deterioration and the Roman Campagna remained abandoned until the eighteenth century (Almagia, 1929).

One of the problems in draining low-lying land on coastal plains is the proximity of the sea. The water table is close to the surface and there may be too little gradient to allow adequate drainage by gravity and natural flow. Even inland, though, there could be major technical problems. Lago Fucino, in the Abruzzi, for instance, was not wholly drained until the middle of the nineteenth century despite efforts in the Roman period, though these were impressive enough. In A.D. 52, under Claudius, a 5½ km gallery was hewn through Monte Salviano to provide an outlet for the surplus water. But the tunnel was not kept clear and despite renewed interest and some new resettlement under Trajan, it was only in 1853 that the entire lake was drained and over 16 500 hectares of land were released for agriculture and settlement. The Romans achieved more on the Po plains though; perhaps because the schemes here were less spectacular, they received rather less attention from contemporary writers (White, 1970, p. 170 and note 50). There is no doubt of the scope in that region for reclamation. Although the swamps north of Parma, through which Hannibal had had to make his way, had been drained by the time he was writing, Strabo could nevertheless compare the Padua district with lower Egypt. In his day it was "intersected by channels and dykes; and while some parts have been relieved by drainage and are being tilled, others afford voyages across their waters" (5.1.5). He went on: "Of the cities here, some are wholly island, while others are only partly surrounded by water." Drainage work on the Po plain under the Romans had started in 109 B.C. with the construction of a number of master canals in the centre of the plain, between Padua and Modena. Later this was extended in the west around Bologna and in the east around Piacenza. A scant note by Pliny indicates that work was undertaken in the Adige region between Padua and Ferrara (III. 119). Other areas of drainage released land for agriculture and settlement in the Veneto, around Cremona, and around Aquileia which, though recently malarial, was outstandingly prosperous under the Empire (Chilver 1941, p. 131).

Through drainage, irrigation and terracing, as well as through judicious crop choice and careful farming methods, the land of Mediterranean Europe could be made, and generally has been made, a land of bounty rather than left as a region of difficulty or hardship. This has been achieved despite regular increases in population and despite, above all, the exigencies of the physical environment. By means of such changes, immense gains to the total economic resource area in most parts of Mediterranean Europe have been made since prehistoric times. Other changes (discussed in Part III) that have affected the condition of the land of Mediterranean Europe throughout the past may have been less intentional; certainly they were generally adverse in effect.

6
Crops

The land of Mediterranean Europe was often praised by the Ancients for its bountifulness. Even in those days, however, this bounty was the result of a careful matching of crops and animals to land and climate. The primary consideration in crop choice is which plants will grow successfully in the somewhat stringent conditions of Mediterranean Europe. The primary consideration in livestock farming is which animals will best fit the farmer's requirements, given the land at his disposal and the exigencies of his cropping timetable. In addition, a farmer's selection of food crops and animals no doubt reflects an elementary desire for variety in diet as well as for self-sufficiency in food supply. Obviously it is important to make the best use possible of the different qualities of land available and at least one writer (Herlihy, 1958b) has seen this ecological aspect as the core of economic history. This may be true on the macro-scale, or for the market-orientated farming of landowners. At household level, or from the peasant farmer's point of view, the land-use question may be seen in a different light. The system under which every family farmed or gained its food and livelihood from the land may be as much, if not more, a function of social structure as of physical conditions. Duby has had similar thoughts in seeing the whole system of agriculture organized, as he put it, to fulfil the social requirements which determined eating habits (1968, pp. 8–9). The well-known crop trilogy of Mediterranean Europe—cereals, vines, olives—is indeed a neat summary of ecological relationships but it records only the supply of dietary variety as well as staple necessities that come from the arable sector. A vital omission are those necessities obtained from livestock. Overemphasis on the classical crop trilogy has tended to be at the expense of its essential complement, the animals, and sometimes this has led to a misunderstanding of the place of livestock in Mediterranean farming.

192

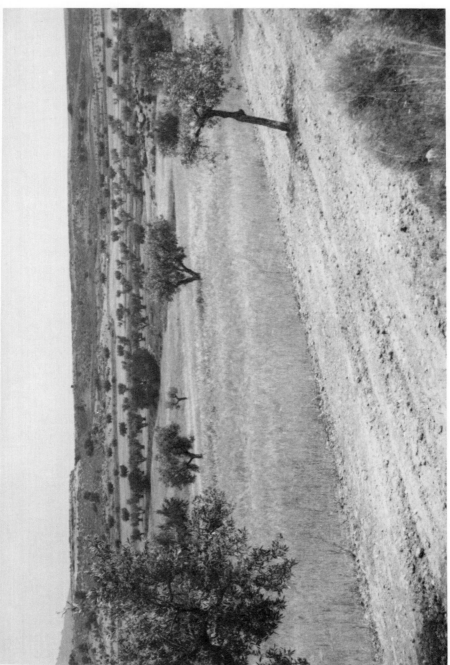

Plate 8. *The agricultural landscape.* Inter-cropping (dry-farmed cereals and olives) on the best soils and grazing on the slopes and rocky outliers in Murcia, Spain.

In this chapter, aspects of the basic cereal and tree crops are considered. Discussion is brief because treatment of Mediterranean food crops and arable farming technology has been more than adequate elsewhere (White, 1963, 1965, 1967, 1970; Brothwell, 1969; Semple, 1932). In Chapter 7, the place of animals and of livestock farming, and the range of farming systems involving livestock that have been traditional in Mediterranean Europe, are examined more fully. Finally, in Chapter 8, the discussion turns to the question of farming systems that may have been found during the prehistoric period in Mediterranean Europe.

The Traditional Cereals

Wherever people have lived in Mediterranean Europe, since the Neolithic, a cereal crop of some sort would normally have been essential, whatever local conditions of terrain or climate. Some remains of threshing floors and other traces of cereal cultivation may be found at altitudes or in localities where none happens to be grown today. In Corsica, grain was once grown on the Niolo plateau, that is above 900 or even 1000 m (Carrington, 1971, p. 241). In the Pyrenees, Neolithic farmers grew grain at Mas d'Azil (700 m) on the French side and at similarly high altitudes on the Spanish side in Catalonia (Chevalier, 1956, p. 114; Cura-Morera, 1976). Wherever climatic or economic conditions permitted the cereal crops tended to be given, and thus defined, what was regarded as the "best" land. As the preferred bread grain, by Roman times at least (Pliny, XVIII. 15), wheat was given pride of place on the ground as well as in the literature. Roman agronomists advised a "heavy, rich, treeless soil" (Cato, VI.1) but there were a number of varieties of wheat as well as of barley which allowed selection according to local or regional conditions. By and large, however, the grainlands of Mediterranean Europe included the better-drained soils of the valley bottoms and of the floors of intermontane depressions as well as the great plains of the lowlands. The gentler, more rounded, deep-soiled slopes of the soft-rocked hill regions have also been good cereal lands.

While all districts had to try to produce at least a self-sufficiency in bread grain, not all could be equally favourable or successful in cereal production. Some gained a high reputation early for the excellence and reliability of the harvest, but the classical writers were interested in wheat above all and noted in detail the "best" wheat-growing areas whilst the excellence of barley or oat districts goes unrecorded. Varro was particularly fulsome in his praise of good wheat districts: "What spelt shall I compare to the Campanian, what wheat to the Apulian . . . ?" (1.11.7). Throughout the last two or three thousand years in general, the island of Sicily, the plain of Foggia, the plain of Alèria in Corsica, the Campidano in Sardinia, and the Guadalquivir plains of southern Spain have all been of outstanding value for regular surpluses and for high-quality grains (notably of grain which kept well). The lowlands of the Po valley were esteemed in Roman times and in the Middle Ages for their grain output. In Roman times it was only the distance of the plain from Rome itself that prevented the Cispadane and even Transpadane districts from becoming one of the city's granaries since it was cheaper for the capital to import grain by sea from tribute-owing Sardinia. In the Middle Ages, grain surpluses could be available here when there were shortages elsewhere. For instance, Faenza consumed in 1504 less than half the grain it produced from its territory that year and in 1524 Rimini kept back 16% of its harvest for seed and 50% for home consumption, so the rest was presumably available for export or storage (Larner, 1965, p. 8). Even when there was a general famine in Italy, Romagna was still in a position to export wheat to Florence or Venice. In the event of a local shortfall, when harvest failed through warfare, flood or for other reasons, grain would be imported from neighbouring Marche or from the south (Apulia).

In other parts of Mediterranean Europe, or at other times, shortfalls in the cereal harvest could be of depressing regularity. Of Spanish Catalonia, Swinburne wrote "The scarcity of corn is sometimes very great, the principality [of Barcelona] not producing above five months provision. Without the importation from America, Sicily, and the north of Europe, it would run the risk of being famished" (1795, p. 65). In 1769 the lower Rhone region of Provence had "grain sufficient for only five months" (George, 1935, p. 374). Again in 1777 the Intendent of Provence wrote that "sufficient [cereal] is never produced in Provence for subsistence for one year, it is always necessary to draw on neighbouring provinces and from abroad". In 1775 at Apt nothing remained from the preceding harvest and wheat from Burgundy and rye brought from Marseilles had made up the shortfall. Such regions, the majority in fact, lived under the constant threat of famine.

One reason for this, only partly to do with the quality of the soil, may have been low yield. This, however, is a highly debatable topic. In the opinion of most writers the average yields in even the most favoured districts were remarkably low from Roman to medieval and later times (see for example, Duby, 1958, 1968; Schlicher von Bath, 1963; White, 1963). A four-fold return is suggested as the basic or average yield for most districts at most times. This is not however wholly consistent with the evidence. It is true that there is plenty of evidence for low returns. Official agricultural statistics for Vaucluse in 1844 reveal an average yield of 5·1 in the *département*, with 7·1 in a good year. Despite the high regard the classical agronomists had for Apulian wheat and the importance of the export trade in it in the Middle Ages, yields on the Tavoliere of Foggia in the early 1960s, under dry-farming, were given as 20 to 30 *quintaux* per hectare, a five- to seven-fold increase on seed sown. In the 1830s in Sardinia, returns at Fonni were four-fold for wheat and six-fold for barley (Casalis, 1833).

Fonni, however, is not only a mountain village but, at over 900 m, the highest in Sardinia and its conditions were at the time said to be fit for the growing only of beans. Returns at lower altitudes were considerably greater. At Barumini, in the rolling country of the lower hills, they were twenty-fold for both wheat and barley. Even the classical agronomists were not so pessimistic as modern authorities. Columella's remarks about a four-fold increase are considerably dubious (Frank, 1933, Vol. V, p. 145). Pliny clearly cannot be taken at face value when he claimed that "At all events the plain of Lentini and other districts in Sicily, and the whole of Andalucia, and particularly Egypt reproduce at the rate of a hundredfold" (XVIII. 95). But his gist is perhaps acceptable, particularly as substantiated by Cicero and above all Varro. According to Cicero, an eight-fold yield was normal in Sicily where, like everywhere else, the land was cropped in alternate years or with a 2-year rest period (Jones, 1964, p. 767). Varro held that normal yields varied from ten- to fifteen-fold (1.44.1). Yet Braudel regarded reports of yields of 20:1 or even 15:1 on the Tavoliere of Foggia in the sixteenth century as probably exceptional (1972, p. 426). Similarly George (1935, p. 377) considered the yields of 16:1 reported as regularly obtained in the early seventeenth century on the fertile soils of the lower flood plain of the Rhone as exceptional in the region.

There are two factors of which greater account may have to be taken than has been hitherto in these discussions of early cereal yields. One is by no means unfamiliar; the possibility of extreme variations of yields from year to year within each district. This means that the concept of "average" is scarcely a realistic one when it comes to the health and welfare of the local population. The other is that returns could be and, it would seem, were, extremely variable even between neighbouring districts. This is because the physical condition of the soil, important a factor though it must be, is by no means the only factor affecting crop yields. Management, as well as farming techniques, may have as large a part to play as soil texture in the question of soil "fertility" and crop yields. In northern France, good manuring practice alone can be shown to have been responsible for yields double the local average (Pounds, 1974, p. 198 citing Richard, 1898). In general, a liberal availability or use of manure is not immediately associated with farming in Mediterranean Europe. One natural factor, however, may have worked in favour of what little manure did reach the cereal fields of the south (mostly from grazing of stubble and fallow), that being the high alkalinity of much of the soils of Mediterranean Europe. A small amount of manure is held to be much more effective applied to an alkaline soil than a similar, or even larger, quantity on an acidic one, at least in our own country (Havinden, 1974).

Two other important points concern the type as well as the use of fertilizers and also the selection of seed. The need to maintain soil fertility artificially has never been ignored in Mediterranean Europe. Cato listed manuring as second to ploughing (and yet more ploughing) as the hallmark of good cultivation (LXI). Arab agronomists in eleventh and twelfth-century Spain may have had a slightly different angle on the question, with their concern that all land, good and bad, had to be coaxed into as good production as possible so that fertilizers were to be reserved for the poorest soils (Bolens, 1972), but their interest was undoubtedly as great. The Roman agronomists discussed at length the relative merits of an impressive range of potential fertilizers (e.g. Varro, XXXVII). The normal practice, where none of these was available, or was not available in sufficient quantity, has been to burn the stubble after harvest. Pliny noted that "farmers north of the Po are so fond of employing ash that they prefer it to dung, and they burn stable dung . . . in order to get the ash." (XVII. 49). To the present day, in Sardinia, the custom is to leave two-thirds of the straw-stalk standing after harvest so that it can be burnt later and ploughed in. These ashes may be the only dressing the land ever receives but that it does do some good may be judged from the report that after such treatment a "fair average crop of wheat is about 12 times the quantity sown" (Tennant, 1885, p. 79). Then there is the question of seed. What was sown was as far as possible the best seed that could be obtained. Whether this was local, a part of the previous year's harvest, or whether it was specially imported appears to have been yet another highly variable practice. In medieval Apulia, Charles of Anjou used, and urged others to use, Sicilian seed (Boüard, 1938). For post-medieval Languedoc, Le Roy Ladurie has revealed the whole complicated structure of importation of seed grains (1966, pp. 54–57). The particular interest in his exposition is not so much his discovery of the tradition that seed grain should always travel from south to north, from Mediterranean Europe into the interior and from hot to cooler conditions, but his observation that this was indeed commonly practised.

An important factor in the creation of a grain surplus was the ability to store the grain. In respect of keeping qualities of their grain, it was the more arid, southern districts of Mediterranean Europe that scored most highly. The best of the hard wheats from the Tavoliere of Foggia, in Apulia, was expected to store for 15 to 20 years without giving problems (Boüard, 1938). Varro asserted that good grain could be kept for 50 years (and millet for 100 years) (I.57.3). Agricultural writers, both ancient and modern, had a good deal to say on the subject of storage (Pliny, XVIII. 301–309; Columella, 1.9.10; Varro, I.56) and granaries are a striking landscape feature in many parts of Mediterranean Europe. In Sicily in the nineteenth century, villages were remarkable for their "storebarns that looked like houses" (Verga, 1883). In some Spanish provinces the most conspicuous building is still the *horreo* (Gutkind, 1967, p. 159). In Varro's day the granary was a separate building "above ground, so constructed that the wind can cool them not only from the sides, through windows, but also from below the ground" (Varro, I.56.3). Elsewhere, the answer to the storage problem was a sub-soil pit or silo (*fovea*). These could be quite small and privately owned. In the prehistoric settlements of the Tavoliere, each domestic compound appears to have had one or more stomach-shaped pits that are presumably for storage. Some silos were municipal. Some of the best described are those of the Tavoliere towns such as Cerignola and Foggia. In the late eighteenth century, Swinburne reported that at Foggia "All large streets and open spaces are undermined with vaults, where corn is buried, and preserved from year to year. The orifices are closed up with boards and earth; the sides within are faced with stone" (1783, p. 138). From these holes, *fosse* or *fovea*, is supposed to derive the name of Foggia. By channelling local harvest into such silos as these, substantial reserves could be built up over a short period from quite modest yields.

The means of production of cereal crops in Mediterranean Europe has by and large seen little innovation and few new developments since Roman times until the twentieth century. In 1963, Delano Smith watched the threshing of cereals and beans in the Apennine foothills in Apulia. The operation, carried out by cantering horses on a circular beaten floor, was the exact counterpart of one of the methods advocated by the Roman agronomists (Varro, I.52). Other classical methods could still be found in use in the nineteenth century or even today. In the last century in Sardinia, Tennant noted that a large flat stone, weighing about a hundredweight, was dragged around the floor 20 yards in diameter during threshing operations (1885, p. 79). Use of the *tribulum* (a sledge with flint teeth set into the underside) survives ''unchanged'' in parts of the Mediterranean (White, 1967, p. 156). In central Spain, flints are used even in modern times to replace broken metal teeth in harrows (Kenny, 1961, p. 61). Farming operations could be exceedingly arduous. In the summer of 1839 at least 50 reapers collapsed and died during the harvest in Apulia (Afan de Rivera, 1845, p. 194). The protective clothing worn by reapers in southern Italy, leather gloves, cane finger-stalls to protect the left hand from the sickle blade, and tough goat or sheepskin aprons (Rasmussen, 1969), could only have added to the heat and their discomfort and stress. Farming operations could also be exceedingly wasteful of manpower. The 2-year fallow was probably the least rewarding of all farm activities. It could demand up to eight annual ploughings without immediate or obvious gain (Le Roy Ladurie, 1966, p. 78). The act of ploughing itself was, as few writers have hesitated to point out, a physically arduous task. The small, lightweight ard might have a share weighing no more than 5 kg. This means that it had to be held, even forced into, the ground, however stony or knotted with vegetation this may have been, wholly by the efforts of the ploughman. Modern use of a mouldboard on the plough, by which the soil is turned rather than furrowed or scratched, began to be adopted in southern France not earlier than the first half of the sixteenth century.

Together with wheat, in the traditional cropping pattern, went barley. But barley has clearly been victim of social fashion. In the Apulian village of Montvarese in the 1960s, barley was being grown but only for its medical usefulness and ''as a food for ailing stomachs'' (Brügger, 1971, p. 35). This disparagement of barley as human food is nothing new. Pliny's comments reveal all: ''Barley bread was much used in earlier days, but has been condemned by experience, and barley is now mostly fed to animals.'' If in the first instance, worthy Romans were obliged to eat barley bread or pottage, he implied, their successors were more fortunate. In their refinement, they eat only wheat bread. Barley was food for the poor of the remoter countrysides. This social distinction persisted (though in other parts of Europe barley was replaced in the eighteenth century by rye) and is observed still. It did not, however, prevent large acreages of Mediterranean Europe being given over to barley. Le Roy Ladurie has shown that wheat and barley were inseparable as the basis of farming in thirteenth- and fourteenth-century Languedoc (1966, p. 179). But he has also shown how the disparagement of barley as human food and the periodic decline of the barley acreage can be related directly to levels of population. If these were low, there was sufficient of the preferred wheat for all. Otherwise the poorest sectors of the peasantry and those farmers (often the same) with inferior land were obliged to turn back to barley.

The Political Significance of Wheat

An interesting duality marked the production of cereals in Mediterranean Europe throughout the historic period as well as in Roman times. On the one hand the cereal crop was the basis of subsistence for peasant farmers and landowners alike. On the other hand, bulk trade in cereal surpluses was a pawn in a game which was above all political.

The perennial shortage of grain within the Mediterranean world as a whole, which was a consequence of locally variable yields and of uncertain harvest, resulted in a tendency to move grain from region to region. The typical pattern, as Braudel explained, was that "grain purchases were made locally, within a closed economy and a small radius. Towns drew on the granaries of the surrounding countryside. Only large cities could afford the luxury of importing such a bulky commodity over long distances" (1972, p. 570). In addition there were speculative dealings in grain. At nearly all levels, individuals have had cause to speculate to some extent. After all, in the final analysis, a well-run farm was one with adequate reserves to fall back on in times of difficulty. The idea of self-sufficiency was to protect the farm, and those dependent on it, from hardship. The Roman agronomists were clear on this point (Varro, 1.69, 1.22.4, 3.16.11). They also commended taking advantage of all opportunities to make a profit by selling the surplus part of the reserve at high prices (Duncan-Jones, 1974, p. 37). There is, however, yet another aspect to the manipulation of grain surpluses. It does not concern farm management or the simple economic question of selling grain to regions of temporary deficiency. It concerns the manner in which certain (if not all) rulers and governments in Mediterranean Europe used to manipulate trade

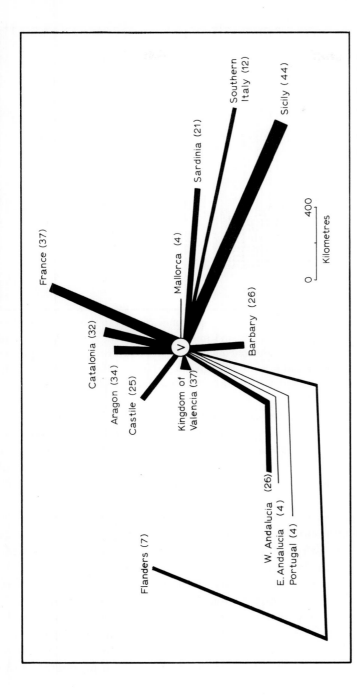

Fig. 28. *Wheat imports at Valencia* between 1401 and 1500 (from data in Rausell Boizas, 1974). The length of each line is proportional to the distance of the source area from the port of Valencia; its thickness reflects the number of occasions (in brackets) on which grain was imported.

Flanders (7)

France (37)

Catalonia (32)

Aragon (34)

Castile (25)

Kingdom of
Valencia (37)

W. Andalucia (26)
E. Andalucia (4)
Portugal (4)

Mallorca (4)

Barbary (26)

Sardinia (21)

Southern
Italy (12)

Sicily (44)

0   400

Kilometres

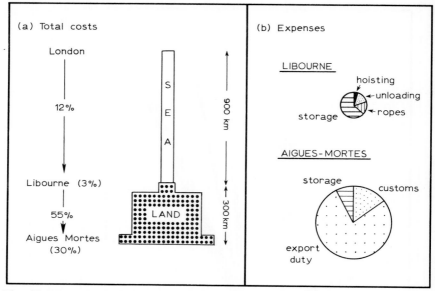

Fig. 29. *Financial profit from trade*. The importance of dues in the wool trade lies not only in their effect on pricing and mode of transport, but in the value of international trade to the royal exchequer. The data, concerning the transport of a sack of wool from London to Italy between 1310 and 1340, are taken from Lopez and Raymond (1955, document 132).

in grain to the point of interfering with normal economic relationships. In this respect, the study of the grain trade, as Braudel put it, "takes us to one of the most vulnerable areas of Mediterranean life and . . . to a greater understanding of that life in all its capacity." This would be as true of Roman and medieval times as of the sixteenth century. The importance of agriculture as the basic source of revenue in Mediterranean Europe from Roman times until very recently has already been insisted upon. It is not surprising therefore that certain regions became "granaries" in view of their capacity to produce and to accumulate a grain surplus. A wide range of factors might account for this. Local high yields might be one. Another was the good storage quality of the hard wheats of southern districts. This is due to a high gluten content which makes them durable and, particularly relevant to the past, well-behaved in ships (Mack Smith, 1969, p. 22). Another concerned districts where the non-agricultural sector of the population was low. In an average district in northern Italy, it has been suggested, only a third of the district's own productive grain might have been consumed locally (Grendi, 1970, p. 110). Where there were exceptionally few towns or there was a low non-agricultural population, a still smaller proportion of the harvest would go for local consumption. Finally, yet another factor that favoured the development of certain regions as grain surplus producers was proximity to sea transport. In this way Apulia and the islands of Sicily and Sardinia gained an economic advantage, while it was distance that had prevented the highly productive Po valley from marketing its grain in Rome (Toynbee, 1965, Vol. II, p. 180ff). Cereals from the Po lowlands would have cost in Rome three times as much as grain from Sardinia or Sicily. Transport differentials cannot have altered radically between Roman times and the early fifteenth century, when the cost of moving cereals by land was nearly 20 times as much as sea transport (figures in Boüard, 1938).

Even the best-endowed of the so-called ''granary'' regions were at risk from hazards affecting the harvest. In addition to weather, flood and warfare, there might be a perhaps unexpected hazard, that of devastation by locust plagues. In 1231, Frederick II was obliged to order each man in Capitanata ''to collect 4 *tomoli* [5 bushels, of locusts] before sunrise and to burn them before special officers'', the penalty for not doing so being one gold *ounce* (Huillard-Bréholles, 1844, p. 71). In New Castile and Extremadura, terrible ravages were caused in 1755-1756 by a plague of locusts that spread from the uncultivated wastes to the well-tilled fields on the edges of towns (Vicens Vives, 1969, p. 505). The Spanish province of New Carthage was also particularly vulnerable to the devastations of locusts and in Visigothic times an earlier harvest date was for this reason necessary, coming between 17th June and 1st August (instead of the usual 18th July to 18th August) (King, 1972, p. 211). In addition to these natural hazards, the grain surplus regions were vulnerable to external threats. After the Second Punic War, for instance, Rome found herself in command of the sea and the shipping routes that could henceforth be used to transport in bulk to Rome the cheaply produced cereals of the new North African territories. By the end of the first century B.C., Egypt was supplying a third of the grain consumed at Rome and the effect on Italian regions such as the Roman Campagna was disastrous (Almagia, 1929; Delumeau, 1957, p. 588; Semple, 1932, p. 369). Home prices were depressed and arable farming was abandoned in favour of viticulture. Since this involved hill country in preference to the plains, the latter tended to be economically abandoned, with only graziers henceforth taking advantage of the extensive level land, now under grass.

The interest of governments and of rulers in cereals and the grain trade operated at three levels. At the lowest level the rulers' interest centred on stored grain. Sometimes the action was genuine and disinterested, taken perhaps to relieve a famine after an exceptionally hard winter, as when Domitian ordered the immediate release of all grain in Roman Asia not needed for sowing or for home consumption (Duncan Jones, 1974, p. 38, fn 3). At other times rulers acted in their own interests. In fifteenth-century Sicily, all towns on crown land were obliged to store the surplus cereals from their territories in designated silos (Mack Smith, 1969, p. 191). The same applied to Sardinia, also under the Aragons, in the following century (Sorgia, 1972, p. 153). Year by year, whenever harvests were good enough, the silos were filled. Yet, as soon as grain prices rose or there was a famine somewhere, it was the ruler who ordered shipments from these same silos and who pocketed the financial gain. In 1224 there had been a major fall in food prices and Frederick II ordered the buying-up of cereals on a massive scale on behalf of the crown (Kantorowicz, 1931, p. 124). In 1240, he was able to sell 50 000 *salme* of wheat in Tunis at a 70% profit. In medieval Romagna artificial shortages were likewise created through enforced storage (Larner, 1965, p. 129) and indeed most instances of government interest in grain shipment and issue must have been vulnerable to allegations of manipulation whether there were grounds or not.

A second level of government interest concerned the export trade. Rulers or governments could insist on a minimum export quota. In Sardinia, the Aragonese insistence on maintenance of such a quota eventually harmed the entire economic state in the island to the point of endangering its domestic food supply. In 1323 the inhabitants of Barletta (Apulia) rioted in protest against the continued export of what they regarded as their own grain (Mickwith, 1941, p. 335). There were the occasions when the exporting government was embarrassed by its own actions. Harvests in southern Italy had been ruined or reduced by the wars of 1266 and 1268 and at the same time the presence of foreign troops needing to be fed aggravated local shortages. Notwithstanding, the Angevin government persisted in its policy of buying up grain wholesale in anticipation of the crusade of 1270. By that year, however, Charles I of Anjou was having to import wheat from Provence. Moreover, he was having to pay between 75 and 80 oncid per hundred *salme* for it, whereas by the following year prices had dropped to a more usual 38 to 40 oncid!

Part of the financial aspect of government interest in the manipulation of an external trade concerns export dues. Given the importance of exports to the central government, access to or control over exporting ports was the vital corollary. In order to be free to carry out monopolistic activities, a government had need of its own ports. The preoccupation of the Hohenstaufen with creating no less than 11 new ports along the Apulian coast merely reflects this need. The importance to the royal exchequer of income from export dues is pertinently revealed in the case of the shipment of Apulian wheat to Little Armenia in 1336 (Renouard, 1935). Pope Benoit XII had made available 10 000 florins for the purchase and despatch of grain to Armenia for famine relief. With the whole of that amount, 12 400 *salme*[14] of wheat could have been bought in Apulia. Alternatively, 6800 *salme* (no taxes paid) or 6300 *salme* (taxes on grain export paid) could have been bought in Apulia and sent to Armenia. But yet another stage in the accounting shows that no more than a miserly shipment of 4100 *salme* would have been sent for that money if all export duty and all freight charges were paid as normal. (Freight charges added 200% to the basic price of wheat but only about half of the cost of freightage actually went to the carriers, the remainder was due to the crown as in the form of the various taxes on shipping.) In the event, 4786 *salme* were despatched. The lesson learnt is that one-third of the cost of the grain eventually sent to Armenia went to the central exchequer.

The third level of government interest in the cereal trade was political. The Venetians, for instance, also had a high stake in ports up and down the Italian peninsula and on the opposite Adriatic coast. But Venice was chronically short of grain and, before its mainland possessions were extended, the establishment of trading *emporia* was a key to the survival of the republic itself. So critical was a reliable supply of grain for the lagoon city that their political affiliation could be bought for the price of a port. Or so Frederick II found in 1239 when he reaffirmed Venice's monopoly of the Apulian ports of Salpi and Barletta in order to gain Venice's military aid and political support against the papacy (Van Cleve, 1972, p. 273; Nicolini, 1965). Much the same view can be taken of the Spanish takeover of Sardinia (Tangheroni, 1972). The island had had a high reputation for its cereal production since it paid tithes to Rome in grain. It had been granted to James II of Aragon by Pope Boniface in 1297 but it was not until a financial crisis 20 years later in Aragon, that the Spanish were provoked into seeking further resources abroad and taking effective control of the fief.

The key to the political significance of cereals in Mediterranean Europe

H

lay in the fact that rulers were well aware how the generally low level of cereal production in the Mediterranean world would mean guaranteed sales at appropriate moments (Renouard, 1935, p. 313). Rulers could take advantage of this order to fill their treasuries. In order to be able to do so however control had to be gained over those regions which could be counted on to produce surpluses and over their ports. A short term consequence of this interference in the grain trade might be the falsification of price levels, as Hamilton found for post-medieval Valencia, Aragon and Navarre (1936, p. 197). But the long-term consequences of this exclusive form of commercial enterprise must be seen as a check on the economic development of the region concerned. Rostow has already concluded that the major factor in the stagnation of "traditional societies" (such as those which succeeded each other in Mediterranean Europe) was the absence of "the notion that surplus when it existed, should be invested to yield a progressive expansion in per capita income" to benefit all levels of society (1975, p. 14). In the context of the underdeveloped regions of Mediterranean Europe, the political significance of wheat (and, arguably, of wool) in post-medieval times surely has more than a transitory implication.

The New Cereals

Nothing has displaced the traditional dry-farmed cereals of classical times in Mediterranean Europe, wheat and barley. But two of the crops introduced since the Roman period have had immense significance in certain localities or circumstances. The rice plant was known to classical writers but only as, in Pliny's words, the favourite grain of the natives of the Indian sub-continent (XVIII. 71). The first sight of maize, however, cannot have been more than a few months earlier than 1500, when it reached Andalucia from the New World (Le Roy Ladurie, 1966, p. 70). The evidence for pre-Columbian maize in Africa, where it could have been seen by early travellers, is far from satisfactory (Brothwell, 1969, p. 104). Both rice and maize differ radically from the traditional Mediterranean cereals in being moisture-demanding crops, although their needs in this respect are very different. It might therefore seem curious that such intruders into the cropping pattern have been able to take such a hold on farming in Mediterranean Europe. The outstanding point is that each is a contribution to the supply of staple, not luxury, foods. Each, too, complemented the traditional agricultural economy at its weakest points. Maize is not only an exceedingly productive grain crop, potentially far more prolific than wheat, but it was also used as a green fodder, available in summer, the season of shortage in the lowlands. Because rice was a wet-land cereal, its introduction into the marshy coastlands and riverlands of Mediterranean Europe meant that land otherwise virtually unusable became available as arable.

Rice appears to have been introduced from the East into Mediterranean Europe by the Arabs. Possibly as early as the eighth century, certainly by the tenth century, it had reached Spain (Lévi-Provençal, 1950, Vol. III, p. 282). Its distribution has been closely associated with terrain naturally flooded or prone to flooding and in many ways the expansion of riziculture in Mediterranean Europe, even in modern times, has been part of the process of land reclamation. This is exemplified in Valencia. The demand for more cereals in the eighteenth century led to the use for rice growing of both higher, well-drained land in the coastal region, that had to be flooded seasonally with irrigation water, and the naturally wet marsh fringes where the rice paddy was part of the reclamation technique (Cavanilles, 1797, cited by Houston, 1949, p. 103). Not all the Spanish *huertas* though were found to be suitable for the new crop. South of Valencia, for instance, the Segura river has too unreliable a regime for the successful establishment of rice growing in the Murcian *huerta*. But rice had spread further north, to the Ebro delta and to Catalonia, by the middle of the eighteenth century. Despite a general welcome from farmers and a hungry population, there were attempts by the authorities to control or restrict the expansion of rice growing in Spain. Much of this stemmed from fear of aggravating the malarial infestations associated with the marshes and increasingly attributed to the new paddies. On the other hand, there were clear-cut cases where the local community could feed its population only by turning to rice. The appearance of extensive new marshes in the territory of Ampurias (Gerona) was a direct result of the River Fluvia's abrupt change of course in 1790. The villagers petitioned the authorities to let them grow rice, as their neighbours were doing, in order to compensate for loss of land and income from milling and other riverine activities (Sunyer, 1963).

In Italy, too, rice had been introduced by the Arabs into Sicily, whence it was disseminated northwards. By the early sixteenth century it had reached the plains of Lombardy and the ill-drained districts of the Po valley. By 1570 there was a steady supply of the new cereal to the city of

Genoa from these districts (Braudel, 1972, p. 69). By 1584 it was being grown on a commercial basis in the eastern parts of the Po lowlands and especially in the Veneto. In the other direction, it had spread along the Ligurian coast to reach Nice by the end of the century. On the lowland itself (still the major single centre of rice production in Europe), the development of riziculture represented less the interests of peasant farmers than those of landowners with considerable investment potential. The re-shaping of existing fields and the extension of irrigation and drainage channels were costly and demanded both skills and coordination of efforts not easily available to all.

In contrast, the growing of maize, despite hesitant beginnings, early interested the peasantry. Provided an individual plot could be irrigated, adoption of the new cereals involved less agrarian reorganization and capital investment than was involved in the creation of a block of rice paddies. The first evidence of maize in Mediterranean Europe is a letter written by Christopher Columbus, dated 1498, in which he refers to *mahiz* ''of which there is already a good deal in Castile'' (Hemardinquer, 1973, p. 227). From Spain, maize spread slowly northwards and eastwards. After 1565 it had crossed the frontier from Galicia into south-eastern Aquitaine, where it was known at Bayonne as a green fodder crop (Le Roy Ladurie, 1966, p. 71). In 1678 the grain was being marketed at Béziers. Thus while it took only 10 years for the new cereal to reach Andalucia from America, over a century passed before the new cereal was diffused over the 200 or so kilometres that separated Béziers and Bayonne.

The new grain reached Italy rather more quickly. By the middle of the sixteenth century, *grano d'Indio* was noted regularly in Tuscan shipping lists, and reports on the Italian famine of 1590–1591 revealed that something called *sorgoturco* was being grown in Apulia and shipped to Venice (Hemardinquer, 1973). Stocks of rye, ''all sorts of dry vegetables,'' millet and maize were held at Benevento for distribution in the same famine. By the late seventeenth century, maize had become firmly integrated into peasant farming and polyculture as an alternative staple cereal, particularly in the damper districts of Mediterranean Europe and towards the Atlantic fringes (Lefebvre, 1933, p. 703). In Piedmont, between 1792 and 1802, large landowners ploughed up meadows and woodland for the new grain rotation in a deliberately speculative venture. Peasant farmers did the same, hoping to gain a surer and better subsistence level. The new crop introduced a profound change, one which concerned the organization of farming routine. In Languedoc, by the eighteenth century, 80% of the total workforce involved in the harvesting and stripping of the cobs (and the gathering of the new haricot beans) was female.

This meant that where there was maize there could be little sericulture. However, the new grain was above all a crop of the plains, and of regions of high population density. Sericulture would have held its own in the hills and in drier and perhaps in the less populated districts. Oddly it is the dish *polenta* made from this novelty that is widely regarded as traditional in Lombardy and other north Italian districts. Southern regions were too dry or too sparsely populated for maize. The flicker of agricultural innovation and dynamism in the northern lowlands failed to be noticed in the south.

The Traditional Tree Crops

Contrary, perhaps, to popular image, Mediterranean Europe is a land of trees. If most of the ancient forests and woodlands have now been removed and reduced to the more familiar scrub, the integration of tree crops with cereal and vegetable cultivation and with animal husbandry and the various forms of *coltura promiscua* ensures still a largely wooded landscape in many parts of the region. Districts with a high grain output can appear from a distance as continuous woodland. Varro remarked that Italy was "so covered with trees that the whole land seems to be an orchard" (1.2.7). The importance of tree crops in diet and in daily life in ancient Rome was early recognized in the planting of a symbolic olive, vine and fig tree in the Forum. The peasant farmer may have had but one orchard, with olives and vines interplanted and even undersown with cereals or vegetables. Estate farmers may have specialized in large-scale production of one or the other and had several hectares under a single tree crop. But even the smallest land holders would try to gain a vineyard and at least a few olive trees.

The vine grows wild in Mediterranean Europe and its fruits have been eaten since prehistoric times. Wine was a staple drink of all social classes by the Roman era, as it is today, but there is little evidence to show whether wine was produced much before the second millennium B.C. Native chieftains in Gaul were said to be drinking water at the time of the foundation of *Massilia* in the sixth century B.C. (Justinus, XLIII. 3.11). It is thought that cultivation of the vine was introduced into Italy by early settlers coming from Greece and other Hellenic regions (White, 1970,

p. 229). Certainly considerable scope remained well into the historic period for improvements to both cultivation and processing techniques. Strabo reported that in Liguria it was the practice to mix pitch with the wine, in order to improve its keeping qualities, and that because of this many Ligurians preferred to import wine from Italy (4.6.2). In the same region, particularly around San Remo, the improved vine was still not universal by the thirteenth century A.D., being regarded a seigneurial rather than a peasant crop (Quaini, 1973, p. 46). The Malvisian and other selected grape stocks were imported into Sardinia only in the early Middle Ages by Byzantine monks (Cherchi-Parba, 1959). In Corsica viticulture remained very primitive until the Genoese introduced new techniques in the seventeenth century (Renucci, 1974, p. 58). But in the better vine-growing districts and above all in Italy an immense variety of vine stock and cultivation techniques were at the farmer's disposal even in the Roman period (Columella, Book III; Varro, I.25; Cato, I.32; Pliny, Book XIV). The various practices of training vines reflect local conditions of soil, micro-climate and risk from other hazards, such as grape-loving foxes. Agricultural treatises, Roman and modern, devoted pages of advice to these matters, to the manner of pruning (one of the most critical stages in the cultivation of the vine) and to the selection of stock suitable to local soils.

The deep-rooted vine is well adapted to survive the long dry season of the Mediterranean summer but young plants have to be nurtured in carefully prepared trenches. All the classical agronomists made this point. Columella gave the greatest detail and suggested that trenches should be 2 feet deep and "as great a width as that of the iron spade permits" (III.13.2). Trenching was standard for all types of soil but where the sub-soil included a hardpan or a calcrete (as in the case of the Tavoliere of Foggia) it would have been essential. The outlines of very straight Roman vine trenches and neatly aligned olive pits, spaced in accordance with the measurements recommended by the agronomists, and of the much more irregular medieval trenches revealed on the air photographs provide a uniquely detailed archaeological record of early land use (Bradford, 1949, 1950, 1957).

For the commercial farmer, viticulture has always been more profitable than cereal farming. Bearing this in mind, Cato ranked vineyards as the most desirable form of farming (I.1). In Visigothic Spain, vineyards were evidently of outstanding importance, receiving especial protection from the law (King, 1972, p. 212). Almost everywhere, vineyards were taxed and leased at much higher rates than was cereal land from Roman times onwards. In medieval Spain the difference could be as much as 20:1, though such a difference was rare. However, there are many disadvantages in large-scale viticulture and it was Pliny who quoted the case of a great fortune lost in a single generation (XVIII.37). Nevertheless, vine-growing expanded greatly in republican times in central Italy, largely in response to the demands of the growing urban market of Rome (Toynbee, 1965, p. 310). Expansion continued into the Early Empire (Dion, 1959). If cheapness of local prices is a reasonable index of overproduction, there is clear evidence for a major viticulture crisis in Italy by A.D. 92 (Duncan-Jones, 1974, p. 35). It was at this time that the Emperor Diocletian issued an order (reported by Cicero in *de Re Publica*, III.9.10) that the acreage of vines in transalpine Gaul should be reduced by half, even if it meant uprooting established vineyards. There is some doubt as to the directness of the relationship between the crisis and Diocletian's order. Another factor would have been the coincident cereal famine. There is no doubt that expansion of the offending vineyards was at the expense of arable land and it is more likely that domestic grain production had been severely curtailed at a time of increased demand from the growing urban market at Rome.

By the late centuries of the Roman Republic, and no doubt much earlier, vines and olives were being grown both on a small scale, as part of every peasant farmer's polyculture system, and on a larger scale, as a commercial enterprise. Cato's advice to the aspiring capitalist farmers of his time was to specialize in vines if the land was suited to a bountiful production of good-quality wine (I.1). But the vine, unlike the olive, produces badly if neglected and is normally one of the most demanding crops of Mediterranean Europe. Vineyards are highly individual in their requirements according to the stock planted and to the subtleties of local soil, micro-relief and micro-climate which determine the time and manner of pruning and picking. It is primarily for this reason that the vine is not a suitable crop for monocultivation on an exceptionally large scale. Cato's advice for a commercial vineyard concerned an estate of 100 *iugera* (25 hectares). Vines under the charge of a bailiff or a host of labourers yield poorly in comparison with those tended with care and devotion by the owner or under his close supervision (Aymard, 1948). Pliny (XIV.48) showed how a case of good husbandry repaid the owner in both quality and in quantity: "everybody was running to behold the heaps of grapes to be seen in these vineyards." Certain districts in Italy had already gained a reputation as wine-producing districts. Columella named the regions of Massa and *Caecuba* (south of Terracina) in southern Latium, Sorrento in Campania, and the Alban hills of Latium as the best in the world (2.2.24). Pliny claimed that of the 80 well-known wines of the Roman world, Italy produced over two-thirds (XIV.87).

Just as each peasant farmer would have been striving for self-reliance in terms of cereal production, so there can have been few farmers in Mediterranean Europe since early Roman times who did not own at least one vine. This single vine would have most likely trailed about the entrance to the house where it could be tended, guarded and admired and where it would provide agreeable shade as well as fruit. Even where the more fortunate could boast of an entire vineyard, it was common to find a few plants set close to the house, destined perhaps for the production of table grapes rather than wine. The same is true in modern times. For Spain in the early sixteenth century, the *Relaciones* of New Castile show how domestic, or peasant, viticulture was formerly very much more widespread than it is today (Salomon, 1964, p. 83). The influence of urban demand for fresh fruit and local wine accounted for an exceptionally high proportion of land under vines in the neighbourhood of major centres such as Toledo. Although some of these old areas of peasant viticulture such as La Mancha have survived, most have vanished in the face of competition from commercial vineyards.

As in the case of the vine, archaeological evidence suggests there was a wild form of olive in Italy and southern France in prehistoric times. Still less than the vine, though, in its wild form the olive yields very little that is useful. Like viticulture, the cultivation of the olive tree was an innovation that eventually reached Mediterranean Europe from further east. Amongst the earliest archaeological evidence for a cultivated olive are finds from the Bronze Age village of Tufariello (Buccino) in southern Italy, dated to the end of the third millennium B.C. (Holloway *et al*., 1975, p. 79). Despite the great care taken by Roman farmers in olive cultivation and in the preparation of olive oil, there have been many districts in Mediterranean Europe where cultivation of the olive tree is, or has become, a casual affair. In Corsica and Sardinia, for instance, the traditional practice is to pay little attention to the trees which, once planted, are left to grow half wild in the rockiest terrain around the arable area. Harvesting consists of picking up the fallen fruit (a practice condemned by the Roman agronomists (Pliny, XV.77)) or, at best, of shaking the tree.

These farmers are exploiting one of the major advantages of the olive, its tolerance of rocky terrain and steep slopes that would otherwise be of little use. In southern France, in the traditional pattern of land use, olives used to be planted on the highest slopes and on the rockiest ground. But for really profitable olive cultivation, attention should be paid to soil quality and to climatic conditions. Cato was quite explicit about which types of olives should be matched to different soil types; for instance, ''In heavy warm soil plant . . . those for pickling . . . Plant the Licinian olive in colder and thinner soil . . .'' (V.7). On the Tavoliere of Foggia, centennial olive groves occupy land that could equally well produce the excellent cereals for which the lowland was formerly renowned, partly because there is little inferior land available. Each tree has been carefully pruned to give a flat-topped, compact canopy supported on three main branches, the whole designed to facilitate picking. Each tree, originally planted in its own pit, is today found 25 and 50 feet from its neighbour, precisely as recommended by Columella (r.r. 5.9.7; de arb 173). The soil beneath is sown with cereals and later manured by sheep grazing the stubble.

In all but the warmest districts of Mediterranean Europe, olive trees are vulnerable to late or to exceptionally severe frosts. For this reason too, the upper slopes, above the level of possible temperatures inversions, are best for olives especially in climatically marginal areas such as the Rhone valley or in districts exposed to cold winds of the Mistral or Bora type. Cato advocated the planting of olives wherever possible on west-facing slopes. Three days of exceptional frost in southern France in February 1956 resulted in destruction or in severe damage to nearly every tree both east and west of the Rhone from which the region has never fully recovered. Each century has had its share of such crises. In 1789 ''the frosts were so hard . . . that they have obliterated for a good many years to come the principal resource of the country, through the perishing of the majority of olive trees, from Aix to Tarascon. For several years there will be no oil . . .'' (Intendant's Report, 1789, cited by George, 1935, p. 394). There had already been two exceptionally severe frosts earlier that century (1709 and 1766), six in the previous century, and at least three in the sixteenth century. A rather less well-known risk, not mentioned by Cato though recognized by Pliny (XV.4), is that extremes of drought can also adversely affect the olive. Unlike the vine, which has at least one deeply reaching root, the olive normally survives periods of drought by virtue of its exceptionally extensive but surface rooting system. Its vulnerability to

H *

Plate 9. *Olive press* in the vaulted ground floor room of a peasant's house in the mountains of Liguria (photograph by courtesy of

exceptionally dry conditions may therefore not be so surprising. Though accounts of these are rare in Mediterranean Europe, a region well accustomed to periodic aridity, it is reported that olive trees were killed or severely damaged in a drought in Spain in the ninth century A.D. (Smith, 1966, p. 442).

It might seem anomalous to include the sweet chestnut as a traditional tree crop of Mediterranean Europe, especially as there are many others (the fig, carob, the citrus fruits, the pomegranate) that have also come to be accepted as part of the Mediterranean orchard. It is true that the weight of evidence for the cultivation of the chestnut and for the use of the flour derived from its fruit as a substitute for bread dates from the eighteenth century. However, there is no doubt that the chestnut was present in at least many parts of Mediterranean Europe throughout the prehistoric period. It is found, for example, in the pollen record in Corsica continuously since the Würm (Reille, 1975, p. 11). If its present-day distribution owes much to plantings in the last two or three centuries, it must also reflect widespread planting during the Roman period.

The Roman agronomists were well acquainted with the usefulness and the cultivation of the chestnut. Those who were writing for the landowning class of farmers, however, were selective in their interest. In the context of commercial or estate farming, the usefulness of the chestnut lay primarily in its coppiced timber. From this came the stakes, props and baskets that were needed on any arable estate but above all in the vineyards (Columella, r.r. IV.30, III.2; de arb XXII.3). Pliny had the most to say on the usefulness of the fruit of the chestnut as a source of human as well as pig food. He listed the nine varieties of edible chestnut and pointed out that, ground up and "roasted", "it supplies a sort of imitation bread for women when they are keeping a fast" (V.92). For this reason, the perennial use of the chestnut as an alternative, if disparaged, source of bread, it is viewed here as one of the traditional tree crops of Mediterranean Europe.

From the climatic point of view, high rainfall and warm equable temperatures are the chief physical factors in the distribution of the sweet chestnut. It is also better suited to siliceous soils. If its fruit rarely appears in the archaeological record, this can be explained by its poor keeping qualities (Brothwell, 1969, p. 95). If there is scant mention of the use of chestnut flour or bread in the general literature or in the archives, this can be explained by the observation that this form of food was enjoyed only by the hungriest and poorest peasants. One can merely surmise that the chestnut forests of the Sila Massif in southern Italy, such as those carefully protected by the villagers of Laino, were in the thirteenth century valued as a source of human food as well as for their pannage for swine and timber and fuel resources. But the documentary record is clearer in fifteenth-century Languedoc. Studies of the *compoix* reveal how in the Cevennol villages in particular the proportion of land under chestnuts increased year by year (Le Roy Ladurie, 1966, p. 212). At Saint Geniès de Varençal, basically a cereal-growing village, chestnuts occupied 11% of the cultivated land in 1526 but 16% in 1566, after which the acreage stabilized; in 1649 it was still only 17%. To researchers such as Le Roy Ladurie, there should be no underestimating the extent of the chestnut forests in the siliceous mountains of Bas-Languedoc in the sixteenth century, despite the modesty of the statistics in general, nor the importance of the chestnut harvest. The fruits were exported even to Italy as well as to other parts of Languedoc. But above all the chestnut was "the chief food of the inhabitants of the Cevennes" whether eaten raw, roasted whole, or ground into flour and made into a heavy, black bread. It was with chestnut foods, too, that peasants "managed to pay the doctor" (*ibid.*, p. 213, quoting Felix Platter, 1892, p. 285 and Almeras, 1960, pp. 110–111).

The point is that in the mountains where the chestnut flourished, terrain suitable for the growing of cereals was nearly always at a premium. Whenever population levels were high or increasing, alternative staple foods had to be found. In this way, by 1792, the mountainous district of central Corsica that came to be known as La Castagnicca was supporting densities of up to 88 persons per square kilometre (Perry, 1967). No commune here had less than half its land under chestnut and in some up to 95% of the land was so planted. The nuts were milled locally and if there was a surplus of flour it was either exported or fed to livestock. The other products of the chestnut tree remained just as important as when the demand for the nuts was lower; timber, charcoal, tannic acid for leather processing, wood for fencing and for fuel were exported from La Castagnicca in return for wine, wheat and olive oil which could not be produced locally in sufficient quantity under the new circumstances. Such was the picture not only in Corsica and Languedoc but wherever chestnut forests flourished; in the Apuan and Ligurian Alps, on the Sila Massif, in the Pyrenees, the Cevennes, and in the Iberian Sierras. In these regions pigs had as pannage only what the human population did not need or could spare. When times were better, it was an easy matter to dismiss chestnut bread as an inferior feed, fit only for Pliny's fasting women! Periodic pressure on the chestnut as a staple food in Mediterranean Europe can begin to be documented for the post-medieval period and surmised, from rather more recent scant evidence, for the Roman. With regard to the poorest members of the peasantry or some of the less fortunate districts of the region, the chestnut should certainly be included as having been a traditional staple tree crop throughout the historic period.

7
Animals

It has been impossible to discuss crops and the arable aspects of farming without at least passing reference to the animal side of farming. The two aspects are very closely if not inextricably related; Afan de Rivera (1832, p. 15) spoke of agriculture and "its inseparable sister", pastoralism, even in the day of some of the most specialized ranching ever known in the history of Mediterranean Europe. In considering the place of livestock in the normal farming pattern of Mediterranean Europe throughout the past, there are four main points to bear in mind. First there is the question of the place of livestock in the agricultural economy in Mediterranean Europe and of the variety of farming systems that have been operated here in the past. Secondly, there is the question of feed resources available from the "local" area and the village territory. The third point individualizes one farming system in particular, that of large-scale grazing with more or less long-distance transhumance. Finally, the fourth point questions the validity of assessing certain types of terrain as having what has been called a pastoral vocation and of regarding land at present uncultivated as land inherently uncultivatable. First, however, there is the question of the relative merits of the animals themselves to the farmers of Mediterranean Europe in the historic past.

Farmers and their Animals

The modern peasant farmer, whatever his status, normally is a possessor of animals to some degree or another. In Sicily, Chapman found that "almost every family keeps a few chickens as a matter of course" and that many villagers also had a goat (1973, p. 32). Several villagers also had a few sheep and swine. All villagers therefore could have access to the livestock products they needed at least for their diet. In Pitt-Rivers' village in southern Spain there were peasants fortunate enough to own cattle as well as goats, swine and sheep, though the cattle were "a hardy, half-brave breed, giving no milk and good only for veal in the market towns or for bull-baiting in the local *pueblos*" (1954, p. 36). Individual villagers, those with larger holdings or otherwise better-off, might have a very much larger number of animals. In medieval Apulia, one peasant household owned a pair of oxen, 20 swine and 20 sheep while another family (owning two houses) had altogether 90 sheep, 12 mares and 17 asses (Camobreco, 1913, document 178, dated 1225; document 213, dated 1287). It was evidently much the same in Roman times. Pigs and poultry would have been as normal on any holding as in later centuries. Together with cattle, these were obviously regarded by the agronomists as the basic characteristics of any decent farm. Cattle were kept primarily for work. As in later centuries, milk came from goats and sheep. The manure produced by all the farm animals was valued as a fertilizer. Whenever possible, the animals, particularly cattle, were confined to pens or stalls so their manure could be the more easily collected. It was for such reasons that a flock of sheep was considered part of "the proper equipment" for an oliveyard, according to Cato (X.1). His advice was that an olive farm of 240 *iugera* (60 hectares) should carry no less than 100 head of sheep.

Cattle, sheep, goats and swine, therefore, have been the commonest farm animals in Mediterranean Europe at all levels since Roman times at least. The predominance of one type of animal over another at a particular locality, or on one farm as opposed to its neighbour, reflects only partly the nature of the physical environment in the area. Far more basic factors were the farmer's economic status, the farming system involved, and, perhaps, his aspirations to betterment. Some of these aspects are elaborated below.

Swine

Of all the farm animals potentially available to each farmer in Mediterranean Europe, it is soon appreciated that the pig is the most readily available, the cheapest and the most useful at the very elementary level of providing the meat element in the normal European diet. A peasant has to be really exceptionally poor not to be able to gather together the feed for at least one pig. In modern "Alcala", Pitt-Rivers found that "it was every family's ambition to fatten a pig or two" in the forests during the autumn in anticipation of winter (1954, p. 37). In Roman times too: "For who of our people cultivate a farm without keeping swine?" asked Varro (II.4.3). At the other end of the scale, a good deal of money could be made from the sale of pigs and pig products, very little effort and expense having been involved in their raising. Pig-keeping can lead to quick profits. A good, 2-year-old, home-reared pig in Sardinia in the last century yielded 400 pounds of meat, a six-month porker weighed 30–35 pounds (Tennant, 1885, p. 83). A pig usually reproduces with abundance, two large litters a year being normal. Salted pork keeps well while remaining palatable and pork has been probably the most common meat at all social levels, except amongst the Moslem or Jewish communities of Mediterranean Europe. In the Middle Ages a common form of tax or rent payment, where this was demanded in kind, was a pig. But the chief reason for the ubiquity and social lowliness of the pig is undoubtedly the ease with which swine can be raised.

There have been basically two traditional ways of keeping swine in Mediterranean Europe. Either they are kept on the farm, in a pen or confined to yards, with occasional or seasonal excursions in search of forage or pannage, or they may be allowed to run half-wild in mountain woods and forests, from where they are rounded up and brought down to the village as necessary. While the former practice is practically ubiquitous, certain districts in Mediterranean Europe have become famed for the gastronomic products of their "wild" pigs. Sardinia supplied most of the pork eaten at Rome (Strabo, V.1.12; Pais, 1923, p. 502). Half-wild pigs still roam the Gennargentu feeding on the "grass, roots, acorns, chestnuts and wild olives, which give the flesh a most delicate flavour" as Tennant found last century (1885, p. 83). Earlier in the nineteenth century, there were reported to be 2000 free-ranging swine (*porci rudi*) in the single Gennargentu commune of Fonni (Casalis, 1833). In addition, there were 350 village pigs (*porci domestici*). In the hill villages and in those of the plain, where the pigs rarely left the immediate environs of the village, the numbers of *porci domestici* were very similar and there can have been few households in each village that had no pigs. For these animals, grazing had to be found from orchard and wayside grass, from vineyard and garden weeds, kitchen crops and the occasional foray further afield, singly or as a herd. It was only in the mountain communes, or in communes with a substantial area of mountain, forest or other suitable terrain within their confines, that advantage could be (or had to be) taken of the extra forage resources.

There is no doubt that swine could be an important, if not the most important, livestock element in upland villages. Of a total of 21 clauses in the Statutes of Laino (Calabria) that dealt with animal matters, no less than 12 were concerned quite specifically with the village's pig-herds (in Cappelli, 1931, p. 428ff). Only three were devoted to sheep and goats and only two to cattle. In pre-Moslem Spain, too, swine were often the main livestock of at least certain villages though there is no evidence of exploitation of stock other than pigs for meat (King, 1972, p. 214ff). In Arab-controlled territories the Moslem population did not raise pigs but non-Moslem farmers evidently did; "bacon-rights" were assigned to Christian traders at Messina in Sicily, such as the Genoese, in the twelfth century (Abulafia, 1977, p. 92).

Overstocking of such free-ranging swine has been blamed for major vegetation changes and deforestation in Corsica since the Middle Ages (Reille, 1975, p. 165). It is difficult to be precise about the pig populations of mountain communes since official statistics bear little relation to reality. For Sardinia in the second half of the nineteenth century the official figure was a total of 51 384 swine for the entire island. On the other hand it was openly acknowledged that this probably represented less than a tenth of stock actually kept. Tennant cited the case of one farmer who had upwards of 1000 pigs pastured in his forest but who returned the number of 100 in order to reduce his taxation. Even so, there is no doubt that densities could have been high; in 1961 some communes in the Gennargentu officially had up to 4000 swine each (Desulo, Villagrande-Strisaili, for example) (Bergeron, 1967).

Cattle

In contrast to the humble but rewarding pig, cattle have tended to be regarded as expensive and therefore prized animals. This is because a cow can be extremely expensive to maintain in adequate feed. Cato may have advised that "there is nothing more profitable than to take good care of the cattle" (54.5) but the uninitiated amongst the new farmers of his age must have been horrified on studying his or Columella's schedules of feed rations for working oxen (clearly summarized in White 1970, p. 219ff). Not all farmers would have followed the advice too closely. In Sardinia last century a feed of straw and beans was all that was normally given in the middle of the day to animals actually at work and except for this all cattle were expected to feed on the pasturage they could pick up, summer or winter (Tennant, 1885, p. 82). On the other hand, it was not in these upland districts that there was the greatest need for plough animals. It was in the grain-growing hills and lowlands that the problem of fodder for plough teams could be desperate, particularly if there were any circumstances artificially aggravating the shortage. Where there was extensive arable land, very large numbers of plough oxen were required; Swinburne saw ''no less than twenty-four ploughs at work in the same field, each drawn by a pair of oxen'' on the rich plains of Andalucia (1795, p. 212). Insufficient or out-of-condition plough teams would mean a reduced harvest and possibly a threat of famine in the following year. One of the commonest complaints registered against the large-scale graziers of post-medieval Apulia concerned the reduction of pasture for the plough teams. Typical was the plight of Bartholomeo de Bagnula (of Canistrella, Foggia) who complained in 1479 that he had insufficient grazing to support the 60 oxen he needed to plough his arable land (Spola, 1953, document 36t). Even crown land was not immune from such problems. Two centuries later, the Spanish king of Sicily was being warned that shortage of draught animals was seriously hampering cultivation of the wheatfields ''whence your Majesty's revenues chiefly come'' (Mack Smith, 1969, p. 187). [15]

Food production from cattle was therefore always a secondary consideration. There were regions, such as the Pyrenees, where cows were not even milked (Chevalier, 1956, p. 297). The small, hard-working Sicilian cow, however, was expected to yield up to 6 litres of milk a day for her masters as well as feeding her calf for a period before she was put back to work in the fields. Beef therefore tended to come from working animals when their life was over. It is generally assumed that a consequence of this was that the meat was tough and unpalatable. White, for example, disparages the quality of the Romans' meat, known to have often reached the butcher's shop by way of the sacrificial altar (1970, p. 277). Birrell (1968) attempted to explain the relativity low price of beef at Berre (Provence) in 1429 as compared with mutton (three and five deniers a pound, respectively) on the basis of palatability. There is no doubt that cattle were killed for meat only after their working days were over or if for other reasons they could also be classed as the bestie inutile of the documents (Jones, 1966, p. 382). Bone refuse from medieval Tuscania shows that most of the beef bones thrown away there had come from beasts aged over four years at death (Barker, 1973, p. 302). If beef is supposed to have been tough because of the animals' working lives, the same might be said of mutton, particularly that which came from transhumant sheep. Dugrand commented adversely on the quality of a *gigot* from sheep which today graze the rocky, dry Garrigues of Montpellier (1964b, p. 218). However, not only are the records from the past silent on this matter, but it is possible that the whole question has been exaggerated. In Sardinia last century, Tennant found that "the flesh of working oxen is scarcely distinguished from that of cows or heifers" (1885, p. 82).

As more evidence comes to hand, another supposition is being qualified. It is becoming clear from archaeological and documentary sources that very much more meat entered the diet at all levels of society than has hitherto been allowed for, at least at certain periods during the last millennium. It has been suggested, for example, that in tenth-century Spain beef cattle were more important than milch-cows (Smith, 1966, p. 445). One of the statutes of the Calabrian village of Laino (number 16) dealt quite specifically with beef butchering (Capelli, 1931). The butchers of Berre in the fifteenth century were sufficiently wealthy to act as moneylenders (Birrell, 1968, p. 131ff). The prosperity of butchers in Languedoc did not escape the notice of Le Roy Ladurie (1966, p. 185), who associated a rise in the price of meat with an expansion in the arable area destined to keep pace with demographic expansion. By the fifteenth century, the improvement in the quality of cattle that Barker has noted in central Italy may have been widespread. If so, a slightly smaller number of animals might maintain a stable level of meat supply. From bone evidence at Tuscania, Barker suggests that one cow could by now provide up to twice as much meat as one goat or sheep (1973, p. 161). As far as possible, meat continued to be eaten. In the sixteenth century the Pope himself intervened in agricultural matters in demanding an increase in arable and promoting experiments in livestock rearing. As a result of these experiments 125 "red cattle" were introduced into the Roman Campagna (Delumeau, 1957, p. 570). In the sixteenth and seventeenth centuries in Sicily, meat reached the table even during Lent and while ecclesiastics were reproached for their extravagance (if not their impiety!), each company of Spanish troops stationed on the island had to be rationed to a maximum of four sides of beef a week (Mack Smith, 1969, p. 187).

The archaeological evidence on livestock, whether raised for meat or for other purposes, comes from bone deposits, from which the proportional importance of the different kinds of animal is noted. This may give a misleading impression of the balance of livestock in the region, since the smaller size of sheep and goats (and swine) tends to be compensated for by larger numbers. From the point of view of grazing and fodder needs, about five adult sheep or goats might be equivalent to a single adult cow. There is little denying, though, that sheep and goats are the animals most readily associated with the traditional scene in Mediterranean Europe.

Sheep

Like cattle, sheep on Roman and later farms had a dual role, the production of wool and the production of manure. The question of foodstuffs (milk and cheese) was, to the peasant in particular, the most important function of sheep-raising. To the commercial farmer, though, wool was the primary object. Columella praised the sheep because of their wool, which he saw as ''our principal protection against the violence of the cold and [which] supplies us with a generous provision of coverings for our bodies'' (VII.2.1). Certain breeds and certain districts became associated with the best-quality wools: Tarentum in south-east Italy, for example, in Roman times, Spain later. The pre-eminence of Spain, and Spanish-ruled Italy, in and after the later Middle Ages, was due largely to the merino. This breed of sheep yields a long-haired silky fleece that has been, and is still, esteemed as amongst the best in the world. The appearance of the merino is associated with the arrival of the North African Berber tribe in Spain in the twelfth century. From Spain the merino was taken into other parts of Mediterranean Europe, either to form pure merino flocks (such as those of Arles in France) or to be crossed with local breeds to improve their wool (as in Sardinia). Merino wool was reaching Genoa at the beginning of the fourteenth century after 1307 which is when the shipping lists make the first clear reference to *merinus*; the earliest definite mention of the merino in Spain is dated no earlier than the fifteenth century (Lopez, 1953). Yet two centuries later the Iberian merino sheep had become ''the pampered favourite of Kings'' and its exploitation was making an indelible impression on the landscape and in the pattern of life in Spain (Klein, 1920, pp. 7, 162). In Klein's words, the entire economic and social structure of that country has been etched by merino sheep more deeply even than by olives or grapes. The native Iberian breed, the *churro*, produces a rather coarse wool and did not attract the attention, except adversely, of the major wool producers.

More than cattle, sheep have been valued for their milk. In the eighteenth century, while Sardinian sheep were still unimproved, La Marmora accounted for the quantity of cheese produced in the island by referring to the successively large numbers of animals rather than to the abundance of their milk yield, which was always, in his view, poor (1839, p. 442). Be that as it may, Sardinia was ranked as a leading exporter of cheese early in the sixteenth century. Cheeses were sent regularly from Cagliari to Leghorn and frequently to Genoa, Naples, Marseilles, Barcelona and Valencia (Braudel, 1972, p. 151). Another region famed for its cheeses was south-eastern Italy. Here cheese-making facilities occupied an important part of the layout of each *masseria di pecore*. In Spain, the despised *churro* yields excellently in milk and the regions of Burgos and Villalon have come to be associated with the production of high quality soft cheeses.

Goats

Goats used to be far more numerous on Mediterranean Europe farms than they are today. They were ranked below sheep, being less profitable and not particularly easy to keep. A goat requires as much food as a sheep and, in view of its agility, still more attention from the shepherd. Its great advantage is that the quality of its food need not be so high as for sheep. Like swine, therefore, the usual practice has been to graze goats on land not required for other stock and to give it a wide range of relatively rough fodder and feeds unsuitable for the other animals. In this way, several goats can be kept cheaply and easily in the vicinity of the house all the year around, an ideal arrangement for a milk-giving animal. Notwithstanding its meat, the goat's pre-eminence in Mediterranean lands is as the poor man's cow. Accordingly there was consternation throughout southern France in 1725 when the *Etats* of Languedoc brought about a restriction on the numbers of goats that could be kept as an attempt to protect the woodlands (Segui, 1946). From east to west, there was a rush to point out that the goats provided ''the only milk available during the summer'' and that often goat's milk was all that was available to peasants ''to season their bread each evening'' (Chevalier, 1956, p. 309). When the edict was repeated in 1896 there were those who insisted that ''not to tolerate goats would be the whole ruin of the population'' in certain districts. Special medical certificates could be obtained in order to gain exemption from the ban on grounds of sickness or of extreme poverty.

Farming Systems

The individual farmer's choice of one type of animal or another is but one, rather small, aspect of a very much more fundamental topic, that of the entire complex known as a farming system. It is one example of what the agricultural geographers and economists refer to as an enterprise, the others being crops and (if counted separately) grasses (Morgan and Munton, 1971, p. 23). The combination of enterprises found on each farm is the set of functionally interrelated elements that constitute a farming system (Birch, 1972) though some call this a type (e.g. Whittlesey, 1936; Symons, 1968). Agriculture is characterized by a large number of small producing units, each one of which, whatever its size, operates as a planned economic and ecological system with decisions made, normally by individual farmers, in the context of their own needs, assessments and experience. Finally, the system has to be stable, remaining in equilibrium or in balance with its environment and capable of continuity.

Each enterprise is characterized by a number of variables. In the present context, the more important of these can be listed as: the type (or types) of animals involved; the numbers of each type; the proportion of one type to the others; and the proportion or balance of the livestock elements of the system to those of the arable. From another angle, and without going into details here, the four relevant factors are seen as being the economic, the technical, the environmental and the behavioural.

Man's primordial need for animals is in the normal manner of things for their contribution to his diet. Which type of the available animals he actually chooses depends on whether he can support the ''expensive'' kinds (sheep and, above all, cattle) or only the more ''economical'' ones (goats or, above all, swine). In this way economic factors come into operation. At the same time, however, the farmer is equally concerned to maintain the cereal side of his diet. His land has to be cultivated and its fertility safeguarded. For this he does not necessarily need animals. On the other hand, although all of the animals in question can aid in the latter respect, by providing manure, only cattle can be used as a means of cultivation. Hence the technical factor is very closely tied to the economic one; a farmer's decision to acquire an ox-drawn plough, for instance, presupposes that either his resources and annual profit or his seasonal workload do in fact justify the expense of keeping the draught animal. Then there is the environmental factor, which may work quite independently of the others. The physical environment of the neighbourhood may be such that the farmer can take advantage of an abundance of fodder resources outside his own farm and indulge in the raising of exceptionally large numbers of livestock. Hence the *porci rudi* of the Sardinian and Corsican mountain villages for example. Finally, there is the behavioural factor. As already noted, a farmer's social standing may be closely associated with, or even defined by, possession of a certain type of animal or a certain number of animals.

A search through the documentary evidence has revealed that at least six different farming systems have been in operation in Mediterranean Europe in the historic past. It showed that all six have existed throughout the two millennia in question. It also showed that all or any of the six could be found in co-existence within any region. Five of the six are represented in Fig. 30 in the right hand column. Each farming system corresponds very closely to one of the social rankings.

At the lowest end of the scale is the system found amongst those members of the rural community who do not really qualify to be called farmers. Most commonly they are the poorest, landless labourers. But into this category would also come those whose livelihood comes mainly from other occupations, such as fishing and mining, and who may be relatively well-off but who have little time for agricultural pursuits. However it is, these have no more than the absolute minimum of agricultural resources; a kitchen garden and an orchard tree or two on the arable side, a pig or two on the animal side, possibly a goat as well. Certainly they cannot afford a cow or even sheep (which is why they are not represented in the figure). Next along the scale comes the small peasant farmer, owning or holding some land, engaged in polyculture, raising a pig or two at home, but also having a small number of sheep as well as a goat or two. Then comes the rich peasant. Rich, that is, in terms of land farmed but also, if he chooses, in livestock. He may himself own only a modest number of animals (say 50) but he may also provide for those belonging to others so that he runs a flock of some size (up to, or over, 100 head). Obviously, the variations amongst the peasants' farming systems in any real situation are more complex than represented here but these suffice to identify the model.

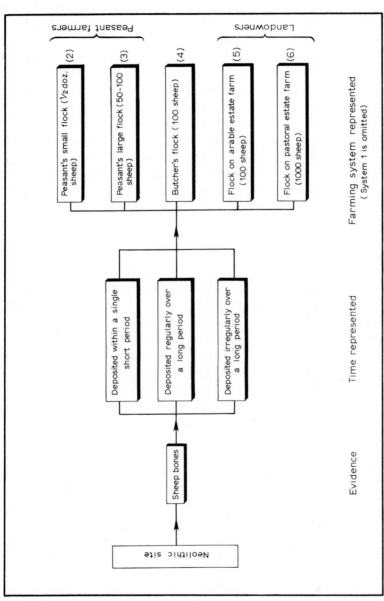

Fig. 30. *Problems of interpretation of archaeological evidence for livestock farming.* Livestock may be present on a single farm in various numbers and proportions and can be managed in a number of quite different ways. The diagram shows, first, how difficult it is to make deductions concerning livestock management, and therefore farming systems, from simple bone finds. The right hand column also summarizes five of the six different farming systems identified and documented as typical in Mediterranean Europe throughout the historic period (see text for amplification and discussion). Because there are peasants

The diagram contains the following elements, reading across:

Neolithic site → Sheep bones →

Time represented:
- Deposited within a single short period
- Deposited regularly over a long period
- Deposited irregularly over a long period

Farming system represented (System 1 is omitted):

Peasant farmers
- Peasant's small flock (½ doz. sheep) (2)
- Peasant's large flock (50–100 sheep) (3)
- Butcher's flock (100 sheep) (4)

Landowners
- Flock on arable estate farm (100 sheep) (5)
- Flock on pastoral estate farm (1000 sheep) (6)

Column headings: Evidence — Time represented — Farming system represented (System 1 is omitted)

The butchers are a race apart, neither peasant farmers nor of the landowners' class but nevertheless owners of sizeable flocks and herds. In the absence of meat-storage facilities, butchers had to maintain the animals they had bought in until these could be slaughtered and in a restricted sense they too were farmers. The charge could be heavy; in 1301 Francesco of Lucera (Foggia) was given 500 cattle and 300 sheep from the huge number of animals seized by Charles of Anjou from the Saracen community, together with another 20 cows which were expressely ''to be used for the food of the soldiers'' that had been sent to the town for the siege (Egidi, 1917, document 638–639). In Provence, at Berre, in the fifteenth century, butchers were not only running flocks of up to 100 animals but were doing exceedingly well out of this. Wool, suet and skins were sold in advance of slaughter on contract and paid for in advance, so the butchers became moneylenders and gained yet further from the interest they charged on money lent (usually half the profit made with the loan) (Birrell, 1968).

The remaining two farming systems involve the landowning class. As has already been noted, the ancient agronomists, and Cato in particular, advised the keeping of sheep on an arable estate. Up to a point this would be normal practice, since any estate farm aimed to be as self-sufficient as possible. Domestic pigs, a few goats and sheep, cattle for ploughing (and horses or mules for transport) were the essential accoutrements of any arable farm, whether it specialized in olives, vines or cereals or was a more broadly based mixed farm. Finally there was the farmer who specialized in animals to the extent of having many hundreds or even thousands. Included in this category, though perhaps worth regarding as a little different, are the speculative graziers, men who owned very little land but who owned or controlled vast numbers of sheep or cattle.

The specialist grazier lived a life and operated a system quite different from any of the other farmers, peasants or landowners, and from the butchers. This was not just because of the excessively large number of animals owned or in his care, numbered in hundreds or thousands, but because his *sole* preoccupation was with livestock. In all other farming systems found in the historic period in Mediterranean Europe the animals were ancillary to arable farming or (in the case of the butchers) to another form of livelihood. The grazier, however, might not even possess land and he certainly was unlikely to have sufficient to support the huge flocks and herds under his control. By the thirteenth century in Provence, there were individuals who owned a single modest flock, a sheep fold, and several pieces of land, although resources from the land were wholly inadequate to provide pasture for the total number of animals in their care at one time or another (Poppe, 1966). The way they managed was by *renting* pasture. In short, the grazier was a speculator, with a way of life far removed from that accepted by the majority of society, from king to lowliest peasant, to whom the precept ''to live off your own'' was the key to their style of life. These speculators apart, though, the landed proprietors were free to raise livestock in outstandingly large numbers only because their food supply, and other necessities, were assured from other parts of the estate. For these, therefore, there really could be an element of personal choice. Each landowner of substance could decide whether to devote the balance of his land surplus to providing for himself, his family and his other dependents, to arable land use or to livestock. Some quite explicitly refused the responsibility of pastoral farming. In the central Pyrenees for example, landowners with extensive forests and natural pastures at middle and upper altitudes made these available as summer grazing to ranchers and graziers from outside the region (Chevalier, 1956, p. 438). Their own herds and flocks remained comparatively small and were essentially for self-sufficiency in regions where survival was often precarious and always difficult. From their point of view, it was to their advantage to pocket the rent paid by the outsiders and to avoid the risks involved in livestock raising in a mountain environment. The outsiders, coming from estates and settlements on the Aquitanian lowlands, were left to the often risky business of moving huge numbers of animals between the winter grazings of their own districts to the high pastures rented for the summer. Given that they had their own lowland estates to rely on for their own livelihood at least, it can be argued that this sort of system was well-adapted to the physical environment, as Renucci has done for Corsica (1974, p. 205). Other landowners, as will be seen, gave themselves wholeheartedly, if not enthusiastically, to livestock raising on a scale that merits classification as ''pastoralism''.

This summary of the very different forms of farming that have been found in Mediterranean Europe serves to underline one very important point. That is, the distinction between the mixed farmer, peasant or landowner, and the specialist livestock farmer. The former was engaged in arable farming and his animals, numerous or otherwise, were an integral part of his total farming operation. Their type and numbers reflected his assessment and experience of available resources and opportunities. The latter, whether also landowner or essentially landless, was a livestock

owner *par excellence* and a full-time cattle or sheep raiser. Not one of the
farming systems, however, was necessarily exclusive of another. Within a
single region several, if not the entire range, would normally be found.
The key issue in all farming involving livestock of any kind concerns their
feed. This is discussed next.

Fodder and Pasture

For farmers of all statures and for graziers alike, the provision of adequate
and suitable feed for their animals all the year round was the gravest
responsibility. It could also be a major problem. The bigger the herd, the
more serious the problem and the more complex the solutions found.

It is beyond dispute that a basic premise in farming in Mediterranean
Europe has always been that animals should be fed from the local area as far
as this could possibly be managed. Columella is quite explicit on this
point: "it is generally better to use the food provided by one's own farm in
feeding one's own cattle rather than those of other people" (VI, preface,
2). Village communities, it will be seen below, spared no effort to make
arrangements for keeping their livestock movement within at least the
local area if not within the actual confines of their territory. Only the
graziers, a race apart, had to recognize from the outset that there was no
hope of a match between the size of their herds and flocks and the capacity
of their own land to feed them.

The problem starts with the better-off peasants and the aggregate of the
village flocks. An individual peasant farmer might own only a score or two
of sheep and goats. However, when all animals in the village are put
together the number can be considerable. [16] In sixteenth-century Castile,
some villagers expressed satisfaction with the grazing available within the
boundaries of their township. Uceda (Guadalajara), for example, had
"much and very good pastures and especially two very good *dehesas*
[common grazing] . . . almost all holm-oak which usually provides good
grass" (Salomon, 1964, p. 139). Others were less fortunate and were
obliged to make arrangements outside their own commune. Several
villages might group into federations for the purpose of sharing grazing
land (inter-commoning). One of the replies to the question of the
Relaciones for Ajofrin (Toledo) reads: [17]

. . . they said that this aforementioned place has very little land [a very small territory], and that the commonland that the inhabitants of the said village can enjoy is only a small amount of land on a sierra, which is called the Celeda, to which can go, and be accumulated, about 30 head of animals and which has no other lands of its own for pasture and [they said] that this village has common lands with a certain usage in a certain part of the sierra and the land, which they call the common, which is two leagues from this village, . . . is the common of the city of Toledo and [of] this village and of 12 other villages and localities . . . (Salomon, 1964, p. 143).

Sometimes the arrangements were specifically for the plough teams. At Alcaudete (Toledo), grazing was ''at the free will of the town of Talavera which gave it to them for their work animals''. Elsewhere the shortage might be seasonal only. The villagers of Carracosa del Camp (Cuenca) stated that ''the town with its lands has some pastures for large and small stock during the summer, august [sic] and autumn but . . . in the winter season, because the land is open and bare for use [as] arable . . . the major part of the livestock go to spend the winter out of the lands of this community . . .''. The same thing was found in Sardinia. In the Arborea district, high pressure on the land for food had shortened the duration of fallow and the village livestock was being sent up onto the nearby Giara plateau from the stubble as soon as this was needed for ploughing (Le Lannou, 1941, p. 195).

Wherever possible the animals were kept as close to the farm or village as possible. Columella went on to emphasize the advantage of the cattle dropping their manure on their owner's land rather than on someone else's. In the Valencian *huerta*, where pasturing regulations forbade the presence of sheep, goats and cattle not strictly needed for domestic use within the irrigated area, provision was made of grazing (*bovalar*) just outside the *huerta* but still within the territorial boundary (Glick, 1970, p. 22). In his survey of present-day peasant farming on the Greek island of Melos, Wagstaff found that ''the great majority [over 75%] of stock-keeping farmers kept their sheep and goats within 5 minutes walking time of their house . . . very few farmers ranged their animals at a distance of more than an hour from home [and] still fewer kept them on distant pastures for the whole year or the greater part of the year, though the maximum distance involved here was about 5·4 hours or about 27 kilometres'' (1976, p. 26). In this modern context, it has been the growing of fodder crops under irrigation that has made such an arrangement possible. Elsewhere, other ways out had to be found. Village codes were designed to ensure some sort of compatibility between

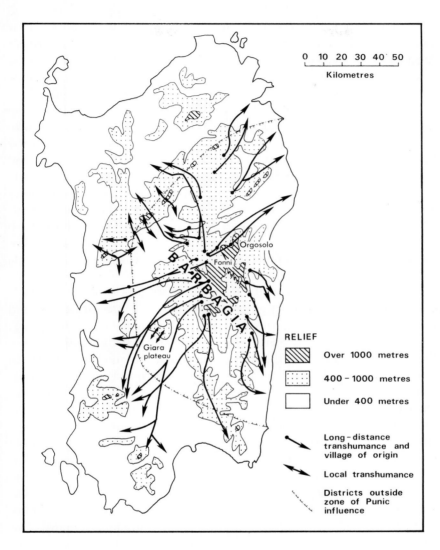

Fig. 31. *Major lines of movement of livestock in Sardinia* in both long-distance and local (or ''reluctant'') transhumance (adapted from Le Lannou, 1941). The Punic–Roman frontier is supposed to explain, as well as to underlie, the traditional division of the island into a civilized, cultivating part and a barbarian, pastoral part.

numbers of stock and available fodder or grazing. According to these and to local usage in Sardinia, villages rich in pasture land were able to allow 1 hectare per sheep while those poorly off could allow only 0·7 hectare per sheep in the lowland district of Arborea (Le Lannou, 1941, p. 195). In the mountains of central-east Sardinia because of low temperatures and snow cover no winter grazing at all is available, and because of the cold, which neither sheep nor lambs would survive, it is simply not possible to keep the flocks at home all the year around. The villagers therefore had to take them to lower altitudes for the winter. The movement down from the Barbagia district starts late in October so that ''not a flock spent the bad season here, and the first bleatings of the returning flocks were hardly heard before the end of May'' (*ibid*, p. 174). These flocks can have quite long distances to travel. From altitudes of 1000–1200 m they move down to 600 m, to the plateau of Giara where they mingle with animals who have moved up from the Arborea villages, or lower still. Between 30 and 60 km separate the winter and summer grazing areas of flocks from most of the Gennargentu villages (Fig. 31).

The use of seasonal grazing can be far more subtle than the simple winter/summer contrast suggests. In Sardinia it is the shallowest and therefore most rapidly warmed soils that are sought out in spring, especially those rich in leguminous plants. These nourish the sheep after the long cold season and the nitrogen stimulates a good milk yield. In summer, grazing is concentrated on the moister and more acid soils, where the grass remains moist, and spring pastures are left to recuperate. Once the temperatures start to fall, as they do rapidly in the autumn, the shepherds move their flocks into districts which receive the earliest rainfall whilst remaining comparatively warm. In the Mediterranean Pyrenees use of the *soulanes* (or *solans*) is very carefully regulated whereas grazing on other slopes is more or less free (Sorre, 1913, p. 433). The *soulanes*, the first pastures exposed by snowmelt, are also the first closed to grazing to avoid spoilation through overuse. These restrictions were applied impartially to local livestock and to the transhumant animals that belonged to ''outsiders''. Elsewhere, priority might be given to the villagers' own animals. In the coastal *huertas* of eastern Spain little grazing was available other than that of the marshes or along the grassy banks of the irrigation canals. So when land was set aside in 1368 at Oliva (Gandia) as common grazing (*dehesas boyales*), regulations forbade the sale of any other pasture to ''outsiders'', the transhumant shepherds (Fontavella, 1952, p. 239).

Any threat to village grazings was therefore a serious matter. A common plaint in the *Relaciones* of Castile was that *dehesas* and other village grazing land was being encroached on, or usurped by, private landowners, particularly those from the nobility (Salomon, 1964, p. 151). In Apulia, more than two centuries after Frederick II had made grants of grazing land in perpetuity to the inhabitants of San Nicandro and of Castel Pagano (Foggia), the two communes were still disputing this land (Spola, 1953, document 4, dated 1478). At the beginning of the eleventh century, no less an authority than the Greek Catapan Boianus was involved in the settlement of the dispute between Troia and Vaccarezia over grazing lands at the boundary of their territories (Trinchera, 1865). On the other hand, livestock owners quite obviously sometimes failed to pay scrupulous attention to local observance. The *Libro Rosso di Monopoli* (Muciaccia, 1906) contains a number of documents from the eleventh to the fifteenth centuries concerned with the safeguarding of arable land and tree crops from damage by livestock. In 1339 the governing body (*Universitas*) of Monopoli was permitted to elect a custodian who would prevent illegal grazing in the olive groves that fringed the shore during the month of February (document XIII). Even so, a few years later, in 1405, the inhabitants of Martina had to be reprimanded for grazing their animals in just these coastlands during the olive harvest (document XXII).

Where there was no, or insufficient, village land, grazing could be rented by individuals. The customary laws of Corsica record a number of ways in which arrangements were made by individuals (Chiva, 1963). Some arrangements covered the entire year, others concerned only one season. For instance, two or three shepherds could form an association that would last from October to May. According to this, the associates placed their animals and made their purchase of pasture in common and divided the profits at separation. In another form, agreements bound the shepherd and the entire village community. Yet another series of arrangements were made between individual flock owners and the pasture owner. On the mainland, in Romagna, the large number of contracts of *soccida* and *colatico* in the archives reflects the difficulties of small landowners in securing satisfactory grazing for their animals during the fourteenth century (Larner, 1965, p. 124). A typical *soccida* would run like the one which records how, in October 1357, Piero Menghi of Gambelaria received three cows from Iacopo Barenci and agreed to give them pasture until they were fattened for market. In return, Iacopo promised to give Piero half the proceeds of sale, having deducted the value of the cattle. Under other arrangements, oxen could be leased for ploughing in return for payment in cash or kind. Similar contracts were drawn up for the provision of manure. Until quite recently in the Pyrenees, grazing livestock were to be grouped into a *tinguda* (300 head of animals) and each *tinguda* was to remain in, and to manure, the designated arable fields for three whole nights (Sorre, 1913, p. 433).

The only detailed account of the process of renting winter grazing comes from the Roman Campagna (Pullé, 1915). There used to be two sorts of contract governing the use of grass on this plain. There were contracts made for the duration of the season, with no time limit, and there were those in which the season was divided into ''winter'' (24th September to 24th June) and ''spring'' (15th March to 24th June) sections. Just before the end of the summer, one shepherd representing the community or the owner of the sheep would leave the high Apennine pastures for the lowland. He headed for wherever he expected, from previous experience, to find suitable grazing. There he inspected the ground and discussed terms with the proprietor of the land. Then, on behalf of the owner of the sheep, he would pay for a bailiff or *vergaro*, who would be in charge of all men and animals that came within the range of a particular *masseria*. The landowner agreed to provide all the materials (such as chestnut pales and reeds) needed in the construction of *capanne*, the shepherds' huts. For as long as he remained in the lowlands, each shepherd cared for about a hundred animals and lived in the *capanne*. When at the end of the season he left for the high Apennines, the chestnut pales of the *capanne* remained ready for the flocks of the following season.

Similar arrangements must have been made in Roman times. Cato offered advice on the terms pasture was to be rented at. According to him, the season ran from the first of September to ''when the pear trees begin to bloom'' on dry meadows or to the start of irrigation, as appropriate (CLX.IX). On the whole, however, the Roman agronomists were more preoccupied with advising on alternative sources of feed for livestock than with discussing the qualities of pasture land beyond the farm. Again, it is clear that no effort was to be spared to feed all the animals as far as possible from local resources. With this in mind Cato duly warns his readers to ''remember how long the winter lasts'' in upland districts (30). The other agronomists emphasized how different animals not only had different requirements but how they could be more or less demanding as regards feed. Most valuable, they said, were the plough oxen. These should receive the best hay during spring ploughing then, in the course of the year, they would receive lupins, beech nuts, clover, beans and vetch (Columella, VI. 3). Sheep "must be supplied with an abundance of every kind of food . . ." and Columella goes on to mention grassy fallow, new growth on arable after the first autumn ploughing and meadow grass as desirable (VII.3.9). For those farmers with poor resources there were advantages in keeping an ass as a beast of burden; according to Columella, "it can be kept even in a country which lacks pasturage, since it is content with very little fodder of any sort of quality, feeding on leaves and the thorns of briar-bushes, or a bundle of briar-bushes, or a bundle of twigs . . . indeed it actually thrives on chaff . . ." (VII.1). An important fodder resource in Mediterranean Europe has been the use of tree leaves. Cato advocated the use of oak and fig leaves as well as elm and poplar. Poplars were to be planted around the borders of the farm, "so that you may have leaves for the sheep and the cattle" (VI.3). The leaves were to be stored slightly moist. Columella gives details about the qualities of the different leaves (VI.3.7) and Pliny gives instructions about the raising of elms from seed (XVII.76). Archaeological evidence from other parts of Europe suggest that the practice of using leaves was no innovation of Roman farmers but had been common practice since the Neolithic.

The stall feeding of cattle has also been, and still is, standard practice in Mediterranean Europe. In the Pyrenees, the onset of winter saw animals brought down to the farmstead (Chevalier, 1956, p. 425ff). The cattle were permanently stalled in low-doored, low-roofed byres that would not be cleared out until vacated in spring. Sheep, however, were taken out daily unless snow was actually covering the ground. Straw and hay formed the basic feed for all these animals. The fear of shortage was a perennial and urgent problem and a fodder famine a constant threat. This could result from poor growth of grass in the preceding autumn occasioning premature use of the home pastures or of fodder reserves, or it could result from a protracted winter or a hard spring. Normally, an attempt was made in the autumn to anticipate the situation and to sell surplus animals but misfortune or a late spring would see the peasants emptying their own straw mattresses and tearing the thatch from the roof in order to keep their stock from actual death by starvation. In the hottest or most arid districts, the season of shortage is in summer rather than winter. In the essentially Mediterranean environment of the Madeiran archipelago, where there were 1·6 head of cattle per declared owner in 1955, not a cow was to be seen out of doors during those months unless it was to browse roadside verges in the more humid areas in the cool of the evening (Delano

J.

Smith, 1968, p. 21). Instead, huge bundles of grass, leaves and bracken are gathered in the mountains and carried down for the animals.

The growing of crops specifically as animal feed was also a recognized if not a common practice in classical times. Only farmers with possibilities for irrigation or with sufficient land to set some aside for this purpose could do this. For them, Columella recommended lucerne as the best crop, followed by the various vetches or a mixture of barley and oats (11.10.24). Lucerne was favoured for several reasons but not least because a single plant was expected to last up to 10 years and to give from four to six harvestings each year, all the time improving the soil and fattening the cattle. However, it requires copious watering. In subsequent centuries, the range of fodder crops remain much the same. In 1478 it was reported that the Count of Potenza had been sowing *ferrayna* (*ferrana*, the same as Varro's *farrago*, a mixture of barley, vetch and legumes for green feed (I.31.5)) on his land at Fiorentino (Foggia) as a feed for his plough animals (Spola, 1953, document 5). In a nineteenth-century agricultural treatise, published in Naples, the chapter on "Artificial Meadows" deals with: various fodder cereals; irrigated lucerne; *lupinella*; Spanish *lupinella* (Sulla); various clovers; *poa* or *fienarola*; and *cavalo* (Molinari, 1880). Even in so intensively farmed a district as the Murcian *huerta*, a small portion of the land used to be reserved for fodder crops. Fortunately a small plot is quite sufficient for such a prolific crop. For lucerne, Columella suggested a plot 10 feet wide by 50 feet long for the average small estate farm.

The fact that there was a problem at all in supplying sufficient feed or grazing for a relatively modest number of animals all the year around results only partially from climatic conditions in Mediterranean Europe. It is due much more to the desire of each farmer to keep his animals on his own fields, or at least within his village's territory. For the vast majority of farmers, animals and crops were integral and complementary elements of a mixed farming system, designed to provide them with little more than their basic needs. Their flocks and herds were in preference sedentary, though local circumstances might impose some movement from pasture to pasture. If it had to go out of the local area, the movement might be referred to as reluctant transhumance. In the case of the graziers, the situation was quite different. The distinction that is insisted on here, that between the village or the arable landowners' flocks, reluctantly transhuming short distances, and those belonging to the graziers, transhuming over sometimes a hundred kilometres, is no mere academic point. The fact that claims made by local arable farmers against the transhumant flocks of the graziers were usually supported by the community (Admiralty, Spain, Vol. II, p. 186) underlines the validity of this distinction.

Pastoralism, Graziers and Transhumance

Few geographical situations have tended to be more misjudged than the nature and place of transhumance in Mediterranean Europe. Associated with a certain form of stock-raising, transhumance has been one of the dramatic characteristics of Mediterranean lands. But it is by no means a peculiarly Mediterranean phenomenon nor should its development be ascribed simply to the complementary possibilities of mountain and plain. The sort of stock-raising which gave rise to the attention-catching, large-scale type of transhumance was that of a highly specialized, capitalist activity, based on the socio-economic status of graziers, and that of a certain number of grazier-landowners.

The word ''pastoralism'' is generally vaguely used. It can be intended to refer to the grazing of animals, the grazeable state of the land, the operations of milking, cheese-making and wool marketing, or even to diet. Somewhere in her writings, the economic historian Joan Thirsk has defined pastoralism as ''an agricultural system where there is an equal or greater emphasis on livestock as a form of income as on arable'' but other authorities would narrow the definition much further, insisting that the word be applied only to a livestock farming system in which arable activities are negligible or non-existent. It could therefore be argued that the term is better avoided altogether and that ''grazier'' should be used where appropriate. This term therefore would include both those individuals who themselves owned no or little land and possibly few animals and yet had control over herds and flocks numbering thousands of head (such as the men of St Christol), and those landlords with extensive estates who chose to use that part of their land not needed for subsistence for ranching rather than arable.

The hallmark of a grazier was that he held stock far in excess of the carrying capacity (taking winter and summer together) of his land. His way of life was very different from that of the peasant farmer. It involved deliberate risks, such as the assumption that adequate pasture would be rentable and that the rent asked would be payable. It involved a different time-scale, in so far as the duration of the season away from home was concerned. It involved delegation of the actual work to professional or salaried shepherds. These may have included, as Le Roy Ladurie found in the case of thirteenth-century Montaillou (Arriège), itinerants, who were often criminal suspects or even unstable "drop outs" (1975, p. 108). It involved great dependence on the external market and notably on the international price of wool. The scale of the grazier's operations can be measured not only by the numbers of animals but also by the distances involved. The transhumance journey itself can be measured as a linear distance (one or several hundreds of kilometres separated summer and winter pastures) or as a temporal distance (journeys took several weeks or even a couple of months). It may also be measured according to the degree of political involvement incurred; whole states were crossed and "foreign" ones entered in Spain and Peninsular Italy for example. Only when such a scale is involved can the assertion that transhumance in Mediterranean Europe was "born of the complementarity of mountain and plain" (Isnard, 1973, p. 21) have any real meaning.

The grazier's interest in livestock was selected with a view to financial gain. In general, the non-peasant farmer was free to select his farming preference. Most commonly this was for cereals, because as Duby put it (1968, p. 273), that was the tradition (by the Middle Ages anyway), or for viticulture because of the special affection Mediterranean farmers have for the vine. But there is yet another Latin tradition. It was not only the agronomist Cato who held the view that the best way to get rich was to be a competent grazier and the second best way was to be a moderately good grazier. Columella, who was reporting this view (VI, preface 4) obviously endorsed it. Both recognized that the financial returns from extensive cereal farming were often unattractive and that the price of wool offered a better prospect. Then there was often the labour question, when labour for arable farming was in short supply. The estate owner might hold land that could not be used for arable (mountain pastures, marshy plains). Or, simply and all other things being equal, it may have been that the livestock side of farming was the most appealing. On this, Varro had a good deal to say. He pointed out that "of all the ancients the most illustrious were all shepherds" (II.1.16). He went on to point out that Greek and early Latin poets praised men who were "rich in flocks", "rich in sheep" or "rich in herds".

The number of animals in a flock owned or controlled by a grazier could run into thousands. It is true that the 257 000 sheep reputedly owned (Pliny, 33.135) (amongst other livestock and probably divided amongst several estates) by the Roman freeman C. Caecilius Isidorus would have been considered extraordinary at the time. But in 1301, during a sale of animals belonging to the unfortunate Saracen community at Lucera, one individual bought 1024 fat cattle and nearly 4000 sheep; two brothers (one a Knight Hospitaller) bought 1216 cattle and calves; a fourth individual (Nicola Cagneto di Barola) bought a modest 1300 sheep (Egidi, 1917, document 638–639). In the same district a century later, a certain Lillius de Civitella was answering for the 2600 sheep and goats he had pastured only at Bonassissa (near Salpi); the vassals of the Count of Fundi had 15 000 sheep near Trani; Count Camerlingo had 11 000 at Montedorisi; one Stefano de Finabellis of Foggia had 4500 animals; and Elizabeth de Anguillaria, duchess of Ascoli, had an illicit 1000 sheep in the territory of the now-deserted *Corleto* (Spola, 1953; various documents, all from the 1470s).

Whether flocks were large or small, the animals have to be kept under control at all times and their movements carefully ordered. Village codes reflect this concern at lowest level. But the passage of animals across the length or breadth of a country required legislation from a higher authority and the national codes supplied this. In these, grazing matters were prominent. The fourth century Theodosian code in Italy contained warnings such as ''we [i.e. the Emperor] learn that . . . animals from our private estates are being kept from the pastures of certain places'' (23rd September, A.D. 365; in Parr, 1952). In Spain, all four of the titles of the Visigothic *Fuero Juzgo* that deal at all directly with agriculture refer to the problem of damage to crops by animals or to the animals themselves (in Kleffens, 1968). Again in Italy, out of a total of 388 titles in the edict of Lombard King Rothar, 77 concern agriculture and rural matters and of these 37 concern livestock and animals specifically (Drew, 1973; M.G.H. *Leges* IV). The same old problems were cropping up again in the same area in the thirteenth century. Frederick II's *Liber Augustalis* contained titles such as ''The restitution of damages inflicted by animals'' (title LVI (36)) or ''How the pledge of security should be given for animals in pasture'' (title LV (34)) (Powell, 1971). Many of these were no more than restatements, in the face of a growing transhumant sector of stipulations given in Lombard times (Dilcher, cited by Powell, 1971, p. 131fn).

Frederick II did not introduce commercial ranching, based on transhumance, in southern Italy in the thirteenth century. It already existed. He may or may not have encouraged the graziers' activities even while controlling them. Certainly there were other rulers, Roman and medieval, who appreciated the potential of their own gain from this form of farming.

Charles I of Anjou, for instance, introduced sheep from North Africa, for breeding in 1278 (Leonard, 1954, p. 86) and although it is nowhere so stated, these are very likely to have been of the merino breed. Crown or demesne land was rented to graziers and, most critical of all, taxes taken from almost every aspect of the ranching operations. Under the Romans, sheep were driven from Apulia into Samnium for summer and were there ''reported to the tax-collector, for fear of offending against the pasturing of unregistered flocks'' (Varro, II.1.16). Flocks so registered were permitted to be grazed on public land on payment of a *scriptum*. In the second half of the fifteenth century in Apulia, the tax rate per hundred head of sheep rose from 6 ducats to 8 and, in 1479, to a proposed 9 Venetian ducats (Spola, 1953).

Abuses apart, this sort of arrangement might be regarded as part of the normal grazier system. The movement of large numbers of animals over long distances has always involved the use of special trackways, resting places and transit pastures. It was only natural that a state sought to derive benefit from providing or permitting the necessary arrangements. It was only to the benefit of all too that the graziers should cooperate in controlling their animals in order to minimize damage to neighbouring crops and lands. The unusual aspect, it is now easy to see, was the institutionalization of these activities in the later Middle Ages. As our own times have demonstrated, institutionalization of an economic or social activity fossilizes it. So long as graziers remained free to act as individuals, the market demand for the product of their activities would have been the strongest influence on land use and on the extent of commercial ranching. For instance, when cereal prices, compared to wool prices, rose steeply between 1550 and 1650, a normal response might be a drop in the area under grass and conversion back to grain. However, in neither of the two countries notorious for the development of extremely powerful grazier institutions, Spain and the Neapolitan kingdom, did this happen. In order to protect his vested interests, the grazier's response to unfavourable wool prices was to run yet more sheep even though this meant more grassland was required at precisely the moment that the local population needed to increase their arable land. In Apulia there was some yielding up of crown grazing land for cultivation but it was of little long-term benefit and the villages in question were eventually abandoned (see below). Under institutionalized pastoralism the pressure was to advance the graziers' interests even if this would be at the expense of cultivators. In Spain under Ferdinand and Isabella, measures were taken to expand the area of pasture land while the attempts of other farmers to improve or to extend their arable were forbidden or hindered. Charles V found it particularly important to maintain his income since his entire policy seems to have been based on finance gained from the export of wool (Klein, 1920, p. 317ff). In short, it would not be too gross an exaggeration to suggest that the modern backwardness of southern Italy and central-south Spain owes much to economic stagnation resulting from the institutionalization of ranching in and after the Middle Ages.

The two grazier institutions in Mediterranean Europe in historic times were the *Mesta* in Castilian Spain and the *Dogana della Mene delle Pecore* in the Kingdom of Naples. The first had emerged by 1273 (Klein, 1920) and the latter was introduced into Italy by 1447 or 1468 (de Dominicis, 1781; Musto, 1964). The *Mesta* was officially disbanded in 1796, the Dogana not until 1806.

The creation of the *Mesta* in 1273 was the first step in the process of exploiting what Swinburne referring to Neapolitan Italy, was to call "one of the richest mines of wealth for the Crown" (1783, p. 143). Although many laws from earlier codes appear to have been incorporated into the *Mesta* charter, the intention was clearly, according to Klein, "to modify the ancient and widespread taxation of the herds" (p. 163). So, whereas early income from graziers had been merely in the form of fines and penalties, levied locally by each town's administration, the *Mesta* began to impose its own form of taxes and dues. The extension of large-scale grazing in Spain played a vital part in the Reconquest and explains the importance of major ecclesiastical establishments as graziers. From at first favouring, and then protecting, the activities of graziers in Spain, with their long-distance tranhumance, the crown turned to taking fiscal advantage and by 1568 it had its own appointees in *Mesta* offices. From the herdsman's point of view, what had been a source of employment for him and a source of income for the livestock owner, had now become an increasingly necessary source of revenue for government expenditure. The distinction always remained, however, between the local "sedentary" flocks and the *Mesta* animals. It may in fact have been a very ancient distinction, going back to Visigothic times. It is known that there was transhumance then though on what scale it is difficult to tell. Visigothic laws, though, allowed

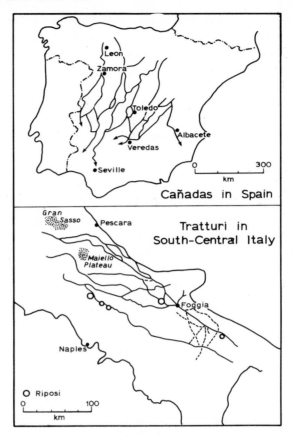

Fig. 32. *Outlines of major routes of transhumance in Spain and Italy*, under the *Mesta* and the *Dogana*, respectively (Atlante Nacional de Espana, 1965; Franciosa, 1951).

for the access of transhumant stock to unenclosed and waste land and these laws apparently survived the Moorish occupation (Smith, 1966, p. 438). The distinction was also expressed in the contempt of graziers, whose flocks were mainly of merino sheep, for the village flocks. These were made up of the native *churro* breed and were ''the object of scorn and abuse for the itinerant herdsmen'' (Klein, 1920, p. 7).

Less has been written, in English, about the Italian grazing institutions than about the Spanish *Mesta* so rather more will be said here. By the end of the fifteenth century there were three *Dogana* institutions in the Neapolitan kingdom, which was by that time ruled, significantly, by Spain.

There was the *Dogana di Napoli*, the *Dogana di Puglia* and the *Dogana di Calabria* (Galanti, 1788, Vol. II, p. 177ff). Only Molise and *Principato Ulterior* escaped organization by one of these. The Apulian institution included the provinces of Capitanata (now Foggia), Terra di Bari, Terra di Otranto and Basilicata. Its full title was *Dogana della Mene delle Pecore di Puglia*. It was created or given fiscal and substantial judicial power in, it is usually thought, 1447 or at the latest by 1468 (Dominicis, 1781; Galanti, 1788; Musto, 1964). At first the institution was based in the ancient town of Lucera but it was soon moved to the more centrally located village of Foggia. For this or other reasons Foggia was to become at about this time "the most opulent place in Puglia" (Swinburne, 1783, p. 139). Today it is the biggest city in northern Apulia. As in Spain, the *Dogana* was the result of deliberate crown policy. Alfonso I of the Neapolitan kingdom had sent an agent to treat with the graziers of the Abruzzi and the landowners of Apulia. The king undertook to supply merino stock from Spain, and to provide winter pasturage (from the demesne) for 7 months a year, drove roads (*tratturi*) that would be not less than 60 paces wide, freedom from royal tolls and very much more besides. He also undertook to compel "all barons and bodies corporate" on the route to furnish herbage. His agent purchased extra pasture or land henceforth to be used as pasture to augment the demesne lettings. In return, the Abruzzi shepherds agreed to bind themselves to come down each year to Apulia and to nowhere else; to submit to the jurisdiction of the *Dogana*; to observe the Dogana's arrangements for the parcelling of the grazings; to pay the penalties as set out by the *Dogana*; and to pay taxes on their own livestock, according to the *Dogana*'s rate.

The *Dogana* therefore acted for the king. It had its own hierarchy of officers and a tribunal for the observance of byelaws or *instruzione doganali*. Every grazing activity was given a price. Demesne and private land could be bought but it was more usual to rent it on payment of *fida*. By 1496 there are references to the different taxes payable for grazing, for watering and for overnight stops (*pascolare, adquare* and *pernoctare* rights). The animals themselves were taxed, as was their entrance and exit from scheduled grazing grounds and from the drove roads (*tratturi*). River crossings were taxed. By 1573, some 157 000 ducats were coming in annually. This rose to 450 000 in 1578 but was forced down by the hostility of the graziers (possibly also by high animal losses due to overstocking) and the *Dogana*'s takings in 1583 were only 241 000 ducats.

This variation in income is also a reminder of the vulnerability of the

J*

livestock to adverse weather conditions. In 1234, after a particularly hard winter on the Tavoliere, thousands of sheep died as a result of starvation and cold. Floods, not infrequent on the Tavoliere, also took a toll. Ranching could be no less unpredictable an activity than cereal farming. A ''bad year'' could mean a dry autumn, such as in 1766 when a *tramontane* wind so desiccated the grass that one-third of the animals were lost, or a heavy snow fall, such as that coming between the 20th and the 28th January 1745 which resulted in the loss of half the Tavoliere livestock. For the graziers as well as for arable farmers, a ''good year'' meant a winter of well-distributed rainfall and therefore luxuriant spring growth.

Under the Aragonese administration of the Neapolitan kingdom, the numbers of animals registered with the *Dogana* amounted to between two and three-and-a-half million. In 1536 and 1541 numbers were down to two and one million, respectively. The peak was reached in 1684 when there were over five-and-a-half million registered animals. The drop in numbers in the third decade of the sixteenth century coincided with a phase of high grain prices and acute shortage of arable land. There was pressure from the peasantry and arable estate farmers alike for more land to plough. To a limited, and usually temporary, extent the balance was redressed. The *Dogana* did attempt to establish a minimum arable acreage and to increase the allowance of grazing earmarked for plough teams, the *mezzana*. In this way, for instance, seven *carrara* of land were taken from grazing at Casalnuovo, San Andrea and La Guardiola and added to the ten *carrara* already in cultivation at Motta della Regina. The move came too late, or was insufficient, to save this latter community, however, and the village was soon abandoned (the others were already deserted). The temporary ''generosity'' of the *Dogana* at this time belied their more usual attitude. Under *Dogana* regulations, arable farmers were entitled to compensation for losses and damage from trespassing animals but there seems to have been very little chance of actual redress. Trees were not tolerated on or near the grazing lands because, it was held, their roots absorbed too much moisture from the soil and so reduced the grass cover.[18] Whole forests were cut down by or as a result of *Dogana* pressures. Pasture for plough animals was restricted to *mezzana* enclosures, all too frequently overstocked and inadequate. Farmers were not even free to work out the details of their operations. The duration of fallow, for instance, was set by the *Dogana* to a minimum of 3 years, so that the graziers could have the full advantage of weed growth.

The land that came under the jurisdiction of the *Dogana* was organized

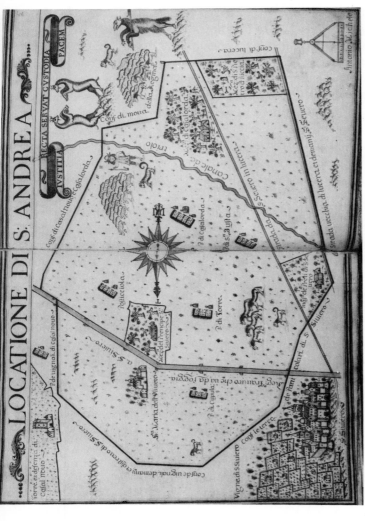

Plate 10. *Organized ranching.* One of the *locationi* in northern Apulia that came under the jurisdiction of the *Dogana della Mene delle Pecore* of Foggia. San Andrea and Casalorda were both taxable villages in 1301, the former on a site occupied since Roman times and earlier. In the neighbouring *locatione* (top left) Casalnuovo was likewise deserted in 1635 (only its tower remains today) but had been a sizeable nucleation since pre-Roman times. Compare the pattern of closes immediately outside the walled town of San Severo with those of the abandoned site of San Lorenzo (Fig. 25). The cartographer manages to say a good deal about the *Dogana* while obeying instructions to survey the *locationi* and map their boundaries, *poste, mezzane,* the *tratturi* and all other matters relating to the *Dogana* (reproduced by courtesy of the Archivio di Stato, Foggia and Mrs P. Bradford).

by Alfonso I into units, each a *locatione*. In 1483 there were 43 of these; by 1548 there were 77, giving a total of 15 500 *carra* (just under 4000 km²). Most of the additional land had come from the territories of declining or deserted villages (such as Casalnuovo, Salpi, San Lorenzo, Corleto) (Plate 10). Demesne land, administered by the *Dogana* on behalf of the crown, was classified as "general". These general *locationi* were by far the most extensive. The private *locationi* were about equal in number but added up to a smaller total area. They were the property of the most rich or powerful of the local landlords or represented land belonging to a few wealthy citizens who owned no animals themselves but who were content to let the land as an investment. The *locationi* were demarcated on the ground by lines of white stones, as are some of the Apennine pastures today, and marked by inscribed pillars. The *locationi* of Apulia were surveyed in 1548, in 1687 and again in 1735. The maps from the last two surveys have survived and are in the Foggia archives (*Dogana*, 1686; 1735–1760).

All movement of livestock on the Tavoliere or across it was closely controlled by the *Dogana*. Entrance was by one of eight *passi*, each corresponding to a major drove road (*tratturo*) in the network running the length of the Apennines down to the heel of the peninsula. Officially only a fixed number of animals was allowed into each *locatione* as a measure against overstocking but this measure may have been disregarded, as in 1603 there were 6425 animals at Salpi and, only 5 years later, 7300. Each spring, in April or May, all the Tavoliere flocks, together with those which had come up from further south, were obliged to pass through the city of Foggia for registration and for payment of outstanding dues. Thence, accompanied by their guardians and by mounted *Dogana* officials, they would set out along the broad *tratturo* towards the Abruzzi and the Gran Sasso pastures. Most of the guardians were Abruzzi shepherds, of whom it was said that they preferred to sleep in the open rather than in huts (*poste*) similar to the *capanne* of the Roman Campagna. There must have been large numbers of *poste* on the Tavoliere even so. At first these were roughly built, using materials that were to hand, such as marsh reeds or the giant fennel that is so typical of the Tavoliere. Later each *posta* was replaced by a permanent dry-stone building, often constructed from blocks of sub-soil calcrete. The focal point of each *locatione* was a single *masseria di pecore*, with its immense complex of stabling, pens, residential quarters, cheese-making rooms and storage facilities.

The role of the central state and the crucial issue of state finances emerge clearly as the key factors in the institutionalization of Spanish and Italian ranching in the medieval and post-medieval period. The absence of a strong central authority in southern France and in non-papal northern Italy may explain why comparable institutions failed to be created there. There were large numbers of graziers in Provence and Languedoc (Sclaffert, 1959; Rouquette, 1913). The pattern was to take the flocks into the Alps, the Pyrenees or onto the Central Massif for summer grazing (Fig. 33). There was an organization based in Arles but its major concern was to safeguard the merino pedigree of associated flocks (Orange and Amalbert, 1924). If there were formalized rights, they were community rights such as the *Esplèche d'Arles* (George, 1935, p. 358; Tardieu, 1860). Local rulers were certainly as interested in the financial aspects of transhumance here as elsewhere. Early in the thirteenth century, Count Raymond-Berenger V of Provence imposed a tax on animals that came down to pass the winter on the lowlands and Charles V of Anjou did likewise. But there was never a comparable institution in southern France to the *Mesta* or the *Dogana*. This perhaps can be explained by the lack of a single big enough and strong enough central authority in a position to take advantage of the graziers' activities. The region was politically fragmented, Languedoc remaining independent of France until 1229 and Provence until 1486, and within each area there was no single local power. By the time central authority was imposed, this was too late and, possibly, too distant.

There was undoubtedly a grazier class of farmers and there was certainly long-distance transhumance in Roman times in Italy. Varro himself owned "large stocks of cattle, sheep in Apulia and horses in the district of Reate" and knew very well that "the same localities are not equally suited in summer and winter to the pasturing of all species which is why flocks of sheep are driven all the way from Apulia into Samnium for summering" (II Introduction; I.1.16). His own flocks "wintered in Apulia and summered in the mountains around Reate, these two widely separated ranges being connected by public cattle-trails, as a pair of buckets by their yoke" (11.2.10).[19] There are a number of references to *latifundia* that may have been used for ranching and to individual graziers. One, for instance, alludes to "all those hills and farms in Apulia, all those pasture lands that tire out the kites" (Juvenal, *Satires* X.54). An indication from the same author that land was relatively cheap in Apulia comes when he mentions a price "for which you might buy a whole estate in some province, or a still larger one in Apulia" (IV.25–30). Parts of Apulia were famed, like the Argolis, for horse-raising. According to Livy, Hannibal was able to

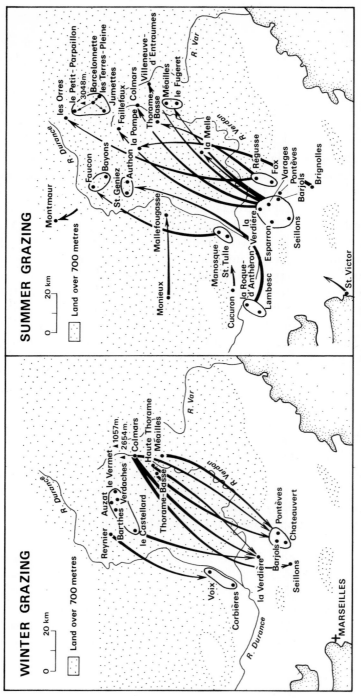

Fig. 33. *Movement of livestock in Provence* in the fifteenth century (from Sclaffert, 1951). The upland villages send their livestock down onto the lowlands of Basse-Provence to escape the winter cold and shortage of pasture. The animals would have travelled together with those belonging to owners resident in the lowland villages who had spent the summer on the mountain grazings. Thus a single transhumant flock masks the operation of at least two possibly quite different farming systems.

WINTER GRAZING

0   20 km

☐ Land over 700 metres

Reynier
Auzat   le Vermet ▲1057m.
Barthes Verdaches   2654m.
le Castellard   Colmars
Thorame-Basse   Haute Thorame
                 Méailles
R. Durance
Voix
Corbières   la Verdière   Barjols
Seillons   Pontèves
                            Chateauvert
R. Verdon
R. Var
✝ MARSEILLES
R. Durance

SUMMER GRAZING

0   20 km

☐ Land over 700 metres

Montmaur
R. Durance
les Orres
le Petit - Parpaillon
3048m.   Barcelonnette
          les Terres - Pleine
Jumettes
Faucon   Faillefaux
Bayons   la Pompe   Colmars
St. Geniez   Authon   Thorame-   Villeneuve-
                        Basse   d'Entraumes
Mallefougasse   Méailles   le Fugeret
Monieux   la Melle   R. Var
         la Roque-   R. Verdon
Manosque d'Anthéron Verdière Régusse
St. Tulle   Esparron   Fox
Cucuron   Lambesc   Varages   Pontèves
                               Barjols
                      Seillons   Brignolles
St. Victor

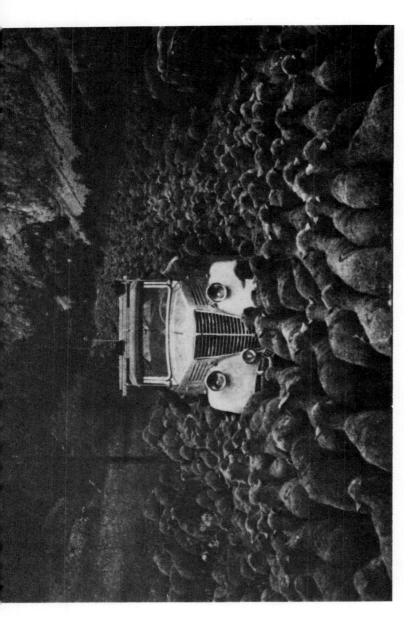

Plate 11. *Transhumance* in France earlier this century. Not surprisingly, one of the factors contributing to the decline of the traditional style of transhumance has been the advent of the motor car and the very great increase in road traffic. Some animals are still moved by lorry or by rail but this method is disliked by shepherds as the sheep no longer have time to adjust to changes in herbage and climate.

plunder the forests of Apulia from his winter base at Salapia (Salpi, Foggia) and to drive off as booty "herds of horses, about 4000 of which were distributed amongst the cavalry to be broken" (XXIV, 20.15). Large-scale grazing was the subject of Seneca's disapproving comment on the "huge herds and flocks that need whole provinces and kingdoms to provide them with pasture" (*de Beneficiis* VII.10). Ranching therefore certainly existed in Roman times. What is noticeable for its absence is any hint of, still less evidence for, institutionalization of the graziers' activities in the manner of the later *Dogana*.

At least by the first century A.D., transhumance and large-scale grazing were well organized. Apart from Varro's explicit comments, there is the famous inscription on one of the gates at *Saepinum* (Altilia, Campobosso).[20] It was right through the middle of this town that the drove road linking Foggia and Benevento with Isernia in the Abruzzi passed. The inscription reveals that livestock owners had complained that their employees (the shepherds and guardians of their transhumant flocks) were being "harassed" by the local population and, most specifically, that the Roman government was interested in the protection of the transhumant livestock. The Roman government, in other words, was as anxious to safeguard its income from a lucrative activity as its medieval successors. On the other hand, such an interest reflects no more than the operation of an efficient government department. The Roman tax-collectors, too, would have been no more than civil servants. In short, there is nothing to suggest the existence in Roman times of a semi-autonomous all-controlling institution comparable to the later ones.

One interesting sidelight to the phenomenon of large-scale commercial livestock farming is the involvement of the urban centres in what might seem by definition to be a rural activity usually associated with the most remote and distant parts of the countryside. Yet the graziers were very closely linked to the urban centres. They were controlled from the towns and this control was not just a matter of issuing directives; it had its physical counterpart. Their animals were counted here for tax purposes and their presence in the urban centres was very real, as at *Saepinum*. Then, the entire marketing system emanated from the towns. This is revealed in the origins of the *Mesta* itself; in calling the shepherds of Castile into a single association in 1273, Alfonso was merely re-organizing and manipulating a pattern based on existing urban charters (Klein, 1920, p. 79). The graziers themselves were townsmen either by origin or by preference, particularly by the seventeenth and eighteenth centuries. The

Plate 12. The *cardo decumanus* at *Saepinum* today; sheep still pass along this road through the heart of the Roman town, though in fewer numbers than in Roman or late medieval times, when the *tratturo* was in full use.

objectives of their profiteering would have been found in the towns rather than, as is evident from the absence of embellishment of or investment in their estates, in the countryside.

The conflict that is so often set out in textbooks or glamorized in literature as characterizing relationships between the livestock and the arable farmer must therefore for many cases be regarded as exaggerated. By and large, all farming systems in Mediterranean Europe have been part of a single spectrum, though it is true that the speculative graziers had little in common, as farmers, even with their estate-based livestock-raising neighbours. The latter, however, resident in towns and cities, would not have stood out so much from the other major landowners, those who gained their riches from viticulture, olive growing or cereals. It was only when their livestock was on the move over long distances and in large numbers, or when these landowners attempted to restrict arable land use, that a conflict of interests might have arisen between rancher and farmer.

The opposition between districts said to be ''pastoral'' and those said to be arable also needs qualification. One of the most deterministically "pastoral" regions of Mediterranean Europe is supposed to be the mountainous interior of the island of Sardinia. Yet even the highest village in the island (Fonni, at 900 m) had its arable land. At the beginning of the nineteenth century, one third of the 744 families resident in Fonni were described as arable farmers, growing mainly barley and beans (Casalis, 1833). Besides this, it is true that the livestock statistics for Fonni make impressive reading: 1200 cattle and oxen (of which at least half were free-ranging); 700 horses and colts; 42 000 sheep and goats; and 2350 pigs. When these animals are apportioned amongst the families, this works out as an average of 1½ cattle or oxen, less than 1 horse, 52 sheep, 3 goats and 3 pigs for each family. At Orgosolo, not far away, the floors and lower slopes of the broad valleys of the district are intensively cultivated even today. Admittedly, in the nineteenth century, the arable was the concern of the women of the village and so designated a socially inferior activity. Nevertheless, the aim at Orgosolo, as at Fonni, had to be self-sufficiency through mixed farming. Until the arrival of Pisan and Genoese traders in the Middle Ages, the local economy of these mountain villages would have been even more "closed" than that of any of the villages at lower altitudes: they had, for example, lain well beyond the trading range of the lowland and coastal centres of Roman and Punic times (Fig. 31). And obviously, the physical nature of the environment cannot be wholly ignored. Adjustments were indeed made: animal fat, for instance, is still preferred to olive oil. The sale of cheeses, skins, blankets and bone or horn utensils is useful in assuring an adequate supply of cereals and other necessities. Status up here has to be judged by ownership of flocks and herds rather than by land held, for most of the land is worth very little. In this context it is not surprising that there is livestock rustling and expropriation of pasture. But the total situation reflects a *modus vivendi* which enabled the inhabitants of these Sardinian mountains to survive and their settlements to continue in existence. In an inhospitable environment, the margin between survival and non-survival is particularly narrow. Reaction to anything seen as a threat to survival might be expected to be intolerant and acrimonious. And so it has been: during the sixteenth century there were apparently 1000 murders a year in an island whose total population numbered no more than 500 000 (King, 1972).

Writers have been quick to associate banditry, in Sardinia or elsewhere, with what they see as a traditional and deep-seated enmity between "pastoralist" and arable farmer. Not only is the dichotomy a false one, even in the case of Sardinia where each mountain commune had its share of arable land, but there are other factors to take into consideration. La Marmora, writing not very long after the event, insisted that the conflict between shepherds and cultivators was due to the government's edict of 1806 which permitted landowners to enclose their holdings, even those in the open fields (1839, p. 389). Insufficient attention had been paid to local usage and to openfield traditions and the new divisions, marked by walls, were often run right across grazing land regarded by the various communities as traditionally theirs or at least available to them by rights of usage (Cagnetta, 1975, p. 138).

The process of enclosure was by no means new in the nineteenth century. There had been government action in 1771; enclosure of land for one reason or another had been common enough since the fifteenth century (Le Lannou, 1941, pp. 133ff, 157ff). Under the best circumstances, the relationship between the individual and the group is potentially antagonizing to one side or the other. In districts as economically precarious as mountainous Barbagia, new pressures that threaten subsistence have an exaggerated significance. Even without enclosure problems, the relationship in Sardinia between the local population and authority had been particularly unhappy. The effective introduction of feudalism in 1326 with the establishment of the Spanish government ushered in a long period of general and sometimes severe economic decline. This is attributable to the poor behaviour of the new fief-holders (Putzulu, 1967; Meloni, 1972). Subsequent periods of difficulty can be associated with financial and economic crises in Spain rather than with matters strictly insular. In short, it would have been always the mountain communities, those with exceptionally large numbers of livestock and discouragingly difficult arable land, that were the most vulnerable to any political or social harassment that had an economic edge and, not surprisingly, the most volatile in their reactions to it.

Together with the banditry of Sardinian, or other, shepherds, the grazier system of farming in Mediterranean Europe has been particularly subject to misunderstanding by geographers, historians and archaeologists alike. It is hoped that enough has been said here to set the graziers, together with their transhumant animals, apart from all the other farmers of the region. Another fundamental distinction introduced here is that between *laissez-faire* ranching and the institutionalized grazier system which operated in specific parts of Italy and Spain within well-defined dates in the later historic period. Finally, although a number of farming systems have been identified for the entire historic period, in not a single case would it be true to say that the physical condition of the land was ever the determining factor. At any level, a farming system is in the last analysis an economic phenomenon and only in part an ecological one. What this seems to have meant in Mediterranean Europe is that man has been primarily responsible for his own way of life, in the past as in the present.

8
Prehistoric Farming

The last 2000 years have seen little real change in the ways in which life was lived and livelihoods were made in Mediterranean Europe. In the preceding chapters it was found that the same range of farming systems, the same ranking of society, the same preoccupation with agriculture as virtually the sole basis of personal and national wealth characterized the Roman and medieval periods and the modern period prior to the major changes of the twentieth century. There have always been, for instance, peasants of some sort; there have always been individuals who were richer or poorer, more or less successful amongst the landowning classes as well as in the peasantry. What was liable to change was not the nature of the individual economic systems or social groupings but their relative importance within any one district from period to period. This sort of change is part of continuity. The continuity of the Mediterranean "way of life" since early Roman times has therefore been confirmed. The question now arises as to whether this continuity dates from the establishment of farming in the early Neolithic or from some time later.

For the prehistoric period, the problem concerns not only the amount of evidence for the geographical past but very particularly its nature. For the historic period, evidence comes from the archives, from literature, from study or even observation of analogous situations, and from archaeological data. For the prehistoric period, only the latter is available. If analogy is used, it usually involves a match of situations separated by immensely long periods of time; the dangers of drawing at random on nineteenth- and twentieth-century versions of "traditional" practice to illuminate activities in the sixth or seventh millennium B.C.. need no stressing. This data problem means that two basic assumptions have to be made from the outset if the argument is not to be abruptly halted at this point. The first is that human capacity, mental and physical, has been of the

257

same order since (at the very least) the Neolithic. The second is that man's basic requirements for survival have also remained essentially the same. The prehistoric farmer, it is assumed, was as concerned as his historic counterpart with providing first and foremost shelter and a varied diet based on animal and vegetable foodstuffs for himself and his dependents. It is not therefore the range of these requirements—precisely those of the model described earlier—that have changed since the Neolithic. The change has been in the means of producing them. Archaeological evidence shows that techniques and equipment changed a great deal over the prehistoric period alone. But archaeology has no direct record of the operational aspects of the economy or of farming systems, any more than it has of patterns of thinking or of religious beliefs. Interpretation of prehistoric farming evidence, therefore, has to lean entirely on historical analogy. At least, it can now be said, the available model is known to be valid for the very respectable time span of 2500 years. It is also known that there is no evidence at all that the model, or any significant part of it, was a novelty at the start of the Roman period. With a mind that is no less open and cautious but also thus encouraged, the argument can proceed from the historical to the prehistorical period.

Territory

Until very recently, a rural community's livelihood normally came mostly from the land immediately around it, its territory. For the historic period it was observed that there can be a good deal of variety in, first, the form of this territory and, second, in its internal organization. It was noted, too, that these aspects are explained by reference not so much to physical as to economic factors and to such matters as convenience of access. That prehistorians have recognized that these elementary economic relationships are not without relevance for the prehistoric period has been vigorously demonstrated in discussions of the territorial concept (Higgs and Vita-Finzi, 1972; Jarman, 1972; Jarman and Webley, 1975; Barker, 1975; Jarman, 1976). Rather less attention, though, has been paid to the factors involved and to the way in which these actually operate. For example, out of a score of papers dealing with settlement location at a major London conference, only five gave top emphasis to economic factors (Ucko et al., 1972; commented on by Willey, 1973, p. 273). The others focused on political reasons (including defence and administration) without showing that these could not begin to operate until the economic basis of settlement had been assured either from its territory or by alternative arrangements.

Inattention to process and to basic economic principles might lead to a mechanical approach to prehistoric land use. An approach advocated in the existing literature is to select an appropriate territorial radius, to centre this on a prehistoric site, and to describe certain aspects of the landscape found therein. Instructions for such "site catchment analysis", as it has been termed, have been published (Higgs, 1975, appendix A). The researcher is told to attempt a map of "potential productivity" but not told what this is. He is merely directed to observe present farming and environment. At worst, the exercise would result in a catalogue of modern pedological and agricultural data which, in the long run, may or may not have much to do with the site's *palaeo*economy. What the researcher needs is a clear directive that physical conditions need not be quite the same today as in the prehistoric period in question (as the final part of this book attempts to demonstrate), that farming techniques quite certainly have altered and, above all, that his particular observations are of little value unless carefully fitted into what is known as the total agricultural environment (see below) and into the appropriate farming system.

It is obvious that the interpretation of prehistoric farming evidence or the analysis of prehistoric site selection has to start from a reconstruction of physical conditions as they were at that time. What is perhaps less obvious is that far more real evidence and hard facts concerning the palaeoenvironment can be extracted from the ground than concerning human activity. The empirical study of palaeoenvironments in relation to the Neolithic and later prehistoric periods in Mediterranean Europe is, however, still in its infancy. What is clear from studies so far made is that the degree or nature of difference between the prehistoric and the present environment need not be great or dramatic to be of significance from the farmer's point of view. The farmer, after all, is immediately concerned with soil conditions, first and foremost, and then with micro-climate; that is the scale of the environment in which his crops grow. Oddly, perhaps, the greatest misunderstandings about the former condition of the land within the territories of prehistoric settlements have concerned the type of terrain most liable to physical change; limestone hills and plateaux (prone to soil erosion) and low-lying coastlands (prone to flooding and siltation). So without some evidence for past soil conditions, the assertion that a Neolithic population living in a limestone area was "unlikely to have been concerned to an important degree with arable exploitation" or that it was composed of "pastoralists" (Jarman and Webley, 1975; Louis, 1948) has little foundation.

Then there is the question of changes in the agricultural techniques, crop strains and farm implements which would have had bearing on the output of the prehistoric territory. In north-western Europe, the adoption of the asymmetrical *carruca* plough instead of the symmetrical *ard*, with its very different capabilities, is probably critical to the understanding of early settlement distributions and terrain potential. In Mediterranean Europe, however, the question of technical change has on the whole less urgency. There was much less change in farming tools and practice in the south even up to the middle of the twentieth century, certainly up to the nineteenth century, than further north. Nineteenth-century agricultural treatises read almost identically to the Roman (see White, 1970, for the latter, and Molinari, 1880, as an example of the former).

There is very little evidence of farm equipment from the prehistoric period. Such fragments of farm tools as have survived tend to be dated no earlier than the last centuries of the second millennium B.C. They show no significant deviation from equipment used in Roman times or more recently. Two certain and one possible Bronze Age ploughs are known from north Italy. One, found by Battaglia at Ledro (Trentino), is illustrated by Barfield (1971) and is reproduced here in Fig. 24. They all concern, or purport to concern, ploughs of the *ard* type. They may seem, as they do to another prehistorian, "incredibly flimsy" but they are in fact not at all different from a great many of the *ard* ploughs currently in use around the world or in many districts of Mediterranean Europe (see Haudricourt and Delamarre, 1955, and articles in *Tools and Tillage*, 1968ff). The lack of prehistoric ploughs may be an accident of survival or it may reflect on the fact that by no means all cultivation, even of cereal fields, has depended on the plough. Various forms of digging sticks or breast ploughs are known in other circumstances and some indeed have been suggested in late Neolithic contexts in Mediterranean Europe (Courtin, 1970, p. 12; Courtin *et al.*, 1976, p. 172ff). In Roman times a wide range of other hand tools (hoes and mattocks) was ubiquitous in Mediterranean Europe. For the smaller fields and higher terraces these are still the only suitable equipment for breaking up the soil and creating a suitable tilth for seeding. Even for farmers with large fields and easier gradients it is no foregone conclusion that an animal-drawn plough would have been used. The fundamental consideration is not the availability of the technology but the economics involved in its adoption. Most critical is the cost of feeding the animal that is to draw the plough. In modern situations it is well known that a minimum agricultural output has to be achieved before the farmer finds it worth his while to employ animal labour (Clark and Haswell, 1966, pp. 33, 53ff). So again the question of the farmer's status is relevant. However, many who cannot really justify the expense in animal terms may decide to acquire an animal-drawn plough in order to alleviate a severe seasonal congestion of the work load. They have to feed the animal as best they can. If they fail, instances of the employ of human traction are not unknown (Le Roy Ladurie, 1966, p. 78).

There must have been certain times in the prehistoric period when a technical change of sufficient importance to lead to a re-assessment of soil fertility in the territory, or to affect its "potential productivity" did occur. For instance, *ard* ploughs can be fitted with wheels to help in the ploughing of heavier land and there is evidence for this having been done in Roman times (Pliny, 18.172; White, 1967b, pp. 141–142). [21] Then there have been immense improvements in crop strains, affecting their yield, resistance to climatic variation and to disease, and their tolerance of weeds. There have been changes in sowing and harvesting methods and in seed storage. One outstanding development would have been the introduction of irrigation. This might make a district "habitable" where it was not so considered before [22] or increase the productivity of an individual farm. It can alter not only the farmer's crop choice but also the arrangement of crops on his land.

Despite the general emphasis given to arable land and to its cultivation, it should always be borne in mind that it is by no means axiomatic that arable land was inevitably the most urgent consideration in the prehistoric farmer's assessment of terrain or in site selection. There have been historic circumstances when, for good reasons, it was the quality and abundance of pasture that was behind the decision to settle at that point. [23] Arable land, after all, is susceptible to considerable improvement through good cultivation; natural grazing is not. Finally, there are circumstances where non-agricultural matters have to be given priority (Chisholm, 1968, p. 106). In short, as it is impossible to read the minds of the prehistoric farmers as they made their decisions, so it is scarcely a useful exercise to attempt to predict a prehistoric settlement pattern on the basis of theory or on the present environment alone.

It may be assumed, however, that a variety of soil types would have been as advantageous to the prehistoric farmer and to his community in general as to his historic counterpart and that it resulted in a certain, broad pattern of land use. In this context, the "site catchment" approach is useful. This is based on Von Thünen's premise that the most economic location of a farm or farming community is as near to the centre of its resource area or territory as possible and that the territory should be as compact as circumstances permit, ideally circular or hexagonal (Von Thünen, 1829; Chisholm, 1968, Chapter I). With this in mind, a selected radius is used to define the prehistoric farm's (or village's) hypothetical territory (Higgs and Vita-Finzi, 1970; Delano Smith, 1972). Where, however, in reality the geological or topographical pattern has a strongly linear arrangement (as in the case of scarpland or basin and ridge relief) and settlement is dense, a compact circular territory is not the most convenient shape. The territory has to be distorted in shape (Hagget, 1965, p. 94; Orwin and Orwin, 1967, p. 26). Considering Neolithic settlement on the river-crossed lowland of northern Apulia, therefore, it was found that a linear territory for each site would be more appropriate (Delano Smith, 1978).

While a variety of soils or terrain types was undoubtedly normally desirable, the variety need not always have been great. On the Tavoliere of Foggia, in northern Apulia, relief is muted and geological contrasts are limited despite the valley network. The significant contrast in terms of economic potential is between the valley-bottom soils (alluvial) and those of the broad, level interfluves (various alkaline or siliceous loams and sandy soils, often underlain by massive forms of calcrete). In the case of the 70 settlement sites analysed, the majority were so located as to be able to take advantage of both types of land. In contrast to this limited range, soil variety is found to be much greater in regions of dissected relief or greater geological contrast. Of the 40 or so circular or near circular territories illustrated by Barker (1975) for Neolithic and Bronze Age sites in central Italy, only seven are found to contain fewer than three land-use classes while the majority contain four to five.

Farming Systems in the Prehistoric Period

The increased sophistication of archaeological techniques and new intensity of research is beginning to provide a factual basis for the rethinking of long-established interpretations and for the emergence of a whole new area of integrated study. One of the established models (Higgs and Jarman, 1969, p. 38) that now has little acceptance in the light of new evidence is the evolutionary or "ladder of progress" idea, according to which prehistoric societies progressed from one economic stage to the next in a pre-ordained sequence; from "hunting-gathering" through "pastoralism" to "agriculture". Instead, new theories are being tried out, such as the concept that geographically remote groups tend to continue a tradition longer than a more centrally placed one (Bender, 1972, p. 104). This seems a reasonable observation in the light of present-day experience but one that must be extraordinarily difficult to demonstrate in a prehistoric context. Another new line of argument is to suggest the distinction be made between "mobile" and "sedentary" economics, with mobility inevitably preceding sedentarism (Higgs *et al.*, 1972, p. 36).

One of the more important points that have been made recently is that the process of evolution from a non-agricultural society into a society with an established farming community probably took quite different courses in the eastern and the western Mediterranean basins (Whitehouse, 1978, p. 78). In the Aegean, it would seem that the first Neolithic people were immigrants who introduced a fully developed farming community there even before pottery was in full use. In the western Mediterranean, the picture is different. It is now recognized that the Mesolithic population was inventing pottery and experimenting with animals at least 1000 years before plant cultivation was introduced. According to Ruth Whitehouse, Italy (including southern Italy) should be fitted into this western pattern. This means that non-farming sites, such as those represented by the earliest levels at Coppa Nevigata and at Grotta delle Mare (Apulia), should now be seen as part of a "ceramic Neolithic" rather than as a precocious or partial Neolithic. Savory was perhaps anticipating these ideas when he wrote about the possibility "that some of the microlith using communities [in Spain] were already in fact to some degree Neolithic by 6000 B.C." (1968, p. 66).

Whatever the finer points of the archaeologists' arguments, it seems that it can be accepted that by the turn of the sixth millennium B.C. crop and animal agriculture was already established in southern France and southern Italy, arriving in Spain slightly later. In the earliest Neolithic, the gathering of wild foods and the products of hunting and fishing made a proportionately greater, if not most substantial, contribution to the economy. As the various branches of farming developed, these activities became at first ancillary and eventually vestigial, as they are today. In this way the inhabitants of one of the earliest-dated Cardial sites in southern France (Chateauneuf-les-Martigues, Bouches-du-Rhone), where sheep were more or less domesticated by 5770 ± 240 B.C. (uncalibrated date) (Phillips, 1975, pp. 48, 52), must have relied wholly on gathering for their cereals, fruits and vegetables.

The first, uncertain signs of cereal cultivation at Chateauneuf-les-Martigues come from the pollen spectrum for the following millennium in the form of the grasses *Chenopodiacea* and *Plantago* and a single cereal grain (Renault-Miskovsky, 1971, p. 36; comment in Phillips, 1975, p. 52). But by and large, the Cardial levels of the Neolithic can be associated with the beginnings of arable farming. Wheat was being grown not far away at Fontbrouega (Var) and from Cardial sites in Aude and Vaucluse comes rather more circumstantial evidence in the form of sickles and of objects interpreted as weights for digging sticks (Courtin, 1970, p. 12; Courtin *et al.*, 1976, p. 172ff). Leguminous crops such as vetch, beans and lentils were making their appearance. In Mediterranean Spain and in northern Italy, a full mixed farming economy appears to have been well established by just after 5000 B.C. (Savory, 1968; Barfield, 1971). Grains found in a Cardial level at the cave of Coveta de l'Or, on the Alicante–Valencia border, have been identified as mainly of Emmer wheat and naked barley and dated to 4560 ± 160 B.C. at the earliest (Phillips, 1975, p. 57).

Identification of crops grown or animals raised at a certain site at a certain date is one thing. Recognition of the balance of these or of the farming system practised at that site, the whole foundation of the life of its inhabitants in other words, is quite another. Barker's survey of Neolithic and Bronze Age sites in central Italy (1975) is one of the most comprehensive analyses of prehistoric economic activity published and the only one so far to shed some light on the operation of farming systems at different stages in the prehistoric period. As a result of his review of available data, the unacceptability of the "ladder of progress" idea is confirmed: "the existing data can no longer be ordered in simple stages applicable to the whole of central Italy and equated with major cultural phases" (p. 158). He also adds substance to the assumption made at the beginning of this chapter, namely that the same kind of complexity was found in the prehistoric economies as in the historical.

A total of 46 different sites were examined by Barker for the Neolithic and Bronze Age (and others for pre-Neolithic times). Only two sites appear to have been occupied continuously, although four were re-occupied at various times. From the archaeological evidence and his assessment (based on a sometimes arguable interpretation of site catchment analysis) of the area surrounding each site, Barker recognized no less than eight different "economic types", as he termed them. These are summarized in Table I.

Close attention to the table shows that several of the so-called "economic types" must have been in fact only parts of a single farming system. In the final analysis two certain, and two possible, farming systems are revealed in Barker's data; the appearance of the greater number of "types" is the consequence of an inevitably incomplete archaeological record. The points raised by the table and leading to this conclusion are several, if sometimes minor. An important point, though, is that not one of the 46 sites appears to have been wholly and exclusively concerned with arable farming. In view of what has already been said about the role of livestock in normal farming life in the historic millennia, this is a not

Table I.

"Economic Type"	Period I (5th-mid-4th millennium)	Period II (late 4th to end 3rd millennium)	Period III 2nd millennium
1. All-the-year settlement: stock, cereals	5	7	17
2. All-the-year settlement: stock, cereals, hunting		2	
3. Settlement/camp: mainly stock	2	4	22
4. Winter camp: stock	4	1?	11
5. Summer camp: stock	1	4	6
6. Spring/autumn camp: stock			8
7. Spring/autumn camp: stock, hunting	3	2	
8. Summer camp: stock, hunting		1	
Total number of sites	16	21	45
Total economic types	5	7	6

unexpected conclusion. Some sites, though, are classified as having been concerned exclusively with livestock. There are two immediate answers to this. One is that even an apparently "wholly pastoral" society is almost always found to have some way of obtaining the products of arable farming, if these are not produced from within that society (Fig. 34). Secondly, a

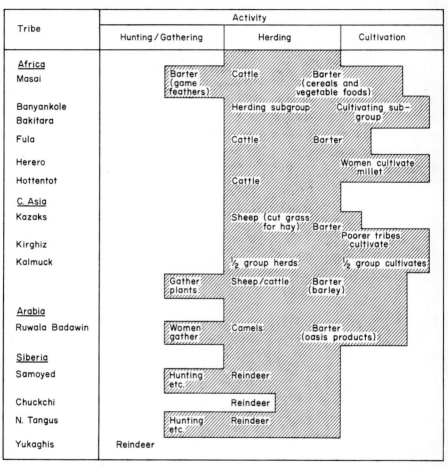

Tribe	Activity		
	Hunting / Gathering	Herding	Cultivation
Africa Masai	Barter (game feathers)	Cattle	Barter (cereals and vegetable foods)
Banyankole Bakitara		Herding subgroup	Cultivating sub-group
Fula		Cattle	Barter
Herero			Women cultivate millet
Hottentot		Cattle	
C. Asia Kazaks		Sheep (cut grass for hay)	Barter
Kirghiz			Poorer tribes cultivate
Kalmuck		½ group herds	½ group cultivates
	Gather plants	Sheep/cattle	Barter (barley)
Arabia Ruwala Badawin	Women gather	Camels	Barter (oasis products)
Siberia Samoyed	Hunting etc.	Reindeer	
Chuckchi		Reindeer	
N. Tangus	Hunting etc.	Reindeer	
Yukaghis	Reindeer		

Fig. 34. *Definitions of "pastoralism".* If the term "exclusively pastoral" (used, for example, by Daryll Forde, 1934, in connection with the Masai) is intended to refer to a mode of life in which cultivation has no place, then this runs counter to the facts. Daryll Forde's so-called pastoralists (in shaded column) are known, in almost every case, to have access to, to rely on, or to cultivate, arable products.

Most of these "pastoral" groups are also described as nomadic.

closer look at the details of Barker's lists reveals that some of these sites (in Marche for instance), classified as having been occupied only seasonally, can be shown to have been associated with others at which there was arable farming (Barker, 1975, pp. 135, 155). Yet another point concerns the place of hunting. Like gathering, of which there is no mention, hunting has had its place in the normal system of peasant farming, as well as supplying sport for the leisured, throughout the historic period. A penultimate point is that each of the sites classified as temporary must by definition either be paired with another or others that are seasonally complementary or be associated with a permanent base. Finally, it is interesting that not at one site was there a radical change in type during the sometimes very long periods of occupation implied by the archaeological evidence.

Barker's data and the eight "economic types" he has recognized therefore can be resolved into evidence for two, three or four farming systems, all except one of which have had a counterpart during the historic millennia. The first system is what might be called the standard one, that of the farmer who lives in a permanent steading, most commonly in a village, and whose livelihood is derived from mixed farming, animals and polyculture. His settlement would have been surrounded by that part of the territory which had been cleared of natural vegetation and was cultivated. Some of the arable would lie as fallow. This, together with the uncleared parts of the territory would have been used to support the animals, all of which would have remained within the territory all the year around. Some animals may have been regularly or occasionally penned, necessitating the gathering and perhaps storage of fodder.[24] There should have been no shortage of this even on the lowlands. If nearly a quarter of the present-day land use in nine of the prehistoric territories examined by Barker (p. 157) is accounted for by woodland, it is a reasonable assumption that no smaller a proportion would have been so available in prehistoric times and even that probably a very much greater proportion of the territories in question would have been wooded in those days.

The second system is only a variation of the first. It too involved mixed farming from a permanent farm or village base. Its only difference is that for one reason or another there was insufficient grazing or fodder at one season or another. Accordingly therefore, some of the animals were sent elsewhere, outside their own territory, for the season of shortage. The sites involved in this system would be some of those classified as all-the-year settlements (economic types 1 or 2) together with some of those classified as a seasonal camp with stock according to altitude. The historic parallels for this system include those communities where "reluctant transhumance" has had to be practised.

The third and fourth systems are identified with rather less certainty. Both concern those sites which Barker indicated as having been occupied only temporarily, at whatever season, and involved in stock raising; in the late Bronze Age (period III of Table I) these accounted for over half the 45 sites then occupied. For the third system it could be argued that the sites represent the camps of full-time herders who had no permanent base, or no significant base, but who moved from camp to camp and back to the first according to the season. In point of fact, however, even amongst the nomads of the world there is usually one base identifiable as a "home base", even if it is not permanently occupied by a holding population, where even a quick crop may be taken (Evans, 1940, p. 75ff; Daryll Forde, 1934). There was no sign of nomadism in Mediterranean Europe for the historic period. It is doubtful that even the Balkan forms of shepherding were ever truly nomadic. They certainly have not been so this century. The shepherds of the Vlachs come from permanent villages where as much arable land is worked as terrain and climate permit (Wace and Thompson, 1914). It is said that the Sarakatsani of Epirus do not own any land (Davis, 1977, p. 20ff, commenting on Campbell, 1964) but they rent pasture from villages and there are two sub-groups who have settled and turned to agriculture, usually in the high mountains of their traditional summer pastures. Another vital link in the modern Sarakatsani's life is the merchant who takes the milk for cheese-making and who gives them the cash needed for payment of pasture rents as well as for the purchase of non-pastoral foodstuffs and other necessities. How much the existence of such agricultural sub-groups and the proximity of merchants are a result of modern government pressure, or how much they are older elements of an economic system more complex than is usually allowed for, is difficult to establish from published accounts.

As far as the possible fourth system is concerned, therefore, the most convincing argument appears to be that at least some of those sites noted by Barker as having been occupied only seasonally might represent yet another of the better-documented systems of historic times, that of the graziers. In this case, the permanent village base might be a 100 or more kilometres away. One would hope that pottery evidence would confirm individual linkages and indeed Barker, as noted above, has already made some observations relevant to this interpretation.

The existence of possible evidence for a grazier system in peninsular

Italy as early as the Bronze Age, if not the Neolithic, deserves attention. There is no need to assume, as is sometimes done, that transhumance had to have occurred at any prehistoric (or historic) site at which sheep or goat bones are found. Once the distinction has been made between livestock-raising on a scale which involves long-distance transhumance (the graziers) and that of the villagers, which involves little or no extra-territorial movement of flocks and herds, the case for the emergence of a grazier system in the prehistoric period raises an interesting question. Sometimes it has been assumed that transhumant livestock-raising was a direct function of the environment alone. In this book it has been suggested that the social, economic or political implications are of far greater consequence in the development of a grazier farming system. What of these factors in the prehistoric period?

For the historic period it was noted that the key to the different farming systems was social status. The grazier was a major landowner or a social aspirant. For the prehistoric period, evidence for so abstract an aspect of life is not available in the same way. The question is not an impossible one and it is much discussed by archaeologists. What has to be presupposed is that a certain number of individuals were in a position whereby they did not have to work for their own subsistence and that these individuals possessed, or had access to, sufficient resources to be able to divert a part of these towards non-subsistence ends. The assumption has to be made, in other words, that there was a social division and an associated economic diversification in prehistoric times. Some archaeologists have no difficulty in accepting that an economic contrast is to be expected between acepholous societies and those with some degree of social differentiation (e.g. Sharrat, 1972, p. 551). The archaeological problem is to demonstrate from the evidence whether such social differentiation existed in the Neolithic and in the Bronze Age in Mediterranean Europe. Some put an emphasis on the appearance of a warrior class in the middle of the Bronze Age (Piggot, 1965, p. 118). Others note the existence, in certain regions, of quite different settlement types, the civil and the sanctuary in Neolithic Sardinia for instance (Lilliu, 1963, p. 47). As a pointer, there are the magnificent megalithic tombs of other districts (Languedoc, southern Spain, south-eastern Italy and Sicily), though to one archaeologist the megalith is not to be seen as the family vault of a prehistoric squirearchy but rather as a communal tomb (Renfrew, 1966).

The case for prehistoric social and economic divisions must in the last analysis rest with the archaeologists and on archaeological data, and with

K

it, the case for a grazier system. All that can be said here in conclusion is that so far as is evident from the data, farming systems in Mediterranean Europe were in general no different in prehistoric times from those of historic times in any essential respect. There was in all probability a landlord class, at least in the Bronze Age if not in the Neolithic. The foundation of society would have been, still more perhaps then than later, the peasantry. None of the evidence from the prehistoric period points away from any of the "traditional" farming systems of the historic period

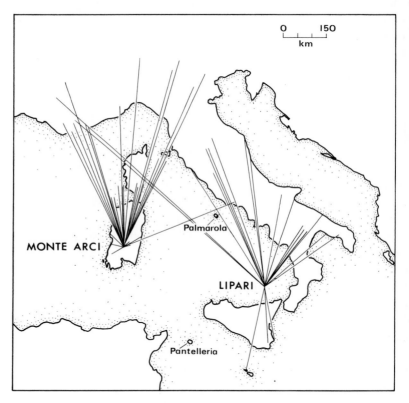

Fig. 35. *Neolithic trade.* Obsidian from Monte Arci in Sardinia and from the Lipari Isles was widely exported in the western Mediterranean in the sixth millennium B.C. It would be difficult to call even the Neolithic economies wholly "closed" or "natural" with this, and other, evidence for exchange or trade in mind. In the diagram, the lines point to find spots of the appropriate obsidian; finds of the volcanic glass from Pantelleria and Palmarola are not shown (based on map in Hallam *et al.*, 1976).

to suggest that there were primitive cultivators rather than peasant farmers in the Neolithic. Admittedly, the nature of the social structure of society and its economic divisions at the very beginning, when the new agricultural systems were just emerging from the desperate events of domestication, remains obscure and this may well have been an earlier period of greater differences. But the first clear signs of widespread trading by the sixth millennium B.C. establishes beyond doubt the existence of some form of market structure which cannot be part of a primitive cultivator's way of life. In its way therefore, the appearance of trade in obsidian Mediterranean Europe (Fig. 35) may be regarded as confirming the existence of peasant farming and as marking *grosso modo* the birth of the region's traditional way of life in all its many facets.

Part III

Changes in the Environment

Even places alter—with uncertain gales
Where once was land the bounding vessel sails
And where the sea once spread, on steady land
Now houses, trees and men securely stand.
Shells far from sea removed are often found
And anchors buried in the mountain ground.
Torrents a valley of the plain have made
And mountains headlong to the sea conveyed.

Ovid Metamorphoses XV

Part II

Changes in the Environment

9

Erosion on the Hills

From the point of view of an individual farmer, whether he lived in prehistoric, historic or in modern times, the relevance of the entire range of environmental factors is summed up in their effect on the soil from which he has to derive his livelihood. Alterations in the environment which in some way or another have bearing on the quality and characteristics of his land are therefore of considerable interest. Small changes taking place on a timescale of a generation or two have more impact on a farmer or his community than larger changes effected over several hundreds of years (the climatic changes of the Holocene, for instance). However, viewing the whole period of mixed farming and settled existence in Mediterranean Europe dealt with in this book, certain changes stand out as having the greatest significance in farming and settlement, namely soil erosion and its corollary, soil deposition or siltation.

Ancient writers were no less aware than are modern ones of the changes even then affecting the environment. In the first century A.D. Pliny wrote that ''the earth is eaten up by herself'' (II.207). He also pointed out that for a very long period of time ''the seas have been encroaching on the land or the shores have been moving forward, and the rivers have formed curves, or have straightened out their windings'' (III. 16). Three centuries earlier Aristotle had also remarked that not only does ''the mainland and the sea change places and one area does not remain earth, another sea, for all time'' but that ''this process must . . . take place in an orderly cycle'' (Meteorology, I. XIV). He also had a good sense of time, noting that the process tends to escape ''our observation because the whole natural process of the earth's growth takes place by slow degrees and over periods of time which are vast compared to the length of life . . .''

As the early writers saw it, the process of environmental change was in essence one of transference of material from the land into the sea. The land

275

is being smoothed and levelled through the action of raindrops, torrents and rivers through the ages. The sea is being filled up by material eroded from the land, carried by the rivers as alluvium, and deposited in the sea, first near the land "so it is possible for the sea to be entirely silted up" (Strabo, I.38.8.53). Modern geomorphologists cannot better the model. They too see a general tendency "for a downward movement of material to fill the oceanic hollows to form a level land surface" (Stoddard, 1969, p. 43). With the greater precision of modern knowledge they can point out that, since the mean elevation of the world's continents is 840 m above present sea level and the mean depth of the oceans is 3800 m, the eventual land surface would be 2440 m below present sea level, allowance being made for the larger size of the oceans.

Some regions are more erodable than others or are more vulnerable to erosion at certain times. So far as Mediterranean Europe is concerned, each year anything from 60 to 600 tons of material per square kilometre might be in process of removal from the land to find its way to the coast and out into the sea basins. The rate at which erosion of the land takes place and the relative importance of one factor or another is part of the geomorphologists' concept of erosion potential.

The single most important factor in vegetation change since the early Neolithic has been man and man-induced activities. So these are the two main aspects of environmental change considered in this chapter. The accumulation of soils along the coasts is dealt with in the following chapter.

The Erosion Potential

The erosion potential is a concept summarizing the final balance of the very large number of factors involved in a place's liability to soil erosion. The salient aspects of this potential are mentioned here. The history and problems of soil erosion in Mediterranean Europe are long and relatively well-documented.

Soil erosion is normally effected by run-off. It is thought for instance that the amount of rainfall held in soil hollows before it overflows as run-off may be as little as 2 mm and is unlikely to be more than 5 mm of the rainfall of any one storm (Kirkby, 1969). The most significant run-off producing characteristic is relief (Morgan, 1969). The role of relief can vary from a hypothetical extreme where 100% of rainfall is lost through run-off to a low where 25% or less flows overland. In all cases the relief factor would account for the highest proportion of run-off (40% in the extreme instance of rugged terrain with an average slope generally over 30%).

In view of relief alone, therefore, Mediterranean Europe in general is at high risk from run-off. Most of Spain (88%) is over 200 m above sea level and much of this is classified as mountain or hill. The same is true of Italy and of southern France. Of Italy, it has been said that "a depressingly large proportion of both main types of relief is either steep enough to make cultivation difficult . . . so steep that cultivation is extremely precarious, or simply too steep to serve as anything but forest land or poor pastures" (Cole, 1964, pp. 97–98). About 20% of mainland Italy is classed as lowland (below 300 m) but only 16% of the islands of Sicily and Sardinia. As a consequence of the mountainous relief alone, run-off tends to be high. Not surprisingly the highest concentration of material in suspension in the western Mediterranean sea (apart from off the Po delta) is found along the east coast of Sardinia where "abundant terrigenous supplies" are swept by run-off from the Gennargentu, a highly mountainous area of impermeable crystalline rocks that receive an average of up to 2000 mm of rainfall per annum (Emelyanov and Shimkus, 1972).

Important as relief may be as a factor of run-off and erosion potential, there are three other factors contributing to run-off. Indeed, taken together, these three (infiltration, vegetal cover and surface storage) are apparently more important than relief alone. Moisture infiltration is affected above all by the dryness of the soil and secondly by its texture. The irregularity of the distribution of rainfall throughout the year in Mediterranean Europe means that soils tend to dry out in summer to considerable depths and to develop a hard-baked crust. This hinders quick infiltration or absorption of the rain when it does come. It also checks the growth or germination of plants which could keep the soil moist with their cover. Clayey soils on the coastal plains of Apulia are annually desiccated to a depth of 1–1·5 m. Soils in the Albacete district of southern Spain may remain dry for 6 months after a long drought and depletion of the soil's reserves of moisture. On such soils, fast-falling rain tends to sweep off as effectively as from an impervious rock.

The second point affecting infiltration rates is texture. Soil texture is largely dependent on parent rock. In his study of soil erosion in southern Italy, Kayser (1961) found it convenient to recognize four groups of parent rock on the basis of permeability. Three of these are to some degree reasonably absorptive. However they are spatially of secondary

K*

consequence, accounting for less than 40% of the total area of the *regione* of Lucania. All other rocks, the *flyschs* and the Plio-Pleistocene clays, are impermeable. Looking at the soils developed from these rocks, Kayser found that these too are overwhelmingly impervious in texture. In the hill and mountain districts of Lucania (already high run-off regions because of relief) 79% of the soils were described as "clayey", "clayey sands", or "clayey loams". Not surprisingly, therefore, half of Lucania is affected by erosion of one sort or another.

It is worth recalling that for these reasons erosion by run-off is not necessarily confined to districts of high altitudes or to the excessively steep slopes of mountain districts. A short slope on rocky terrain can suffer from soil loss but so can a quite gentle slope on unconsolidated strata, which may be heavily gullied by an occasional downpour. On the lowland of northern Apulia where there is little vegetation cover and ploughing runs up and down the slope, ridges and valley bluffs are sometimes heavily gullied. Here too, much of the soil is clayey in texture. Only three of the nine soils found on the Tavoliere of Foggia can be officially described as alluvial or clayey but these three alone account for half the total area (Consorzio).

A relatively dense vegetation cover would not only check the impact of raindrops reaching the soil, facilitating infiltration, but also the speed of overland flow or run-off. This is chiefly because forest litter, or the herbaceous layers of more open vegetation, holds the water until it is absorbed. Researchers have found that the drier the regional climate, the more important it is that the soil should be protected by vegetation. (Kirkby, 1969, p. 235). Only where the average annual rainfall is not less than 600 mm is the density of the vegetation cover a relatively unimportant factor in the context of run-off. Once the plant cover has been removed or severely reduced, however, these upland regions become particularly vulnerable because there is nothing to hold the soil on the steep slopes under a high rainfall regime. In turn the increased run-off gives rise to floods further down.

One of the best-documented rivers for flooding in the historic period is the Tiber. Inevitably its flooding has been associated with loss of vegetation and with soil erosion of the hills and mountains upstream, where the majority of the rocks are soft and unconsolidated Tertiary strata. In the first half of the final century B.C. an increased tendency to flood was noted (Frank, 1933, Vol.I, p. 174). There were serious floods in the years 203, 202, 193 and 192 B.C. In the latter year the Tiber swept away two bridges in the city of Rome as well as some houses in the countryside. Then in 189 B.C. the river overflowed no less than 12 times. The main cause of this new flood hazard is ascribed to the deforestation of its basin during the third century B.C. In that century timber was being cut for a growing industrial sector and for ship-building in particular. Land was being extensively cleared to make room for quite new urban centres and for the growing suburbs. The demand for building materials stimulated the brick and mortar industry which needed fuel for firing and for lime burning. Land was also being cleared for the new agricultural estates that were springing up all over Etruria. Then at Rome itself, the third century was marked by major urban development and this meant a heavy demand on upstream suppliers just for roof timbers and for scaffolding in the initial phase alone.

In most of Mediterranean Europe, therefore, whether drier lowland or humid mountain, changes in the vegetation cover have played a major part in the rate at which hill slopes are eroded. In accounting for natural vegetation cover, climate is an obviously important factor. On the drier lowlands one of the problems is the slowness of vegetation growth and regeneration. The more arid the region, the thinner the plant cover and the fewer the species present. Yet saplings of even the best-adapted species, the xerophytes, need a period under "nursery conditions" for germination and until they are established. Normally these conditions are created by the micro-climate of the parent trees so if these have been cut down, spontaneous regeneration of the dominant tree species can be exceedingly slow and precarious. On the other hand, very few parts of Mediterranean Europe are in fact so dry as to be classified as semi-arid. Only in a few parts of Spain are exceptionally dry conditions indicated by the predominance of plant associations typical of hot steppes (alfa or sparta steppes) instead of sub-arid Mediterranean scrub of oleander or *thuya* (callitris) (Birot and Gabert, 1964, p. 255). The interior Ebro basin, the Levantine coast between Cape Gaeta and Capo Palos, and the Segura basin south of Albacete are so marked. Elsewhere in Mediterranean Europe, the particular disposition of local relief and geological characteristics may result in a regional climate that comes close to the arid margin, as is the case of the lowland of Apulia and the Taranto district further south. But in general, by far the greater part of Mediterranean Europe is climatically capable of bearing forest vegetation.

One of the best-known characteristics of the Mediterranean climate is the torrential nature of so much of its rainfall. This is yet another factor promoting soil erosion. The total amount of annual precipitation in a given district may be relatively low but what happens is that the total number of days on which rain falls may be so few and the storms so severe that well over half the annual total of that region's rain falls in a few hours. The figures are disturbing. Three examples are given in Table II. Note that these storms can occur in any of the seasons. Even allowing a maximum rate of infiltration, it is possible that between 80 and 95 % of each storm's rain is lost through non-absorption. Evaporation accounts for some loss but most simply runs off the land, carrying the soil with it. This means quite simply that, in regions where a high proportion of annual precipitation arrives as storm rain, the proportion of the annual total that is really effective and that is absorbed into the soil can be very low. For example, the

Table II. Annual precipitation in three regions.

| | *Murcia* | | *Montpellier* | |
| | 24-h total | Annual Total | | 24-h total |
Date	(mm)	(mm)	Date	(mm)
Oct. 1952	38·6	235·7	27.9.1857	130
Nov. 1953	42·7	390·5	11.10.1861	70
Dec. 1954	104·5	376·9	11.10.1862	233
Nov. 1955	63·6	237·3	3.10.1864	300
Nov. 1956	32·1	208·0	30.11.1955	147
Jan. 1957	59·8	309·1	(Annual average 770 mm)	
Oct. 1958	51·0	227·6	(altitude 10 m)	
May 1959	45·6	402·8		
June 1960	28·6	312·8		
Nov. 1961	19·9	137·4		
(Annual average 53 mm)				
(Altitude 295 m)				

Moliterno (Potenza)

In 20 min,	25 mm of rain fell on 3.10.35
In 1 h,	36 mm of rain fell on 2.10.35
In 6 h,	61 mm of rain fell on 4.12.35
In 12 h,	100 mm of rain fell on 4.12.35
In 24 h,	104 mm of rain fell on 3.12.35

(Average annual rainfall 1070 mm)
(altitude 880 m)

rainfall record for 1964 in the Foggia province shows that between 67 and 74% of the annual total of 470 mm could have been "lost" in this way.

To say that there have been fluctuations in the climatic characteristics of Mediterranean Europe since early prehistoric times, as elsewhere, is probably less contentious than to suggest that there have been changes of climate. Conditions of rainfall, temperature or cloudiness for example have not been stable throughout the seven millennia of interest in this book. Even within each century there are phases of "good" and "bad" weather. From the point of view of the erosion potential in Mediterranean Europe, changes in regime, rather than in annual totals or the overall effect, might have considerable significance. For instance, all other things being equal, a shift towards a regime of high intensity summer rainfall would probably increase the erosion potential (Kirkby, 1969). The question of climatic fluctuations in post-Neolithic Mediterranean Europe is not enlarged on at this point, however. Rather, some of the evidence found in the soils and in the ground for past climatic conditions will be mentioned as being of particular relevance to the fieldwork of geographers and archaeologists alike. The two topics considered are the palaeosols and the calcretes.

Palaeosols

By and large, the palaeosols of Mediterranean Europe are either red or black. A considerable literature already exists on the former. The debate as to the extent that the process of rubification may take place under present-day climatic conditions, however, seems little settled. It is accepted though that the bulk of the *terra rossa* soil so characteristic today of the limestone and calcareous regions of Mediterranean Europe is in fact a palaeosol, revealed only through the loss of more sombre-hued covering soils.

The essential factor in rubification is without doubt the existence of a well-marked seasonal contrast that ensures a protracted dry season in a relatively humid year. That the formation of *terra rossa* should be associated with a warm, moist climate overall is substantiated by malacological studies of soils in the Rhone valley. In one study there were found to be two generations of soil, the underlying red earth and a younger brown earth (Bourdier, 1963, p. 325). In the red earth only 30% of the molluscs were xerophytic species whereas 60% of those in the overlying brown earth, normally associated with the climax Mediterranean forest dominated by evergreen oaks, were xerophytes. Some red earths, such as those of the forest of Valbonne in the same area (George, 1935, p. 275) also have a calcareous hard pan or zone of calcareous nodules, presumably associated with some form of leaching or other vertical movements of soil moisture.

It seems advisable to reserve the term *terra rossa* for the bright orange-red soils found on compact white limestones and in the karstic features of those strata (the joints or diaclases, dolines etc.). In the opinion of some pedologists the purity of these *terra rossas* points to the slowness of the decalcification process which produced them. The residue from hard, massive limestones is thought to be in the order of 0.01%, which would yield not more than 1 m of soil for every 100 m of rock weathered (Curtis et al., 1970, p. 100). These soils would owe their formation to a geological rather than to a pedological process. From the human geographer's point of view their date of origin belongs to the geological rather than the historical time scale. Dugrand (1963b) ascribed some of the red-coloured soils found on the Languedoc Garrigues to the Tertiary era but most to the Quaternary interglacials.

In addition there are red earths thought to be to some degree lateritic. Yet others are described as loessic in origin. Both these too are of ancient formation, belonging more properly to a discussion of the Quaternary. It is interesting to note, however, that their distribution is not without consequence for the historic period. For instance, certain forests and woodlands apparently owe their ecological characteristics and their survival as relict forests directly to the presence of such palaeosols. The forest of Ventoux (Vaucluse) grows in a clayey lateritic red earth that is unusually rich (in comparison with neighbouring soils) in silicates and aluminates (George, 1935, p. 273). This means that the soil is cool and moist even though it overlies limestone and that it serves to isolate the vegetation from the effects of such a bedrock.

In a few districts today it is possible to find a red earth below a quite well-developed brown earth carrying forest or mature scrub vegetation. This would have been the normal situation in earlier times, before soil erosion removed the brown earth and exposed the red palaeosol (Fig. 36). In short, the redness of what has come to be regarded as the typical Mediterranean soil is generally a certain indicator that soil erosion has taken place to a considerable extent. Prehistoric man would have seen little of these red earths without digging deeply.

The black palaeosols of Mediterranean Europe are most common in the

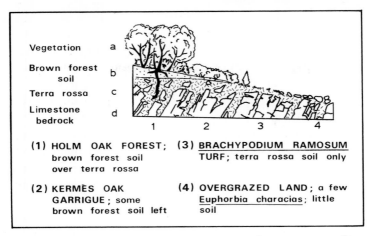

Vegetation   a
Brown forest   b
   soil
Terra rossa   c
Limestone   d
   bedrock
                   1   2   3   4

(1) HOLM OAK FOREST; (3) BRACHYPODIUM RAMOSUM
    brown forest soil   TURF; terra rossa soil only
    over terra rossa

(2) KERMÈS OAK   (4) OVERGRAZED LAND; a few
    GARRIGUE; some   Euphorbia characias; little
    brown forest soil left soil

Fig. 36. *Vegetation degradation and soil erosion in profile* on compact limestones
(based on Braun-Blanquet, 1936).

coastlands or along the major rivers, where soil drainage is poor. They are
more sporadic and far less spectacular than the red earths. Their colour is
not a function of climate so much as of edaphic (soil) conditions, and may
be due to a high content of manganese, often associated with salinity and
more important as a colourant than a high content of ill-decayed organic
matter (Birot and Gabert, 1964, p. 112). Some palaeosols are grey rather
than black. Kayser observed several instances of a palaeo-grey soil in valley
alluviums in Lucania (1961, p. 114). They were up to a metre thick and
graded from a sandy horizon spotted with rust-coloured marks into a
similarly spotted grey clay. Most, if not all, of these black or grey
palaeosols are demonstrably of Neolithic or post-Neolithic date. In
Languedoc, where three "black" horizons, each no more than 20–30 cm
thick, mark former periods of high water table or soil saturation, one is
dated by its pottery content to the Mailhacian (Late Bronze Age) period.
The others are stratigraphically younger.

Calcrete

Quite apart from any hardpan they may (occasionally) contain, soils in
many parts of Mediterranean Europe rest on a more or less continuous substratum of almost pure calcium carbonate, known generally as calcrete.

The formation of calcrete is thought to be related to past rather than to present climatic phases (Montarlot, 1960; Coque, 1962; Birot and Gabert, 1964; Goudie, 1973; Vaudour, 1975). Those of Mediterranean Europe have so far escaped systematic examination. What has to be borne in mind is the variability in appearance, in mode of origin and in the date of origin of the calcretes. Some appear to have been formed from precipitates in former lagoons or other expanses of shallow, highly calcareous and clean water. Others seem to result from the seasonal movement of moisture within a former, also highly calcareous, soil. Judging from their stratigraphic relationships, some of the most impressive formations must date from the Pleistocene while others, thin but very hard, can be shown to be post-Roman. Some are pure white in colour, some yellow, even brownish. Some are very hard and exhibit a crystalline texture, others are floury in texture and nodular in structure. They are found from sea level up to altitudes of 300–400 m above sea level. Some are of quite local occurrence, some appear to cover several square kilometres. They are found in southern Italy, southern France, central and eastern Spain.

As in the case of the red soils, the key factors in the origin of calcretes must involve temperature and rainfall. There must have been a sufficiently marked seasonal contrast at the time of formation to give a hot, dry, evaporative period, and there must have been low rainfall.[25] Other factors could include those that affect the movement and behaviour of soil moisture, such as phyto-climate, micro-relief, cultivation techniques and settlement features.

Amongst the most impressive calcrete formations in Mediterranean Europe are those of the Tavoliere of Foggia in southern Italy. In at least half of this vast lowland, calcrete formations of one sort or another, known locally as *crosta*, are found. The hardest are always closest to the ground surface. In this form, the calcrete may be only 2–4 cm thick with banded colouring and crystalline texture, forming a carapace to a thicker horizon of less-resistant, even soft, material. It has been suggested (Vaudour, 1975, p. 58) that the process of hardening took place after, and possibly long after, the initial formation of the calcrete. The hard form can be found alone, sealing a Roman vine-trench in Apulia, for example, or in post-Roman deposits. The softer horizon is commonly 2–3 m deep but in some places the whole formation is known to be at least 8 m deep. It has a nodular structure which suggests that precipitation of the calcium carbonate was polarized on an object such as a pebble or a shell. These block formations are quite easily broken up with a pick-axe and provide a cheap, handy building material that has been much used in dry-stone walls since the middle Neolithic.

Because the carapace of the Apulian calcretes had not been extensively damaged until recent agricultural developments and the introduction of a deep tractor-drawn plough for the purpose, it has preserved a unique archaeological palimpsest. Almost any trench, pit or ditch dug into the calcrete since the Neolithic was revealed in astonishing clarity through crop and soil marks on war-time aerial photographs (Bradford, 1946, 1957). Both in Apulia and in southern France (Languedoc) the oldest-known features cut into the calcretes date to the middle Neolithic (Chassey in Languedoc) and this archaeological dating provides a *terminus ante quem* for their formation. East of the Rhone, early Chassey artefacts have been reported from below what was described as a ''strongly concreted crust'' attributed to the Atlantic climatic period (Montjardin, 1970). More interesting still is the fact that the entire Cardial (early Neolithic) layer of the prehistoric village of Escanin (Bouches du Rhone) was said to be separated from later ones by calcrete. Without field inspection, however, it is difficult to know whether the calcrete in question is of restricted occurrence, confined perhaps to the area of settlement, or part of a regional feature, as in the case of the Lansargues or the Tavoliere of Apulia, and whether it is the hard, carapace variety or the massive, nodular formation. The interpretation is bound to be different according to the identification. In all eventualities, the study and dating of calcrete will provide a useful indicator of past climatic and general environmental conditions in many regions of Mediterranean Europe.

The Spread of Settlement

The occupation of Mediterranean Europe goes back a very long time. Before the final glaciation there was Neanderthal man, known from such sites as Saccopastore (Campania). After the Würm episode there was a substantial population of hunters and gatherers. These are known from a number of sites widely distributed over Mediterranean Europe, the better-known ones including those at Mas d'Azil in the Pyrenees, Grotta Coruggi in Sicily, Hoga de la Mina in southern Spain, and Arene Candide on the Ligurian coast. But even making very generous allowance for the incompleteness of the inventory of Palaeolithic and Mesolithic sites it is doubtful that, however profligate of natural resources these early inhabitants may have been, or however long the period of time involved, or however high the erosion potential, the pre-Neolithic population made as significant or lasting impact on the environment of Mediterranean Europe as did Neolithic farmers and their successors.

By, or about, 5000 B.C., the first fully Neolithicized mixed farmers had made their appearance in south-east Italy (Whitehouse, 1968a, b, 1978; Guilaine, 1976). By the end of the fifth millennium the new farming economy had reached virtually the entire region, from Italy to Spain. From the point of view of environmental change, the new farming economy was revolutionary in three major respects. First, it not only enabled but indeed demanded a normally sedentary way of life. Second, partly as a result of this fixing of human habitation it led towards an intensification of human and human-induced activity focusing on these settlements and making eventual vegetation degradation and soil erosion a very real possibility. Third, there are the arguments in favour of a Neolithic demographic explosion.

Evidence for a Neolithic population explosion can only be in the form of an increase in number of contemporary habitations. Attempts to illustrate this with data gathered from even a single region by way of example fail, partly because of the incompleteness of the archaeological record, and partly also because different regions show quite different chronologies as concerns the intensification of settlement pattern. The expected model, a noticeable multiplication of settlement sites reaching a peak in the middle Neolithic, is found in some districts on the Tavoliere of Foggia in the fifth millennium for instance. It is found in Provence too, where, it has already been pointed out, hardly a cave remained unoccupied and the number of open-air villages grossly multiplied (Courtin, 1970, p. 30). In other regions the noticeable increase of habitation sites comes very much later. In the province of Valencia, for example, it takes place only in the Bronze Age, when there does seem to have been a veritable burst of colonization, or of demographic increase. In some districts there is no evidence at all for any explosion at any time. On the low-lying terrain bordering the lagoons of eastern Languedoc, population levels appear to have been as high in the late Bronze Age or early Iron Age as they were in the middle Neolithic, to judge from the number and size of the sites. On balance, however, it may be fair to say that most regions of Mediterranean Europe became relatively densely occupied for the first time in human history by the mid-Neolithic, that is, well before the end of the fourth millennium B.C.

These newly occupied parts of Mediterranean Europe were by no means confined to what might be regarded today as especially favourable terrain. Sites of Neolithic settlement are found in very different environments, at almost all altitudes for a start. The middle zone of the Pyrenees was quite densely inhabited to judge from the evidence at Mas d'Azil and from the large number of megalithic burials in the department of Ariège. There were arable and livestock farmers even higher in the mountains by the early fifth millennium, in the Cerdagne for instance, where although the plain is about 1000 m above sea level, the encircling peaks tower over it at up to 2400 m (Guilaine, 1976b; Rovira i Port, 1976). There were Neolithic people living high in the Cevennes. Two occupation sites lie on what are today bleak moor-covered slopes on the northern side of Mont Aigoual (Lozère) at over 1200 m (Hughes, 1960; Salles, 1960). In Corsica, of the ten early Neolithic settlement sites so far known, at least one is at 1100 m (Col de Vizzavona) while the highest of the 30 or so late Neolithic sites are at Piano de Levie (800 m) and on the Niolo plateau (between 1000 and 1400 m) (T. Liègeois, personal communication). In central Italy too there were permanent late Neolithic settlements at quite high altitudes, such as Grotta a Male (950 m) and Val di Varri (at 800 m but with surrounding land at over 1300 m). Some early sites still higher up, such as the Bronze Age shepherds' camp at Campo Pericolo (2000 m), were apparently occupied only seasonally (Puglisi, 1959; Barker, 1972).

At the other extreme, Neolithic settlement was also widely established near sea level and even on terrain so low-lying as to be vulnerable to inundation. This fact has only very recently become demonstrable. It used to be generally assumed that heavily forested, damp-soiled coastal plains were deliberately avoided by Neolithic settlers, principally because of the inadequacy of their tools and equipment to deal with the vegetation and soils. For Languedoc, it was suggested that "at this time the plain is hardly colonised" in contrast to the lighter forests of the limestone plateaux which were seen as "much more welcoming [and] already swarming with humanity" (Dugrand, 1963b, p. 201; after Louis, 1949). Another writer asserted, for the same plain, that "man did not try yet to make use of the Pliocene soils and lowlying land, presumably covered with a forest denser than the garrigue, an obstacle for clearance" until after the Bronze Age (Daumas, 1951, p. 70). The contrast between plateau and plain is indeed strongly marked. But current archaeological investigation is revealing that the number of lowland or scarp-foot settlements in Provence and Languedoc has been hitherto under estimated (Fig. 38). Chalcolithic sites,

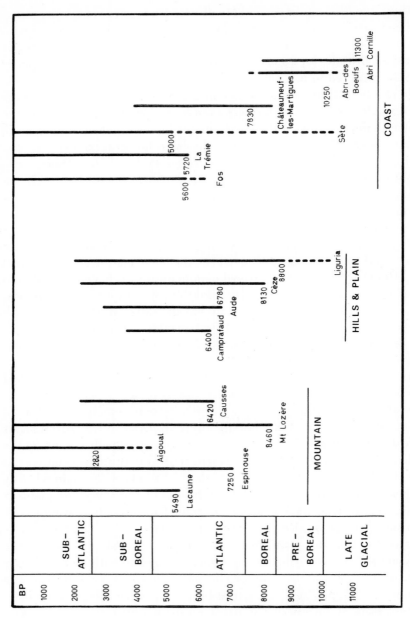

Fig. 37. *The altitudinal spread of prehistoric settlement in Provence* (from Planchais *et al.*, 1977).

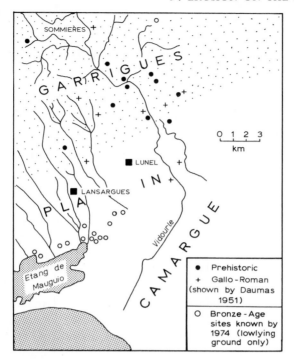

Fig. 38. *The distribution map of prehistoric settlement revised.* At the time when Daumas sketched his map, it was assumed that the lack of evidence for prehistoric sites on the coastal plain in general, and along its low-lying lagoon fringe in particular, meant that these areas were deliberately avoided by early farmers. Recent fieldwork, for example at Lansargues, has shown this view to be no longer tenable. Although only Bronze Age sites (the *terremares*) are shown, there is as much Neolithic and Hallstattian occupation in the same area.

for example, are being found below a shallow but effective masking of soil, not more than half a metre deep (N. Mills, personal communication). Other archaeological evidence coming to light since the late 1960s shows that even the marsh fringes of these plains were at least as densely settled by the middle Neolithic as at any other time in the prehistoric period (and far more so in prehistoric times than since the Middle Ages) and as densely occupied as the limestones further inland.

So even in the earliest Neolithic there were people living on the seaward margins of the coastal plain of Languedoc. Cardial pottery has been found from what would at that time have been an island in the lagoon of Leucate (Aude) (Freises and Montjardin, 1974–1975). Twenty-five kilometres from the coast but still on the plain is the site of Le Pouget, the first lowland Cardial site known in Languedoc. In fact, in the whole of the district around the lower valley of the Hérault, no fewer than 31 hitherto entirely unsuspected Neolithic sites have recently been reported, four of them showing signs of occupation as early as the Cardial, the remainder middle Neolithic (Chassey) in date. Further east along the coastal plain and towards the Camargue, eight Neolithic, eight Bronze Age, and six early Iron Age occupation sites have been discovered within a single 10-km^2 zone in the marshlands of the commune of Lansargues (H. Prades, personal communication).

In southern Italy, the Tavoliere of Foggia was early recognized as an unusual lowland in having "one of the densest concentrations of prehistoric settlement yet known in Europe" (Bradford, 1949, p. 60). The average altitude for these settlements works out at about 40 m although a great deal of the lowland lies at 100 m. Here too it was the general assumption that the apparently unoccupied areas could be explained by the unsuitability for permanent settlement of the broad valley bottoms and of the coastal wetlands. In these coastal zones, the land bordering the lagoons lies mostly below 5 m and it certainly has been marshy and liable to regular flooding. A single prehistoric site was known, Coppa Nevigata, occupied from very earliest Neolithic times (the date of initial occupation is now given as 6200 B.C. in Guilaine, 1976) and situated on a rocky shelf 10 m above sea level at the foot of the Gargano. However, fieldwork in the coastal zone in the early 1970s revealed half a dozen hitherto unknown Neolithic or Bronze Age habitation points at altitudes mostly below 5 m (Delano Smith and Smith, 1973; Delano Smith, 1975b, 1978, p. 120ff). The story is the same for eastern Spain too. Recent additions to the distribution map of prehistoric settlements show that lagoon sides and valley bottoms were early occupied. The Bronze Age site of Navarre (Valencia) for instance lies now beneath marsh formations on the floor of a narrow valley in the hills just behind the coastal plains (Chocomeli, 1945; Tarradel, 1975, p. 42ff). Two Mesolithic sites near Anna, in the same province, have also been discovered, similarly marked by the natural infill of, in this case, a lake created artificially between the tenth and the thirteenth centuries A.D. (Perez, 1975). Other pre-Neolithic occupation sites have recently been identified along the former shores of the Almenara lagoon near Castellon (Rossello Verger, 1975). In Sardinia, the lagoons of Cagliari and of Cabras are proving to have been surrounded by a large number of Neolithic settlements, many of which are today less than 2 m above present sea level. In Corsica, Neolithic sites are in the process of erosion by water in the Etang de Diane (Roth and Congès, 1976).

Early prehistoric settlement took place not only at all altitudes but also on all types of terrain. The low-lying lakeside or lagoonside locations have been mentioned above. Other settlements spread over limestone hills and plateaux that are today so barren of soil and vegetation cover as to be the despair of planners. When Arnal was writing his monograph on the Neolithic of the department of Hérault he listed over 180 open-air habitation sites in this department alone, every one of which is to be found on the limestone plateaux of the Garrigues of Montpellier or on the limestone outlier of La Gardiole (Arnal, 1936). The same went for the number and distribution of megalithic burials. This restricted distribution had already so struck another archaeologist that he formulated what he saw as a "law". To Temple (1936) it was clear that since over 80% of Neolithic burials in the two *départements* of Hérault and of neighbouring Gard were on limestone, prehistoric settlement can only be interpreted as having been "motivated, voluntary and reasoned". With this conclusion, though less with the manner in which it was arrived at and not at all with the intended implications, it is hardly possible to disagree.

Farming and Food Gathering as Factors of Degradation

The newly established settlements would at once have become centres of activities which to a greater or lesser extent, in longer or shorter term, would eventually have an adverse effect on the environment. The first to be affected is the vegetation (Fig. 39). The flora of Mediterranean Europe is very rich; the French botanist Flahault counted at least 4000 vascular species for southern France, about a third of which are annuals (1937, p. 13), but these are thinned out in the process of degradation. Eventually the soil is but patchily masked and scantly protected from erosion. As the plant population is reduced in density so it is also reduced in variety and in ecological status. The most degraded scrubs and heaths, therefore, are those with little vegetal cover and very few species. Most of these are typically low, wiry or with leathery or spiney leaves as an adaptation to the now unmitigated heat and aridity of their exposed situation.

There are also many bulbous plants. The typical pattern of vegetation degradation, and its concomitant soil erosion, is radial. Concentric zones of varying intensity of degradation focus on the village, town or farmstead (Fig. 40). As long as the density of settlement remained relatively low and each settlement relatively small, each zone would have comprised only

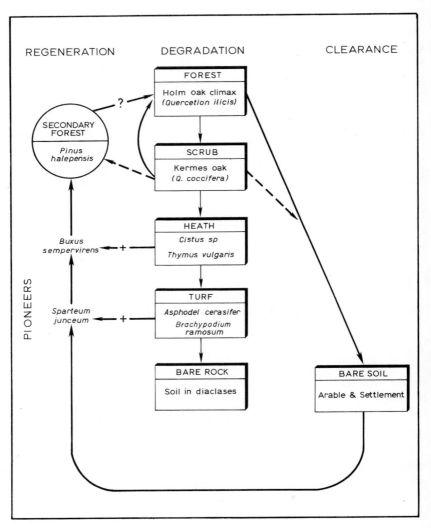

Fig. 39. *The temporal model of vegetation degradation and soil erosion* (based on Harant and Jarry, 1960).

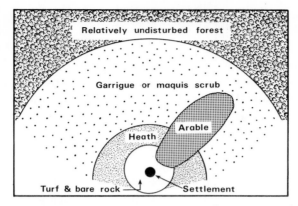

Fig. 40. *The spatial model of degradation and erosion.* The intensity of domestic and agricultural activities is normally at its greatest in the immediate proximity of the settlement and decreases with distance.

isolated patches of degradation in the climax vegetation. However, with population increase, multiplication of settlements and diversification of economic activities, each "island" of clearance and erosion gradually expanded to merge with others to affect entire districts. Farming, ancillary food gathering and industry are the three major branches of activity of the rural population that were carried on in prehistoric as well as in historic times and that led directly to vegetation degradation.

Farming

The first step in creating farm land is the deliberate clearance of as much of the plant cover as possible from the area intended as the arable fields. The herbaceous layer is removed entirely, shrubs are uprooted and canopies lopped from the very big trees. Trunks and stumps are left in the ground to rot. After clearance come years of cultivation, carried out in a manner that may or may not protect the newly exposed soil from erosion. Crops do afford some sort of protection but this is by no means as effective as the original vegetation. Cropping is seasonal and during their months of immaturity the plants cover only a small part of the soil. Then the soil is left bare, as fallow until a weed cover develops, scarcely adequate as a protection against erosion even after a year or two. The practice of inter-cropping arable and tree crops may favour soil protection in hill districts as long as the orchard rows and plough furrows (if any) are not aligned up and down the slopes.

One of the key activities in good husbandry, in the eyes of the Roman agronomists as well as in the modern view, is the maintenance of a good tilth. Most of the farmer's activities in the fields are directed in one way or another to this end. Repeated ploughing, harrowing and hoeing do not necessarily lead to soil erosion. A good tilth means a good rate of infiltration and less danger of run-off. The depth of soil disturbed is not great. Even ploughing, so long as it is with an *ard*, does not normally penetrate deeper than 25–30 cm and there need be no down slope furrows to channel soil-wash and run-off and lead to gully erosion; cross-ploughing is normal with the *ard*. The Roman agronomists recommended a minimum of four ploughings each season and noted that no fewer than nine altogether might be needed on particularly heavy soils, as in Tuscany (Pliny, XVIII.XLIX.182). Similarly, in the eighteenth century, six ploughings were advised for the heavier soils of the lowlands of eastern Languedoc whereas four sufficed on lighter land (Daumas, 1951, p. 253).

The effect of other cultivation techniques on the soil has been greatly discussed amongst soil scientists and modern agronomists. In modern practice, the use of the hoe between ploughings is usually associated with weed control but the point has been made that as it aids the formation of a tilth it can also be seen as an aid to the conservation of soil moisture (Baver, 1956, p. 182ff). Mulching and manuring, both practised in Roman times, are on the whole regarded as beneficial; excessive diurnal ranges are modified and an otherwise bare soil is protected from raindrop impact. Moreover, once ploughed in , the manure should also increase the porosity of the soil and in this way improve the infiltration rate. The burning of stubble is a more contentious issue. It is often held that the soil's micro-fauna is killed by the passing of the fire but in Mediterranean Europe much of this takes refuge from the summer drought far down in the soil profile, where the soil remains moist. Insects shelter under rocks and stones and need not be disturbed by the quick passing of the fires. A much more serious objection concerns the loss of structure-forming humus but the straw is rarely entirely burnt to ash and plenty of unburnt sections and roots remain to be ploughed in. Yet another objection concerns the transient nature of the benefit; rainfall is blamed for removing most of the potassium, for instance, before it has had time to improve the soil. But unless there is exceptionally heavy soil-wash soon after burning, Mediterranean soils are not likely to risk impoverishment through leaching. A much greater if less expected threat to soil health in Mediterranean Europe may come from irrigation. Incautious flooding and inadequate cultivation result in the formation of a hard surface crust on the soil which certainly has an adverse effect on plant growth. It also hinders or checks the soil's absorptive capacity and thus positively encourages run-off. Soil drainage, on the other hand, is rarely anything but beneficial provided the water table is not over-lowered. Soil aeration is increased and therefore so is bacteriological activity, together with the rate of infiltration.

On balance, the total effect of the clearance of virgin land of its natural vegetation is generally regarded as adverse. The production of organic matter is significantly decreased while its rate of decomposition is increased. There may be more leaching than before. The bared soil is completely exposed to raindrop impact. The constant mechanical manipulation of the soil by instruments of tillage tends to disturb it and is rarely carried out advantageously. Baver (1956) reports research which shows that the porosity of a clay soil may be reduced by as much as 18% after the first 40 years of cultivation simply because up to 40% less organic material and nitrogen has been received, meaning that the soil's structure contains fewer of the beneficial aggregates and soil pores become blocked by clay-silt particles (*ibid.*, p. 184).

The extent of land wholly cleared of vegetation for use as arable tends to fluctuate according to the fortunes of history and, more directly, to the level of population. Phases of demographic pressure are ecologically recorded. A period of easing of the pressure results in an abundance of pioneer plants (such as the gorses and brooms, ready colonizers of abandoned arable land) and in progressive vegetation associations. Phases of pressure lead to renewed clearing. By the beginning of the seventeenth century, for instance, the authorities in Provence were alarmed at the rate by which not only old *agri deserti* and areas of secondary growth were being reclaimed but also at the rate by which the area of forest was being seriously reduced through the clearance of assarts. Associated place-names (Issarts from *eyssart* for example) and place-names to do with burning (Cremade, also in Gard) testify to similar pressures on the land across the Rhone in Languedoc (George, 1935, p. 305).

Forests, however, can come as well as go. While clearance is more or less instantaneous in effect, ecologists have found it difficult to be certain about the length of time needed for the vegetation to regrow after clearance and to pass through the succession of progressive ecological stages that leads to the re-establishment of the climax forest. Much, of course, depends on the state of vegetation at the moment when pressures are relaxed, as well as on local soil conditions, on relief, and on such matters as the prevailing weather pattern. It has been suggested that, in an area of Languedoc receiving not less than 700 mm of rainfall each year, some 70 to 80 years are necessary for a favourable soil on abandoned arable land to become spontaneously reforested by a fully developed *Quercus ilex* association (Barry, 1960). But Flahault reported remarkable progress at the end of last century in several localities in southern France (1937, p. 25). The massif of Saint Baume, near Marseilles, was so heavily grazed prior to 1860 that it had already taken on the grey-white hue of the most denuded limestones. Sheep owned by villagers and farmers at le Plan d'Aups were held responsible, for there were no fewer than 2000 of them. But once the numbers of sheep had declined and much of the land enclosed or protected (*en defens*), the vegetation's recovery was rapid. Thirty years later there were pine (*Pinus sylvestris*) and oak (*Quercus sessiliflora*) trees with young beech and yew, dominants in the former forest, already making an appearance in their protection. Elsewhere, land abandoned in 1874 was already covered with young Aleppo pine and holm oak just 20 years later, the new vegetation being no different from that of the neighbouring forest, 1200 m distant.

In addition to their arable farming activities, farmers in Mediterranean Europe have also had their livestock. The animal side of farming has no less an adverse effect on the natural vegetation albeit a more complicated one. Quite apart from the foliage, shoots, fruits and plants eaten by the animals, or gathered for them, one long-standing practice has been the burning of the entire herbaceous layer at certain times of the year as a means of improving the quality of the turf for grazing. Lucan related how, when Apulian farmers burnt the old grass after the summer drought to stimulate autumn regrowth, "Monte Gargano and the fields of Vultur and the pastures of hot Matinus light up the countryside with a blaze of fire" (IX. 182ff). More vividly still, Silius Italicus described "the multitude of fires that the shepherd sees from his seat on Mount Garganus, when the uplands of Calabria are burnt and blackened, to improve the pasture" (Punica, VII.364ff). The problem is a familiar one. Once vegetation has been degraded to a particularly low status, those plants that survive are the most hardy of that association's component species and by definition the most unpalatable for grazing animals. One of the most tenacious of the Mediterranean grasses is *Brachypodium ramosum*. It is a pyrophyte, able to survive burning, with branching leaves that in summer dry into a turf that is tough and unnutritious. Burning becomes the only way of getting rid of the wiry thatch and promoting lush new growth with the arrival of the first autumn rains. Inevitably, since other grasses and herbaceous plants cannot tolerate such treatment, the district is left with a turf composed solely of *B. ramosum* which thenceforth has to be burnt each year and which, moreover, is less suitable for feeding cattle than for goats and sheep. On the other hand, it has been argued that, where the vegetation has not been allowed to degrade below shrub status, the carrying capacity of forests may be greatly improved by burning because the shrub layer is opened up to the benefit of the understorey vegetation and herbaceous plants (Mellars, 1976).

Food Gathering

Peasant farmers, and the rural population at large, have not hesitated in the past to take advantage of the wild fruits and fauna available from the countryside. Today it is only in the poorest sectors of the population or amongst the unemployed that a livelihood may have to be sought wholly from gathering activities in a way that must be very close to those of pre-farming societies (Dolci, 1959). Otherwise, although nearly every midden excavated by archaeologists, whether from a prehistoric, classical or medieval settlement, contains evidence of the hunting or snaring of small game (hare, fowl, tortoise, wild pig) or the seeds and fruits of wild plants, gathering remained ancillary to farming.

Rather than hunting, it is the gathering of wild plants and their fruits that could locally have considerable and direct impact on the vegetation. It seems that few plants did not have their uses. The ancient writers certainly appreciated the wild plants of Mediterranean Europe as much as the peasants have done in more recent times (see Pliny *Natural History;* Polunin and Huxley, 1965; Harant and Jarry, 1960, Vol. II). Grasslands and pastures yield plants valued for their leaves and gathered during the cooler, wetter half of the year. These include the chicory family (*Crepis bulbosa, C. feotida* and the blue-flowered commercial chicory *Cichorium intybus*); the lettuce family (*Latuca perennis*); and dandelions (*Taraxacus sp.*) which can be eaten raw or cooked. From rockier terrain comes the wild asparagus (*A. acutifolius*). The leaves of the sow-thistle (*Sonchus oleraceus*) are edible and so are those of the milk-thistle (*Silybum mariana*). Some plants, such as wild leeks (*Allium*) are dug or pulled from the ground. Others, such as salsify (*Tragopogon porrifolius*) and creeping campanula (*Campanula rapunculus*) are valued only for their roots. The fruits of many plants, shrubs and trees are edible. The berries of the black nightshade (*Solanum nigrum*) can be eaten raw (and its leaves cooked as a spinach). The ash (*Fraxinus ornus*) provides "manna", an exudate for which the tree is cultivated in Calabria and Sicily. Gums from the pistachios (*Pistacia terebinthus* and *P. lentiscus*) are used in wine preservation as well as by fishermen as a sealant for their boats. The *Arbutus unedo* tree is nicknamed the strawberry tree because of its fruit. The sloe (*Prunus spinosa*), the hawthorn (*Crataegus oxycantha*) and another very common shrub of the drier lowlands, *Pirus amygdaliformis*, all produce edible fruit. Acorn flour has not been unknown though chestnut flour is preferable. A variety of mushrooms and fungi are found in the damp litter of the forest. Yet other plants have been exploited for industrial or medicinal use. Since the eighteenth century at least five species were said to have disappeared from the garrigue vegetation around the vicinity of Montpellier, seat of an old and eminent School of Pharmacy (Flauhault, 1937, p. 162, citing (and qualifying) M.E. Planchon).

Not all gathering activities need be destructive to the natural vegetation. Some of these plants would otherwise be regarded as weeds in vineyards and on fallow. Some come from field edges and roadside verges. But the gatherer tends to concentrate on those parts of the plant involved in its propagation or survival, such as roots and seeds, or on the youngest, most tender, growth. Grazing animals do exactly the same. Different but complementary grazing habits of the different livestock ensure that almost every plant in a herbaceous layer is close cropped, that many plants and saplings are uprooted, that new growth is cut back by nibbling, bark is damaged, roots are chewed, and the seeds and the fruit of the dominant trees gobbled up. Reille attributes deforestation in Corsica directly to the excessive numbers of swine allowed to range freely there since the fourteenth and fifteenth centuries (1975, p. 165). Damage to the dominant tree species through the grazing of swine, sheep and goats can be almost irretrievable.

Early Industries and the Environment

By early classical times the industrial sector was being held responsible for adverse changes in the environment. Pliny was the most open on the undesirable effects of mining on the land. In Spain, he noted that ''the solid matter thus caused by the water [used in the washing of ore] is poured into the sea and the broken hill is washed away'' (33.66). But it was the vegetation that received the full force of the demand for industrial fuel. Strabo records that ''In ancient times the plains of Cyprus were thickly overgrown with forests and therefore covered with woods and could not be cultivated'' and goes on to identify the reason for their disappearance; ''The mines helped a little against this since the people would cut down the trees to burn the copper and silver and . . . the building of fleets has helped'' (XIV.65).

Mining and metallurgy was by no means a new economic development in the Roman period. Exploitation of copper had begun in the Neolithic and was certainly worked in Mediterranean Europe by the fourth millennium B.C. [26] A full distribution of the earliest workings will never be known but it can be assumed that wherever there were ores and minerals reasonably close to the surface, these were worked in prehistoric and Roman times as they have been more recently (Fig. 41). The shortage of information on the sites of old metal workings is not surprising considering that techniques of prospecting, ore-getting and processing scarcely changed before the nineteenth century.

By the late Neolithic and the appropriately named Chalcolithic period, copper exploitation and working would have been widespread. In Languedoc there are a number of localities known to have been worked in the prehistoric period as well as later or that one can reasonably assume to have been used. The copper deposits of the Cevennes, most particularly in the vicinity of Le Vigan, would have been no further than about 40 km distant from the metal workers at the Chalcolithic village of Fontbouisse (Gard) (Roudil, 1972, p. 18). At Neffiés and at Cabrières (Hérault), veins of dolomotized limestone traverse red-coloured Devonian strata. The veins contain blue and green copper carbonate (azurite and malachite) and are thought to have been exploited early in the Bronze Age if not already in the late Neolithic (Vasseur, 1911, cited by Bourdier, 1963, p. 323). Gallery mining was also known in the prehistoric period and at Neufbouches (Hérault) veins were exploited in this way to a depth of 12 m (Louis, 1948, p. 126). In eastern Spain, copper deposits in the Mediterranean coastal regions are thought to have been worked by the Neolithic builders of the collective tombs in Almeria. This is suggested by finds of copper slag at El Garcel (Savory, 1968, p. 80). That this part of Spain is in fact exceptionally well endowed in mineral resources was well

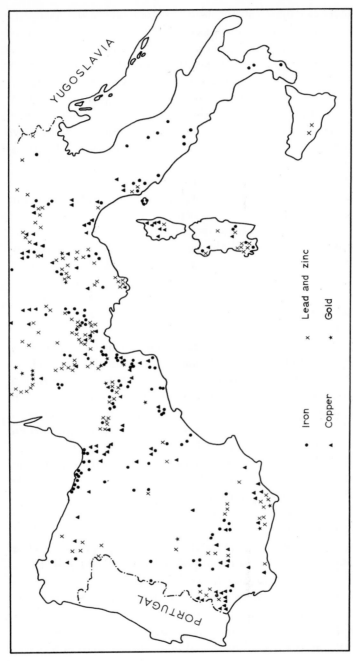

Fig. 41. *The distribution of metals in Mediterranean Europe* gives an idea of how widespread early and historic metal-working was. The relative paucity of mineral occurrences in Italy, especially in the south, is misleading. Iron was exploited in the thirteenth and fourteenth centuries at Longobucco (Calabria) and in the district of Reggio Calabria itself where Charles I of Anjou was anxious to develop the mining industry. The new *Carte Métallogénique de l'Europe* (UNESCO) was available only for Spain and France at the time of going to press.

known to the Greeks and Romans. Strabo was exceptionally enthusiastic: "neither gold, nor silver nor yet copper, nor iron has been found anywhere in the world in a natural state either in such quantity or of such good quality" (3.2.8). On the other hand, Italy was not exactly wanting in minerals either. In northern Italy the foothills of the Apennines east and west of the Adige contain many deposits of copper and silver which were probably the source of metal objects that have been found in settlements on the Po plain occupied during the third millennium (Barfield, 1971). Some of the late Neolithic communities in the same area had copper objects and it can be surmised that these came from the same deposits.

Perhaps second to Spain but still one of the greatest mining and metal-producing regions of Mediterranean Europe at all times has been Sardinia. Together with south-eastern Spain and Tuscan Italy, Sardinia ranked as a foremost producer of an enormous range of minerals. This is due to the importance of volcanic activity in the island's geological history. Metamorphic as well as volcanic rocks are rich in mineral veins and deposits. Fara listed nearly 20 minerals and deposits that were known and exploited in the sixteenth century. The list includes copper, gold, silver, molybdenum, antimony, pyrites, mercury and lead. But the earliest product of mining in Sardinia was not mineral but the volcanic rock itself, the glassy obsidian. Obsidian was being widely and in no small quantities exported in Neolithic times into southern France and into Italy (possibly via Elba) (Hallam et al., 1976). Copper was worked in the Bronze Age. The Romans worked mainly silver and lead. Medieval interests were concentrated on silver, to judge from the activities of the Genoese. These worked in small, private groups, formed for the purpose. For instance, in 1253 a group of six Genoese organized themselves into a mining company and acknowledging in writing "that they have jointly made among themselves a *societas* to last forever for the purposes of buying mines, furnaces or veins for the production of silver in Sardinia or wherever . . ." (Lopez and Raymond, 1955, document 99). After the Genoese, the Spanish maintained an interest in Sardinia's metal reserves. Their highly profitable "island route" was based on the export of cloth and coral from Catalonia and a return cargo of Sicilian wheat and Sardinian silver (Vicens Vives, 1961, Vol. II, p. 330).

Because of the widespread occurrence of mineral-bearing veins in Sardinia, early mineral workings are widely distributed over the island but because of their small scale or superficiality they tend to escape notice and when identified are still more difficult to date. One of the better known mineral areas is Barbagia, where mining appears to have been particularly important during the nuraghic period of the Bronze Age (Guido, 1963, p. 152). In this area shallow quarries for open-cast copper working, galleries that followed the metalliferous veins, and shafts that could sometimes be over 20 m deep, have been found and identified. Only one area in the island might have deserved early designation as an "industrial zone", and that is the Iglesias district. This district may be outstandingly well-endowed in mineral (and coal) resources but its major advantage lies in its accessibility from Cagliari, whence most of the island's ores and metals used to be shipped. At least 14 mines in the Iglesias massif have been identified as definitely of Roman origin and although only a single Roman foundry is known there is evidence for at least nine smelt works of the same date (Vardobasso, 1939; Binaghi, 1939).

The environment in Sardinia has suffered from the process of ore extraction and processing and serves to illustrate what happened more generally in Mediterranean Europe. The Barbagia district has been described as "a wild and desolate region . . . completely denuded of its natural forest by copper miners. . ." (Guido, 1963, p. 152). The vegetation provided the much-needed pit props, and above all vast quantities of fuel used in firecracking in the mine and in the smelting of the ores. The Iglesiente is today similarly treeless. An idea of the effects of mining on soil erosion is available from this district where, as a result of present mining operations, something approaching 200 000 tons of detritus is swept into local streams, the Piscinas and the Naracauli, each year (Spano and Pinna, 1956, p. 169). In addition, these rivers carry 900 000 m ^{3} of turbid water. In fact, comparatively little of the suspended material actually reaches the sea. Most is deposited on the bed of the stream; water in the Rio Naracauli contains 30 g of solid matter per litre of water at a point just below the mine's outflow but only 7 g at its mouth.

One of the most environmentally destructive techniques still employed in surface mining in various parts of the world is hushing. This involves collecting water in a dam in order to release it in a directed rush. The hillside is scoured of its plant and soil cover and the bed rock is thus bared for inspection for traces of minerals. Hushing was commonly practised in Roman times. Strabo revealed that "they flood the waterless districts by conducting water thither" in the gold-bearing districts of Andalucia (3.2.8). Pliny referred to "the bringing of rivers . . . for a hundred miles" for ore-washing (XLIX,66–78). Hushing has the most devastating effect on the landscape, being nothing other than an artificial process of gullying. As a consequence huge fans of debris develop and these divert the courses and create floods. The washing of ores has a similar if more modest effect in the short term. But for long periods mining was carried out in regions of naturally high erosion potential. As Strabo noted, it happens that "the regions which contain ores are necessarily rugged as well as rather poor in soils". The long-term effect of mining on the environment should not be underestimated.

Moreover, metal smelting was normally carried out with charcoal. Since the quality of the fuel is the controlling factor for raising and maintaining the temperature in the furnace, timber felling was by no means indiscriminate. Locally the demand for fuel could be concentrated on one or two tree species according to industrial specification. According to Theophrastus the "best charcoal is made from the closest wood such as the holm oak . . . they last longest" while the other oaks produced too much ash (*Hist. Plant* V.9). Old trees are better than young, again because they give sustained burning. It even mattered, according to Theophrastus, on which side of the mountain the tree had been growing before it was felled: "better charcoal comes from trees in a sunny dry position with a northern aspect". The different industries asked for different charcoals. In historic times iron workers preferred the charcoal of sweet chestnut, silver smelters asked for pinewood, and blacksmiths wanted fir rather than oak because, although it gave a cooler fire, it could be blown more easily into a flame which was conveniently fierce (Forbes, 1950).

So the forested areas of Mediterranean Europe were also populated with charcoal burners. The effect of charcoal burning on the vegetation and the soil in Languedoc has been studied in great detail by Blondel (1941). The timber which was most in demand here in recent centuries was the climax species, the holm oak (*Quercus ilex*). Like most oaks, the *Q. ilex* regenerates from the trunk and can be coppiced, though periodic resting is necessary. When it happened that demand outstripped the rate at which the coppice could be cut in one locality, the charcoal burners moved on to another, returning to the first area after an appropriate interval (perhaps 12 years). What they left behind was not just a clearing in the forest but a zone in which there had been intensive physical and chemical changes to the soil. In the first place, the ground may have had to have been terraced in order to provide a level working area. Where the soil cover was thin, this would have meant baring the rock at one point in order to have sufficient soil to pile up at the required spot. At the site of the burning itself the soil was now sterile and all its seeds and humus content destroyed. Instead a scatter of charcoal remained, the dark colour trapping the heat of the sun to such an extent that the micro-climate was altered and the soil's heat was excessive by the afternoon. The chemical contribution of this charcoal was not advantageous to plant regrowth, nor was the increase in alkalinity resulting from calcification. All these changes meant that seed germination and vegetation regrowth was held up until the soil had a chance to return to more normal conditions. Meanwhile, however, the clearing lay bare and unprotected. In all too many cases it was not long before storm rains were sweeping the soil away and yet another patch of soil erosion was initiated.

The ancient world was not short of fuel in general. Much of Mediterranean Europe remained closely forested until the fourteenth or fifteenth century A.D. But there could be acute local shortages because of the selective nature of the demand for industrial fuels. In southern France in Roman times the effect of the shortage of fuel on the roasting operation was particularly noticeable because "the second roasting is carried out with charcoal instead of wood" (Pliny, XXXIV.96). If however cheap local supplies did run short, there were two ways out of the problem. Timber could be imported, at the risk of raising costs, or the site of the metallurgical operations moved to a new place. Both solutions were employed in Mediterranean Europe at various times. In addition, restrictions on timber felling and on its sale came to be commonplace. In early classical times, the Greek island of Delos had become an important timber and charcoal intrepot in the third century B.C. (Forbes, 1950). Timber was sent to Delos from Macedonia but its resale there was severely regulated by law: "No-one who does not use the public wood-scales is to sell charcoal or logs or wood". Modern public wood-scales, dating from the last two or three centuries, may still be found in many areas, in the Garrigues of Languedoc at Les Matelles (Hérault), for instance. In Languedoc the urban centres had become insatiable consumers of wood. In the sixteenth century, Thomas Platter reported that the inhabitants of Montpellier had to have wood brought in from Verrières de Saint Paul, a distance of over 18 km from the city (p. 204). By 1788 there was "a terrible shortage of wood . . . prices are exorbitant" (cited by Dugrand, 1963b, p. 209). Across the Rhone, in Provence, villagers' rights to cut wood had been restricted since the fifteenth century, and in later centuries no villager was permitted to sell wood without licence (George, 1935, p. 305). In the Cerdagne, high in the eastern Pyrenees, nearly half the communes (12 out of 28) had no forest at all by 1764 (Flahault, 1937, p. 21).

Because of the fuel problem many, if not most, early industries had to be highly mobile. The glass-making industry was an activity greatly favoured by the aristocracy. Charles I of Anjou had a French glass master, one Pelligrino, working for him in a pavilion in the royal park at San Lorenzo (Foggia) and even today the ploughsoil of this long-deserted village site can yield fragments of exceptionally fine glass. In Languedoc, there were "gentlemen glass workers" at La Peyrière near Montpellier, but their kilns were moved "when the timber immediately around the *mas* was used up". Not far away, the glass works at Assas were abandoned "for more propitious areas" when the proprietor bought, in 1432, rights to timber in the still heavily wooded areas around the Pic St Loup (cited by Flahault, 1937, p. 6). In Provence, notwithstanding abundant lignite supplies, the glass masters insisted on the use of charcoal.

Because of the fuel problem, too, the metal industries were also mobile. The consequence of this was to spread more widely their damaging effects on the vegetation and eventually on the soil. In Provence, placenames such as Ferrasières (of which there are at least two), La Ferraye and Ferrière testify to medieval or later iron exploitation and iron working as a major contributor to the disappearance of the formerly extensive forests of Mont Vaucluse (George, 1935, p. 306). In medieval Tuscany, the spatial sequence of the iron industry was highly organized. In the early thirteenth century, one of the largest of the many professional groups in Tuscany consisted of 125 participants (Herlihy, 1958, p. 129). These took an oath and the group operated under the company name of Fabri. During the summer the men worked in Pisa itself, making metal tools and implements. During the winter they went in search of their raw materials, iron and above all wood. They went south to Gigli, Almo and other places between the mouth of the Arno and Rome, avoiding Maremma after the month of May, and to Elba. They also went to Corsica. In all of these places they had gathering points for the timber they themselves cut and the ores they themselves produced.

Together with metal-working and charcoal burning, ship-building was one of the oldest major industries in Mediterranean Europe. In prehistoric times, the Bronze Age in particular was an age of maritime trade, while the Mediterranean throughout the classical period and in the later Middle Ages has been famed for the sea-faring activities of its inhabitants. Cities such as Genoa and Pisa in the Middle Ages, Syracuse in the Roman period,

Punic centres such as Cagliari in Sardinia or Cartagena in Spain were very important centres of ship-building. Even inland cities could be directly involved in supplying timber. Perugia and *Clausio* are recorded as having supplied ships for Scipio's fleet in 205 B.C. (Frank, 1933, Vol. I, p. 174). The island of Sicily yielded timber and naval stores throughout the Greek period in immense quantities. For instance, in little over 1 month, the shipyards of Syracuse produced 220 ships for Hiero in the third century B.C. (Pliny, XVI. 192). Not far along the same coast Messina too had ship-building and ship-repair yards. The demand could not be sustained by the island's resources of tall timber. Although Verres had a merchant vessel built here, it is perhaps significant that the timber for this had to be brought over from the mainland (Cicero *Verres* 5.57). What would have happened was that each coastal city would have had its own shipyard together with a particular supply area. Such shortages in trees suitable for ship construction may therefore have been only local. Certainly Sicily had forests for many centuries after.

In each district there would be a whole range of industries and demands on the forests for fuel or for some product. The leather industry needed tannic acid, which was extracted from oak trees in preference to any other. In Provence in the historic period the preferred method of obtaining the necessary young holm oak was simply to uproot whole young trees (George, 1935, p. 306). Large-scale production of tannic acid in Corsica in the late nineteenth century involved bark stripping. It is estimated that 150 000 m ^{3} of chestnut wood were used to produce 10 000 tons of acid (Perry, 1967). Wherever possible the older and injured trees would be used and there was even a good deal of replanting. The industry had been obliged to turn to chestnut only because there was no holm oak left. Then there were the building industries. Even when timber was no longer used for city houses in Tuscany in the thirteenth century, there was still a demand on the forest since the bricks had to be fired and lime burnt for mortar (Herlihy, 1958, p. 25). A host of domestic and farming demands had to be supplied from the forests. Only oak wood, for instance, was considered sufficiently durable for wine presses and strong enough for bridges. Cork oak was much used in Italy as a hardwood for the wheels of carts and carriages, as well as for charcoal.

There were many minor industries which were carried on by villagers to whom rights of access to the forests had been granted by the landowners. In medieval and post-medieval Provence there was, for example, widespread distillation of essences such as oil of cades, juniper and lavender. There was the distilling of pine-pitch. All these demanded fuel. At least 20 of the pitch-distilling sites known on the Causses of southern France were of Roman origin, and to these has been attributed a good deal of the responsibility for the treelessness of the present-day landscape in their vicinity (Aymard, 1941).

Each form of industrial, agricultural, human and human-induced activity could hardly have avoided leaving a mark on the vegetation cover of Mediterranean Europe. At best, the effect of any one was an alteration in the status of the vegetation that, if not pushed too far, might right itself with time. However, the full pressures of these activities together, in certain districts at least, could not be accommodated by normal ecological resilience and vegetation degradation was followed by soil erosion, and any forested landscape could become "une montagne pelée" or "l'Arabie petrifié" of denuded Languedoc. Yet it was more than just landscape and scenery that was lost. The forests themselves were needed by all classes of people, farmers and city dwellers, for their resources.

The Vegetation in the Past

By taking account of local conditions and of those factors that have been effecting changes in the vegetation of a particular region, a good idea can be arrived at of the vegetation in past times. A vegetation mosaic, the pattern of the different plant associates, is in itself an historical document. The stability of vegetation is compromised by human activity above all, and each ecological group reflects this instability and localizes it. Unfortunately the vegetation document is not a palimpsest, recording everything that has gone before. By its regrowth, vegetation obliterates signs of the past, replacing one element in the mosaic by another. So the mosaic can record in detail the history of the vegetation only for an ecological generation, the length needed for the development and maturity of the climax tree species, say 100 years or so at most. Only with the aid of pollen analysis can the history of vegetation be traced further back, as far back in fact as the glacial periods.

Mediterranean Europe, however, is comparatively poor in pollen records, particularly from the lower and middle altitudes that have carried most of the settlement and economic activity of the past six or seven millennia. Current research by palaeobotanists is actively remedying this situation. Meanwhile, the outlines of vegetation history in Mediterranean

Europe are traceable and make an important contribution to the geographical understanding of the past.

Three main factors can be held responsible for the vegetation mosaic at any moment in time: relict species, climate and factors of degradation. Even where there has been a quite significant change of climate, individual plant or tree species may survive and remain in the locality. They owe their survival under new conditions either to their own adaptability or to some peculiarity in the local area. Thus the forests of Valbonne and Vaucluse in southern France owe their individuality and survival to the presence of lateritic soils, as already noted. The beechwoods of the Foresta Umbra on the Gargano peninsula in southern Italy are today unique at such a low altitude (450–600 m) but again they are regarded as relicts of mid-Holocene conditions. Normally, the vegetation pattern reflects the climate of the present day. This means, in Mediterranean Europe as elsewhere in the world, that increasing altitude gives rise to a series of vegetation zones that correspond to the vertical zonation of the climate. In the mountains of Mediterranean Europe it is possible to pass from warm temperate, even almost sub-tropical, conditions and vegetation through a cool temperate zone (characterized by the familiar vegetation of southern Britain) to a cold zone and even, on the highest summits, to an arctic zone above the treeline. Finally, relict species and species of the climatic climax alike are liable to be affected by the factors of vegetation degradation just discussed and by soil erosion. Accordingly, the vegetation pattern at all altitudes will contain plant associations of different ecological status. Reconstruction of the vegetation pattern for any period in the past must be based on these three factors.

In Mediterranean Europe today, the zonal succession starts at sea level in the warm temperate zone. The vegetation here is therefore typically evergreen and xerophytic. Without degradation, the climax species in most places would be the holm or evergreen oak, *Quercus ilex*. Not only towards the upper margins of the zone but in locally cool positions, such as on high *ubac* (shady) slopes, a deciduous oak may be intermingled, the brownness of its dead leaves standing out strikingly in winter against the grey-green tones of the evergreens. In exceptionally warm and moist districts it is the cork oak (*Q. suber*) that predominates. This vegetation reaches the sea (where it has not been cleared) except where the ground is very low-lying and where edaphic conditions result instead in open halophytic and hygrophilous (marsh) associations.

The phyto-sociology of both the climax holm oak forest (*Quercetum ilicis*) and of its sub-associations, the result of degradation, has been very well documented, notably by French botanists (Emberger, 1930; Braun-Blanquet, 1936; Flahault, 1937; Kuhnholtz-Lordat, 1938, 1958) and summarized in many texts (Birot and Gabert, 1964; Houston, 1964; Harant and Jarry, 1960; *Touring Club Italiano*, 1958). The degraded scrub associations are dominated by species that would normally be merely elements of the climax forest, such as the kermès oak (*Q. coccifera*), various junipers, lentiscs, cistuses etc. Very degraded heath associations are typified by small bushes of rosemary, thyme and lavender. These in turn give way to heathlands of asphodel and euphorbia and to turfs of *Brachypodium ramosum*. These are all the garrigue (in Spain *matorral*) associations, found on limestones. Maquis associations are found on siliceous soils (or on limestone soils which for a particular reason, such as through dolomitization or because of aspect, are exceptionally cold and moist). In a maquis scrub the associations tend to be dominated by box (*Buxus sempervirens*) or by individual genera of the ilex association such as *Juniperus communis* and *Pistacia lentiscus* instead of *J. oxycedius* or *P. latifolia* which are very common in the limestone garrigue associations. Lower status maquis associations contain much heather. Today the *Quercetea ilicis* zone also contains a good deal of Aleppo pine (*Pinus halepensis*). The role of this tree is thought to be crucial in the process of the present-day re-establishment of a fully developed holm oak forest (Nahal, 1962).

As altitude increases, the oak forests become increasingly deciduous and the plant species change until the natural vegetation is wholly characteristic of the cool temperate zone. Here are found tree species familiar to natives of northern France or Britain, the deciduous oaks, elm and sweet chestnuts for instance. Higher still in the zonal sequence the associations of the cold climatic zone are reached. These are dominated by larch, firs and birches. Only on the highest mountains of Mediterranean Europe do the forests gradually thin out until there is only open, treeless, alpine vegetation. Permanent snow is found only on the highest parts of the Alps or Pyrenees.

In each country and within the different regions, the limits of each zone are found at different altitudes (Fig. 42). This positioning reflects above all latitude and aspect in relation to the general climate. What the prehistorian and palaeogeographer need to know, bearing in mind the changes of general climate in the later Holocene, is the exact position of each vegetation belt in the different regions at any given time in the past. For this, however, many more pollen analyses are required, above all from

L*

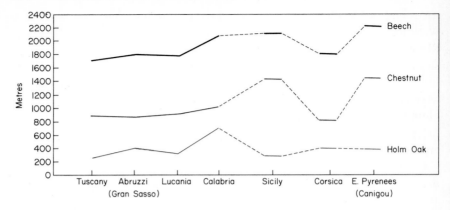

Fig. 42. *The upper limits of some of the major forest species* of Mediterranean Europe, showing how aspect and local conditions as well as latitude can affect the zonal distribution of forests.

the low altitudes where, unhappily, the problems of pollen preservation are most acute. The general picture, though, is reasonably clear. During most of the prehistoric, Roman and the early medieval period, by far the greater part of Mediterranean Europe would have been covered by forest associations. Flahault pointed out (1937, pp. 138–139) that even in this century only about a third of southern France is cultivated, and less than that in *départements* such as Var and Alpes-Maritimes. In the uncultivated areas, possibly only some 20% of the vegetation cover is not of secondary or degraded status. The Tavoliere of Foggia in southern Italy, in contrast, may have been one of those regions where many of the interfluves would have been more or less permanently deforested very early on, in pre-historic times, because of its climatic marginality and lowland nature, which made it particularly susceptible to changes in the position of the water table (see Sarfatti, 1953, on the latter point). Neolithic settlement here may have been amongst the densest anywhere in Mediterranean Europe and there was also a dense and prosperous population on the plain in the early part of the last millennium B.C. By Roman times, though, the plain was left ''lifeless . . . where no tree revives under the summer breeze'' (Horace, *Odes* 1.22.13). Away from the settled areas in the surrounding hills, the forests of ''wooded Daunia'' remained and Horace was able to boast of the ''broad oak forests'' of his native province.

Few of the forests of Mediterranean Europe would not have been marked to some extent by anthropogenic activity during the prehistoric millennia. By Roman times there may even have been a considerable extent of secondary forest in certain areas. Vita-Finzi points out that forests were more extensive in Greece in Imperial Roman times than in the classical period (1969, p. 108, fn 1). Even so, despite local shortages of good timber for ship-building or for the building industry, or of suitable fuel for the production of charcoal, there was undoubtedly sufficient forest in Mediterranean Europe in Roman and medieval times to attract attention. The forests of Sicily had supposedly awed Odysseus with their ''tall pines and crested oaks'' (Homer, 9.186). There are relics of these forests still in the Nebrodes mountains. Etna remained wooded at least until Imperial times (Strabo, 6.2.8) and the mountains around Palermo were forest-covered until the first century A.D. (Silius Italicus, 14.262). In the Palermo forests, the tall oak trees were said to produce ''acorns of remarkable size, twice as big and copious as any where else on earth'' (Diodorus, 4.84). There can be little doubt, as Frank has pointed out (1933, Vol. I, p. 171) that the deforestation of Sicily is a modern or at least post-Roman phenomenon.

The same can be said for the other parts of Mediterranean Europe. Ovid described the poplars of the Po (*Amores*, II. 17.32; *Met*, II.325ff) and Tacitus related how the woods around Cremona helped the Romans in the battle of *Locus Castrorum* in A.D. 69 (Histories, II.24). These forests were still standing in the Middle Ages. It was the fourteenth or early fifteenth century which saw the first modern phases of colonization and clearance. On the Arno lowlands, too, the forests survived into the Middle Ages at least. Strabo (V.2.5) had spoken of ship-building timber from Pisa and yet in about 1050 a German poet was able to comment on the ''wood brought from Lucca'' while in 1286 the woods of Pisa's Stagno district were still thick enough to harbour thieves (Herlihy, 1958, p. 23). One forest, that of San Rossano, stretched unbroken from one river to another, from the Serchio to the Arno.

There had been changes in the vegetation pattern of Mediterranean Europe prior to the Roman period. Up to a point this was due to anthropogenic activity. But on a much broader scale, there were also shifts in the altitudinal positioning of the major vegetation zones in accordance with the changes in the general climate that characterize the post-glacial period, together with a certain amount of adaptation of the local vegetation to the new conditions. The identification of these climatic phases is based above all on palaeo-botanic studies but the accepted sequence is largely based on data from north-western Europe. Only recently are corroborative details for a certain number of places in the warm temperate zone of Mediterranean Europe becoming available.

In general terms, the sequence marks the gradual improvement of climate from the end of the last glacial to a peak (the "climatic optimum") at about 5500 B.C. or just a little later (the Atlantic phase). Recent work on the pollen record from southern France (Escalon de Fonton, 1969; Renault-Miskovsky, 1969, 1970, 1971; see summary schema in Guilaine (ed.), 1976; Arribas, 1968) tends to confirm this from local data. One point is of critical interest in the history of the farming populations of Mediterranean Europe. The establishment of the favourable Atlantic phase in Mediterranean Europe by about the middle of the sixth millennium B.C. means that the long and complex process of "Neolithicization" (summarized by Guilaine, 1976) and the Mesolithic–Neolithic transition would have been coinciding with the climatic and ecological change from Boreal to Atlantic conditions. The Boreal was a period of relatively cold winters, rather dry conditions, and a marked continental tendency. The burgeoning of the new mixed farming economy of the middle Neolithic therefore accompanied, or immediately followed, the establishment of the Atlantic type of climate, so suitable for vegetation and plant growth.

It was the Atlantic phase that saw the establishment of the forest cover of Mediterranean Europe. The evergreen holm oak however at this stage occupied only a relatively restricted position at low altitude (Fig. 42). By far the greater part of the climax forests at middle altitudes and higher up in the mountains was dominated by deciduous oak species. This woodland would therefore have been very much denser, with a closer canopy than holm oak forest. As conditions changed and the Atlantic climate became established in the central Apennines, cold-tolerant species, such as juniper and pine established in the Boreal at quite modest altitudes of 500 m, were displaced to higher altitudes by a mixed deciduous oak wood of oak and beech (Frank, 1969). In Languedoc, the sub-arctic birch forest on Mont Aigoual (at 1300 m) was replaced in the Atlantic by a mixed oak forest containing *Quercus sessiliflora* and *Q. pubescens* (Firbas, 1931); similarly in Corsica. On the Rotondo massif, near Lac Creno, and on other mountains at over 1200 m, deciduous oak woods spread up from lower altitudes pushing the established pinewoods (*Pinus larico*) yet higher (Reille, 1975). By the end of the Atlantic, the landscape of Mediterranean Europe would have been one of a heavily forested region. Mainly deciduous forests spread from near sea level to 1300 or even 1400 m. Oak and beech were the dominant species. At the lowest altitudes there was some holm oak but probably only on the driest soils; on the interfluves, perhaps, in Corsica; and on limestone plateaux and hills on the mainland. In Corsica tree heath (*Erica arborea*) was more common than holm oak at sea level. It flourished here in particular because of the moist climatic conditions and the generally siliceous soils of the island.

The holm oak did not gain the ground it has covered since then until the Sub-boreal, when annual precipitation decreased slightly. This small change in climatic conditions would have had maximum impact on the vegetation of the climatically or geologically drier districts, towards the sub-tropical margin for instance or on limestone and other free-draining terrain. Here, with its better tolerance of seasonal aridity, the holm oak had a distinct advantage over the deciduous species. Where human activity introduced drier local conditions, through degradation or forest clearance, the holm oak gained ground. It has been noted that the Sub-boreal saw the development of a much more marked environmental contrast between coast and interior in western Provence (Planchais *et al.*, 1976). Some of this can be explained by the presence of hills and mountains not far inland, but in large measure the new dryness of the coastal zone may have reflected a greater degree of human settlement and activity here.

The Sub-boreal lasted from about 3000 to 2500 B.C. to the early centuries of the last millennium B.C. (800 or 700 B.C.). If the Atlantic phase had seen the establishment of a prolific forest cover over virtually all Mediterranean Europe, it was the Sub-boreal that saw the establishment of those characteristics associated with this forest cover to the present day: the dominance of holm oak and its associations at lower altitudes (up to 300, 400 or even 600 m according to latitude, aspect and terrain), its ecological precariousness and vulnerability to degradation; and, consequent on that, the considerable variety of the vegetation mosaic which reflects the activities of increasingly dense human settlement pattern.

Most of the Chalcolithic and all of the Bronze Age would have coincided with the duration of the Sub-boreal. In Corsica, cereal pollen appears in the spectrum at Lac Ninon (1770 m) (Reille, 1975). It would have been carried up-valley from fields lower down in the valley. From near sea level, at the southern end of the island, comes another series of pollen diagrams, recording an entire cycle of vegetation clearance and regrowth at Grotta d'Araguina (Bonifaccio) (Gagnière *et al.*, 1969). This cave lies at the bottom of a steep-sided and narrow combe, facing north. It has a long history of prehistoric occupation and a certain amount of forest clearance must have taken place in the Neolithic. Certainly by about 2000 B.C. there was little full forest in the immediate environs of the cave. There were some trees but no undergrowth and 10% of the total pollen rain represents tree species. These were species associated with the holm oak associations, oak itself (probably holm, possibly also cork), box, olive, pistachio and pine. Three or four centuries later there was some undergrowth but no stands (only 2% was tree pollen) and there is little doubt that what natural vegetation there was around Grotta d'Araguina was a low maquis. But by the end of the millennium farming activities had been so reduced that the forest had regrown and tree pollen accounts for 24% of the pollen rain. It was by no means the same forest as before however. Conditions, either climatic or edaphic or both, were evidently cooler and moister and there were hazel and alder as well as oak and elm.

The Sub-Atlantic phase started about 700 B.C., possibly as late as 500 B.C., and continues today. The climatic "change" involved was not very great though regionally it, like earlier changes, may have had some significance. Annual precipitation increased sufficiently to make the distinction with the Sub-boreal and to put an end to any tendency to excessive drought. Temperatures were cooler than they had been during the Atlantic. There were to be periods of unstable weather or very slight climatic fluctuations. For example, the post-medieval period (from 1550 up to 1850) is thought to have been marked by two centuries of relatively cool and moist conditions and increased storminess. In north-western Europe this phase is recognized as the "Little Ice Age" (Lamb, 1966) but it seems to have had a counterpart in Mediterranean Europe. Earlier, in the fifth and sixth centuries A.D., there may have been a similar "worsening" of the general climate, as suggested by documentary and sedimentary evidence. By far the most significant change during the two-and-a-half millennia of the Sub-Atlantic, however, is unquestionably that associated with anthropogenic activity. Reille offers a terse summary of the situation. He found more profound changes in the vegetation of Corsica in this one phase than over the entire post-Würm period prior to the Sub-Atlantic (1975, p. 87).

The story of Corsican vegetation changes serves well to illustrate the sort of changes that were going on over virtually the whole of Mediterranean Europe during the historic and proto-historic periods. At

← Time B.P.

Altitude (metres)		Sub-Atlantic	Sub-boreal	Atlantic	Boreal
Present		2500	4500	7500	6700
Alpine	2500				
Sub-alpine	2000		*Pinus larico*		
		Fagus abies	*Fagus*		
		Pinus larico			
Mountain	1500	*Fagus abies*	*Fagus* *Taxus baccata*	*Taxus baccata* Deciduous *Quercus*	
(L. Creno)		*Pinus larico*	Deciduous *Quercus* (*Betula verrucosa*)	(*Alnus glutinosa*)	*Pinus larico*
Supra-Mediterranean	1000	*Castanea*	Deciduous *Quercus*	Deciduous *Quercus*	*Pinus larico*
		Quercus ilex (*Erica arborea*)	*Quercus ilex* (*Erica arborea*)	*Erica arborea*	
Mediterranean	500	*Quercus ilex* *Erica arborea* *Quercus suber*	*Quercus ilex* (*Erica arborea*)	*Erica arborea* *Quercus ilex* ?	?

Fig. 43. *Altitudinal zonation of vegetation in Corsica since prehistoric times* (from data in Reille, 1975, kindly checked by M. Reille).

the beginning of the Sub-Atlantic in Corsica, at high altitudes, clearances were being made in the oak forests, probably by burning. By A.D. 500 the vegetation at these altitudes was relatively undisturbed and the forest was in process of redevelopment. Beech, however, replaced oak. Reille explains this by the fact that beech mast germinates more quickly than do acorns and that beech saplings are not eaten by pigs whereas young oak shoots are, whether growing from acorns or from the bole. The beech forests were not destined for a long life. By 1200 or so the marked increase in pine (*P. larico*) was at the expense of beech. It can be explained, Reille suggests, by a period of climatic coolness, high cloud cover and humidity. The next period of change, starting in the late fifteenth century, was the most radical. The newly established pine forests were felled as timber, the surviving oak woods were cut for charcoal, damaged by bark-stripping for the tannin industry, or degraded by overgrazing. The consequence of these last few centuries is that, for the first time since the early Atlantic, there are no extensive deciduous oak forests at middle and high altitudes in Corsica.

If the beech woods have survived better this is only because, so long as it was possible to find some oak or pine, beech timber was considered too branched for carpentry and not the best for charcoal. But Reille has little hesitation in singling out the pig as the single most effective agent of the destruction of the Corsican oak forests since the Middle Ages. In Corsica, as elsewhere in Mediterranean Europe, swine were not only permitted but encouraged to roam half-wild in the mountains. During the warmer months they ranged high up in the oak forests. Here the acorns of the *Q. sessiliflora* fall early in the season. The oncoming cold and the first snows forced the herds down to lower altitudes, and they passed the winter in the chestnut woods, or lower still, in the holm oak forests. A small number of grazing swine would do little permanent harm to the vegetation but even today their numbers in the Corsican mountains are considered excessive. Not less than 16 hectares should be allowed for each mature pig and it is calculated that the mountain zone of Corsica (land over 600 m) should not carry more than 4300 swine at any one time. The declared or official number today is 30 000. There is little reason to think it would have been much less during periods of intense population pressure in the post-medieval period.

Away from the mountains in Mediterranean Europe and on the lowlands or in the lower hills, where the holm oak forests would reign supreme were they not subject to clearance or degradation, there can be a surprising amount of deciduous vegetation; deciduous oaks, elms, poplars, ash and sycamore. These trees, and their associated shrubs and grasses, are tied to the edaphically cool and moist conditions of valley bottomlands (Tchou, 1948; Sarfatti, 1953). Formerly there would have been extensive deciduous woodlands on the broader flood plains but clearance for agriculture has reduced these to, at most, a discontinuous belt of trees bordering the river courses. Despite its reputation as a treeless plain, the Tavoliere of Foggia still has one substantial floodplain forest at Incoronata, protected by the sanctuary. The dominant trees are deciduous oaks (*Q. pubescens* and *Q. apennica*). The herbaceous layer and lower shrub strata are luxuriant and even lush compared with the xerophytes of the higher valley terraces and on the surrounding interfluves. In earlier times such woodlands, with their fresh green summer foliage, would have been of immense importance to farmers for their livestock. It would have been from these woods, the ''fierce forests'' of medieval Tuscany, that the elm and ivy leaves used in summer to feed the stalled cattle and other domestic animals were gathered.

Right up to the last three or four centuries, speaking very generally, the farmers and citizens of Mediterranean Europe lived in a land forested to a degree that is often difficult to imagine today. But the forests confronting early Neolithic man by no means resembled those of historic times, particularly at middle and lower-middle altitudes. They would everywhere have been, or have seemed, very much denser. The major landscape difference between deciduous woodland and the xerophytic forests is that the canopies of the dominant tree of the latter rarely touch and the forest is a strangely open one to northern eyes. In most of the region, moreover, there would have been much less variation in the status of the vegetation. Except in one or two areas, anthropogenic degradation was still comparatively slight in effect and spatially restricted. But by the middle or later Bronze Age, the more familiar vegetation zonation was being established in Mediterranean Europe. The present vegetation mosaic is one of the youngest and least stable elements of the "traditional" landscape and environment of Mediterranean Europe.

Valley Infill

Loss of vegetation cover can lead quite quickly to soil erosion, particularly in areas of high erosion potential. It may be true that in many of the cases where scarp-foot Neolithic sites have been successfully located beneath colluvial sediments, the depth of the overlay is not great and does not seem, to some, to have any bearing on the amount of soil loss from the uplands thought to be implied. It is nowhere suggested, however, that the original depth of soil on the uplands was great or that the soil cover was everywhere complete or of equal depth. Even today there are considerable areas of arable land (often no longer cultivated for economic and social reasons) in the shallow depressions that are typical of the massive limestone regions of Mediterranean Europe. These soil-filled hollows are separated from each other by rocky, scrub-covered expanses. What is envisaged is that such soil-filled basins would have been of greater extent and possibly of more frequent occurrence, prior to the (well-documented) centuries of vegetation degradation and soil erosion. It is perfectly possible to cultivate shallow soils though such arable land would not normally be counted amongst the best. With regard to the scarp-foot sites, a number of factors may account for the present depth of the colluvial covering. One set concerns the nature and size of the drainage basin (or the ''hinterland'' of the site with regard to its covering sediments). Another set concerns the degree of compaction (texture, humus content, humidity etc.) and yet another, the exposure of the site itself to soil loss (through wind blow, soil wash or erosion).

Most of the material swept off the uplands as a consequence of deforestation and erosion is eventually deposited long before it reaches the sea. Increased run-off and soil-wash gathers into streams that, as one of the ancient writers expressed it, ''tear up trees and rush headlong down''. Coarse debris is dropped as the streams graded to upland slopes emerge onto the plains. Finer material is swept along and deposited as alluvium by spreading floods. The hazard of these floods has helped make otherwise desirable lowlands and plains a sometimes less than comfortable environment in which to live and to farm. Flood-plain soils have tended on the whole to have been avoided both for settlement and for cultivation. It is, after all, regular flooding that brings the sands and silts that accumulate in the valley bottoms and that are built up slowly into the flood plains. A particularly severe flood will leave its trace in a band of unusually coarse debris, pebbles and gravels. It may be anticipated that over the last seven millennia the total environment of the valleys of Mediterranean Europe has been somewhat changed. The record of these changes is, unlike the case of vegetation, preserved in the phenomenon itself. Detailed and careful sedimentary analysis in the valleys has yet to yield a wealth of information about the past environments of Mediterranean Europe.

Since the Pleistocene, let alone the early Neolithic, there have been changes in river behaviour that can be linked with the continental or even world-wide factors of climate and sea level. It is important to realize however that a valley cannot be considered as a single unit in this context. That part of a valley affected by a change in sea level, whether this causes aggradation and the build-up of sediments or stream erosion and down-cutting, is of limited extent, confined to the lowest reaches. In contrast, a change in precipitation or temperature at the head of a river basin tends to affect stream behaviour, and to result in aggradation or erosion as appropriate, for the greater part of the length of the valley but above all in the middle and upper sections. Butzer noted that aggradation on a stream bed can continue inland even when sea level is falling (1964, p. 178). Earlier, Gortoni had come to the conclusion that there was no direct relationship between eustatic sea level change and valley alluviation in the

Italian Alps (1950, p. 311). From his observations he surmised, correctly as it now proves, that climatic conditions at the head of a river basin have far greater control over the stream behaviour and the valley's alluvial history than does sea level. Vita-Finzi has also put the emphasis on a climatic fluctuation "as the only acceptable mechanism for the erosion of the older [valley] fill" in the Mediterranean (1969, p. 98). What he did not make clear is that this holds good primarily if not only for the upper and middle reaches of a valley.

It has been noted that the major phases of alluvial deposition during the last 100 000 years have coincided with periods of low sea level. This is now explained by associating the lower sea level with a withdrawal of water from the sea in a period of glaciation. Away from the glaciers and ice caps themselves, climatic conditions were highly erosive, being very wet or with low, rock-shattering temperatures. These phases tended therefore to result in an increase in the amount of debris and sediment carried by the rivers. In order to maintain a rate of flow concomitant with this increased load, the rivers attempted to build up the gradient of their courses, and large-scale alluviation was the result, inland that is. A decrease in the load resulted in a period of stream erosion or downcutting. The normal pattern of river behaviour therefore is that periods of alluviation and valley infill alternate with periods when rivers cut into their own sediments. As a result of downcutting, part of the flood plain is left high above the new level of the river as a terrace. The terrace series of Mediterranean valleys has been amply documented. There are usually four in evidence, each marking the position of a former flood plain (Fig. 44) (Judson, 1963b; Vita-Finzi and Judson, 1964; Vita-Finzi, 1969; Cherkauer, 1976; Birot and Gabert, 1964; Cuenca and Walker, 1974, 1976). The characteristic profile, in other words, of the major valleys of Mediterranean Europe, its

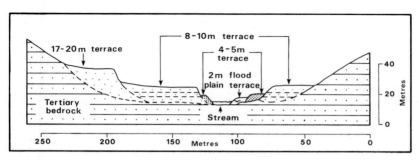

Fig. 44. *Cross-section of the Gornalunga valley, Sicily* (after Judson, 1936b).

overall breadth, its stepped cross-section, and the broad, shallow, often braided and meandering channel, is a direct consequence of late and post-glacial sedimentary history.

In this sedimentary history, various factors have played a part, notably anthropogenic activity, climatic change and fluctuations in sea level. But these factors are not of comparable order. However important man-induced erosion may have been in one region or another, the evidence (as available at present) does not show consistent intensity or, more importantly, synchronous incidence of valley sedimentation in Mediterranean Europe. Potter has pointed out, for example, that in south Etruria, while a period of major valley alluviation began in the third century A.D., the extensive land clearance for farming that would account for the increase in stream load had taken place over 800 years previously (1976, pp. 212–213); the clearance is documented in the pollen record (Bonatti, 1963, 1970; Frank, 1969) and from archaeological evidence (Ward Perkins, 1961, 1963, 1968, pp. 14–17). The work done in Etruria on valley infill (Cherkauer, 1976) illustrates how the Mediterranean area is one of the few parts of the world where the record of human activity is long enough and sufficiently detailed for interactions between man and man-induced effects and the phases of valley sedimentation to become apparent.

It may be accepted that the observed alternation between stream erosion and stream aggradation is in the first place the normal pattern of behaviour for rivers in their natural state and that although it may not be possible to identify an ''immediate cause'' for the incidence of one phase or the other, as Cherkauer suggests (p. 108), it may be expected that the episodic behaviour of rivers relates to variation in the interdependent factors of climate and of sea level. So far, the emphasis in the literature on Mediterranean valley changes has been very much restricted to the possible relevance of climatic changes to valley infill (e.g. Vita-Finzi, 1969; Bintliff, 1975; even Cherkauer, 1976 and Potter, 1976). What is lacking is an integrated study of a single valley, from coast to headwater, accounting for the entire range of possibly relevant factors. General factors—climatic change, changes in relative land-sea levels, stream phase (erosional or depositional)—should prove to be synchronous but the human-induced changes, insofar as these can be isolated, will be independent, unpredictable, and different from region to region.

Geomorphologists accept that the major phases of glaciation led to the lowering of sea level in a world scale. What is less well discussed or documented is the relationship between post-Neolithic climatic changes in the Alps and Pyrenees and sea level within the western Mediterranean basin in particular. Some ideas may be derived from the study of Alpine glaciers. Le Roy Ladurie summarizes physical and historical evidence from the Alps. Since the late Sub-boreal, the five major advances of Alpine glaciers have been: 1400 to 1300 B.C.; 900 to 300 B.C.; A.D. 400 to 750; A.D. 1200 to 1300 or A.D. 1150 to 1350; and A.D. 1550 to 1850 (the Little Ice Age) (Mayr, 1964, cited in Le Roy Ladurie, 1972, p. 274ff). To judge from the last advance, that of the Little Ice Age, the actual changes in temperature could be very modest, involving no more than one degree centigrade. The change in overall weather pattern, however, could be considerable, with ''bad'' weather, higher rainfall and snow incidence and increased storminess (Lamb, 1966). While in the mountains the snowline advanced and glaciers encroached on fields and farmsteads, lower down farmers had to contend with unusually cold and wet growing conditions. For this there is abundant if not always coherent documentary evidence. If such a phase of climatic deterioration happened, in a particular district, to coincide with a phase of deforestation or intensive vegetative degradation, the resultant soil erosion could be of major order, leading to the aggradation of the flood plain and the infilling of the valley.

Between the cool fluctuations and the periods of glacial advance there were warm phases. These cool and warm phases are the two main types of secular climatic oscillation known for the historic and late prehistoric periods. During the last three-and-a-half millennia they have each been reproduced five times (Le Roy Ladurie, 1972, p. 247). But the periodicity is highly irregular. Whether mild or cool, the phases have never been of the same duration. One phase of glacial advance lasted a good two-and-a-half centuries (1590–1850), another scarcely more than one century (1150/1200–1300). They are, however, homogeneous and, however long or short, each type of phase is apparently consistent. The climatic history of Mediterranean Europe as illuminated by the behaviour of glaciers provides part of the background for valley and coastal sedimentation and for the other environmental changes that have directly affected historic and prehistoric farmers. The inherent instability of stream behaviour falls into place as part of a wider scale and more general environmental dynamism.

The only record of stream behaviour is contained in the details of the infill sediments themselves. As yet there are few studies to complement Cherkauer's excellent examination of the Treia at Narce in south Etruria

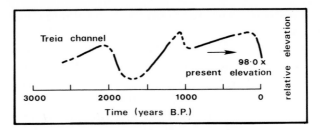

Fig. 45. *Stream behaviour in a Mediterranean valley since prehistoric times.* Trends of the River Treia channel show phases of aggradation (represented by a positive but only relative slope) (from Cherkauer, 1976).

(1976). Here he is able to show how lateral shifts of the channel gradually took the stream bed higher and higher as the alluvium built up (Fig. 45). Finally the regime was altered and instead of deposition there was erosion. Between 1000 B.C. and the present day, three downcutting phases of the Treia can be documented in this way: a major one between about 0 and A.D. 500, a minor one about A.D. 1000 and the present phase, which looks as though it may be another major one. The Treia sediments, and those of other valleys in Mediterranean Europe that have been similarly considered, show that the valley infills bear witness to an eventful geomorphological history in the last few millennia alone. Looking at the full depth of the sedimentary infill of Mediterranean valleys, Vita-Finzi (1969) provided an outline classification for the valley sediments based on just two categories, Old Fill and Young Fill. Obviously, such a simple classification does not attempt to take account of the details of environmental change since the beginning of the Neolithic but it does provide a useful basis. It also raises a number of questions.

According to Vita-Finzi, the Old Fill dates from the Quaternary. It is in fact what Butzer had already described as "a heterogeneous class of colluvial silts and alluvial gravels" (1964, p. 297). Other authors had attempted to sub-divide it into older and younger phases. Ottman, for Corsica, suggested an Old Alluvium I, of reddish colour, and an Old Alluvium II, very much browner in colour (1958). For Vita-Finzi it is all one, deposited before the melting of the last glacial (between 50 000 and 10 000 B.C.) (1972). He admits that the fill can be very varied, forming strong, heavy soils in areas of coarse and even angular detritus. In thickness it varies up to 20 or 40 m. Today this Older Fill constitutes the terraces which flank the sides of Mediterranean valleys, resting on the bedrock of their interfluves and which are advantageous in terms of human occupation in being safely above flood level.

The deposition of the Older Fill was interrupted by the melting of ice-caps and glaciers and the associated rise in sea level. This rise in sea level, the Flandrian transgression, culminated in a post-glacial maximum at different dates in different localities (because of variable isostatic tendencies). After about 6000 B.C., *grosso modo*, there was a general slackening of the rise in sea level and sediments, and the Young Fill began to be deposited in the valleys. It is the Young Fill therefore that is relevant to that part of the prehistoric period considered in this book and to the historic period. The new or Young Fill is duller in tone and darker in colour than the Old Fill, being mostly grey or buff. It is of more homogeneous texture, described by Vita-Finzi as a silty, fine sand. Vita-Finzi has also suggested that it offered a much more fertile soil to post-classical farmers than most prehistoric farmers would have had in the valleys or, more pertinently, on the higher terraces. Before accepting this judgement, however, two points have to be borne in mind. One is that these new soils, being part of the actual flood plain, may not have been much used in early times for cultivation, for fear of flooding or because of their heaviness as compared with interfluve or valley-side soils. Secondly, granulometric analysis has revealed (p. 357) how variable in texture even post-Roman alluvium can be.

According to Vita-Finzi, deposition of the Younger Fill started at very different times. There is a gap of four-and-a-half centuries between the onset of deposition in Morocco and Greece (Fig. 46). The only point that emerges convincingly is that valley aggradation always started in the historic period and usually early in the first millenium A.D. In North Africa, the commonest date of onset appears to have been about A.D. 300. In Greece it was about A.D. 400. Further west, in Mediterranean Europe, it was earlier, at the turn of the millennium in Spain and at about A.D. 100 in Italy. For Greece, Bintliff agrees with Vita-Finzi and comments on what he sees as the ''consistent dating'' for recent hinterland and upstream alluviation which points to a late Roman commencement and an early modern cessation (1976, p. 258). Vita-Finzi himself merely insisted that ''what is certain is that the [Younger] fill was being laid down during the Middle Ages, and that it is now being eroded'' (p. 102). More recently he has suggested an even broader phase for this period, running from A.D. 0 to 1650 (1972).

The variation in the date of onset of one of the most important changes

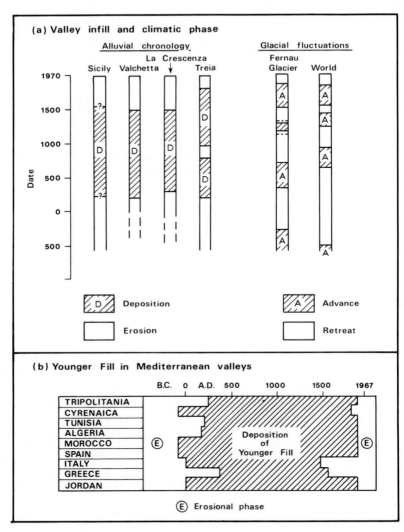

Fig. 46. *Chronology of valley infill.* (a) Some Italian streams compared with each other and with climatic fluctuations as represented by the behaviour of glaciers (Cherkauer, 1976). In (b) the date of onset of deposition of what Vita-Finzi sees as a single major phase of valley infill covering most of the historic period is shown (Vita-Finzi, 1969).

in the valleys of Mediterranean Europe in the last 2000 years tells its own story. Although Vita-Finzi, followed by Bintliff and others, look to the climatic factor, two points are against expecting this to be satisfactory as a monocausal explanation. The first is this variability in date of onset. The second is the *detailed* history of the historic fill, unobserved or ignored by Vita-Finzi but illustrated by the Treia sediments (and from coastal sediments described in the next chapter). Unquestionably, the climatic factor is of immense importance but it has to be considered together with the human one.

The late Roman-medieval period is undeniably one of the most complicated and eventful in human and environmental history. More studies as careful and as detailed as that made of the Treia sediments at Narce are needed to observe the past behaviour of rivers and the nature of valley infill. Similarly detailed and complementary studies of coastal siltation are also needed in order to elucidate the links between climate, sea level and fluvial changes. Only when a number of these become available might it be possible to make a start in chronicling the major changes in the environment of Mediterranean Europe and to have a "fixed" context for the ecological changes wrought by man himself and which may also be recorded in the sediments.

10

Siltation along the Coasts

The sea has been as important in many ways to the inhabitants of Mediterranean Europe as the land. Strabo summed up with acumen the land–sea relationship in Mediterranean Europe when he referred to his contemporaries as "in some ways amphibious and inhabitants as much of the sea as of the land" (1.1.16). Despite the proximity of the sea, though, the coastal zone was assessed, in the first instance, for its potential as an agricultural resource area, just as the inland districts were. Specifically coastal or marine resources, like fish or salt, were regarded as bonuses to be taken advantage of as compensation for some shortfall in the agricultural land. But besides this lowest level of economic significance there was a more abstract measure of the importance the Mediterranean Sea had for the inhabitants of its bordering lands. Braudel elaborates on the strength and profoundness of the relationships between individual regions of the Mediterranean world which had been woven through the commercial use of the sea (1972, p. 276ff). The acquisition, maintenance, or severing of these relationships started in the Neolithic with the obsidian trade. By Roman times they were expressed not only in the exchange of commodities but in diplomacy. The interplay of political affairs throughout the historic period was often expressed in economic measures that were liable to be felt in the daily lives and social well-being of the lowliest inhabitants of Mediterranean Europe.

From Neolithic times onwards, people have lived, or have tried to live, near the coasts of Mediterranean Europe. For most of them, the coastal resources or maritime activities were ancillary to the normal agricultural way of life. For a minority, for the sailors and ship-builders, and the merchants who awaited the safe arrival of each cargo vessel, it was the sea that provided their direct livelihood rather than the land. Their activities led to the polarization of interest and investment on specific points along the seaboards, the ports and landings. It must be expected that physical changes to coasts, affecting the functioning of these points, would be critical to the success of their role in the local economy. In the final analysis, however, it is found that the most far-reaching consequences of coastal change are those that have affected the coastal zones as a whole, and in particular their quality as areas for permanent settlement and agriculture.

There is often ambiguity in the use of the word "port". It may be used to designate a harbour or equally a town or place that possesses a harbour. But not all coastal places had a harbour. Leaving out of consideration those villages which turn their backs on the sea although within sight of it, a very large number of coastal places have (and still more have had) no formally laid out harbours but only landings—a beach furnished with at most a rocky or wooden jetty. For a harbour to enjoy a reputation as a "good port", it needed only to provide shelter from high winds and full seas, from enemies and from pirates. It was not necessarily deemed good because of substantial or complicated dock structures or protective works. Even coasts described as harbourless (south-eastern Spain (Strabo 3.4.8) for instance) in fact had innumerable landings. By preference, most of these were near, even in, the mouth of a river, the essential requirements being a good beach, a nearby supply of fresh-water, and an overseeing hill or promontory. Given such a location, and the simplicity of so many early harbour structures, it is far from surprising that harbours have proved to be amongst the most vulnerable of all man's establishments: that sort of harbour is at the meeting point of two of the most unstable of all geomorphological environments, the shore and the river channel.

On the other hand, the failure of a harbour installation is a technical point and it should not be thought that problems with siltation or erosion lead inevitably to the decline of the urban centre associated with the harbour, still less to its total demise. All ports face both ways. The efficacy of coastal changes in influencing the fate of harbour installations in Mediterranean Europe since earliest times is undeniable. What has to be explained is why the coastal regions of Mediterranean Europe contain veritable graveyards of towns and port-cities, defunct in the last 2 or 3000 years and maybe earlier. The full story of the coastlands, the coastal cities, and the ports of Mediterranean Europe, has not yet been told. What will certainly emerge is that the factors of change in these coastal districts are often as much human as physical. Meanwhile this chapter seeks to open up some of the questions concerning the vulnerability of both the coast*lines* and the coast*lands* behind to human perception as well as to physical change.

Coastal Changes

The ancient writers seem to have had a clearer understanding of coastal changes than of inland erosion. Pliny recalled Theophrastus's reference to the island, as it was then, of Circeo in 314 B.C. and pointed out that by his own time it had become joined to the plain of the Pontine Marshes (III.V.58). He also described the way the coastline of southern Spain was changing because of the mining: "thus the earth carried along in the stream [from the mines] slides down into the sea and the shattered mountain is washed away, and by this time the land of Spain owing to these causes has encroached a long way into the sea" (XXXIII.66). Entire lands, he said, can be born "through the conveyance of soil by streams . . . or by retirement of the seas as once took place at *Circei*" (Monte Circeo). Strabo

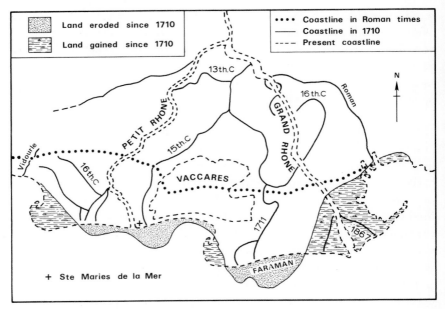

Fig. 47. *Changes in the Rhone delta in the historic period* (adapted from Blanc, 1977).

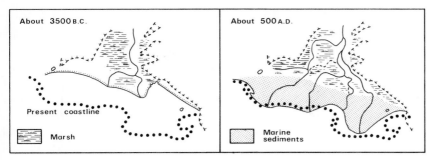

Fig. 48. *Changes in the Rhone delta since the prehistoric period* (Bourdier, 1963).

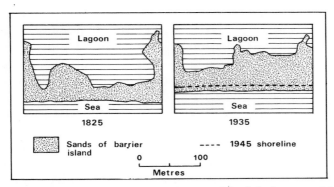

Fig. 49. *Changes in barrier islands.* The evolution of the lido between Maguelone and les Aresquiers (Hérault) from 1825 to 1945 (adpated from Galtier, 1958).

also referred to coastal change in Spain and to "the alluvial deposits that are discharged by the river [*Beatis* or Quadalquivir]" (3.1.9).

More recently it has been claimed that the coast of Valencia has gained nearly 4 km since Roman times (Houston, 1959, p. 170); that the Llobregat delta (Barcelona) is 3 km further out than it was in Roman times (Marques and Julia, 1977); that the Apulian coast near Manfredonia has gained a third of a kilometre since 1870 (Pecora, 1960); that the Tiber delta has been pushed seawards over 4 km since Roman times (Bradford, 1957, his Fig. 23); and that the Rhone delta advanced at the rate of 55 m each year between 1700 and 1710 but rather more slowly thereafter (Russell, 1942, p. 221). Shore sediments have not only gained in extent as these examples show but they can be much deeper too. There are now over 4 m of material over the medieval beach within the port of Genoa (Milanese, 1976) and over 2 m of silt have buried a Roman tiled floor near the Tour du Vallat in the Rhone delta (Russell, 1942, p. 243). A century ago archaeological investigators at Sybaris (Calabria) had to dig through over 8 m of alluvium before they could reach the door of a tomb dating from the fourth century B.C. (Grimal, 1964, p. 227) and recent archaeological work here has had to contend with depths of up to 12 m of alluvium at the mouth of the Crati (Meyerhoff, 1967; Ward-Perkins, 1964). Thinking about the Jucar and Turia rivers and their contribution to the infilling of the Albufera lagoon of Valencia, Rossello Verger engaged in a hypothetical sum to account for the infill. This envisages up to 400 metric tons per square kilometre being eroded in the basins of these rivers each year since the Flandrian transgression and carried down into the once-extensive lagoon (Rossello Verger, 1972).

Much less is heard of the retreat of coastlines, possibly because of the difficulties of obtaining measurements for something that has vanished. Reclus estimated the erosion of the limestone cliffs east of Marseilles as 820 feet since the time of Caesar (cited in Russell, 1942, p. 231). The Rhone delta has one of the most rapid rates of progression in the world but paradoxically this is accompanied by active erosion in some parts (Blanc, 1977, p. 1). At Les Saintes Maries, for instance, the shore was about 4 km away from the village in 1710 but over 700 m was lost in less than two centuries, 50 m having been eroded during the last decade and a half alone, and the sea now is very close (*ibid.*, p. 32). To judge from underwater research (and the plans in Patroni and Flemming, 1969), something like 3 hectares of the built-up area of the Punic and Roman city of Nora in southern Sardinia have been submerged, possibly, in this case at least partially, due to the earthquake that occurred in March 1000 and which has been held to account for the abandonment of the city (La Marmora, Vol. I, p. 232). In Provence, dunes cover part of the former Massiliot colony of *Tauroentum* (Var) but another part of the town now lies beneath the sea. In the nineteenth century, Lenthéric saw at least a square mile of ruins just beneath the surface of the water (1869, his plate 3). Further along the same coast another Massiliot colony, Olbia, has suffered a similar fate (Baratier *et al.*, 1969). In Italy, the sea has claimed two generations of ports in the Gulf of Gaeta. For the second, a replacement for an earlier, small port lost by submergence, the Romans had to excavate an estimated 60 000 m^3 from the surrounding tufa (Schmiedt, 1964, p. 30). Nor has it been only small harbours that have been lost by erosion. The Punic port of Malaga in Spain was famous for its sea walls but these have almost wholly vanished through marine erosion (and some siltation?) (Leon, 1969).

Yet another form of coastal change has been the infilling of estuaries and lagoons and the isolation of ports sited on their inner shores. Roman Fréjus (Provence) was so sited but although vessels under 50 tons continued to reach the harbour up to the middle of the seventeenth century, today 2 km of dry land separate the Roman ruins, ''Caesar's port'' and the Augustan moles from the present shore (Fig. 50). Lenthéric was able to show, from early references, that the material that blocked the lagoon was in process of deposition as early as the first and second centuries A.D. (1859, p. 275ff). Along the Levantine coast of Spain there was formerly a huge gulf opposite Elche, similar to another major embayment in French Catalonia which used to contain the Gulfs of Narbonne and of Capestang (Fig. 51). Both these are now almost wholly infilled and with extensive areas of dry or reclaimed land. Pliny's reference to ''the Ilicitan Gulf'' (III.20), however, makes it clear that a substantial body of water open to the sea remained in the Gulf of Elche as late as the first century A.D.

In Roman times it was possible to reach Pisa, now nearly 10 km inland but perhaps only 6 in Roman times, from the open sea. Ships would pass either by way of the Pisana lagoon (now the Prata marsh) or across a lagoon between the barrier island and the Coltura dunes (now the Padule di Stagno) (Schmiedt, 1964, p. 34). This means that one of Pisa's outports, Porte alle Conche, was itself probably a lagoon or river port and never a sea port. Similar changes were going on on the other side of the Italian peninsula at the end of the last millennium B.C. Ravenna ''passed from a

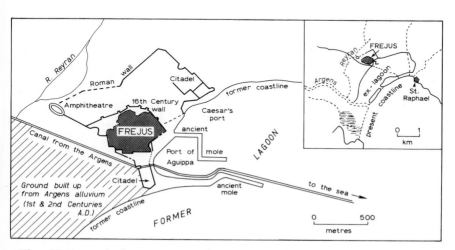

Fig. 50. *Lagoon sedimentation at Fréjus, Provence* (based on Lenthéric, 1859).

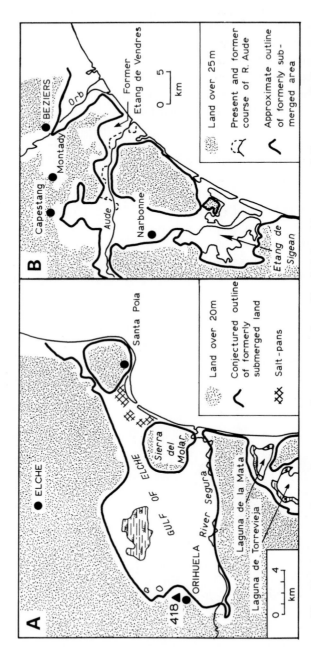

Fig. 51. *Changes in the coastline since prehistoric times:* the gulfs of Elche (Alicante) and Capestang (Narbonne).

A

ELCHE

Santa Pola

Sierra
del
Molar

GULF
OF
ELCHE

River Segura

ORIHUELA

418

Laguna de la Mata

Laguna de Torrevieja

Land over 20m

Conjectured outline
of formerly sub-
merged land

Salt-pans

0   4
km

B

BEZIERS

Orb

Capestang

Montady

Aude

Narbonne

Former
Etang de Vendres

Etang de
Sigean

0   5
km

Land over 25 m

Present and former
course of R. Aude

Approximate outline
of formerly sub-
merged area

sea town position to that of a land town'' (*ibid*, p. 39). Here marine accretion led to the broadening of the barrier island on its seaward side at the same time as sediments were being brought down by the rivers into the lagoon, contributing to the infilling of the lagoon. Not far to the north of Ravenna is the site of *Adria*, formerly a pile-supported lagoon-side town that can be regarded as an early ancestor of Venice. Originally, *Adria* had been easily approached by ships but by the third century B.C. its maritime functions had been transferred to Altino and Aquileia, a consequence, it can only be presumed, of navigation problems due to siltation. The site of *Adria* is today over 20 km from the open sea. As at Ravenna, the broadening of the barrier island by the appearance of a second barrier 5 km further east during the fifth and sixth centuries B.C. contributed to the isolation of the former port.

Problems and changes at Venice since the Roman period have had as much to do with flooding as with siltation. Excavations on the northern island of Torcello have revealed evidence for a major transgressive phase, approximately from A.D. 450 to 550, when slowly accumulating alluvial muds covered the Roman occupation levels (Leciejewicz and Tabaczynska, 1969/1970). From 1740 one of the main preoccupations at Venice was the provision of protection from the sea and an immense effort was put into the construction of walls, dykes and palisades. Just the two lidos of Pellestrina and Sottomarina were protected by over 5 km of such walls (Luzzatto, 1950, p. 27). Nevertheless, siltation also created problems. By the end of the thirteenth century the increased density of bankside housing, the number of timber-built bridges and landing stages, and even the scaffolding erected out in the canals during the construction of a house, all contributed to a deceleration of flow in the canals and to an acceleration of deposition of river sediments. By the fourteenth century, Venice's only real port, San Nicolo di Lido, was suffering from excessively shallow water and throughout the century there were discussions about the dangers of the sand banks that had appeared at the entrance to the lagoon. However, notwithstanding such vicissitudes, the Venetian lagoon has remained open and today the major threat is one of flooding. Artificial closure is discussed as a protective measure, and there is not much threat from desiccation or infilling.

Some formerly open estuaries have been closed and almost entirely infilled since classical times. In Apulia, Lago Salso remained a more or less open gulf until about the late sixteenth century. Strabo's description of it suggests that it was also open in Roman times (6.3.9). The presence of a

M

major embayment along the coast would explain the directions given to travellers going south from Sipontum in the Peutinger Itinerary (third century A.D.) (Delano Smith, 1978. p. 93). The coast road of the day would have had to follow the foot of the Gargano (where it can still be traced) in order to cross the Candelaro river at the point where it empties itself into Lago Salso, before skirting the lagoon of Salpi (Fig. 58). If closure of the Candelaro estuary was very recent, across the Italian peninsula the joint estuary of the Ombrone and Bruna rivers had been closed off from the sea before the *Via Aurelia* was built in the second century B.C. Four or five centuries earlier this too had been a wide, open gulf (Schmiedt, 1964, p. 22 and his Fig. 29). In Spain, most of the estuaries and river mouths described by Strabo as not only open but navigable far inland (Book 3) are now closed or so restricted by sedimentation that navigation, even by small craft, is not practicable.

A much less common form of coastal change in Mediterranean Europe has been the drowning of a lagoon by the sea. This is because the geomorphological conditions for lagoon formation and for submergence are so different that only a major tectonic displacement would normally overtake the accretion that results in a lagoon. Yet this is precisely what appears to have happened along the west coast of Sicily, where the formerly lagoonal island of Motya is now an island in the open sea (Isserlin, 1971; Schmiedt, 1965, p. 259ff and plan). Since, however, this sort of coastal change appears to have been quite common along the Atlantic coast of northern France (Ters, 1977; Pinot, 1974), it may be that the paucity of examples from Mediterranean Europe is due to insufficient submarine research.

A variety of coastal changes involving sedimentation has occurred in Mediterranean Europe during the last two millennia or so. It is matched by the instability of beach regimes over a matter of a few decades. The recent behaviour of observed beaches shows that coastal advance and retreat can be going on simultaneously within a remarkably short stretch of coast. The Rhone delta has already illustrated this point; the detailed study of beaches in Sardinia amplifies it. Excluding the offshore islands, Sardinia has 1400 km of coast, of which about one-third is low-lying and with beach accumulations. Spano and Pinna (1956) studied 30 of these. Three different states were identified: beaches can be described as in retreat, advancing or stable. To judge from their observations, few beaches in Sardinia have remained in the same state since the middle of the nineteenth century. Most have swung from one state to another, the phasing being roughly synchronous. Three major periods suggest themselves: from 1845 to about 1895; from 1895 to about 1935; and from 1935 to the date of the study (1954). However, it was rare that neighbouring beaches behaved similarly except perhaps within the gulfs. Moreover, it was common to find different parts of a single beach behaving quite differently from each other.

The lessons elicited from Spano and Pinna's study of Sardinian beaches are seen from other studies (e.g. Albani, 1933) to have general applicability. This means that different beach regimes and patterns of behaviour within quite short stretches of coastline are to be expected. Secondly, few beaches maintain a characteristic regime permanently but the phasing of changes may be less easily identified. Sometimes the change is no more than a seasonal adjustment. Sometimes it can be easily explained, as when a headland finally ceases to shelter a bayhead or when a river begins to bring down to the sea so much material that accumulation outstrips a tendency to erosion. Another lesson learnt is that changes from one regime to another can, and do, occur within very short periods of time. The Sardinian beaches have had three different regimes within little over half a century (Fig. 52). Finally, Spano and Pinna's observations show that the factors responsible for these changes in beach behaviour are both natural and artificial and that they can be of local or more general effect. On the whole, man-induced changes tend to be local.

One of the significant factors in beach behaviour and coastal changes is the wind, in so far as there is a close relationship between wind speed and wind direction on the one hand and wave direction and surface currents on the other. Shallow waterbodies, such as lagoons and estuaries, may be particularly susceptible but some sort of seasonal variation in sea level along a whole stretch of coast is normal. For this reason, the mean highwater mark is a more practical measure of the security from flood of a low-lying coast than mean sea level. In the *étangs* of the Rhone delta and in the lagoons of the Languedoc coast for instance a few days of a strong on-shore wind can result in widespread flooding along the inner shore while strong off-shore winds appreciably lower their level. Along the Faramon section of the Rhone delta, storm waves can raise the level of the sea by half a metre and even, for a few hours, by as much as one metre (Blanc, 1977, p. 42, citing R. Dumas). Occasionally, high seas break right through a barrier island and form a new, if temporary, *grau* (Galtier, 1958, p. 132). It is common to find that some *graus* regularly close up during the summer and exist only during and after the winter's storms. Fishermen in lagoons,

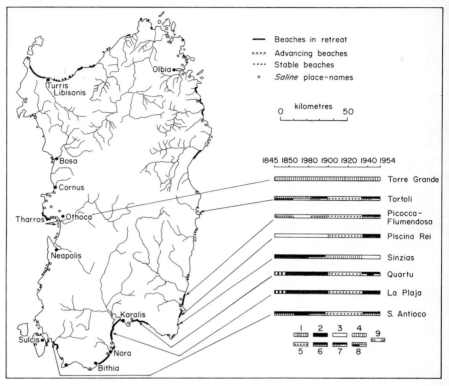

Fig. 52. *Beaches of Sardinia*, showing behaviour since the first part of the nineteenth century (Spano and Pinna, 1956). Punic ports are also shown.
1. advancing; 2. retreating; 3. stable; 4. probably retreating; 5. probably stable; 6. partly advancing, partly retreating; 7. mostly retreating, some stability or advance; 8. mostly advancing; 9. mostly stable, some advance.

like those of Cagliari and Quarto (Sardinia), may find they are unable to sail even flat-bottomed boats during periods of persistent off-shore winds (La Marmora, 1839, pp. 113–115). Surface currents too reflect weather conditions and wind direction. Seasonal variations in the behaviour of spits at river mouths are commonplace. The sudden disappearance of the Padrigiano sediments that were blocking the entrance to the Gulf of Olbia (Sardinia) near the end of last century were probably due to a change in wind and current directions (p. 371). An onset of north-easterly winds and gales is known to reverse the direction of surface currents in the Bay of Manfredonia (Stanley, 1972, p. 336). Since sands moved northwards in this bay (under normal conditions) are of different colour and mineral content from those moved south, it can be suggested that the final closure of the barrier island at Sipontum (Manfredonia) was due to a prolonged phase of unusual weather conditions (see below, p. 358).

Another factor to be accounted for is the possibility of a change in the relative position of land and sea. Because more than one interpretation is possible from the same datum, and because of the unequal distribution of analysed data over the whole world (Pirazzoli, 1976, p. A2), the question of sea-level changes in general and eustatic change in particular is an extremely difficult one. Nor does the very substantial literature help much when the question is a local matter along the coasts of Mediterranean Europe. Very little of the work on sea-level changes has concerned this area specifically. Extrapolation from the Atlantic or Baltic shores of western Europe provides a shaky basis for discussion. Moreover, the literature reflects at least three different views on Holocene changes in sea level (summarized in Jelgersma, 1966). There are those authorities who hold that sea level in the world rose from the post-glacial minimum (at -100 m) to a post-glacial maximum and has remained steady subsequently. There are those who hold that world sea level has continued to rise but that the rate of rise is slowing down. And, finally, there are those (led by Fairbridge, 1961) who see the post-glacial sea-level rise as a series of oscillations, the amplitude of which may have been decreasing during the last two or three millennia. One of the initial problems applying to all three views is that the geologist's and the historian's scales may be of such different order as to be virtually unrelated. In the context of palaeo-environments, a timescale involving oscillations lasting no more than a century is appropriate while the vertical scale is measured by the fact that displacements of centimetre or decimetre importance can be shown to have had noteworthy repercussions on human settlement and on economic activity in the coastal areas of Mediterranean Europe.

Faced with the possibilities of coastal changes in Mediterranean Europe, the first objective, diagnosis of a transgressive or regressive phase affecting the local area sometime in the past, might seem simple enough. But even this is not straightforward. Some types of transgressive sediments (chenier deposits for example) can result from a single if exceptional storm surge or from a protracted period of high water level. Or a period of "wetness", as recorded by marsh deposits, might equally well reflect saturation from a water table raised as much by excessive run-off and flood from further inland as by a rising level of water in the neighbouring lagoon or in the open sea. A second objective, the measurement of the displacement involved, might seem tempting in some cases but even here there are complications. One problem is the highly localized and unpredictable nature of the tectonic displacements (land moving in relation to the sea) characteristic of the geologically unstable Mediterranean basin. Another is that of sediment compaction. Yet another is rate of sediment deposition. In the last analysis only might a third objective be taken up. This would be to attempt to attribute the cause of the transgression or regression to one of the major factors, such as tectonic displacement, eustatic oscillation, climatic effect or sediment compaction. As far as the local area is concerned, the causal factor is of little more than academic interest at this stage. Only when a sufficient number of comparable observations become available specifically for the north-western part of the Mediterranean basin may the significance of each causal factor emerge.

Notwithstanding these difficulties, and the very early stages of present research into the recent coastal changes in Mediterranean Europe, the fact that there have been distinctly "wetter" and "drier" phases in low-lying coastlands since the Neolithic, cannot be ignored. Where these phases have been dated or assigned a period, some sort of synchronization is already emerging. For instance, the weight of evidence available so far tends to centre on the Roman period and to identify one or even two "wet" periods or transgressive phases. The first concerns the early Roman period.

For the eastern Mediterranean, Pirazzoli (1976b) documents a rise in sea level from 300 B.C. to A.D. 150. Caputo and Pieri (1976) show a rise of mean sea level from 600 B.C. to A.D. 100, also on the basis of archaeological evidence.[27] Sedimentary investigations carried out in southern Italy and southern France, and on the islands of Corsica and Sardinia, detailed below, similarly suggest a pre-Roman or early Roman "wet" or transgressive phase. What is less clear is how much change there was in the intervening period before the next clearly identifiable "wet" or transgressive phase, that of about the fourth and fifth centuries A.D. Then, the case for a major regressive phase, or relatively low sea level, during the Neolithic is an increasingly strong one too. Yet another "wet" or transgressive phase in the prehistoric period appears to coincide with the later part of the Bronze Age. A modern one may have taken place in the eighteenth century or be still happening.

One of the few things that can be said with conviction on this topic of post-Neolithic coastal change, is that the fate of one stretch of coast is by no means a certain, or even useful, guide to the fate of another stretch of coast, even a neighbouring one. The range of variables involved in coastal change is not only great, but many factors are closely interdependent while others cancel each other out. Some operate on a global scale, so non-Mediterranean studies can be relevant. Others are regional or local in effect and should only be observed locally. One of the major factors is also one of the most unpredictable, the anthropogenic one.

Lagoon Sediments and Early Settlement

It is arguable that the most challenging, even the most significant, changes come from the low-lying, lagoon-strewn coasts of Mediterranean Europe. For all its mountainousness, Mediterranean Europe is also renowned for its wetlands and coastal lakes and gulfs. There is, for example, the Camargue with the Etang de Vaccarès; the Albufera of Valencia; the Venetian lagoon; the Pontine marshes, the surrounding plains of which have been a byword for unhealthiness; the Roman Campagna; the Tavoliere of Foggia (''tomb of the Abbruzzi''); and the Maremma of Tuscany and of Etruria. Immense efforts at artificial drainage, land reclamation and resettlement, aided by the arrival of the tractor, have resulted in the transformation of all but the most persistent of the wetlands and lagoons into agricultural land or even land for building.

The outline of these aggrading coasts was established during the Pleistocene. Broad or narrow, strings of sandy barrier islands (*cordon littoral*) emerged then, separating the lagoons from the sea. In detail, however, there have been considerable changes. Sometimes the change concerned a shift in the position of the barrier island or, more accurately, the formation of a new one as at Ravenna in the second half of the last millennium B.C. More commonly, it has been a question of consolidation and the joining up of the numerous small islands and sand banks into a single continuous barrier. At the same time there were changes in the outline, extent or depth of the lagoon behind. Of all the changes, those that would have been of primordial consequence to the local population were those that took land away or those that periodically transformed dry land into wet land. It is now established that these types of environmental change have had at least as much effect on human settlement and economic activity at low altitudes by the sea as erosion in the uplands. For Latium it has been shown how the frequency of inhabited centres in the coastal zone has altered through the course of time (Terresu Asole, 1960). In the Roman period there was a nucleated settlement about every 9 km. In the

Plate 13. *Silted coastlands.* The lagoon at Posada, Sardinia, has been much reduced by infilling and only a small waterbody remains. Some of the surrounding land has been reclaimed for arable, some has been enclosed in a curious but characteristic corral-like fashion for grazing. Just inland is the site of Roman *Feronia*, supposedly also a Punic colony.

Middle Ages there was one only every 24 km. Today it is again one centre for, more or less, every 9 km.

If vegetation is the key to ecological stability in the hills, so the water table is the critical factor in the health of the coastlands as a living space for man. Lagoon and wetland sediments are typically very mixed in origin. They may have come from the sea, from rivers, or from the lagoon itself. As a source of information for the environmental history of the district they can be very rewarding. Quite small fluctuations in the water table, measured in tens of centimetres or less, are quickly translated in these marginal zones into a different depositional environment and a succession of sedimentary horizons is therefore a record of these changes. Each deposit has a characteristic colour, texture, faunal and floral content according to its depositional environment. A practical advantage is that the total depth of the sediments tends to be modest, particularly compared with infill in a valley. A section of 3 or 4 m at most in the coastlands is usually sufficient to reveal the depositional history of the last six or seven millennia. This shallowness can be explained by the fact that most of the sedimentary material that arrives on the lagoons or that is swept over the bordering flats is in suspension. On contact with the salt in the lagoons, the suspended material flocculates into particles (of 0·001–0·002 mm diameter) that are then deposited in the form of mud (Galtier, 1958, p. 159ff). It does not necessarily remain there for long, however. Whenever the water becomes agitated, by winter storms for example, much of the mud is disturbed into suspension once again and a large part of the suspended material eventually escapes from the lagoon through the gaps in the barrier island into the sea. Thus the lagoon-side muds represent only a small proportion of the total fine matter originally brought down by the rivers.

Lansargues (Hérault)

The first and most detailed local study to be described comes from the coastal plain of Languedoc. [28] From the Rhone almost to the Pyrenees, the coast of Languedoc is low and flanked by a series of lagoons (*étangs*), some interconnecting, some now quite separate. The ancient Gulf of Capestang has, except for the Etang de Vendres, totally vanished, and only the *étangs* of Bages, Sigean, Ayrolle and Gruissan remain of the Gulf of Narbonne. Further east the combined deltas of the Vistre, Vidourle and a Rhone distributary have isolated the Etang de Mauguio from the Camargue. This lagoon remains a substantial expanse of shallow water, amounting to about 3600 hectares. Up to the Middle Ages, when it formed part of a much more open network of channels and waterbodies known as *Stagna*, it was possible to navigate from the open sea, across the lagoon and up the minor channels to the port of St. Gilles, now 25 km from open water (Russell, 1942).

At the north-eastern corner of the Etang de Mauguio is the commune of Lansargues. The village lies well back from the lagoon shore but its territory runs from the marshes inland to the coastal plain proper. Like the other villages of this part of the plain, the territory of Lansargues includes a succession of terrain types corresponding to the different geomorphological units. The coastal plain, here about 40 m above sea level, includes the Villafranchian terrace. Minor streams drain from this terrace in more or less parallel courses to the lagoon; the Dardaillon, the Viredonne, the Berbian and the Lunel canal run across the territory of Lansargues. From the Villafranchian terrace, the land slopes to about 6 or

M*

7 m, the Nizzan terrace. This is where the lagoon villages are found, not only Lansargues but also Candillargues, Mauguio and the *bourg* of Lunel. Away from the villages, towards the lagoon, the land slopes down again to a broad, wet flat, only half-drained even today, scarcely more than 1 m and at most 2 m above sea level. The vegetation on these flats is typically that of drier marsh formations, with *Salicornia* sp., *Juncus* sp., *Arthrocnemum glaucum* and *Aeluropus littoralis* (Arnal *et al.*, 1977). The wetter areas are marked by *Phragmites* and *Scirpus maritimus*. From this wetland vegetation are derived the local terms for these flats, *le Cayrel* or *les Cayrelles*.

Except to wildfowlers and fishermen, neither the Cayrel flats nor the drier marsh areas are very inviting. The featureless levels are bleak, damp and windswept. Soils tend to be affected by salt, the water is brackish. There is a constant threat of flooding from bankful ditches and rivers. When, late in summer, the water table is as much as 1 or 1·5 m below the surface of the ground, this is only because of massive extraction further inland of stream water for crop irrigation. The lagoon itself is reached only with difficulty across a zone of reeds and rushes. Between these permanent marshes and the coastal flats, however, there is an irregular line of dry points, low knolls or islands, scarcely perceptible in the general flatness but marked by the *cabanes* of the wildfowlers and fishermen (Cabanes de Gasgon, Cabanes de Forton) (Fig. 53). Presumably these represent a former cordon or levée. If today they are the only dry points for the *cabanes*, so sometimes in prehistoric and proto-historic times too they provided the only sites suitable for permanent settlement. At Camp Redon, at the southern end of the knoll at Gasgon, late Bronze Age (Mailhacian) occupation was followed by Iron Age (Hallstattian) and then by Gallo-Roman. The sequence is similar at Forton and, east of the Lunel canal, at La Rallongue. But there is clear evidence that there were times in the prehistoric period when permanent settlement spread away from the cordon and was widely distributed over the area now known as the Cayrel flats. There is a broad zone of Chassey occupation (about 3000 B.C.) to the north of Gasgon. There is a Chalcolithic (2300–1400 B.C.) site on the north side of the knoll at Forton. The densest scatter is of Hallstattian occupation (900–500 B.C.), spread over the flats and across the Cayrel areas.

The discovery of these sites is very recent. For the last decade and a half, archaeologist Henri Prades has walked the entire lagoonside region, from Lattes to Lunel, with his assistants. The cutting of new drainage channels was a fortuitous but magnificent bonus. Buried stratigraphies and, most importantly, buried prehistoric sites were revealed. The results have been, even so far, astonishing. Within a 10 km ^{2} area that covers just the coastal flats at Lansargues, the total cull of prehistoric and proto-historic sites so far is (according to Prades):

Neolithic	{ Chassey	5 occupation areas (3 with hut foundations)
	{ Chalcolithic	3 occupation areas
Middle Bronze	Polada/Apennine	3 occupation areas
Late Bronze	Mailhacian	5 occupation areas
Iron Age	Hallstattian	6 occupation areas
	Gallo-Roman	5 occupation areas

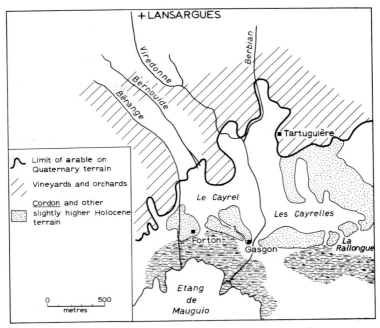

Fig. 53. *General map of Lansargues (Hérault) today.*

The message is clear. First, there can be no denying that the density of Neolithic and later settlement could be as great down on those flats as up on the limestones of the Garrigues further inland. And second, periods of wetness led to retreat of settlement onto the dry points of the cordon while in periods of dryness the inhabitants could, and did, disperse their dwellings and their activities widely over the lower ground. Archaeological details confirm that these people depended on farming no less than did their contemporaries inland. The details of the changes in their environment, from dry land to wet land and vice versa, are recorded in the sediments.

The story must start with reference to the time when the entire coastland was part of a lagoon. The evidence for this proto-Etang de Mauguio comes from the calcrete (*taparas*) that almost everywhere underlies sediments, even in the Cayrel flats. It is absent only at abruptly defined intervals which, it would appear, correspond to the courses of former streams (which have eroded the calcrete) or to channels within the lagoon (which prevented its formation). Typically, the calcrete here takes the form of a yellowish, nodular or blocky stratum, less than a metre below the surface of the ground and not usually more than 2 m thick. The upper surface of the stratum is hard. Its lower surface, very rarely visible, being permanently below the water table, appears to rest on or to emerge from white lagoonal clays. In some localities the calcrete is so ill-formed as to be represented by a similarly yellowish clay horizon containing only nodules of calcium carbonate.

Whatever the date of the formation of the calcretes of Lansargues, and of the former lagoon, they had not only been formed but constituted dry land by the Neolithic. The presence of the calcrete substratum is therefore of inestimable value to the archaeologist and in the study of the changing environment throughout prehistoric and historic times. It provides a clearly defined and visually obvious *terminus post-quem* in the field. It also preserves archaeological features. Any pit or trench dug into the calcrete has remained and can be dated from its archaeological contents. Although the earliest occupation on the calcrete is Chassean, the earliest-known pit is of Chalcolithic date (at Forton). This means that the sediments that have accumulated over these features are of post-Neolithic date.

The post-Neolithic sediments at Lansargues are well stratified (Fig. 54). They can be grouped into five classes or series. For reference purposes the basal calcrete and its clay equivalent constitute the A series. Sediments classed in the B series attract attention by their dark colour. They are dark grey or black. This is sometimes an overall impression gained from the blackness of patches of partially decomposed organic matter in a lighter olive-grey clay matrix, but more typically the sediment is a

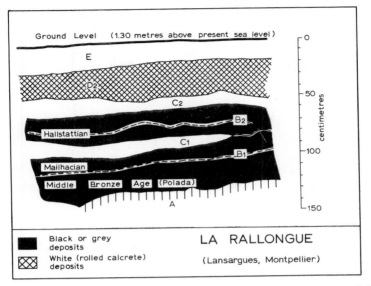

Fig. 54. *Sediments and archaeological levels at Lansargues* (data made available by H. Prades).

homogeneously dark, even black, mud rather than a clay. Granulometric analysis shows sediments of the B series to be poorly sorted loams of mixed origins (sample 28, Fig. 55), the degree of mix being greater in the vicinity of a stream (as at Forton). This fluvial element is reinforced by the molluscal content of the sediment.[29] At Forton, the same sample contained gastropods typical of brackish habitats (*Hydrobia ventrosa*); a number of *helicella*, terrestrial snails which live in dry grassy places, such as dunes or banks, or in calcareous places and which would have been carried downstream to Forton by the Bérange; and some marine molluscs, small *cardium* (*Cerastoderma glaucum*) and some *rissoa*. Away from the streams there were fewer of the fluvial gastropods in samples taken from the B series. At Gasgon the predominant species was *Phytia myosotis*, a gastropod of brackish habitat.

Sediments of the B series are characteristic of wetland conditions. They were the result of permanent saturation or regular flooding. The water was distinctly brackish, which shows that the contribution made by the lagoon to their saturation was by no means insignificant. Around a prehistoric site, the B sediments may be exceptionally rich in occupation debris. Artefacts and pottery date the first of the B horizons to the middle

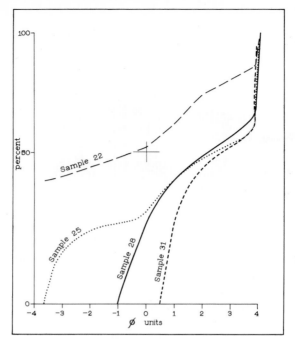

Fig. 55. *Granulometric profiles from sediments at Lansargues.*

and, above all, late Bronze Age. Often it appears that this earlier B deposit rests directly on the calcrete (as at Forton). In this case it has to be supposed that whatever sediments were covering the calcrete in Neolithic and early Bronze Age times have been incorporated into or subsequently transformed by the conditions of saturation that gave rise to the B sediment.

In contrast, the C series of sediments at Lansargues are pale grey or pale olive in colour. Sometimes they are even whitish from tiny soft concentrations of calcium carbonate, sometimes they are mottled like a gley. They tend to be on the fine side but are only "reasonably" and often only "poorly" sorted (sample 31). At La Rallongue they have been described as "non-organic, clayey-sandy loams" or just as "clay-loams" (Arnal *et al.*, 1977). Compared with the B sediments they are very poor in molluscal content. The samples from Forton contain a number of lagoonal *rissoa* but also some land species that could only have reached Forton in floodwater from the Bérange. The C sediments are archaeologically sterile. They represent conditions associated with an extensive lagoon; quite deep submergence by water sufficiently well-stirred to maintain its oxygen content and good aeration. The first of the C series identifiable at Forton were deposited after the Mailhacian (L.B.A.) B horizon but before the dry period of Hallstattian times.

Deposits of the D series are rather singular and will be discussed out of turn. The remaining E series differ from sediments so far discussed in being predominantly fluvial in origin. At La Rallongue they have been ascribed to the flooding of the Vidourle; at Forton, they must have come from the Bérange. They are the most recent deposits, ubiquitously topping the profile. They are silts and loams, sometimes of very mixed particle size (sample 25). At Lansargues they are everywhere grey in colour, whereas much further west, in the Lez flood plain, the modern alluvia have a distinctive yellow colour. They are all archaeologically sterile and also devoid of significant floral or faunal content.

The D series class together two deposits solely on the basis of their individuality. Neither is like the other nor like any of the B, C or E sediments. D1 is in fact a layer of shells; D2 an unusually coarse deposit composed of calcrete fragments, shells, archaeological and other debris. The latter is of more or less continuous, though well defined, occurrence, showing a clear stratigraphic discontinuity where it overlaps other sediments. The former is very local in extent.

The D1 shell deposits clearly represent local shell beds. At Forton, the shell layer is in places 2 or 3 cm thick and stands out clearly in the ditch section for its whiteness. It is composed overwhelmingly of the intertidal *Cardium glauca* though other brackish gastropods (*Bithium cerithium*, *Hydrobia* sp. and *Lymnia* sp.) are present. The extraordinary feature is that almost all the *cardium* are immature and that in many cases the two valves have remained paired even though the hinge ligament has long since vanished. There is little doubt that this deposit represents a colony of young cockles who had ventured into a perhaps rather marginal embayment of the lagoon, survived there a year or two quite successfully, but then had been suddenly overwhelmed by some disaster which resulted in an untimely and abrupt death. The deposit also contains numerous plaques of gypsum. The presence of these suggests that the cockles died of asphyxiation due to the excessively high temperature of their water. What cannot be stated is whether the heating-up of the water was due to an exceptionally hot summer or to a sharp decrease in the depth of the water for other reasons.

The D1 deposit near La Rallongue is similar except that it concerns mussels (*Mytilius edulis*) and there is no gypsum. The mussels are of impressive stature, some up to 10 cm in length, indicating full maturity. All that can be said with certainty about them is that there was formerly a sufficient depth of water at that point in which they could flourish, and that they too may have come to an abrupt death. Apart from the oxygen content and temperature of the water, beds of mussels are known to have been killed by siltation. Judging from the number of buried wooden stakes in the vicinity, it has been suggested that the mussel beds may have been artificial or cultivated. Certainly there used to be fishing near La Rallongue, when the lagoon stretched much further inland than it does today, for numbers of crude stone weights (of the sort still used by local lagoon fishermen) are turned up in the plough soil.

The outstanding characteristic of the D2 deposit, apart from its white colour and its coarse texture, is that all the material it contains shows signs of having been rolled. There are shells, mostly full-grown *cardium*, but they are often broken and almost always worn. Potsherds of Gallo-Roman date, where recognizable, are distinctly rounded. There is an element of finer material, silts and small gravels (sample 22) but the bulk of the coarse material comprises rounded fragments and lumps of calcrete. This D2 deposit is found from Forton to La Rallongue in the commune of Lansargues, and clearly it marks a former boundary between lagoon and shore. In other words, it is a *chenier* deposit, revealed by ploughing.[30] Such *cheniers* normally represent temporary strands of the lagoon, though it would not be too difficult to imagine a thinner deposit of this nature being thrown up by an exceptional storm surge. In either case, the outline traced by the D2 deposits in the marshes of the coastal flats of Lansargues, discernible as a whitish zone in the plough soil of such land as it is cultivated, effectively records an early extent of the lagoon. At La Rallongue, these soil colour changes show up the sinuosities of the former strand, its islands and *graus*. Much more fieldwork and detailed mapping is needed but the *chenier* must represent the lagoon as it was at an earlier stage, probably in the Roman Empire; the youngest datable pottery is given as A.D. 50 (H. Prades, personal communication).

The sediments and the prehistoric sites at Lansargues reveal the nature and, more approximately, the timing of the changes that have affected this section of the Languedoc coast and its lagoon-side lands. Once fully studied and carefully mapped, a more detailed and assured chronology of the changes can be attempted. Meanwhile, only the barest outlines can be suggested. During the Neolithic period (fourth and third millennia B.C.) the entire area of what are today the coastal flats of Lansargues was dry land. It is assumed that this "dry" phase, if no other, was due to an appreciably low sea level. The lagoon therefore would have been quite small and its shore much further away. The depth of the soil covering the calcrete may not have been considerable but even if it were less than half a metre this would have provided perfectly good land for cultivation. A number of streams crossed the area, perhaps in channels in the Cayrel areas today marked by an absence of calcrete. The farmers therefore could select their settlement sites relatively freely, without major physical constraints. In Chassey times there may have been a village of sizeable proportions on the flats immediately north of the *cordon* at Gasgon. In Chalcolithic times it was the practice to excavate pits, trenches or storage silos in the calcrete even, as at Forton, on the lower ground.

It was after the Neolithic-Chalcolithic period that conditions began to change. In fact, there probably never has been a full return to the state of the ground as it was in the Neolithic. While the early centuries of the Bronze Age are usually thought of as having been climatically very dry, even exceptionally dry, sea level was rising and with it the water table in low-lying areas like those of the Cayrel flats at Lansargues. By the last centuries of the second millennium B.C. and the late Bronze Age, ground conditions at Lansargues had become distinctly wet. Low-lying land was permanently saturated and, presumably, regularly flooded. Settlement was restricted to the elevations of the *cordon*. Wherever there was exceptionally low land (the wettest parts of the Cayrel areas today) or along stream courses and, perhaps, close to artificial ditches, there was permanent saturation giving rise to the black muds which form the first of the B series. Where such wetland ran close to the settlements, it was used for the dumping of household rubbish (and an occasional corpse). Stones might be set in the ground to provide a solid foundation, for movement or for other purposes. By the turn of the millennium the inhabitants would have already have adapted themselves to their new, wetland environment.

It would be erroneous, however, to consider these sites as economically or socially marginal, isolated from the mainstream of their civilization by the physical environment. On the contrary, the very same muds have revealed the economic importance of the late Bronze Age villages at Lansargues and the high quality of life in the wetlands. The Mailhacians here "lived well, certainly depending on fish and shellfood but also devouring tortoises (whence the name Domaine de Tartugière), deer, pig

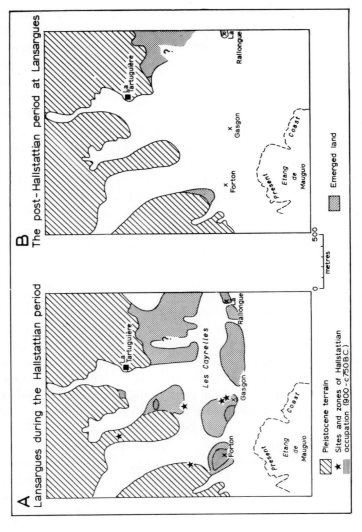

Fig. 56. *Tentative outlines of post-Neolithic lagoon changes:* the northern shores of the Etang de Mauguio, at Lansargues, in the last millennium B.C.

or wild boar, ox, the small ruminants, horseflesh and cheeses, while basalt quernstones show that cultivation had not been abandoned . . ." (Prades, 1973, p. 7). There was bronze casting, too, at several of the other Lansargues sites as well as at Mauguio, and pins, axes, pendants and other tools and ornaments were locally produced. A total of eight casts have been found from these sites, sufficient evidence to negate Roudil's assumption (1972, p. 189 and elsewhere) that the objects in bronze found in these marsh sites could only have been imported. One detail that has emerged clearly from the archaeological material is the importance of the horse; even in these early times, the characteristic way of life of the nearby Camargue was being formed.

For one or two centuries after Mailhacian occupation of the higher sites at Lansargues, it would seem that there was a total inundation of the Cayrel area, the drier marshes and even of the *cordon* sites themselves. The occupants would have had to move their houses to higher land on the land-ward side of the now extended lagoon. It is unlikely that they would have relinquished their territorial claim and before the end of the Hallstattian period (about 700 B.C.) the level of the water had retreated sufficiently for the flats to be considered sufficiently dry for widespread re-settlement. Pits and shallow trenches containing Hallstattian pottery are numerous, even on the lowest land (Fig. 56).

From all the evidence, and not just that of Lansargues, it might appear as though the thousand years from, roughly, 500 B.C. to A.D. 500, were exceptionally eventful in terms of changes in the coastal areas of Mediterranean Europe. It could be argued that this is only because the sedimentary record becomes very much clearer. The problem with the sediments at Lansargues is that since about A.D. 500 they are overwhelmingly of fluvial origin (a significant enough fact in itself) and as such they fail to record the subtle changes of water table or lagoon level as previously. Whatever the full explanation, it is clear that during the proto-historic and the Gallo-Roman periods at Lansargues there was another period of extreme wetness, even inundation. The *chenier* deposits overlap grey, lagoonal, clay-silts of the C series. It is unlikely therefore that even if the *chenier* itself resulted from a short-lived phase of extreme wind and wave conditions it fails to mark the maximum extent of the lagoon of Mauguio in historic times.

About this time a villa was built, complete with mosaic floors, on a tongue of high ground at La Rallongue. As it turns out, this appears to have been the last permanent settlement on the coastal flats at Lansargues.

For the last millennium and a half, riverine flooding has dominated the area's sedimentary history. Sea level, and the level of the water in the lagoon, must have continued to affect the position of the water table and the effectiveness of the natural drainage network. A still more relevant factor has been anthropogenic activity much further inland. Deforestation and soil erosion on the Garrigues, clearance and cultivation on the coastal plain, and wetter or drier phases of weather became the major factors in the post-Roman sedimentary history of the Lansargues wetlands. And wetlands they obstinately have remained, despite efforts at reclamation. In the eighteenth century the authorities despaired of making good use of some 5000 *sétérées* of newly drained land or of the remaining marshes (Daumas, 1951, p. 260). At least the local population rejoiced, as it is recorded, since they gained the right to pasture their livestock on the marshes and on land bordering the Etang de Mauguio. Very recently, an attempt has been made to drain some of the land for arable farming but the indications are that this too may not be of permanent duration or of great profit.

Sardinia and Corsica

It is not in every part of the coastlands of Mediterranean Europe that archaeological and sedimentary conditions combine to yield so easily the record of environmental change since the Neolithic. One practical problem that has to be faced is that the oldest sediments are generally now below the level of the water table and the chances of obtaining a complete, datable profile are rather small. Such was the case in most of the preliminary investigations into coastal change carried out in the islands of Corsica and Sardinia. In Sardinia at the Punic port-city of Neapolis, to take just one example, sedimentary information could be obtained only from the most recent deposits. Nevertheless, this is not without interest for what is revealed about conditions of deposition in particular and environmental circumstance in general. For the more recent past, attention is focused on two problems. One concerns the growing amount of sedimentary evidence for a period of exceptional erosion and, by implication, climatic wetness not more than a couple of centuries ago. The second concerns changing water levels in the lagoons.

The sediments at Neapolis have bearing on the first question. Most of the deposits at the foot of the slope on which the ancient city of Neapolis is situated are silts covered with colluvial materials. But not far below the surface of the ground is a layer of coarse gravels and flat but well-rounded pebbles (see Fig. 62). The pebbles, each 3–4 cm in diameter, are of micaceous sandstone. The local rock, however, is basalt. The pebbles can only have reached Neapolis in strongly moving water and whether the sea or the Mannu river was involved, a phase of bad weather may be inferred. This conclusion is strengthened by the fact that this occurrence of a layer of relatively coarse material just below the surface deposits is by no means peculiar to Neapolis. Across the Gulf of Oristano is the lagoon of Cabras. Investigations along its shores, near the Neolithic site of Currura de Aruif, revealed a similar sedimentary sequence. In this case there were no large pebbles but gravels that must have been brought into the lagoon by marine agencies, possibly when the lagoon was more open to the Gulf of Oristano. It would appear that they had originated in the Tirso valley and had reached the Cabras lagoon through the effect of long-shore drift, which here is anti-clockwise under storm conditions. In the neighbouring island of Corsica, the coarse layers found at Propriano (west coast) and Figarie (south coast) are composed of growan, an angular debris associated with the decomposition and erosion of granites. In each case the local rock is granitic so the material at Propriano and at Figarie has not travelled but represents local erosion. At Propriano, nearly 50 cm of growan were found overlying marine and lagoonal deposits, the infilling, as Caesari has shown, of the inlet used as a harbour in Roman times (Caesari, 1974). At Figarie, investigations were made in the vicinity of the badly eroded site of a Roman villa, an area of rocky outcrops and small lagoons and marshes that largely dry out in the summer. Below half a metre of lagoonal muds (exactly the same depth of cover as at Propriano) is another half-metre of growan. The growan in turn rests on an earlier series of dark lagoon muds and clays.

From these observations it would seem that there has been, at least in these two islands, a fairly recent phase of intensive erosion. It may be suggested, from what is known of recent economic and demographic problems in the islands, exemplified by developments (already described) in La Castagnicca in central Corsica, that this erosive period was associated with the late seventeenth and eighteenth century phase of extreme land hunger and demographic pressure. Increased forest exploitation and clearance would have coincided with the phase of relatively bad weather known as the Little Ice Age. A reduced vegetation cover would have offered scant protection to the soils of such mountainous islands as Corsica and Sardinia under conditions of higher rainfall and increased run-off.

The second question, that of recent changes in water level in the lagoons of Sardinia and Corsica, was raised by sedimentary profiles from the shores of the Cabras lagoon, not far from the Neolithic site of Currura de Aruif. These revealed the position of two former water levels. In fact, the overlapping of bank and lagoon bottom deposits strongly suggests recent changes in relative land and sea levels (Fig. 57). At Currura de Aruif there is, first, nearly a metre of coarse, very yellow sand, comprising the bank deposits. These contain the layer of gravels alluded to above. Then there is a series of lagoonal muds. These are so pale as to be almost white. They contain, unlike the overlying sediments, abundant molluscal debris, mostly of bivalve species. Normally, such pale sediments are indicators of the well-aerated depositional conditions typical of fairly deep water and certainly of water that is well stirred and very clean, conditions not at all consistent with the marshes which today fringe this shore and which give rise to black or very dark muds. Below these is another series of bank deposits. The overlapping of these very different sets of deposits, each representing quite different depositional locations, points to two water levels (Fig. 57). A similar discordance was noted near the Roman villa site of S. Agatha on the south-western shore of the Etang de Diane in Corsica. Here it is also suggested that the Etang formerly extended at this point some 20 m further inland than does today.

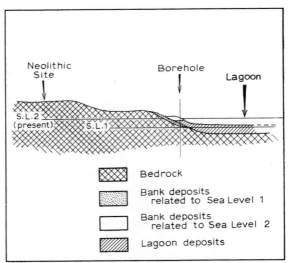

Fig. 57. *The lagoon at Cabras, Sardinia* showing shore sediments and the location of the Neolithic site at Currura de Aruif.

Foggia (Apulia)

The sedimentary events that have contributed to the history of settlement and economic activity on the coast of the province of Foggia, in south-eastern Italy, have already been published in detail (Delano Smith, 1978; also 1973, 1975, 1976). A summary is given here only as a contribution to the present discussion on coastland changes.

About 300 km² of flat, low-lying land borders the Bay of Manfredonia (Apulia, Italy). Most of this area is below 5 m. Prior to the middle of the nineteenth century there were extensive lakes and lagoons in the area: Lago Salpi in the south; Lago Salso, into which the interconnecting lakes of Versentino and Contessa drained, at the mouth of the Candelaro; and finally there was a tiny lagoon lying between the ancient port-city of Sipontum and the sea. Surrounding each lagoon was a belt of marsh varying in extent according to the season. In recent centuries, the whole coastal zone has been scantly populated. Yet medieval records and fieldwork confirm that there were at least five nucleated settlements here up to the fifteenth or sixteenth century. For instance, the city of Salpi (*Salapia*) was a not-insignificant lagoon port of Roman foundation which continued to function until 1547, when the bishopric and other offices were transferred to Trani. In pre-Roman times there were two major cities, a yet earlier, Daunian Salpi and another settlement that can be called *Anxanum* (as listed in the Peutinger Itinerary) in default of certain identification. In prehistoric times there had been much more permanent settlement, mostly Neolithic, around the margins of the lagoons than has been hitherto suspected. After the Middle Ages, however, the formerly firm outlines of the lakes and lagoons of the Foggia coastlands were obliterated and with the decline and eventually the disappearance of the medieval villages (*Cupola, Rivoli, Salpi, Salinis, Sipontum*) was lost all chance of an objective assessment of the quality of these coastlands as a living space in the past. Sedimentary research has shown that the prehistoric landscape here was quite different from the recent one which lies beneath the surface of modern marsh and reclaimed alluvium. Evidence for it, however, has to be sought below ground level.

A good deal of Lago Salpi has been drained and reclaimed since the early nineteenth century. But about 3 km inland from the former shore of the lagoon lies the extensive site of the pre-Roman city, Daunian Salpi (Salpi I). Most of the occupation was contained within the ramparted area but there was some extra-mural development particularly on the northern

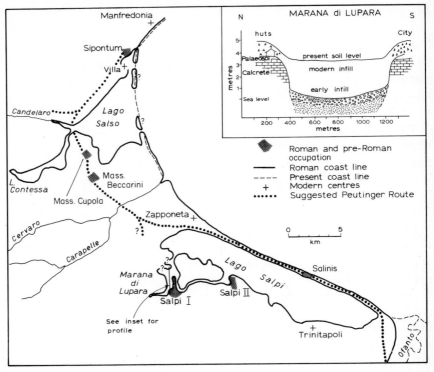

Fig. 58. *Coastal changes in the province of Foggia, Apulia* showing the formerly open gulf of Lago Salso and the channels and lakes at Daunian Salpi (Salpi, or Salapia, I). The Peutinger Table mentions *Salinis*; medieval Salinis was further south along the barrier island but there are grounds for suggesting that the indicated location of Roman *Salinis* was in the vicinity of the present Torre Pietra (Delano Smith, 1978). The inset shows the sedimentary section across the Marana di Lupara from north to south.

side (Fig. 58). Out here one particular group of huts was first occupied, like the city itself, in the ninth or eighth century and, again like the city itself, abandoned in the second century B.C. (Tinè and Tinè, 1969). This was when an entirely new city site was laid out by the Romans 4 miles away and actually on the shores of Lago Salpi.

The ground between the huts and the ramparted city is today still largely under marsh though a small part has been reclaimed for cultivation. It is known, appropriately enough, as the Marana di Lupara. It presents the typically bleak aspect of a wetland. Even the low knoll on which the huts are found would pass unnoticed were it not for changes in soil colour. The buried landscape however is far more interesting. A series of hand-augered boreholes provided a cross-section across the Marana from approximately north to south (inset, Fig. 58). These revealed that the proto-historic inhabitants of those suburban huts would have been separated from the main area of the city by a small but freely-flowing lagoon. The profiles all started with the white lagoonal muds and clays, representing the bottom deposits of the former lake. The infill, which started quite abruptly, is of fluvial origin; clayey loams of rather coarse texture, grey in colour but becoming increasingly olive-hued up the profile. The youngest sediments are also markedly stickier and heavier.

This change of texture between older and younger infill sediments is of particular interest. According to granulometric analysis, the difference between the two sets of loams is small. The older loams have a mean distribution of 2.31 *phi* units compared with 1·97 *phi* units for the younger, and a skew index of $-0·02$ as compared with 0·27. This means that the most recent loams contain a significant amount of the finest silt and clay particles that are normally carried in suspension in river water. Under normal conditions they would reach the sea and be deposited there as off-shore mud. Part of the artificial process of marshland reclamation, however, consists of the ponding of all the flood water in shallow basins (*vasce*) until the entire sedimentary load, including the material in suspension, is deposited. This process results in a highly characteristic type of alluvium, typically poorly sorted and with a "positive skew". Even with modern farm machinery, alluvium resulting from *colmate* makes a very heavy soil. The tractors used for ploughing are usually caterpillar tracked. The soil is classed as second or even third grade in contrast to the other "natural" alluvia which rank as of first quality. The upper horizons of the infill at Marana di Lupara are typical *colmate* alluvia.

At the northern end of the Bay of Manfredonia is found the site of ancient Sipontum (Manfredonia). Sipontum is known to have flourished in Roman times and continued to do so into the twelfth century. About the middle of the century it was described as "a good port" in the *Compasso di Navigare* (Motzo, 1947). The precise location of the harbour is not certain but it is a reasonable surmise that the shore immediately below the city walls was used at one time or another. Owing to the development of a southward-growing spit and probably several off-shore barrier islands, there was a small, open lagoon here by the beginning of the first century A.D., about a kilometre long and half as wide. The port must have had some importance or the environment was pleasant because in the middle of the first century A.D. a sumptuous *villa urbana* was built on a low-lying promontory at the southern end of the lagoon. The villa was designed so as to make the best of its location. Like those on the shores of the Bay of Naples or, in particular, Pliny's villa at Ostia, the walls of the Sipontum villa were built out into the lagoon to support rounded terraces directly overlooking the water. Today this villa is a kilometre from the sea. Since 1939 the entire ex-lagoon has been under cultivation.

The interesting question at Sipontum, apart from that of the existence of the *villa urbana*, is the manner and the dating of the closure of the lagoon. From reasonably reliable cartographic evidence, the final blocking of the barrier island can be said to have occurred during the last quarter of the sixteenth century. What the sediments have revealed is that the sands that caused the definitive blocking did not have the same origin as those which had formed the barrier island and which still form the beaches. These came up the coast from the Ofanto moved by the clockwise current system operating in the Bay of Manfredonia. The former, however, could only have come from the opposite direction, swept south by anticlockwise currents. As already pointed out, current reversal in the Bay of Manfredonia is not uncommon and is associated with an increase in the frequency and the severity of winds from the north-eastern quarter. The arrival of yellow sands therefore from the Gargano coast replacing the black Ofanto sands and blocking the entrance to the lagoon right up to the villa must record a period of exceptionally stormy weather. If this indeed occurred in the late sixteenth century, the climatic change can be associated with the general post-medieval worsening of weather all over Europe in what is usually referred to as the "Little Ice Age".

Another point is that the intruding yellow sands are today found as much as 40 cm above present sea level by the villa. They contain many of the large, brittle shells of *Mactra corallina*. Despite their brittleness, however, the shells show no signs of having been rolled nor are they broken. It seems therefore that shells do not represent beach debris so much as a sub-tidal deposit, more or less *in situ*. This would imply that there has been a relative displacement of land and sea levels in the order of 1 m since their deposition. Now the ancient city of Sipontum lies almost athwart one of the most important geological faults in northern Apulia and earthquakes are all too common. The earthquake of 1745, for instance, severely damaged the Knights Templars' monastery of San Leonardo di

Sipontum, just 7 km south-west of the ancient city. Land and sea level changes in locations such as Sipontum are as likely to be at least in part a consequence of tectonic displacements as of eustatic oscillations.

Silted Ports

The factors affecting the fate of ports in Mediterranean Europe are complex but can be summarized into four sets of conditions or circumstances. Three are man-made: harbour layout (or type); the technical status of harbour facilities; and the vigour of the urban economy. Fourthly, there are the physical changes to which that particular stretch of coast is liable, which may be erosive or depositional. The designation of *portus* in early documents and maps reveals little about the nature or the status of the feature. Little can be guessed about the capacity of the harbour or the range of its activity, or even whether the associated settlement was a village or a major city.

The situation of the port-city and its harbour may have been in the true sense coastal or it may have been ''inland''; that is, some distance up river, at the head of a gulf or on the mainland shore of a lagoon. As regards layout, the early harbours of Mediterranean Europe fall into two very elementary categories (Fig. 59). There were those created from a beach, the strand type, and there were those created out of small inlet, the *cala* type. The size of the artificial structures making a harbour may have a

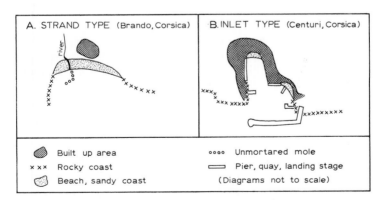

Fig. 59. *Mediterranean harbours*: the two basic types of harbour layouts, based on two present-day examples from northern Corsica.

bearing on its survival. The technical simplicity of what must have been the majority of village and small town harbours made them particularly vulnerable to burial or erosion by natural factors whether in inlets or on the open strand. The importance of the third factor, the dynamism of the port-city itself, can be illustrated by reference to the history of port developments at Marseilles (ancient *Massilia*) (Fig. 60).

The first known installations at Marseilles were substantial ones. In the sixth and fifth centuries B.C. the Greeks at their new colony seem to have been content with the beach at the head of the *cala* more or less as it was, but the Romans equipped *Massilia* with a whole dock complex including, according to Strabo (4.I.5) a dry dock, that led to the early ranking of the port as one of the finest in the Mediterranean world. This first harbour remained in use until the fourth century A.D. when it was abandoned and silts began to bury the structures. In the Middle Ages the rest of the inlet, known as the Lacydon and now as the *Vieux Port*, served again as one of the most important ports in the Mediterranean. By the beginning of the

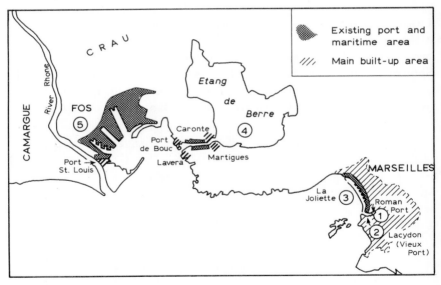

Fig. 60. *The persistence of a port* is due above all to human endeavour. Developments and extensions of what has become the *Porte Autonome de Marseilles* testify to the efforts and investments underlying the maintenance of the port of *Massilia*—Marseilles as a leading Mediterranean, and now world, port throughout over two-and-a-half millennia.

second half of the nineteenth century the opening of the Suez canal brought promise of greater traffic than could be accommodated in the old harbour. Accordingly, work started on a third harbour, La Joliette. A narrow marshy strip of land at the bottom of the hill on which the old town stands was artificially built up and extended in order to make room for a long line of quays and basins and its entire length was protected by a magnificent breakwater, 800 m long. With the coming of the petroleum era, yet new demands were made on harbours and these could not be met at La Joliette, so by the 1920s, a fourth harbour area was being built around the Etang de Berre, where there is the requisite land, as well as the water frontage. Finally, at present, a fifth harbour is in process of development (at Fos) in order to meet the most modern criterion for a successful port-city, that it should also be a major industrial centre. As a result of these efforts and investments, Marseilles is today the third port of importance in Europe and fifth on the world scale. In Roman times and throughout the historic period it had also ranked amongst the leading ports in the Western world. The point is that such status was not maintained solely by virtue of the physical nature of the original harbour but with continuous effort, considerable capital expenditure, and a real desire for improvement.

Good Ports and Bad Ports

Looking about the shores of Mediterranean Europe today, one can find many examples of simple landings, the strand type being the simplest. At Brando (Cap Corse, Corsica), a small stream reaches the head of a sea where a high rocky headland swings out to the south. This headland protects the beach at Brando from the worst of southern winds and swell. All that has been provided artificially at this place is an angled line of boulders which aid loading and discharging. As a breakwater against a real storm from the north-eastern sector, the quay is ineffective.

Many harbours of Greek and Roman construction in Mediterranean Europe are little more than a more substantial development along these lines. A harbour may be formed by a single breakwater, curving or angled, or by two or three so arranged as virtually to enclose a spacious expanse of well-sheltered water. The breakwaters are solid and well-built, usually of mortared blocks. The harbour of Cap Baeo, one of three at *Lilibeum* (Marsala, Sicily) had two curving moles which enclosed a spacious harbour of 24 hectares (Schmiedt, 1964, p. 54). The inner shore may have been built up to assist landings but this was not necessarily the case in harbours of this type. The harbour was sheltered not only by its breakwaters but also by the high rock of the citadel. Some of these strand harbours have suffered siltation. *Lilibeum* itself has been submerged.

Probably the most sought-after location for a harbour has been the rocky inlet. At Centauri (Corsica) a natural inlet, rocky and surrounded by only low hills, was simply supplied as the need arose with jetties and quays. The most recent addition is a single mole aligned across the mouth of the inlet to provide shelter when the sea and the wind are particularly strong from the south-west. The harbour at Centauri is of local importance only and the village has remained small. For such a settlement to develop into a major urban or commercial centre depends not so much on the physical nature of the inlet itself (its depth, degree of shelter, ease of entry etc.) as on its accessibility from the landward side. The more dissected and mountainous the coastline, the more likely the inlet is to be an attractive one. But at the same time the ruggedness of the interior is a disadvantage to the development of commercial functions. As the case of Marseilles shows, the success of the major port-cities of Mediterranean Europe commonly represents a compromise between finding the best harbour in terms of the natural inlet and an accessible situation for the associated settlement.

The early harbour at Palermo, in Sicily, was in an inlet, or *cala*, that was originally at least 1 km long. It was narrow, not much more than 300 m wide, but there was an advantage in this. Boats moored at the head of the inlet would have been little disturbed by high seas and bad weather outside the inlet. At Palermo, the winds and waves coming from the stormy north-eastern sector would have roughed the water at the seaward end only. What happened at Palermo, though, over the centuries also happened at many inlet harbours: siltation at the head of the inlet progressively shortened its length. By the seventeenth century the *cala* at Palermo was less than half its original length. The consequence of this truncation was that boats were having to moor in that part of the inlet that was liable to disturbance by heavy seas. Eventually an outer mole was decided upon to give protection to the inlet from the worst seas, those driven by the north-easterlies more or less straight into the inlet. This had been provided by the early seventeenth century (Fig. 61).

At Bonifaccio (Corsica) there has been no such problem. The inlet here is as long as was the Palermo *cala* originally but it is sinuous and its entrance faces almost due west while the heavy seas come mostly from the

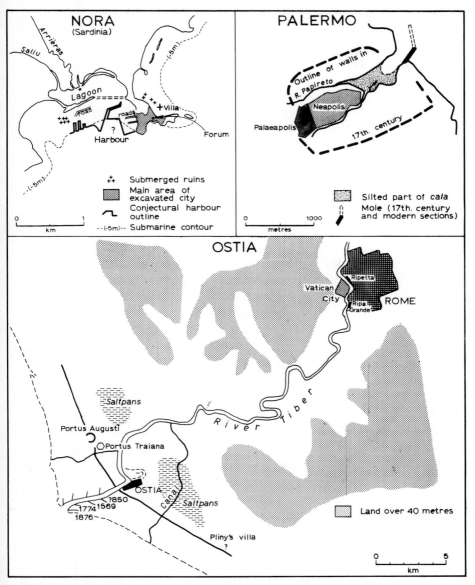

Fig. 61. *Some Mediterranean ports:* Nora (Sardinia, Palermo (Sicily) and Ostia near Rome. The fate of Nora is an example of submergence, the others of problems of siltation. Nora is after Patroni and Wilkes, in Flemming (1969); Palermo is adapted from Schmiedt (1965); Ostia is based on Meiggs (1973) and Bradford (1957).

south-east. Rough water therefore does not reach far enough along the inlet to disturb ships at their moorings and, accordingly, there are no major harbour structures at Bonifaccio, either for protection or for landing. The modern car ferry leaves for Sardinia from nothing more ambitious than a wooden pontoon. Fishing boats (and now pleasure craft) tie up at the historic quay two-thirds of the way towards the head of the inlet. Compared with Palermo, there has been little siltation at the head of the Bonifaccio *cala*.

Where a navigable river reached the sea, preferably in an open estuary, a port might be found at some distance upstream. Rome had an outport at Ostia but there were important landings within the city itself, at Ripetta and Ripa Grande. These remained in use throughout the eighteenth and nineteenth centuries. Contemporary paintings and engravings show that these river ports were humble affairs even in the grandest of cities. By the late eighteenth century the river bank at Ripetta was architecturally splendid, with flights of curving stone steps leading up from the river. But for the boats there was nothing other than a narrow built-up frontage for them to tie up to (D'Onofrio, 1970, his plates 57–64). In earlier centuries, Ripetta, like Ripa Grande, consisted of shelving, muddy banks cut by small staircases and ramps which were only sometimes paved. There were many river or estuarine ports of this sort in Mediterranean Europe. In Sardinia, Punic Neapolis and Roman Bosa were inland ports of this type. In Languedoc there was Lattes, of which more is said below. Thanks to the daily efforts of a dredging machine, Lattes was still functioning in the 1590s as an outport for Montpellier but its Roman city was wholly abandoned by the time Thomas Platter saw it. It might be expected that all such inland harbours, fluvial or lagoonal, were particularly vulnerable to interruption and threat from siltation. A large number, it is true, disappeared even before Pliny's time, but others were maintained open and useful against, sometimes, major physical odds.

Prior to the nineteenth century, a "good" harbour was not so esteemed because it was big or because it was deep. Even the best harbours could be astonishingly small. The inlet type, especially, were usually very narrow. Neither the *cala* at Palermo nor the Lacydon at Marseilles measured much more than 350–400 m across at any time. In both cases by modern times the length of the inlet had been halved by siltation at the head. But cramped space was not a major impediment. Swinburne's eye-witness description of the port of Marseilles at the end of the eighteenth century gives an idea of the density of shipping in the most important harbours. Like most others of the period, the Lacydon was shut up with a chain at night or in times of insecurity. "Ships of war", Swinburne related, "or heavy burden usually ride at anchor in the road between the islands and the main land but there is always a great crowd of smaller vessels in the port; the usual number to be seen amounts at least to five hundred . . ." (1787, p. 465). Admittedly, Marseilles was one of the leading ports of the Mediterranean. In comparison, the harbour at Barcelona was entered by no more than 1000 vessels yearly, at about the same time (Townsend, 1791, Vol. I, p. 152). The Greeks and Romans were also accustomed to packing shipping tightly into their harbours. The Roman dock that comprised the port of Massilia had a surface area of nearly 2000 m². Considering Flemming's suggestion that up to 50 vessels of Mycenean size (10–12 m long) could berth bow on in an area of 100 metres square (10 000 m²) (1972, p. 66), Roman Massilia could have accommodated ten vessels in its dock alone. Boats remained small throughout the historic period, particularly those involved in coastwise trade.

Nor was shallow water necessarily a problem in these early ports. According to Flemming (1971, p. 105), a stable rowing boat draws one-third of its beam. Even the heavy cargo boats of the Roman period, with a beam of 10 m and a length of only 30 m, would have needed little more than 3 m of water. Earlier, to judge from Mycenean paintings, boats had been shorter and narrower in the beam "so a useful harbour need only have been 2 metres deep" (p. 60). Again, bearing in mind the smallness of boats in the historic period, this would have been true in most cases until the nineteenth century. The thirteenth century *Compasso di Navigare* states that the depth of water off-shore at Sipontum increased by one *passus* for every *passus* gained from the shore (Motzo, 1947). Sipontum was described by the same authorities as a "good port". In the same century, boats were still able to reach the harbour at Morgoro, on the northern shore of the lagoon of Cagliari (Sardinia) (Terresu Asole, 1974; Day, 1973). In the same island, Neapolis was also classed by the medieval authors of the *Compasso di Navigare* as a "good port". By the seventeenth century this had been qualified. Neapolis had become merely "a good port for galleys", meaning for shallow draught boats only (Crino, 1945, cited by Schmiedt, 1965, p. 244). Even so, it was only when the depth of water was down to 1 m that navigation on the Cagliari lagoon was completely halted (La Marmora, 1839, p. 113).

By no means were all ancient ports and harbours optimally situated. Even some quite important ones were what can only be described as distinctly bad from the point of view of their physical circumstances. In these cases their survival reflected the scale and dynamism of the urban centre responsible for the trade handled by the port. Two outstanding examples spring to mind, the case of medieval St Gilles and its successor at Aigues-Mortes in Languedoc, and that of Ostia, outport for Rome in Italy.

The medieval port of St Gilles cannot on any criterion have been considered satisfactory even in its early days. Today St Gilles is 25 km from the open sea. In the Middle Ages it was one of the chief ports of departure for pilgrims and, according to some, one of the busiest ports on the south coast of France between the eleventh and late twelfth centuries (Russell, 1942; Oldham, 1925). It was reached from the sea by what must always have been a difficult passage along the lagoons and channels of *Stagna*. But the coast of Languedoc has always been short of good ports and St Gilles was the most easterly point available to the King of France after that part of Languedoc had been ceded by the Count of Toulouse in 1226. So in large measure the significance of St Gilles depended on politico-economic circumstances, not at all on its advantages as a harbour. In part too, its importance lay in its association with pilgrimages and with crusading. Any other port could have fulfilled these needs, and to fulfil them less satisfactorily was scarcely possible. By the thirteenth century navigation to St Gilles had become so difficult and so uncertain because of shoals and sandbanks as to be virtually impossible. Marseilles was the answer, but Marseilles was in Provence and Provence was not yet French. So in what can only have been something amounting to desperation in 1248 a new port was created at Aigues-Mortes by the French king, Louis IX. On the face of it Aigues-Mortes was little better than St Gilles, being set amongst the same lakes and marshes of the Rhone delta, but at least it had one advantage, it was close to the open sea. Aigues-Mortes served as a crusading and a commercial port for as long as it was needed. English wool was obligatorily routed through Aigues-Mortes, for instance, on its way to the cloth towns of northern Italy. Once a better alternative became available, as it did when Provence became part of France in 1490, the *raison d'être* of Aigues-Mortes was removed and the town declined. Toulon was developed as the base for the French navy and Marseilles took over its trade.

The case of Ostia is in all essentials similar. Physical conditions in the lower Tiber area would have always been more or less unsuitable for a port. But as a major economic centre Rome desperately needed a maritime outlet and the only answer was Ostia. Significantly, the earliest reference to Ostia is not to any port or city but to a small settlement established in order to control and to protect the local salt industry (Meiggs, 1973, p. 17). The exact site of this early salt settlement is not known. It was only after Rome had gained control over the whole lower Tiber area (still in the fourth century B.C.) that a settlement nearer the mouth of the river was deemed necessary for the new purposes of defence and for general trade and shipping.

According to Dionysius, writing at the end of the first century B.C., conditions were not so bad as that. He suggested that sailing vessels of up to 78 tons capacity (or capable of carrying 3000 measures or *amphorae*) could enter the mouth of the river and then be towed up to Rome (Dionysius Hal. iii.44). But Strabo, also writing in the first century B.C., was more critical. He condemned Ostia as ''harbourless because of the silting up which is caused by the Tiber'' (5.3.5). Larger ships, he said, had to ride out to sea and only the smaller ones could enter the river mouth. There was another problem, the narrowness of the river itself and the inevitable congestion of shipping. To minimize these problems, a new harbour was built by Claudius in A.D. 42. Two centuries later, even this had had to be thoroughly overhauled, though some problems were due to neglect. Despite all efforts, by the eighth century, in Meiggs' words, ''the sand had probably won'' (1973, p. 121) and today the Claudian harbour is nearly 3 km inland. Instead, a master canal draining the Pontine Marsh was used as an alternative route. It bypassed the river mouth and was easier to keep open for navigation. Ships did pass right down the Tiber in 1117 but by the end of the century the river mouth was deemed unnavigable and only the canal provided access to the landings of Rome.

Environmental changes at the Tiber mouth have been of the first order. The river is estimated to carry down 4–5 million m^3 of silt per annum (Le Gall, 1953, p. 22). This is a huge amount for an Italian river, third only to the Arno and the Po. It reflects the nature of the basin of the Tiber and of its tributaries, which includes some of the most unstable and most easily eroded strata in the peninsula. It also coincides with some of the wettest parts of the Apennines. Inland erosion meant coastal siltation. So century by century the delta advanced, each extension being recorded in the dune lines revealed so clearly by aerial photography (Bradford, 1957, his Fig. 23). Today the sea is in places 4½ km away from the villas that in the first century A.D. were on the coast. But the river is not alone responsible. The line of dunes on the delta is a witness of the activity of wind and sea in piling the sediments back onto the shore instead of dispersing them to the bottom of the sea.

Ostia is an eloquent reminder that ports were only as prosperous as their urban centres made them. Once Roman trade abandoned Ostia, the process of decline, which had always threatened, set in: "Without Rome, it could support itself neither as a port, sea-resort nor even a *castrum*." (Bradford, 1957, p. 241). The same has been said in the two cases of St Gilles, whose abandonment in the twelfth century was in no way proof of the advance of Rhone sediments, and of Aigues-Mortes, created for, and abandoned by, trade.

In the last analysis, then, a port is a man-made feature and it is on human factors that its survival must depend. The physical changes and problems brought by siltation or erosion should be measured in terms of cost and effort. This is not to minimize the problems that must certainly have beset coastal towns and their harbours in Mediterranean Europe in the past. The archaeological evidence, as well as the documentary, speaks for itself on this count. For a better understanding of the decline and abandonment of so many port-cities around the shores of Mediterranean Europe, the focus should be turned to the fortunes of commerce, of urban administration, and of national economic and political organization. Even so, no better a starting point is afforded than with the sediments themselves, those within the harbours of ancient port-cities.

Sardinian Ports

There were a dozen Punic port-cities in Sardinia by the seventh or at the latest the sixth century B.C. (see Fig. 52). All were in that third of the coast classed by Spano and Pinna (1956) as low-lying and therefore were mostly on the west and south coasts. Only two have modern successors: *Karalis* (Cagliari) and the settlement at Olbia, the only one on the east coast. It is possible that there was also a Punic foundation at *Turris Lisibonus* (Porto Torres) on the north coast but this has not yet been confirmed by excavation. The most characteristic siting for a Phoenician or Punic port-city was astride a promontory so that, it is said, either of the bays might serve as a harbour according to weather and sea conditions (Contenau, 1926, p. 287; Pesce, 1960, p. 15). In Sardinia only Tharros and Nora conform in this respect. The excavated ruins of these two cities, spread over long rocky peninsulas now much narrowed by erosion, are amongst the most pleasant sites to visit. The Punic settlement at Olbia was also on a promontory but as this is at the head of a deep gulf the effect is not the same. Bosa and Neapolis were "inland" settlements, with at least the urban centre several kilometres upstream, even if the harbour was closer to the open sea.

The site of Neapolis is in fact over 6 km inland. The nucleus of the former city occupies the seaward edge of a rocky shelf 11 m above sea level. Although overlooked by the sombre ruggedness of the basaltic ridge of Serra Longa, it is itself a useful vantage point. Despite references noted above to port activities still being carried on in the eighteenth century, nothing has yet been discovered of the harbour or landings that served Neapolis in either ancient or more recent times. It is possible that there was an outport further down the inlet, at Su Stangioni, for instance, where Puxeddu reports the remains of several Roman buildings (1975) or still further down towards the sea and below the nuragh at Priogusu, as Schmiedt suggested (1965, p. 249). On the other hand, certain features are discernible on air photographs of the site which could be interpreted as harbour basins immediately below the city (area A, Fig. 62) and on the

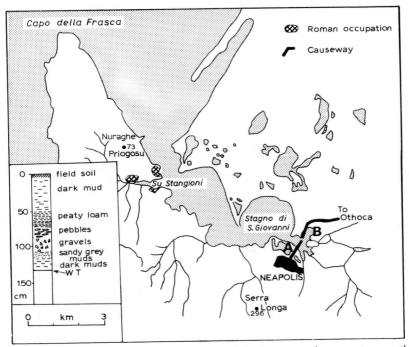

Fig. 62. *Neapolis, Sardinia* showing the site of the Punic settlement, its possible harbour basins (A and B) and (inset) a sedimentary profile from just below the city site and on the seaward side of the causeway (map from Schmiedt, 1965).

opposite side of the inlet (here known as Stagno di S. Giovanni) close to the causeway (Area B).

This causeway was constructed either by the Punic founders of Neapolis or by the Romans. It leads from what must have been the northern gate of the town in a straight line across the inlet Stagno di S. Giovanni for about 750 m. On the other side of the inlet, the road makes an angular turn to the north-east, the direction, it is thought of *Othoca*, another Punic centre of uncertain location. It is still possible to walk along the causeway despite the encroaching marshes. Built of large blocks of local basalt, it is at most 8 m wide (according to Puxeddu; Schmiedt says 12 m). There are two gaps in the causeway which were presumably originally bridged and which were intended to allow a free flow of water from the Mannu and Mogoro rivers. Possibly too, they allowed the passage of small craft. Most of the surface of the causeway is, in summer today, just less than a metre above the level of water in the marshes.

The causeway at Neapolis has contributed to the pattern of siltation and to the development of marshes in the inlet, particularly on its inland side. It checks stream flow so that the rivers' sedimentary load tends to be deposited in the quiet water between the shore and the causeway. Both rivers are liable to carry heavy sedimentary loads. The Mannu rises in the heavily mined Iglesiente massif, at over 2000 m altitude. It drains an area of arenaceous schists and granites that would have early suffered from the vegetation degradation associated with mineral working. The Mogoro starts near Monte Arci, another area of early and heavy mineral exploitation, particularly in Neolithic times for obsidian. It drains hills composed of soft Miocene rocks, marls, conglomerates and limestones, before it reaches the Campidano lowland.

On the north-eastern coast of Sardinia, at Olbia, both river and sea have contributed to sedimentary changes. The Roman port is known in outline but no investigation has been made into the sediments filling up the former harbour, which occupied a small inlet on the north side of the town (Fig. 63). This is now dry land, 2 and even 3 m above sea level. The main inlet, the Gulf of Olbia, is one of the largest in Sardinia and continues to serve as an industrial as well as commercial harbour. One inconvenience is the narrowness of the entrance into the Gulf, only 250 m wide and rocky. Not surprisingly, it has proved to be an effective silt trap. Towards the end of the last century, *The Mediterranean Pilot* warned that the entrance was "so choked with rocks and sands as to admit only small coasters and fishing vessels, the channel having only 4 and 5 feet of water". Spano and Pinna's

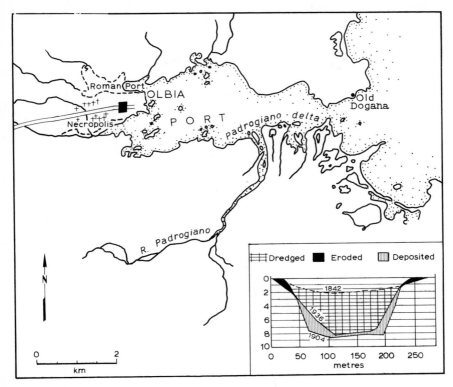

Fig. 63. *Olbia, Sardinia*: problems of siltation (map based on Schmeidt, 1965; section from Spano and Pinna, 1956).

study of Sardinian beaches showed that the offending sediments came above all from the Padrogiano river. This mountain stream debouches inside the Gulf, on its southern shore. Its delta therefore is usually little disturbed by the main coastal currents and acts as a reservoir of sediment that from time to time is moved about the Gulf, blocking its entrance and impeding navigation. This is what had happened in 1847. By 1855, however, the blockage had vanished of its own accord. This would have been due to a change in currents or winds outside the Gulf that affected sub-tidal conditions inside sufficiently to disperse the prograded section of the delta. In the 1870s, however, the silts were again affecting navigation and a channel was dredged through the bar that was blocking the navigation channel in the Gulf (Fig. 63).

Emporion (Ampurias, Gerona)

The first settlement at Emporion in Spain was established in the sixth century on what appears to have been a rocky islet close to the shore. The shore here is backed by low cliffs of Tertiary strata. Immediately north of the islet the River Fluvia used to flow into the sea until 1790 in which year it changed its course to debouch some 6 km up the coast (Sunyer, 1963). South of the islet, the coast swings out to sea in a blunt headland. Together the headland and the islet, strategically placed with regard to winds from

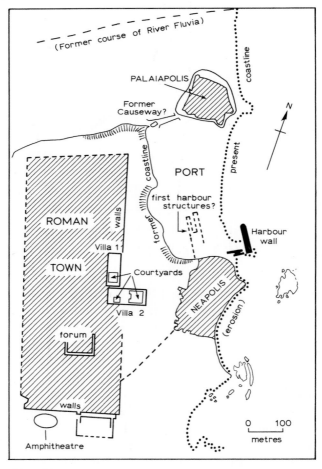

Fig. 64. *Greek and Roman Emporion (Ampurias, Spain).*

the north-eastern quadrant, created a small bay which served as the harbour of Emporion (Fig. 64).

The islet was first occupied as a Massiliot colony in or about 550 B.C. (Almagro, 1968). Expansion of the settlement and of its demographic activities meant that these could no longer be contained within the Old Town (Palaiapolis) on the island and a New Town (Neapolis) was laid out on the headland just across the bay sometime in the middle of the fifth century. The resources of the interland gave economic prosperity. Strabo emphasized the fertility of the territory controlled by the Emporions and the importance of the flax industry, as well as the high quality of the harbours along this stretch of coast (3.4.8–9). In addition to the Greek colony at Emporion, there was a pre-existing native settlement, *Indika*. This was separated from the New Town of the Massiliots, Strabo tells us, only by a wall. About 150 years after the establishment of Roman authority in this part of Spain (in 49 B.C.), Caesar installed a colony of veterans on the site of the Iberian town and laid out a second new town. This was spaciously designed, even if the outline was characteristically rectangular. Only about a sixth of the intra-mural area has been excavated so far but a considerable part of this is taken up by the forum and by the gardens and courtyards of the only two *villa urbana* complexes so far uncovered.

The harbour at Emporion is probably most appropriately classified as of the strand type. There may have been other ports in the vicinity. Strabo mentioned one at the mouth of a river whose "outlet serves as a port for the Emporitans". [31] The old course of the Fluvia remained navigable until 1757 for boats carrying no more than 400 *quintaux* in weight as far as the old mill (Sunyer, 1963). Even so, the indentation of the coast between the Old and New Towns at Emporion itself made a perfectly suitable small harbour just below the city walls. While the islet provided shelter from the worst of the storms coming from the north and north-east, some artificial provision had to be made on the southern side. Accordingly, a high mole was constructed. Originally it ran out from the shore and then bent parallel to the shore but the landward section has since been removed by erosion (and perhaps by stone robbing). The surviving section (Plate 14) is one of the most impressive surviving pieces of marine architecture from the classical era. [32] Built of cut blocks around a cemented rubble core, it is 85 m long, 6 m wide and 7 m high. Potsherds bedded in the cement suggest that the date of construction was between 175 and 150 B.C. Signs of what may represent an earlier, smaller and now completely buried harbour can be traced on air photographs. Within the little bay that

N *

used to contain the harbour, the infill sediments are composed wholly of marine sands and gravels. Close to the islet of Palaiapolis, but north of a line joining it to the mainland, the sediments near to the surface offer a striking contrast. They are dark grey-black, very sticky, fine grained muds, rich in fluvial and brackish muds. North of the islet too, close to where the mouth of the Fluvia would have been, a well-bore shows that there are up to 13 m of what have been described as alluvia, grey lagoonal clays and fluvial sands and gravels resting on a thick calcrete, which in turn rests on hard-packed shelly gravels. [33]

The contrast in the sediments can only reflect two formerly contrasting environments. What is of interest is the obvious inference that has to be made, namely that some sort of feature, now buried or vanished, kept the two depositional environments quite separate. There is no evidence that the river Fluvia or flood water ever passed (in recent centuries at least) between the islet and the mainland to mix with the sands of the harbour bay. The suggestion therefore, is that the islet was not in early times free standing but was attached to the mainland by a narrow low but natural causeway. That this was indeed the case is considerably substantiated by

Plate 14. *Surviving Roman harbour structures at Emporion, Spain,* and a sand-filled harbour. The landward end of the mole has been removed by the sea or by stone-robbing.

the report that below the first metre of material forming the present road surface (unmetalled) is a stratum of hard, yellow *grès*, a naturally cemented sand that is exposed as bedrock higher up in the excavated areas of the Roman city. Such a causeway would have completed the bay which formed the city harbour of the Emporions.

Massilia (Marseilles)

The most detailed archaeological documentation of the sediments inside one of the ancient harbours of Mediterranean Europe comes from Marseilles. Not long ago Roman dock structures were discovered beneath the silts and marshes of an area known as La Bourse right at the head of the inlet of the Vieux Port (Gallia, 1969, 1972). Excavation has revealed a quay 150 m long enclosing a wedge-shaped dock whose total area cannot have been much less than 2000 m² (Fig. 65). Close to the head of the dock is a square cistern, 2·60 m deep and so today well below sea level. Its purpose was to hold fresh water for embarking ships. It was built of relatively soft limestone and the ropes scored heavily into the rim of the basin. The natural shoreline has been found, 20 m beyond the northern end of the Roman dock. This was the strand that served in Hellenistic times. The only fixed features appear to have been a line of stakes driven into the beach to aid the drawing up of boats. Just behind the beach is the city wall.

The Roman dock was built during Vespasian's reign, during the first half of the last century B.C. It continued in use, with alterations, until the third century A.D., when it was deliberately destroyed. Evidently this was a move to forestall the installations, and the supplies stored in the area, from falling into hostile hands. Dockside silos and storehouses were levelled, their bricks and tiles thrown into the dock. Food stores too were jettisoned in the same hurried manner; *amphorae* fell unbroken onto the mud at the bottom of the dock and remained there, complete with their contents and with lids sealed, until found by the excavators. The dock was never used again though there was still water in it. In due course marine deposits and marine molluscs (oysters and whelks) covered the *amphorae* and the debris.

The surviving quay of the Roman dock is today 4·4 m high but this was not its original height. At "some time before" A.D. 300, three new courses of stone blocks had been added to the original six-course wall. Each new block, highly decorated, was over 40 cm thick so the total effect was to raise the quay by 1·40 m. It is true, as has been pointed out, that the

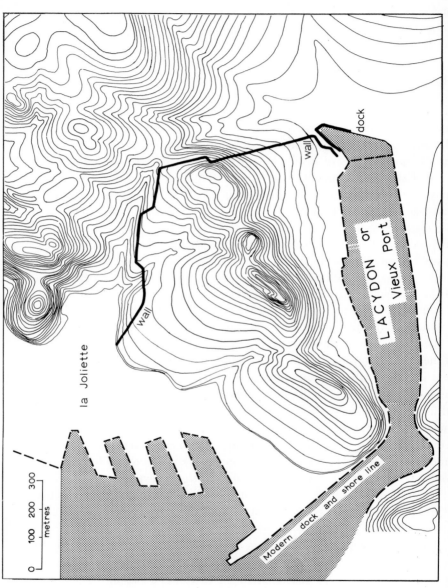

Fig. 65. *Marseilles (Massilia)* showing the *cala*, with the Massiliote and Roman port at its head, the contemporary wall, the medieval port of Lacydon, and the modern built-up part of La Joliette.

draw of water in the dock had been reduced by 2 m by the muds and sands
accumulating in it despite regular dredging. But this could not be held to
account for the raising of the sides of the dock. This can have been for one
purpose only, to keep water in. The level of water in the dock was, by
implication, considerably higher than it had been in the first century B.C.
when the structure was first built. This suggests that sea level was at that
time rising in relation to land level.

The sediments themselves and other details corroborate this interpretation.[34] The level of water in the dock when it was first built is
recorded on the side of the dock itself by a line of *saxicavous* markings on
the sixth course (the highest of the original wall) (Gallia, 1969, p. 427).
This line is now from 30 to 35 cm below sea level (more precisely, the
level of water in the Vieux Port), but it meant that the original draught in

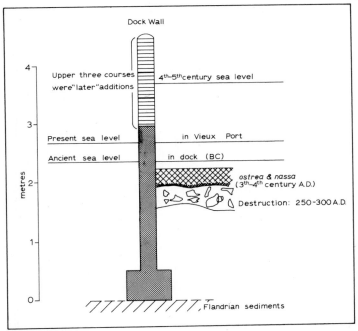

Fig. 66. *Roman harbour structure and former sea levels at Marseilles (Massilia),* Place de
la Bourse. The Roman sea level has a radiocarbon date of A.D. 100 ± 75 and
stands at about 30 cm below N.G.F. This was established on an 1885–1896 base
so the Roman level is only about 10 cm below today's (Pirazzoli, 1976, p. 258).
The Roman level is clearly recorded on the limestone dock wall by the marks
made by destructive marine organisms (saxicavous, such as *Sabellaria alveolata*).

the dock was just under 2½ m. If sea level (relative to the land) had remained unchanged for the next three-and-a-half centuries, by the time the *amphorae* were thrown into the dock the draw would have been reduced by siltation to about 75 cm. However, this clearly was not the case. Immediately overlying the destruction layer is the marine deposit with the molluscs, over which is a layer 40 cm thick of sandy clays. The molluscs show that when the *amphorae* were thrown in (late third century A.D.) there was quite enough clean water for the molluscs to prosper in. This was not likely to have been the case had there been no alteration in the level of water, as 75 cm is normally too shallow for oysters. In short, the sedimentary evidence suggests that at about A.D. 300, the level of water in the dock at Massilia must have reached between 35 and 65 cm *above* present-day sea level (Fig. 66). The rise would have been noticeable for some length of time previously. It was therefore the threat of flooding that prompted the addition of three more stone courses to the dock walls "some time before A.D.300".

Lattara (Lattes, Montpellier)

The river port of Lattes, ancient *Lattara*, output for Montpellier in the early Middle Ages, is only 70 km from Marseilles. But it is on the other side of the Rhone trench and in an entirely different geological zone. Its sedimentary history takes quite another form from that at Massilia. Even so, there are parallels.

There was Neolithic (Chassey) occupation at Lattes but it is the proto-historic and Roman site that attracts attention. It covers a well-defined area, of some 32 hectares, formerly walled (Arnal *et al.*, 1974). There was also extra-mural expansion in Roman times. The earliest levels of the proto-historic occupation date from the Hallstattian period (700–500 B.C.). As at Lansargues, not far away, there was by this time active trade in high-quality pottery with Etruria. This "Etruscan level" is now about 0·5 m below present sea level. Throughout the Roman period the city prospered but by about A.D. 200 there were major changes in its fortunes. Much of the city was in decay or even in ruins. Sufficient of its port, if not the settlement, survived into the Middle Ages when the new and growing town of Montpellier used Lattes as an outport. But by the end of the seventeenth century even this slender link with the past had gone. Thomas Platter, visiting the area in 1595 and 1596, noticed that the dredging machine was at work daily to clear the Lez of weeds and keep it open for navigation. He described Lattes as ''a small, ancient, ruined town, almost uninhabited nowadays. There is nothing to be seen but gardens and a single inn . . . Its encircling walls still stand . . . and the harbour adjoins one of the gates of the town'' (1963, p. 55ff). He also noted that the town ''belonged to Montpellier''; it was very soon after this that the urban nobility began to acquire the land at Lattes in the manner already commented on.

The Lez is a notoriously unstable river even today, and throughout the historic period has changed its course several times. In effect, Lattes was an island city in Roman times, encircled by branches of the river. It is clear that, as at Rome or at Venice, there were specific landing places for individual cargoes and that loading and unloading were carried on at several places around the city. The excavated landing, by the south-western corner of the city, is therefore but one of several that would have constituted ''the port'' of Lattes.

In early Roman times the south-western corner of the city would have been at no great distance from the open water of the Etang de Mejean. The landing there seems to have been in the lowest reaches of the river channel, before it opened out into the lagoon (Fig. 67). It appears to have been a simple, business-like affair. The city wall here follows the edge of slightly higher ground. Immediately below and parallel to the wall, there was an unmortared stone wall or quay in the bank of the Lez. The quay survives to a height of 3·5 m and dates to the ''Etruscan'' period. A timber pontoon, built of white pine and at least 5, probably originally 6 m long, served as the landing itself. When found, it was 2·04 m below the surface of the ground, which means it is today only 30 or 40 cm above present mean high sea level. The pontoon was added in the second half of the first century B.C. Just opposite, 15 m away on the other side of the river, a second wall had been built a long time after the first but, like the pontoon, also probably in the first century B.C. (evidently a period of considerable redevelopment at Lattes). Like the dock wall at Massilia, the new wall at Lattes was built in the approved Vitruvian style with cyclopean blocks and a base of blocks laid transversely and resting on pebbles and gravels that were either part of the river bed or that had been dumped there for the purpose. Again as at Massilia, the new wall at Lattes was added to at a later stage, in a different style and with smaller blocks. This addition raised the wall by about 60 cm. Finally, again as at Massilia, all landing arrangements in this part of Lattes fell into disuse by the end of the third century A.D., a coincidence that is unlikely to have been merely accidental. Another

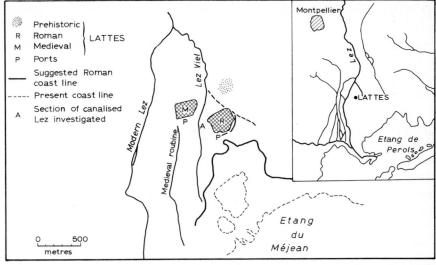

Fig. 67. *Lattes (Lattara).* The river port-city of Roman Lattes was formerly much nearer open lagoon water. Siltation of the Lez and other streams has led to a build-up of land at the head of a formerly pronounced bay (Etang du Méjean) on the northern shores of the lagoon. Siltation of the Lez Viel itself led to the cutting of an artificial channel so that the medieval port could continue to function as an outport for the newly developing town of Montpellier. The inset is taken from Cassini's map of the area (1791).

canalized section of the Lez at Lattes was uncovered by archaeologists further upstream and altogether 30 m of canal wall were traced (Plate 15). This wall had been built during the first century B.C. in Vitruvian style and apparently remained usable until about or after A.D. 150. There was a flight of steps down into the canal and, in one section, a re-entrant. A bollard-like stone was also recovered. Not counting the transverse foundation blocks, the wall was 1·90 m high. It was of limestone, with each course neatly laid and decreasing in size towards the top. Each block had been chipped on the spot for a perfect fit and (as at Massila) the limestone flakes had dropped into the deposits at the bottom of the canal.

The most noticeable feature reflected by the sediments that have not only infilled but entirely buried this section of the canalized Lez is the contrast between conditions at the time of the construction of the retaining wall and those of a few centuries later. As at the downstream landing, the wall rests on an artificial foundation of gravels and stones that

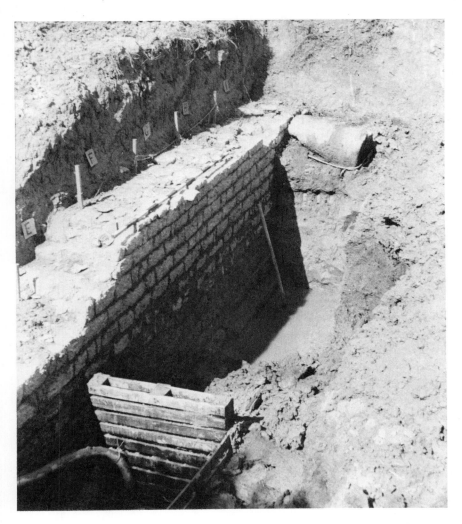

Plate 15. *Lattes*. Roman wall of canalized Lez in process of excavation under very difficult conditions. The grey clays level with the top of the wall, filling the channel, are rich in occupation debris and are associated with the ruin or abandonment of much of the city about A.D. 300 (present ground level is seen top left).

is now just below sea level. The natural bed appears to have been mostly coarse sand with a few patches of mud and was exceedingly rich in molluscs besides the limestone flakes chipped during the building of the wall. Thirteen species of molluscs have been identified, all but two species are characteristic of fluvial, perhaps faintly brackish, water. They are also numerically the most important in the sample. The two species are non-aquatic, and could have been swept into the stream from the dry ground around. Rather less happily for the excavators there was vigorous flow of bitterly cold water from the old river bed showing that a "ghost" Lez continues to flow unsuspected well below present-day ground level.

At the time of these major improvements to the navigability of the eastern branch of the Lez, there was plenty of water in the stream and flow was steady if not particularly fast. That this was the case is suggested by the presence of molluscs of the *Limnes* species (*L. peregrinus, L. palustris*) which tend to live in water that is fairly still. During the next few decades the stream continued to deposit lenses of coarse sand, gravel and mud in a sandy silt. By the end of the first century A.D., however, the canal bottom was becoming covered by deep, light-grey muds. These continued to accumulate until the depth of the canal had been reduced by half. Evidently the river's rate of flow was very much slower, although it seems to have been carrying plenty of fine matter to deposit as clay. Very few molluscs were found in these deposits. One reason for this change in river regime (at this point) and in the depositional environment could have been that a higher level of water in the lagoon was leading to the ponding back of river water in the lowest reaches of the Lez. Whatever the cause, this situation continued from the late first century to about A.D. 300, when the channel was entirely filled up and its retaining wall buried.

Another change occurred about this date. After A.D. 300 clays continued to accumulate over what was the canalized section of the river. But they are of different colour, very much darker, and are also rich in occupation debris, all of which show signs of heavy rolling. Evidently this was a period of heavy flooding and surging currents. To judge from the amount of debris, parts at least of the city were already in ruin and abandoned. The Lez may have shifted the course of its main branch but it was still capable of sending extensive floodwater over the old, easterly, canalized course for a long time. Eventually conditions quietened down and yet another pattern of sedimentation was established which continues to the present day. This is the deposition of the yellow-brown flood plain loams that are so characteristic of the Lez today.

Conclusion

As the number of detailed accounts of the sedimentary histories of ports and of sections of coast around Mediterranean Europe slowly increases, two points become evident. One is that certain physical changes which have taken place in the coastal environments begin to be encountered in different places, perhaps at obviously different times. But even where they appear to concern a specific period, precise synchronization is elusive. There are still too many obstacles in the way of even aiming at a total explanation of the changes that can be seen to have affected the coastal areas of Mediterranean Europe since the Neolithic. Not the least is the inadequacy of present data. Another is the difficulty of obtaining an absolute date for a sediment or even for appropriate archaeological features. Most of the structures buried in or associated with the sediments are walls or parts of buildings, elements that are either undatable or that can be ascribed a date so broad as to be of little help. Even an artefact with a precise date, such as a potsherd, is in these contexts of little use because sediments are liable to be reworked and redeposited. On another scale is the problem of the tectonic instability of the land surface. Too many changes may be explained by any one of a number of causes, often interdependent. Changes in the deposition of environment may be the result of a change in attention paid to artificial drainage systems. The destruction layers at Massilia and at Lattes, for instance, may coincide not only with what appears to be evidence for a relatively high sea stand but also with the arrival in southern France of invaders. As it turned out, neither Franks nor Alans did in the event actually lay waste to south-eastern Gaul in A.D. 253 or 276 but the threat their presence posed was real enough for the authorities to have possibly decided to take action. Certainly the end of the third century marks a turning point in the history of the Roman Empire in general and of the Gallic provinces in particular (Baratier, 1969, p. 75). The main years of destruction came after A.D. 400 with the appearance of, above all, the Vandals (Nimes was sacked in 408, for example). But even without destruction, administrative disruption and the failure of law and order, especially economic order, are as powerful agents of environmental change, on the scale we are considering, as changes in the height of the water table or a climatic deterioration. All that can be said with certainty is that the history of the environment and the history of man cannot be satisfactorily divorced.

The Quality of Coastal Living

The archaeological record demonstrates that people have lived, and sometimes lived most handsomely, in low-lying coastal areas that in modern times have been wetlands. Tradition, in this case, is an upstart. The association of the dangers and discomforts of the marshes, of the hazards of flood, or of the perniciousness of malaria and "bad air" with such districts is not wholly without foundation but has been much misunderstood and even exaggerated. The sedimentary record shows that this sort of adversity was neither a permanent nor an inevitable consequence of the low-lying nature of the land and of the proximity of lagoons and open sea.

Not enough is known about the organization of settlement and economic activity in the wetland areas of Mediterranean Europe when these were inhabited in the past. The Mailhacian villages at Lansargues were surrounded by sluggish streams or drainage ditches. Were these channels in fact natural or artificial? It makes a difference to the assessment and the understanding of that Bronze Age society and of its capability to organize itself to ensure a reasonable standard of living. In our own times, the Danes in the colder lands of eastern Jutland and the Dutch in their province of Holland have shown what can be done to make a "satisfactory" human environment out of an "unsatisfactory" physical one. Why, then, after at least 2000 years of continuous occupation in the Foggia coastlands did the situation suddenly become intolerable? There had been physical changes in the prehistoric period no less than in the historic but it was only after the Middle Ages that occupation really declined: whereas in 1301 there were five taxable towns or villages in the wetland district (listed in a letter from Charles II demanding taxes from "all towns and places in Capitanata" (Egidi, 1917), by the late sixteenth century there was not one. Yet at the end of the eighteenth century despite the "bad air" and the floods, investment was being put into an entirely new foundation (Zapponeta). The quality of an environment as a living space, it must be said, lies not only in its physical attributes but also in the minds and attitudes of its inhabitants or potential inhabitants.

Malaria

One of the factors usually called on to explain the neglect and abandonment of the coastal plains since Roman times is malaria.

Unfortunately, unlike the sands of an encroaching beach or the mud carried in flood water, malaria leaves no direct physical trace either of the illness or of the mosquito that carried the infection. Documentary evidence is often ambiguous and a fever or *ague* could be the result of many conditions or infections yet, to judge from comments by modern travellers, the entire fate of formerly rich coastal plains hung on the balance of this uncertain factor. At least one historian has drawn attention to what he sees as the immense significance of the state of health of a given population at crucial moments in human history (McNiell, 1977).

Not all areas infected by malaria in the nineteenth and twentieth centuries were necessarily unhealthy in earlier times. True, the Romans did not deny the unhealthiness of the district around their city. As in modern times, wealthy Romans were in the habit of migrating to their hill farms or to their sea-coast villas but this was to escape the depressing heat of summer in a city rather than malaria (Lanciani, 1897, p. 7). Some regions were described by Roman writers as unwholesome or pestilential; e.g. the Pisan Maremma (Strabo, 5.6.1) and Apulia (Caesar, Civil War, 3.2; Cicero *de lege agraria* 2.27.71). But there were others that were perfectly wholesome, such as the Ravenna marshes (Strabo, 5.1.7).

The origins of malaria in Mediterranean Europe are not known (see discussion in Brunt, 1971, Appendix III). The few words of description that are needed for its certain identification are available in one of the earliest scientific medical documents extant, namely Books I and III of the *Epidemics*, ascribed to Hippocrates. The book is datable at the latest to B.C. 400, so ''we therefore know that [malaria] was rife then in the Eastern Mediterranean'' (Charles Singer in a letter to John Bradford, 1953). One view is that malaria was brought into the Mediterranean from Africa (Tramonte, 1949, p. 16). No direct evidence for malaria in the prehistoric period can be expected because it is a disease which affects the soft parts of the body. However, Singer does point out a possible link where prehistoric graves contain an undue proportion of teenage and younger children. Deaths at those ages are relatively rare in a non-malarial society and this may possibly be confirmatory of the idea of malaria in Neolithic settlements.

The environmental aspects of malaria are exceedingly varied. There are apparently 50 important *Anopholes* vectors, and not all mosquito species are vectors. Of the 12 species found in Italy, only three are important as vectors (May, 1961). Some breed in quiet waters, others in fast-running streams, still others in tepid water only. Some tolerate salinity, others do not. Rainfall winds and temperature changes affect species adversely or favourably. The pattern of human behaviour also has different effects on different species; the smoke from cooking keeps mosquitoes away but depending whether cooking is done indoors or outdoors, as well as on the habits of the mosquito, the insects may be imprisoned indoors. The height of the house is advantageous only if the flight level of the *Anopheles* is known. The practice of sleeping out of doors (e.g. to guard sheep) increases the chances of being bitten. Amongst this wealth of detail, one point stands out; that many of the breeding places of these malaria-carrying mosquitoes have been created by human society. Those of *A. superpictus*, a mountain species found in Calabria and Sicily and which breeds in streams with rocky or pebbly beds, liking the sun, are natural but the other two common Italian species prefer to breed in quiet water or in tepid water. [35] Quiet or tepid water is found not only in natural features such as lakes and ponds but also in possibly far more extensive man-made water bodies, canals, drainage ditches, saltpans, reservoirs.

There is no easy guide to the extent of an infected area or degree of its infection (Magistris, 1930, p. 46). Professor Monti outlined the four sets of conditions that have to be fulfilled before malaria becomes a real problem (1921; cited in Magistris, 1930, p. 44). First, obviously enough, the species of *Anopheles* capable of propagating malaria have to be present. Second, the ambience has to be suitable for its life, reproduction and spread. Third, the infection has to be present (it may be of recent arrival) in the blood of carriers or agents. And, finally, there has to be an opportunity for the insect to bite people. An epidemic increases or decreases according to the fulfilment of all these conditions together. Any one condition can change the epidemic quite abruptly. So it has happened that certain districts appeared to be unsuitable for malaria and were traditionally free of the infection, until recently. Magistris quotes as an example of this, the case of Collina di San Colombano in Lombardy. There was no malaria here and not even any mosquitoes until the second decade of this century. Between 1910 and 1915 there were problems of acute water shortage in the vineyards of the district, particularly for mixing the copper sulphate spray. So over 2000 tiny reservoirs were constructed in the vineyards. It was these reservoirs, one on each plot, that became infected with mosquitoes from rice paddies lower down on the Po flood plain. Similar examples of the late appearance of malaria can be found in Spain. At Ampurias (ancient Emporion) malaria developed only after 1790 when the river Fluvia changed its course, leaving the old channel and its environs marshy and stagnant (Sunyer, 1963). Further south along the

Levantine coast, the high incidence of epidemics of malaria in the eighteenth century was thought to be associated with the spread of rice growing and limits were placed on the extension of paddies (Houston, 1959, p. 181). The outstanding point noted from a list of larval habitats is that over half are man-made (Bates, 1965, p. 165).

Changes in land use and in farming or other rural activities therefore can have a significant effect on the incidence of malaria. In countries such as Italy where the commonest malarial vectors are species preferring open country, the clearance of forest for arable and its degradation into low status scrub must have contributed enormously to the spread of the disease (G. Macdonald in a letter to J. Bradford, 1953). The importance of all these anthropogenic factors in the incidence of malaria lead to the conclusion that there would have been very much less, even no, malaria in prehistoric times.

Changes in weather conditions from year to year or from season to season, can also affect the incidence of malaria on the area affected. An exceptionally dry spell will result in the scarcity of pond or marsh species (Bates, 1965, p. 163ff). The direction of the prevailing winds immediately after the breeding season can blow the insects much further inland than they would normally range. Their timing can determine the onset of illness. The lagoons of Languedoc were prolific breeding grounds for malaria-carrying mosquitoes. In April and May the winds tend to be strong from the south-east and the newly hatched adults are blown inland as far as the city of Montpellier (Harant and Jarray, 1962, p. 164). According to one visitor, the inhabitants of Montpellier were quite green with unhealthiness at this time of the year!

The problems brought by a high incidence of malaria could be very real. Although malaria is a debilitating rather than a killing disease, once immunity has been obtained it must account at least in part for the demographic trends of the lagoon communes of Languedoc. Alone, population numbers are not very revealing, although they can be dramatic. At Aigues-Mortes the population in 1709 totalled 3500 persons but by 1774 it was down to 1600 (Galtier, 1958, p. 245). There could be many reasons other than malaria for this but more telling are the statistics for age at death in the infected districts. The national average for life expectancy in France in the middle of the nineteenth century was 35 years. In the coastal areas, however, this could fall to 25 years or even lower. It was lowest at Palavas (15·4 years) and Mireval (18·5 years), not so bad in Mauguio (22·8 years) and better further west, at Capestang and at

Vendres, for instance (25·6 and 26·0 years, respectively) (Regy, 1867, cited by Galtier, *op. cit.*).

Because of the uncertainties in interpreting the evidence for malaria in the historic past, reasons for the periods when epidemics and infections were particularly bad have to be surmised rather than proved. However Celli was able to draw up a graph showing the variations in the incidence of malaria from the eighth century B.C. to the twentieth century (1925). The graph shows four peaks: one during Republican Roman times (fifth to third centuries B.C.); a second in Imperial times (fifth and sixth centuries A.D.); another in the late Middle Ages (end of the tenth to early thirteenth centuries); and finally the best documented, that of modern times (seventeenth to mid-twentieth centuries). In Braudel's view there was also an increase in marsh fevers at the end of the fifteenth century and early in the sixteenth century (1972, p. 65). Most of these dates have already been mentioned in discussions of climatic fluctuation or sea-level oscillation. Despite, or rather in addition to, the importance of human activities in the spread and intensity of malaria in Mediterranean Europe in the historic period, these physical factors may also prove to be vital in explaining the total situation at any one moment in time.

Lagoon Resources: Fish and Salt

Despite, sometimes, the fears of malaria, the low-lying coasts of Mediterranean Europe were not devoid of positive attractions. Of these, fish and salt are perhaps worth singling out for brief mention. Lagoon waters tend to be amongst the richest of fishing grounds because of the variety of habitat they offer. In the Albufera of Valencia 22 species of fish can be found and four types of eels (Pardo, 1942). The 2000-hectare lagoon at Cabras is still considered the best stocked of Sardinia's lagoons and amongst the most productive in Italy (including the Venetian and the Ortobello lagoons) (Spano, 1954). Up to 250 fishermen with 40 or so boats earn a living from it between the months of October and April. Five species in particular are fished, including mullet, eel, carp and tench. In Apulia, most of the formerly well-stocked lagoons are today silted, drained and farmed but Lago Lesina is still associated with the fishing industry. In 1923 there were plans to reclaim this lagoon. The idea was dropped only after angry protests from the fishermen's condominium and pressure from Anglo-American interests (Colaccico, 1955, p. 55). Though Lago Salpi is now half-dry, and the other part is used for salt production, it should be remembered that the original intention at Lago Salpi was to restore its fishing industry (Afan de Rivera, 1832, 1845). By 1764 the lake had become shallow and saline through insufficient dilution with fresh water. Neither fish nor plant life could survive and the putrid stench was overwhelming. The idea of the new canal was to stimulate circulation of water in the lagoon, improve oxygenation and therefore living conditions for the fish. In the event it had to be admitted that the new canal was bringing more silt than water and that Lago Salpi would never be the rich fishing ground it was formerly.

The second major gain from lagoons and low-lying coastlands is salt. This is so vital a commodity that since Roman times the production of salt has tended to be a government monopoly. One way of arranging this was for the government to nationalize a lagoon in its entirety. This was done in Spain, where James the Conqueror acquired the Albufera of Valencia on 21st January 1250. It was he too who accorded to the inhabitants of the city of Morella (Castellon) the salt collection rights that are at the origin of the present day *Comun de Pescadores* (Pardo, 1942, p. 100). At Lago Salpi Frederick II took care to reinstate a long-existing state monopoly (Candida, 1951, p. 14ff). This lagoon had always been valued for its salt production. There was salt production in Roman times, to judge from the place-name *Salinis* in the Peutinger Itinerary. At the end of the eighteenth century it was allegedly frustration at losing an estimated 100 000 ducats each year through contraband in salt that spurred the Neapolitan government into buying the lagoon, rather than any real concern for the fishermen's hardships (Afan de Rivera, 1845, p. 27ff). Still more galling for the government was the fact that most of the salt smugglers came from two new villages created as part of the Bourbon reforms in Apulia. In Provence, Charles of Anjou added to his fiscal unpopularity by making salt taxable at the place of production rather than at point of distribution (Baratier *et al.*, 1969, p. 44). The practice was to buy up the entire output from the salt works on behalf of the crown, at crown prices, and then to resell the salt at specially appointed depots (*gabelles*) for as much as five times the original price. The *gabelle* documents constitute an exceptional archive. They also show the enormous scale of salt production in some of the major salt pans in the fourteenth century. A total of 15 000 metric tons a year came from the saltpans of the Camargue (Arles, Stes Maries, La Vernède); from those at Berre 3000 tons; from Toulon and Six-Fours 1500 tons; from Var and Hyères 8–11 000 tons. Provençal salt was exported by way of the Rhone valley and its tributaries into the Alps, where it was much in demand for livestock as well as for domestic use. Some went by sea to Tuscany and Liguria but this had to compete with salt exported from Languedoc, in particular the vast saltpans of Peccais at Aigues-Mortes, and from the Adriatic where salt production was headed by the saltpans of Lago Salpi.

Not all salt production was on this scale. Records of the disposal of property in the Middle Ages show how commonplace it could be for a peasant family to be the owners of a single small pan at the marsh edge. Two or three of these were acquired by the monastery of San Leonardo (Manfredonia) for instance in the twelfth century and later (Camobreco, 1913, documents 25(1146), 36(1154), 247(1325) for example). Such pans would be quickly overrun if neglected and leave little permanent trace. They are virtually impossible to date too, so any distribution map of salt production in historic or prehistoric times is bound to be a gross understatement. Despite no less than 32 place-names associated with the word *salinas* in Sardinia (see Fig. 52), only one early salt pan is known with certainty, at Golfo di Palmas (Mori, 1950, p. 49). It has been identified as Punic. All salt producers, whatever the scale of their operations, would have shared one fear in common. The onset of a period of increased siltation or flooding could threaten disaster. One is led to wonder whether the disposal of saltpans to San Leonardo in the Middle Ages was merely a series of chances or whether it has any sinister implications in terms of physical changes affecting the lagoons at that time.

The Neolithic Landscape of Mediterranean Europe

It is perhaps still too early to attempt a full geography of Mediterranean Europe in the Neolithic. However, it is possible to begin to establish a few points. It would be a truism to start by saying that at the beginning of the period the environment was very different from that of the present day or even of the last few centuries. The pattern of post-Neolithic vegetation change has already been sketched out. Compared with changes in the coastlands, these ecological changes might be regarded as qualitative rather than quantitative. Along the coast there have been not only changes in the quality of the environment (wetland, dry land) but also changes measurable in absolute terms. Land has disappeared through erosion or submergence. It has also been created through sedimentation and aggradation. In short, the coastal outline of Mediterranean Europe must have been in places very different in the sixth or seventh millennium B.C. from the present one.

There is no serious disagreement about the observation that relative sea level was appreciably lower some time during the Neolithic than at any time subsequently. What is in question is the amount by which it was lower. Flemming has researched extensively in the Mediterranean and visited some 2000 coastal or off-shore sites. His conclusion is that there has not been a net change in the eustatic level of the sea over the last 2000 years but he does provide evidence for a lower Neolithic sea level and he suggests that it would have been about 3 m below the present day level. Any other variations in land/sea relations he holds to be local and due to tectonic movements. Bintliff, from evidence in Greece, has argued for a Neolithic sea level that was as much as 6 m lower than the present one (1976, 1977). However, most of the archaeological evidence from Mediterranean Europe that is today found below sea level is rarely lower than 1 or 2 m.

A low sea level occurring during the Neolithic would have represented a downward oscillation after the maximum level reached by the Flandrian Transgression. The date of the latter varies but 6000 B.C. may be taken as a guideline, when much of what is now coastal plain or estuary was then submerged. One has to envisage, therefore, a far more indented coastline and a much more restricted area of coastal plain in the landscape of the pre-Neolithic period. Any coastal landings made in the pre-Neolithic period (assuming there was navigation) would have been at points now possibly quite far inland. After this, sea level dropped to the low point reached during or by the middle Neolithic. As it dropped, so an increasing width was exposed of what was to become (and what has partially remained as) coastal plain.

Precisely how much "new" land became available in the Neolithic period is difficult to determine, at least at this stage. In the first place, all depends on the profile of the land. Where gradients were low, a quite small displacement of the relative level of sea and land would have exposed extensive tracts of gently shelving land. It has been suggested (in a rather different context) that where there is an average slope of 1 % in the Gulf of Lyons, the shore would be prolonged by 2 or 3 km (Denizot, 1957, p. 85). West of the Rhone, such a gain could add up to a very large area of coastal plain. Its surface could have been something like that described for Lansargues in the Neolithic. On the other hand, where gradients are steep off-shore, a lowering of sea level would add little to the land area. But it could have another significance. East of the Rhone, for example, many of what are today islands would have become attached to the mainland.

The quality of the new land need not have been so poor as has been suggested for the Atlantic and Channel coasts of France. A drop in sea level there would have left, according to Ters "vast, sandy, muddy or marshy expanses (according to locality), up to 10 kilometres broad" (1976, p. 180). Not only is the climate very different in Mediterranean France but much of the Languedoc coast, for example, may have had a calcrete substratum as at Lansargues. The humid, warm conditions of the Atlantic period might have been a positive aid in stimulating prompt colonization of the mud flats by plants and a speedy ecological progression from mud to marsh to dry land. More certain is the effect of a drop in sea level on the lower reaches of rivers and in their estuaries. This would have been to initiate a phase of channel degrading or incision. As the river beds dropped, so would the level of the water table, and surface drainage on the new lands could have been quite efficient. So much, however, is conjectural. Accumulations of off-shore sediments since the Neolithic mask the early land surface and so its gradient is never known, only surmised (tentatively) from present-day submarine contours.

After the Neolithic, the level of the sea rose. Again, by how much is a matter for disagreement amongst coastal geomorphologists. According to the evidence at Lansargues (making no allowance for tectonic movement), it rose sufficiently to submerge most of the coastal plain of Neolithic times. The coastal population had to make adjustments. Territorial boundaries need not have been affected but the sites of particularly low-lying settlements had to be exchanged for ones on higher land. There may have been something of a wave of recolonization further inland, providing there was room, but many people may have preferred to continue to exploit their territories as best they could in the new circumstances from new sites. Total abandonment of a permanent home and well-established village involves a decision not taken lightly. By and large, as has been seen in these chapters, the forces of continuity have been strong in the historic period, and would have been no less so in the prehistoric period.

11

Continuity or Catastrophe? Concluding Remarks

Of course, the conclusion cannot be avoided that continuity is the foundation of historical reality. The persistence of human life, settlement and economic activity in the regions discussed in the preceding chapters need no further emphasis. If England can be described as "An Old Country" by 1086 (Lennard, 1959)—and few would seriously dispute this—how much more so were the countries of Mediterranean Europe by the time of the Roman takeover? Half-truths of school history, like the suggestion that the Black Death "wiped-out" whole populations, dissolve when stripped to the facts; no district or community is known where there was 100% fatality directly attributable to the disease. Even in the worst cases, there were survivors.

What is true as a generalization, or on the macro-scale, does not inevitably hold good for individual localities or on the micro-scale, a point instanced often enough in this book. Survivors of the Black Death, to pursue this convenient example, have been known to change homes and even villages, taking advantage of general or personal circumstances to move to a better holding or property, or being forced to do so by some overlord. If a sufficient number of the survivors moved away, for whatever reason, the former village may become eligible for classification as deserted. [36] Even a case of total abandonment, however, need not be an instance of catastrophe, if by this word is meant an adverse event or circumstance of such nature that a break or discontinuity is involved. The former community's territory, for example, does not disappear into some historical Black Hole. It is appropriated by another community, informally or formally as the case may be; one of the most frequently

393

observed instances has been for use as grazing land. The tract in question therefore may indeed be abandoned in the sense that it is no longer used to sustain a group of farmers living in the ill-fated settlement but just because a distant grazier or a group of squatters send livestock there instead it in no way becomes a less real part of the district's total economic structure. On the contrary, of such instances is the very nature of change. Only in regions truly describable as uninhabited would it be possible for a true break to occur. In short, to establish settlement discontinuity, it is not sufficient to establish a break in permanent occupation at some (or any) point of the territory. It has also to be established that the territory itself has ceased to exist both in its own right *and* as part of another; and that, in country such as Mediterranean Europe, which was old well before the Romans, would have been a rare possibility. A common enough phenomenon is the re-occupation of deserted settlements; of all the places mentioned in this book, Ordona (Apulia)—a settlement twice deserted since Iron Age times—may provide some of the best archaeological documentation of settlement decline. Important, too, in the history of settlement are site changes, as opposed to total abandonment of territory.

The nature of apparent discontinuities in the past therefore may need closer examination. One way of approaching this was suggested in the preface of this book; that is, the separation of what might be called the "durables" of human life and livelihood from what might be called "matters of the moment". These can be paired. For instance, one set of "durables" are the basic human needs (food, shelter etc.) while parallel "matters of the moment" are the actual nature and design of these and the technical means of their production. The former does not change, the latter does; so much so as sometimes to disguise the underlying continuity. Similarly, there are aspects of human behaviour which are durable (gregariousness, social stratification, for example) and aspects which are temporary, the moeurs of the moment. Then there is a vast array of features which can be divided into the durable (circumstance in general) and the temporary (circumstance in particular). Some instances of the former have emerged in the preceding pages: the core–periphery dichotomy; the effect of price revolutions; the manipulation of cereal production and trade; the implications of urban development; the commercial tendencies of rural society; the country mentality of some citizens; etc. The latter are made up of the actions of specific individuals at named places and at specified times. Into this last category might be put the entire concept of feudalism, to all appearances a wholly post-Roman innovation (so far as Mediterranean Europe is concerned) with no earlier parallel, and certainly such events as the Reconquest of Spain or the Hannibalic War in Italy. Even so, these last two events also contain within themselves type situations that are permanent or durable, as has already been noted in the discussion of the emergence of a certain type of *latifundia*.

A second approach to an understanding of the true nature of some of the greater changes that have marked the history of Western Mediterranean Europe would be to focus on the mechanics of change. This exercise is receiving attention from mathematicians. Their illuminating study of the continuance of change has received an unfortunately conceived title, that of "catastrophe theory".[37] The concept is valuable, however, in the context of historical geography if only because it draws attention to two points in particular. First, to the composite nature of the set of circumstances that are usually rather loosely recognized as a "change". And, second, to the observation that the key factor or catalyst need not be in itself an obvious or even a particularly noteworthy event or happening; it is its position in the sequence that gives it, in retrospect, its significance. The process of change has at least three basic stages normally of very unequal duration. There is first the antecedent or build-up stage; followed by the crisis (containing the moment of decision or the single decisive event); and finally the period in which the consequences of the decision are put into effect or during which the implications of the event become apparent, a stage of manifestation in other words. To the mathematicians, the process of change is amenable to much subtler analysis, portrayed in the three (or more) dimensional model as a cusp. To the historical geographer, or indeed to the historian, their approach might be of help in achieving a balanced and objective explanation of changes in the pattern and in the quality of life in the past. The way it might help is through focusing attention on the responsible factor or factors and separating them from those that can be regarded, for that particular moment, as merely circumstantial.

No issue should be forced. The use of analogy, models or a theoretical framework is legitimate in the study of the past only as a guideline, to be discarded or adopted as the evidence eventually shows. To this geographer at least, it seems axiomatic that the better known (by definition normally the most recent) has to be used in an attempt to illuminate the less well known and the more distant or obscure periods of the past. What does become clear from a study of the past of this nature is that change is neither just accidental nor wholly controllable. It is not something that happens with passing of time. It is in fact as much a prerequisite of successful living as an inevitable aspect of the physical environment. To stop the environment from changing at all is impossible; to check social or economic change is to invite difficulties. Learning, perhaps from Croce (1970, p. 146), that a greater understanding of the past is derived if history is considered not the result of natural causes but as a moral drama, the historical geographer in Mediterranean Europe finds himself watching a very long-playing drama. Moreover, it is a drama which repeats itself, with new actors, in a scenario that seems familiar but that has from time to time been altered just enough to make a difference to the *denouement*.

Notes

1. According to Toynbee's analysis of the extant Roman censuses, six or seven of the given total figures can be regarded as severely questionable and a number of major caveats apply to all. There are obvious errors of transcription (for example, the reversal of figures for the 179/178 and 174/173 B.C. censuses). There are also occasions when two or three totals are recorded for a single date. It is nowhere recorded which classes or groups of the population were excluded from the census counts (slaves certainly would have been) or what territory was included. There are problems concerning the accuracy of the original counts, the possibility of bias at the time of the census or of deliberate falsification of the published figures by the Roman government subsequently. What is clear is that the figures that have been handed down since Roman times represent no more than compilations made from the original census data.

2. Modern municipal statutes define a *vecino* as " 'any male Spaniard *emancipado* [i.e. one who is over 18, living apart from and independently of his father] who habitually resides within the municipality and is included on the electoral register' " (quoted by Kenny, 1961, p. 12). A coefficient of 4·5 is commonly taken for north Italian *focularia*, and a lower one for *boccarum* where a salt-consumer is assumed to be a person aged over 3 or 4 (Herlihy used a coefficient of 1·22 for rural communes of Pistoia (1967, p. 66); but see discussion in Mols (1954, Vol. II, p. 110ff on *bocche* and Vol. I, p. 25ff on *feux*) for a measure of the problems involved.

3. This total includes 16 hours applying weed killer. Hand-weeding could double the total number of hours spent, depending on local conditions.

4. In southern Italy in the twelfth century three classes of rights were distinguished (Evoli, 1931). These were: essential rights; useful rights; and *domenicali*. Essential rights were strictly personal and related to the subsistence needs of each citizen. They included separate rights for the grazing and watering of beasts, the overnight parking of livestock, the collection of fuel and timber, even for the "occupation" of ground space taken up by a dwelling. Useful rights

included rights of timber for other than house-building or domestic fires, for the gathering of acorns and chestnuts and of fruit still on the trees. The third class of rights implied participation in the produce of the fief in general and might be granted in respect of selected crops, vegetable or cereal, or of taxes or as permission to pre-empt dues payable by the inhabitants for any of the other rights. Land alienated from the operation of these rights was referred to in Italy as in *defesa* (''properly defined as closed land in which no one at any time could exercise *usi civici* [rights]''); in Spain as *la dehesa* (Salomon, 1964, p. 136), and in France as *dévèses* or as land *mise en défense*. Evoli sees any alientation of these rights as parallel to the enclosure movement taking place in England at about the same time.

5. Information kindly supplied by Monsieur Mayre of Lansargues, Hérault.

6. Yet another factor in their economic stagnation at this time. Taorimina, for example, lost half its population of 6000 between the two censuses of 1583 and 1653 (Mack Smith, 1969, p. 196).

7. This figure of 6000 for Pistoia is a total estimated for 1351, a year too close to the Black Death to have much resemblance to the real total for 1344 (Herlihy's own note).

8. Professor G. D. B. Jones has suggested a date early in the beginning of the third or even at the end of the fourth century B.C.; I am indebted to him for most of the archaeological information on the Foggia centuriation system.

9. In comparison, under post-war agrarian reform laws, allocations normally vary from 4 to 13 hectares according to the region's population pressure and to opportunities for supplementary income.

10. But Raper (1977) and Eschebach (1970), whose land-use classification Raper follows for Pompeii, ignore agricultural land use despite the archaeological evidence.

11. Interesting to find, therefore, in 1976 at least one landowner in the process of deliberately reverting to tradition by clearing a rocky garrigue for a 30-hectare vineyard in order to liberate what he considers still the ''best'' soil on his estate (that on alluvium) for irrigated lucerne (Monsieur Guizard, Montpellier, personal communication).

12. Agrarian reform in Greece in the early 1960s promoted the planting of the new earth-banked terraces with lucerne (Delano Smith and Watson, 1964, p. 340).

13. Few species of the *Graminaceae* family (except rice) tolerate saturation at their roots. As the plants grow and their roots push downwards, interstitial air is pushed down through the soil by the growing roots until held up by the water-

table. Insufficient room for the displaced air means stunted growth in the plant. At first, yields suffer, then finally the plant itself. The balance between a well-watered and a saturated soil is therefore a very fine one.

14. One hundred *salme* was equal to about 160 litres or $4\frac{1}{2}$ bushels.

15. This shortage of draught animals could have been contributed to by the competitive price of beef.

16. See Hoskins (1965) *Provincial England*, p. 8, on this point for fourteenth-century England.

17. This, and other extracts from the *Relaciones*, were kindly translated for me by Professor J. P. Cole.

18. They may have had a point. The root system of a tree is an incredibly lengthy network of main, secondary and minor roots and spurs; masses of these roots in a wood can, it has been suggested, retain up to 1000 tons of water per acre. In addition, as much as 27% of rain or snowfall may be held in the canopy, and a further considerable volume of water passes from the roots to the top of the tree and is there evaporated (R. Arvill (1967) *Man and Environment*, p. 33. Penguin Books, London).

19. The straight-line distance from Reate (Rieti) to Foggia is over 500 km.

20. "Scriptae a Septimiano ad Cosmum.—[Cum] conductores gregum oviaricorum qui sunt cura tua in re presenti subinde mihi quererentur per itinera callium frequenter injuria [m] se accipere a stationaris et magg. Saepino et Boviano, eo quod in transitu jumenta et pastores quos conductos habent dicentes fugitivos esse et jumenta abactia habere [retineant] et sub hac specie oves quoque dominicae [si] bi [pe]reant in illo tumultu, necesse habebamus etiam scribere quietius agerent ne res dominica detrimentum pateretur . . .". (A. Grenier (1905) *La Transhumance des Troupeaux en Italie du Sud et son role dans l'Histoire Romaine. Mélanges d'Archéologie et d'Histoire*. Vol. XXV, p. 307,fn 4. Paris and Rome).

21. The absence of reference to anything that could possibly indicate the presence on these wheeled ploughs of a mouldboard or a coulter of some description would put the existence of a wheeled *ard* beyond doubt.

22. Analysis of the process of settlement in Lapmark (northern Sweden) revealed that some relatively favourable but small zones failed to attract settlement until the 1830s although in many cases they were surrounded by settlements established as early as the 1770s. Only when new crops and farming techniques were adopted (notably, the growing of potatoes and the irrigation of hay, which increased yields from two to ten fold) did it become possible to earn a living from a far smaller acreage than previously and so these small unclaimed areas were late settled.

23. In S. C. Powell's (1964) *Puritan Village* it is shown how under certain circumstances (for example, those of colonization in New England in the early seventeenth century) good meadowland would be prized above arable soils. The latter at Sudbury (Mass), were in fact of very indifferent quality but were deemed capable of improvement. The decision to settle was taken in view of the extensive area and outstanding quality of the meadowland so urgently needed to maintain the plough oxen and breed their replacements.

24. What Barker has termed, rather ambiguously, a "stock-economy" operating at Narce (Tuscany) from the end of the second millennium onwards must be interpreted, according to his own description, as an example of this farming system. For he makes the point that there it seems "to have been successfully adapted to the particular constraints and resources of the area around the settlement, for it lasted virtually unchanged until the end of the following millennium" (1976, p. 303).

25. Phases of red earth formation might be expected to have alternated with phases of calcrete formation according to the wetness or dryness of the climate. On the Tavoliere zonal calcretes are sometimes overlain by a reddish soil. But some pedologists believe that both calcrete and red earth can be formed at the same time and even in association with one another (Durand, 1952; Boulaine, 1957; see discussion in Birot and Gabert, 1964, p. 111). The situation will undoubtedly become clearer when the much-needed detailed classification of Mediterranean calcretes is established. The confusion may arise if a red earth contains a hardpan, a calcareous horizon, which is not at all genetically the same as a zonal calcrete. Such concretions have been observed in the red earths of the forest of Valbonne in southern France (George, 1935, p. 275).

26. Recent evidence from Israel dates mines and smelters there to about 4000 B.C.

27. For the record it might be noted that Fairbridge (1961) has a "high" sea level at about 200 B.C., as do other researchers for the north-western seaboards of Europe (Mörner, 1971; Andrews *et al.*, 1973; Morrison, 1975; Ters, 1977).

28. I should like to record my thanks to Monsieur Henri Prades for showing me Lansargues (and Lattes) on many occasions and allowing me to work on the sediments. I am also grateful to Monsieur Mayre for his help and for information on Lansargues.

29. I am greatly indebted to B. W. Sparks (University of Cambridge) for help in identifying molluscs from my several fieldwork campaigns in Mediterranean Europe and to Dr Taylor and Mrs Whybrow of the British Museum (Natural History) for comments on the marine molluscs.

30. A *chenier* is defined as normally a sand and shell ridge occurring slightly discordantly on a marsh surface (J. T. Greensmith and E. V. Tucker (1973) Holocene transgressions and regressions on the Essex coast, Outer Thames Estuary. *Geologie en Mijnbouw* **54**(4), 195).

31. L. T. Jones's identification of this river, the *Clodianus*, as the Muga is clearly an error. The Muga reaches the sea some way to the north, near the supposed site of *Rosas*, the other Massiliot colony in the Gulf of Rosas.

32. There was an eighth-century mole at Delos, Greece, which was 100 m large and "built up from massive rough-hewn blocks of local granite" (Casson, 1971, p. 362).

33. I am grateful to Sig. Ruberto for this information and for discussions on the harbour of *Emporion*. Corroboration awaits further investigation.

34. I am grateful to Monsieur Guèry of the University of Aix-Marseilles for details of the stratigraphy. The interpretation is largely my own.

35. *A. labranchiae* is found in the southern half of the peninsula, and in Sicily and Sardinia; *A. sacharovi elatus* used to infest the Pontine Marshes and is still found around Ravenna.

36. Basic definitions concerning deserted and shrunken villages are now widely accepted on the continent as in Britain. In the former case, desertion leaves no more than three steadings; in the latter, as many as six may survive on the site. Rather less attention, it would seem, has been paid to definition of the feature that has been deserted and there is a good deal of scope for confusion in this respect, particularly in Mediterranean Europe. In the modern Italian censuses *masseria* and other forms of estate centres are not included with nucleated settlement even though their populations may be substantial. It has been pointed out elsewhere (Delano Smith, 1975) that if this were to be the rule in discussions about deserted villages a certain amount of confusion would be avoided. From ground evidence alone it may be impossible to distinguish the site of a former *masseria* from that of a monastery, for instance, yet as social or political centres (if not purely functionally), these two features may have quite different implications in the total settlement pattern and farming structure of the district. Klapisch-Zuber and Day are carefully explicit about their definition of a deserted village as having been at lowest level "a hamlet of several hearths" (1965, p. 420).

37. In connection with Catastrophe Theory as a summary of certain types of change, see Thom (1969, 1975) Zeeman (1976) and Wagstaff (1978).

References

Abulafia, D. (1977). *The Two Italies: Economic Relations between the Norman Kingdom of Sicily and the Northern Communes.* Cambridge Studies in Medieval Life and Thought. Cambridge University Press, Cambridge.

Acton, H. (1956). *The Bourbons of Naples.* Methuen, London, 2 vols.

Admiralty (1939–1944). *Italy* Geographical Handbook, Naval Intelligence Division, London, 4 vols.

Admiralty (1939–1944). *Spain and Portugal* Geographical Handbook, Naval Intelligence Division, London, 3 vols.

Afan de Rivera, C. (1832–1833). *Considerazioni sui mezzi da restituire il valore proprio ai doni che la natura largamente conceduto al Regno delle due Sicilie.* Fibreno, Naples, 2 vols.

Afan de Rivera, C. (1838). *Memoria sui mezzi di ritrarre il massimo profitto dal lago Salpi coordinando questa impresa a quella piu vasta di bonificare e migliorare la pianura di Capitanata.* Fibreno, Naples.

Afan De Rivera, C. (1845). *Del bonificamento del lago Salpi coordinato a quello della pianura della Capitanata, delle opere eseguite e dei vantaggi ottenuti.* Fibreno, Naples.

Albani, D. (1933) *Indagine preventiva sulle recenti variazioni della Linea di Spiaggia delle Coste Italiane,* Ricerche sulle Variaziooi delle Spiagge Italiane, I, Anonima Romana, Rome.

Albèri, E. (1839–1863). *Relazioni degli Ambasciatori Veneti durante il secolo XVI.* Florence, 15 vols.

Alberti, L. (1550). *Descrittione di tutta Italia* . . . A. Giccarelli, Bologna.

Almagia, R. (1929). The Repopulation of the Roman Campagna. *Geographical Review* **XIX**, 529–555.

Almagro, M. (1968). *Ampurias, Guia Breve de las Excavaciones y Museo.* Barcelona.

Anati, E. (1964). *Camonica Valley.* Jonathan Cape, London.

Andrews, J. T., King, C. A. M. and Stuiver, M. (1973). Holocene sea level changes, Cumberland coast, northwest England: eustatic and glacio-isostatic movement. *Geologie en Mijnbow* **52,** 1–12.

403

Angioni, G. (1976). *Sa Laurera: Il lavoro contadino in Sardegna*. Editrice Democratica Sarda, Cagliari.

Arnal, J. (1963). Les Dolmens du Départment de l'Hérault. *Préhistoire* **XV**, Presses Universitaires de France, Paris.

Arnal, J. (1973). Le Lébous à Saint-Mathieu-de-Tréviers (Hérault). Ensemble du Chalcolithique au Gallo-Romain. *Gallia-Préhistoire* **XVI**, 131–200.

Arnal, J. and Prades, H. (1969). Les chars mailhaciens à Camp Redon (Lansargues, Hérault). *Annales de la Société d'Horticulture et d'Histoire Naturelle de l'Hérault* **109** (3), 134–139.

Arnal, J., Bailloud, G., Riquet, R. (1960). Les Styles céramiques du Néolithique. *Préhistoire* **XIV**, 211. Presses Universitaires de France, Paris.

Arnal, J., Martin-Granel, H. and Sangmeister, E. (1964). Lébous. *Antiquity* **XXXVII**, 191–200.

Arnal, J., Majurel, R. and Prades, H. (1974). *Le Port de Lattara Lattes, Hérault*. Institut International d'Etudes Ligures, Bordighera-Montpellier.

Arnal, J., Arnal, H. and Prades, H. (1977). L'implantation de terramares ou ports langunaires sur la rive nord de l'Etang de Mauguio, Hérault. In *Approche Ecologique de L'Homme Fossile* (H. Laville and J. Renault-Miskovsky, eds). Bulletin de l'Association Française pour l'Etude du Quaternaire, Supplément.

Arribas, A. (1968). Las bases economicas del Neolitico al Bronce. In *Estudios de Economia Antigua de la Peninsula Iberica* (M. Tarradell, ed.), pp. 33–60.

Arrighi, P. (ed.) (1971). *Histoire de la Corse*. Privat, Toulouse.

Ashby, Th. (1927). *The Roman Campagna in Classical Times*. Benn, London.

Audibert, J. (1962). *La Civilisation Chalcolithique du Languedoc Oriental*. Institut International d'Etudes Ligures, Bordighera-Montpellier.

Aymard, A. (1941). Remarques sur le déboisement des Grandes Causses dans l'Antiquité. *Revue Géographique des Pyrénées et du Sud-ouest* **12**, 115–128.

Aymard, A. (1948). L'interdiction des plantations des vignes en Gaule Transalpine sous la République Romaine. *Mélanges offerts à D. Faucher*, 24–47.

Aymard, M. (1973). Chiourmes et Galères dans la Méditerranée du VIᵉ Siècle. *Histoires Economiques du Monde Méditerranée 1450–1650: Mélanges en l'honneur de Fernand Braudel*, pp. 50–64. Privat, Toulouse.

Aymard, M. and Bresc, H. (1973). Problemi di storia dell' insediamento nella Sicilia medievale e moderna, 1100–1800. *Quaderni Storici*, 24, Anno VIII, fasc. III 945–976.

Balabanian, O. (1975). Les openfields lanièrés de Zarza-Capilla et de Cabeza del Buey. In *I Paesaggi Rurali Europei*, pp. 17–26. Atti del Convegno Internazionale, Perugia 1973.

Baldacci, O. (1952). *La Casa Rurale in Sardegna*. Ricerche sulle Dimore Rurali in Italia, VIII, Centro di studi per la Geografia Etnologica, Florence.

Baldacci, O. (1962). *Puglia* Le Regioni d'Italia, Vol. 14, U.T.E.T. Turin.

Baratier, E. (ed). (1969). *Histoire de la Provence* Privat, Toulouse.

Baratier, E., Duby, G. and Hildesheimer, E. (1969). *Atlas Historique Provence, Comtat Orange, Nice, Monaco.* A. Colin, Paris.

Barfield, L. H. (1971). *Northern Italy before Rome.* Thames and Hudson, London.

Barker, G. W. (1972). The conditions of cultural and economic growth in the Bronze Age of central Italy. *Proceedings of the Prehistoric Society* **38,** 170–208.

Barker, G. W. (1973). The economy of medieval Tuscania: the archaeological evidence. *Papers of the British School at Rome* **XLI,** 155–177.

Barker, G. W. (1975). Prehistoric territories and economies in central Italy. In *Palaeoeconomy* (E. S. Higgs, ed.). Papers in Economic Prehistory, Vol. 2, pp. 111–175. Cambridge University Press, Cambridge.

Barker, G. W. (1976). Animal husbandry at Narce. In *A Faliscan Town in Southern Etruria* (T. W. Potter, ed.), pp. 295–307. British School at Rome, London.

Barker, G. W. (1977). The archaeology of Samnite settlement in Molise. *Antiquity* **LI,** 20–24.

Barry, J. P. (1960). Contribution à l'étude de la végétation de la région de Nîmes. *Année Biologique,* 311–550 (Thèse d'Université, Lettres, Montpellier).

Bates, M. (1965). *The Natural History of Mosquitoes.* Harper, New York, (reprint of first edition, Macmillan, 1949).

Baver, L. D. (1956). *Soil Physics,* 3rd edition. J. Wiley, New York.

Bazzana, A. and Guichard, P. (1974). *Recherches sur les Habitats Musulmans du Levant Espagnol.* Centre d'Archéologie Médiévale de l'Université de Lyon II (cyclostyled).

Beloch, K. J. (1937–1961). *Bevölkerungsgeschite Italiens.* Berlin and Leipzig, 3 vols.

Bender, B. (1972). *Farming in Prehistory.* John Baker, London.

Benoit, F. (1940). Le delta du Rhône à l'époque grecque. *Revue d'Etudes Anciennes* **42,** 567–572.

Bergeron, P. (1967). Problèmes de la vie pastorale en Sardaigne. *Revue de Géographie de Lyon* **42,** 311–328.

Betancourt, P. B. (1976). The end of the Greek Bronze Age. *Antiquity* **L,** 197, 40–47.

Biagioli, G. (1970). *Agrarian Changes in Nineteenth-century Italy. The enterprise of a Tuscan landlord, Bettino Ricasoli* Univ. of Reading, Institute of Agricultural History Research Paper No. 1.

Binaghi, R. (1939) La Metallurgia in età Romana in Sardegna. In *Sardegna Romana* (A. Taramelli *et al.*, eds), Vol. II, pp. 40–53. Istituto di Studi Romani, Rome.

Bintliff, J. L. (1975). Sediments and settlement in southern Greece. In *Geoarchaeology: Earth Science and the Past* (D. A. Davidson and M. L. Shackley eds), pp. 267–275. Duckworth, London.

Bintliff, J. L. (1976). The Plain of Western Macedonia and the Neolithic Site of Nea Nikomedeia. *Proceedings of the Prehistoric Society* **42**, 241–262.

Bintliff, J. L. (1977). *Natural Environment and Human Settlement in Prehistoric Greece*. British Archaeological Reports Supplementary Series 28, Oxford, 2 vols.

Birch, J. W. (1972). Farming systems as resource systems. In *Agricultural Typology and Land Utilisation*, pp. 13–20. Centre of Agricultural Geography, University of Verona, Verona.

Birot, J. and Gabert, J. (1964). *La Méditerranée et le Moyen-Orient: Volume I Généralités, Péninsule Ibérique, Italie*. (2nd Edition). Presses Universitaires de France, Paris.

Birrell, J. (1968). La Ville de Berre à la fin du Moyen-Age. *Cahiers du Centre d'Etudes des Sociétés Méditerranéennes* **2**, 109–168.

Bishko, C. J. (1963). The Castilian as plainsman: the medieval ranching frontier in La Mancha and Estramadura. In *The New World Looks at its History* (A. R. Lewis and T. F. McGann, eds). University of Texas, Austin.

Blanc, J. (1977). *Recherches de Sédimentologie Appliquée au Littoral du Delta du Rhône, de Fos au Grau du Roi*. Centre National Pour l'Exploitation des Océans, Marseilles.

Blanchet, A. (1941–1946). *Carte archéologique de la Gaule Romaine* Forma Orbis Romana, Fasc. VIII Gard 1941; Fasc. X Hérault, 1946.

Blanchet, G. (1958). Les petits profits de la garrigue. *Annales de la Société d'Horticulture et d'Histoire Naturelle de l'Hérault* **98**, 83–88.

Bloch, M. (1931). *Les Caractères originaux de l'Histoire Rurale Française*. Colin, Paris (English translation, Routledge and Kegan Paul, London, 1966).

Blondel, R. (1941). *La végétation forestière de la région du St. Paul, près de Montpellier* S.I.G.M.A. (Station Internationale Géobotanique Méditerranéene et Alpine) Montpellier, 79.

Blumer, W. (1964). The oldest known plan of an inhabited site dating from the Bronze Age, about the middle of the 2nd mill. B.C. *Imago Mundi* **XVIII**, 9–11.

Boe, G. de (1975). Villa romana in località "Posta Crusta". Rapporto provvisorio sulle campagne di scavo 1972 e 1973. *Notizie degli Scavi di Antichita* Rome **29**, 516–530.

Boira, V. G. (1975). *El Tribunal de las Aguas de la Vega de Valencia 960–1960* (4th edition). Valencia.

Bolens, L. (1972). Engrais et protection de la fertilité dans l'agronomie hispano-arable XI-XIIᵉ siècles. *Etudes Rurales* **45**, 34–60.

Bolkenstein, H. (1958). *Economic Life in Greece's Golden Age*. Leiden.

Bonatti, E. (1961). I sedimenti del lago di Monterosi. *Experientia* **17**, (252), 1–4.

Bonatti, E. (1963). Stratigrafia pollinica dei sedimenti post-glaciale di Baccano, lago craterico del Lazio. *Atti della Società Toscana di Scienze Naturali*, Pisa, **XL**, 40–48.

Bonatti, E. (1970). Pollen sequence in the lake sediments. In *Ianula—an account of the history and development of the Lago di Monterosi, Latium, Italy* (G. E. Hutchinson, ed.). Transactions of the American Philosophical Society 1x (4), 26–31.

Bonnassie, P. (1966). Un contrat agraire inédit de Sant Cugat. *Anuario de Estudios Medievales* **3,** 441–450.

Boscolo, A. (1967). *Il feudalesimo in Sardegna.* Testi e documenti per la storia della Questione Sarda, 4. Sardu Fossataro, Cagliari.

Boüard, M. de (1938). Problèmes des subsistances dans un état Médiéval: le marché et les prix des céréales au Royaume angevin de Sicile (1266–1288). *Annales d'Histoire Economique et Sociale* **54,** 483–501.

Boudier, F. (1963). *Le Bassin du Rhône au Quaternaire* C.N.R.S., Paris, 2 vols.

Boyd, C. E. (1952). *Tithes and Parishes in Mediaeval Italy.* Cornell University Press, Ithaca, New York.

Bradford, J. S. P. (1949). "Buried landscapes" in Southern Italy. *Antiquity* **XXIII,** 89, 58–72.

Bradford, J. S. P. (1950). The Apulian Expedition: an interim report *Antiquity* **XXIV,** 93, 84–95.

Bradford, J. S. P. (1957). *Ancient Landscapes.* Bell, London, 297 pp.

Bradford, J. S. P. and Williams-Hunt, P. R. (1946). Siticulosa Apulia *Antiquity* **XX,** 77, 191–200.

Braudel, F. (1972). *The Mediterranean and the Mediterranean World of Philip II* Collins, London, 2 vols (English translation from 2nd revised edition 1966; first French edition 1949).

Braun-Blanquet, J. (1932). *Plant Sociology.* Translated and revised by G. D. Fuller and H. S. Conard, Hafner, New York and London (facsimile edition in 1965).

Braun-Blanquet, J. (1936). La forêt d'yeuse Languedocienne. *Mémoires de la Société des Sciences Naturelles de Nimes* **5,** 147p.

Bresc, H. (1973). Documents on Frederick IV of Sicily's Intervention in Malta: 1372 *Papers of the British School at Rome* **XXVIII,** 180–200.

Brigaglia, M. (1976). *Profilo storico della città di Sassari* (2nd edition). Chiarella, Sassari.

Brögger, J. (1971). *Montevarese: A Study of Peasant Society and Culture in Southern Italy.* Universitets Forlaget, Oslo-Bergen-Tromso.

Brothwell, D. P. (1969). *Food in Antiquity.* Thames and Hudson, London.

Brunt, P. A. (1971). *Italian Manpower 225 B.C.–A.D. 14.* Clarendon Press, Oxford.

Bullock Hall, W. H. (1898). *The Romans on the Riviera and the Rhone.* London.

Burns, R. I. (1967). *The Crusader Kingdom of Valencia. Reconstruction on a 13th century Frontier.* Harvard University Press, Cambridge, Mass., 2 vols.

Burns, R. I. (1975). *Medieval Colonialism. Post-crusade exploitation of Islamic Valencia.* Princeton University Press, Princeton, N.J.

Butzer, K. W. (1964). *Environment and Archaeology.* Methuen, London.

Bylund, E. (1960). Theoretical considerations regarding the distribution of settlement in Inner Northern Sweden. *Geografisca Annaler* **42**, 225–231.

Caesari, J. (1974). *Rapport à M. le directeur des antiquités historiques de la Corse sur les sondages archéologiques effectués à Propriano, Corse* (unpublished).

Cagnetti, F. (1975). *Banditi a Orgosolo* (new edition of *L'Inchiesta su Orgosolo* 1954). Guaraldi, Rimini and Florence.

Cahen, C. (1940). *Le Régime Féodal de l'Italie Normande.* Paul Geuthner, Paris.

Callahan, W. J. (1972). *Honor, Commerce and Industry in Eighteenth Century Spain.* Baker Library, Harvard Graduate School of Business Administration, Cambridge, Mass.

Calomonico, C. (1970). *La Casa Rurale nella Puglia.* Ricerche sulle Dimore Rurali in Italia, 28, Olschki, Florence.

Calvini, N., Putzulu, E. and Succhi, V. (eds) (1957). *Documenti Inediti sui traffici commerciali tra la Ligura e la Sardegna nel Secolo XII*, Padua.

Calvo, G.-T. F. (1975). *Continuidad y Cambio en la huerta de Murcia.* Academia Alfonso X al Sabio, Murcia.

Campbell, J. K. (1964). *Honour, family and patronage. A study of institutions and moral values in a Greek mountain community.* Clarendon Press, Oxford.

Camobreco, F. (1913). *Regesta San Leonardo di Sipontum.* Regesta Chartarum Italia, 10, Rome.

Candida, L. (1951). Saline Adriatiche *Memorie di Geografia Economica.* Anno III, Vol. V, Naples.

Cappelli, B. Laino ed i suoi Statuti *Archivio Storico per la Calabria e la Lucania* n.s.I. 405–450.

Caputo, M. and Pieri L. (1976). Eustatic sea variation in the last 2000 years in the Mediterranean. *Journal of Geophysical Research* **81**, 33, 5787–5790.

Carabellese, F. (1924). *Il Commune pugliese durante la monarchie normanno-sveva.* Commissione Provinciale di Archaeologia e Storia Patria, Documenti e Monografie, Vol XVII, Bari.

Cardona, J. M. (1976). *La Conquista Catalana de 1235.* Institut d'Estudis Eivissencs, Eivissa.

Caro Baroja, J. (1964). *Los Pueblos de Espana.* Barna, Barcelona.

Carrère, P. and Dugrand, R. (1960). *La Région Méditerranéenne.* Presses Universitaires de France, Paris.

Carrington, D. (1971). *Granite Island. A Portrait of Corsica.* Longman, London.

Carrion, P. (1932). *Los Latifundios en Espana.* Ariel, Barcelona.

Caruso, A. (1963). *La Dohana Menae Pecudum o Dogana di Foggia e il suo Archivio.* Miscell. giuridico-economica meridionale, Serie: Dogana e Tavoliere di Puglia, C.E.S.P., Naples-Foggia-Bari.

Casalis, G. (1833ff). *Dizionario Geografico-Storico-Statistico commerciale degli stati di S.M. il Re di Sardegna* 28 vols.

Cassan, abbé, and Meynial, E. (1900). *Cartulaire de l'Abbaye d'Aniane*. Société Archéologique de Montpellier, Montpellier.

Casson, L. (1907). L'administration communale aux XIV et XV ème siècles dans quelques communautés dépendant des Abbayes d'Aniane et de St Guilhem du Désert, Montpellier. *Mélanges d'Histoire Locale* **V**, 186–259.

Casson, L. (1971). *Ships and Seamanship in the Ancient World*. Princeton University Press, Princeton, N.J.

Casta, F. J. (1974). *Le Diocèse d'Ajaccio*. Beauchesne, Paris.

Castillo, A. Del (1965). El manso medieval A de Vilosiu. In *Homenaje a Jaime Vicens-Vives*, Vol. I 218–228. Barcelona.

Cavanilles, A. J. (1797). *Observaciones sobre la Geografia Agricultura y problacion del Reino de Valencia*. Valencia.

Celli, A. (1933). *The History of Malaria in the Roman Campagna from Ancient Times* translated by A. Celli-Fraentzel, Bale, London.

Chalandon, F. (1907). *Histoire de la Domination Normande en Italie et en Sicile* 2 vols. Paris.

Chapman, C. G. (1973). *Milocca: a Sicilian village*. Allen and Unwin, London.

Chapman, G. P. (1974). Perception and regulation: a case study of farmers in Bihar. *Transactions of the Institute of British Geographers* **62**, 71–93.

Cherchi-Parba, F. (1959). Lineamente storici dell'agricoltura Sarda nel secolo XIII. In *Studi storici in onore di F. Loddo-Canepa* Vol. II, pp. 119–216. Bibliotecha della Deputazione di Stori Patria per la Sardegna, Nos. 1 and 2, Florence.

Cherkauer, D. S. (1976). The stratigraphy and chronology of the river Treia alluvial deposits. In *A Faliscan Town in South Etruria* (T. W. Potter, ed.), pp. 106–120.

Cherubini, G. and Francovich, R. (1973). Forme e vicende degli insediamenti nella campagna Toscana dei secoli XIII-XIV. In Archeologia e Geografia del Popolamento, 877–904, *Quaderni Storici*, **24**, Ancona.

Chevalier, M. (1956). *La Vie Humaine dans les Pyrénées Ariègeoises*. Génin, Paris.

Chilver, G. E. F. (1941). *Cisalpine Gaul*. Clarendon Press, Oxford.

Chisholm, M. (1968). *Rural Settlement and Land Use*. (2nd edition) Hutchinson, London.

Chiva, I. (1963). Social organisation, traditional economy, and customary law in Corsica. Outline of a plan of analysis. In *Mediterranean Countrymen* (J. Pitt-Rivers, ed.), pp. 97–112. Mouton, Paris.

Chocomeli, J. (1945). La primera exploracio palafitica en España. *Archivio de Prehistorica Levantina* **II**, 93–114.

Chorley, R. J. (ed.) (1969). *Water Earth and Man*. Methuen, London.

Christaller, W. (1966). *Central Places in Southern Germany* (Translated by C. W. Baskine). Prentice Hall, Englewood Cliffs, New Jersey.

Ciasca, R. (1928). *Storia della Bonifica del Regno di Napoli*. Laterza, Bari.

Cicco, P. di (1964). *Censuazione ed Affrancazione del Tavoliere di Puglia* (1789–1865). Quaderni della Rassegna degli "Archivio di Stato", 32, Rome.

Cipolla, C. M. (1965). Four centuries of Italian demographic development. In *Population and History* (D. V. Glass and D. E. C. Eversley, eds.), pp. 570–587. Arnold, London.

Clark, C. and Haswell, M. R. (1966). *The economics of Subsistence Agriculture* (2nd edition). Macmillan, London.

Colacicco, G. (1955). *La Bonifica del Tavoliere*. Consorzio Generale per la Bonifica e la Trasformazione Fondaria della Capitanata, Foggia.

Cole, J. P. (1964). *Italy*. Chatto and Windus, London.

Colmeiro, M. (1965). *Historia de la Economia politica en Espana*. Taurus, Madrid 2 vols.

Conzorzio — *I caratteri generali del Comprensorio consortite: l'attiva Bonifica*. Consorzio per il Bonifica della Capitanata, Foggia (cyclostyled).

Contenau, G. (1949). *La Civilisation Phénicienne* (2nd edition) Paris.

Conzen, M. G. R. (1962). The plan analysis of an English city centre. *Land Studies in Geography* Series B. No 24, pp. 383–414.

Coque, R. (1962). *La Tunisie présaharienne, étude géomorphologique*, Paris.

Courtin, J. (1970). Le Cardial récent de Provence. *Les Civilisations Néolithiques du Midi de la France* Actes du Colloque de Narbonne 15-17 Février 1970, Laboratoire de Préhistoire et de Paléthnologie, Carcassonne.

Courtin, J. (1970). *Le Chasséen Méridional* ibid. 27–31.

Courtin, J. (1976). Les civilisations néolithiques en Provence. In *La Préhistoire Française* (J. Guilaine, ed.), Vol. II, pp. 255–266. Les Civilisations Néolithiques et Proto-historiques de la France.

Croce, B. (1970). *History of the Kingdom of Naples* translated by F. Frenaye, University of Chicago Press, Chicago and London.

Crino, S. (1945). Un portolano inedito della prima meta del secolo XVII *Atti dell' V Congresso Geografico Italiano*, I, 605ff.

Cuenca, A. P. and Walker, M. J. (1974). Commentarios sobre el Cuaternario Continental en al centro y sul de la Provincia de Alicante (España) *Actas de la 1 Reunion Nacional del Grupo de Trabajo del Cuaternario, Madrid, Oct. 1973*, Madrid, 15–38.

Cuenca, A. P. and Walker, M. J. (1976). Pleistocene finale y Holoceno en la cuenca del Vinalopo (Alicante). *Estudios Geologicos* 32, 95–104.

Cura-Morera, M. (1976). El Grup Cultural de les Cistes néolitiques del Pre-Pirineu Catala ("El Solsonia") *Cypsela* Diputacion Provincial de Gerona Servicio de Investigaciones Arquelogicas, 49–52.

Curtis, L. F., Courtney, F. M. and Trudgill, S. (1976). *Soils in the British Isles.* Longmans, London.

Dainelli, G. (ed.) (1939). *Atlante Fisico Economico d'Italia.* Consociazione Turistica, Milan.

D'Arms, J. H. (1970). *Romans on the Bay of Naples.* Harvard University Press, Cambridge, Mass.

Daryll Forde, C. (1934). *Habitat, Economy and Society.* Methuen, London.

Daumas, M. (1951). Le Lunellois. *Bulletin de la Société Languedocienne de Géographie* **22,** 185–291 and **23,** 3–150.

Dauzat, A. and Rostaing, C. (1963). *Dictionnaire des Noms de Lieux de France.* Larousse, Paris.

Davico, R. (1972). Baux, exploitations, techniques agricoles en Piémont dans la deuxième moitié du 18ème Siècle. *Etudes Rurales* **45,** 76–101.

Davies, O. (1935). *Roman Mines in Europe.* Clarendon Press, Oxford.

Davis, J. (1973). *Land and Family in Pisticci.* L.S.E. Monographs in Social Anthropology 48, Athlone Press, London.

Davis, J. (1977). *People of the Mediterranean.* Routledge and Kegan Paul, London.

Davity, P. (1617). *Les Etats, Empires et Principantes.* du Monde, Paris.

Day, J. (1973). *Villaggi abbandonati in Sardegna dal trecento al settecento: Inventario.* C.N.R.S., Paris.

Day, J. (1976). Villaggi abbandonati e tradizione orale: il caso Sardo. *Archeologia Medievale* **III,** 203–40.

de Dominicis, F. N. (1781). *Lo Stato Politico ed Economico della Mena Pecore in Puglia* Naples, 3 vols.

Delano Smith, C. (1968). The land use of eastern Madeira. In *Four Island Studies* World Land Use Survey, Monograph 5, pp. 3–30. Geographical Publications, Bude.

Delano Smith, C. (1969). The Tavoliere of Foggia in the Middle Ages. In *Apulia Research Report* III Society of Antiquaries of London (unpublished).

Delano Smith, C. (1972). Late Neolithic settlement, land-use and *Garrigue* in the Montpellier region, France. *Man* **7,** 397–407.

Delano Smith, C. (1975). Villages désertés dans les Pouilles: le Tavoliere *I Paesaggi Rurali Europei* Atti del Convegno Internazionale Perugia May 1973, 125–140.

Delano Smith, C. (1976). Sfruttamento dei terreni agricoli e fattore socio-economici dell'agricoltura preistoria e romana in Capitanata. *Rassegna di Studi Dauni,* Foggia, **4,** 5–16.

Delano Smith, C. (1978). *Daunia Vetus.* Foggia, Amministrazione Provinciale di Foggia.

Delano Smith, C. and Smith, C. A. (1973). The Bronze Age on the Tavoliere, Italy. *Proceedings of the Prehistoric Society* **39,** 454–456.

412 REFERENCES

Delano Smith, C. and Watson, V. (1964). La Géographie et l'histoire dans la région d'Argos (Grèce). *Méditerranée* **4**, 329–340.

Delumeau, J. (1957-1959). *Vie économique et Sociale de Rome dans la seconde moitié du XVI siècle*, Paris, 2 vols.

Dematteis, G. (1965). Le casa rurale nella pianura vercellese e biellese *Studi Geografici su Torino e il Piemonte* **2**, 7–100.

Denizot, G. (1951). Les anciens rivages de la Méditerranée française. *Bulletin de l'Institut Océanographique*, Monaco, **48**, 1–56.

Denizot, G. (1957). Le rivage de Provence et Languedoc au temps des Ligures. *Revue d'Etudes Ligures* **23**, 5–50.

Denizot, G. (1961). Les côtes de France et en particulier du golfe du Lion depuis 6,000 ans. *Actes du 86ème Congrès des Sociétés Savantes, Montpellier*, 145–151.

Desamparados, C. P. (1977). *El "Repartiment" de la Cuidad de Valencia*. Temas Valencianos, Valencia.

De Sanctis, G. (1907–1964). *Storia dei Romani*. La Nuova Italia, Turin and Florence, 4 vols.

Desplanques, H. (1959). Contribution à l'étude des paysages ruraux en Italie centrale: l'arbre fourrager. *Géographie et Histoire Agraires* Actes du Colloque de Géographie Agraire, Annales de l'Est, Nancy 97–99.

Desplanques, H. (1969). *Campagnes ombriennes: contribution à l'étude des paysages ruraux en Italie centrale*. A. Colin, Paris.

Despois, J. (1959). Pour une étude des terrasses de culture dans les pays méditerranéens. *Géographie et Histoire Agraires* Actes du colloque de Geographie Agraire, Annales de l'Est, Nancy 105–117.

Devic, Cl. and Vaissete, J. (1872). *Histoire Générale de Languedoc* (2nd edition). Toulon, 10 vols.

Dienne, de (1891). *Histoire du Dessechement des Lacs et Marais en France avant 1789*. Paris.

Dilke, O. A. W. (1971). *The Roman Land Surveyors*. David and Charles, Newton Abbot.

Dion, R. *Histoire de la Vigne et du Vin en France des origines au XIXème siècle*, Paris.

Dohr, H. (1965). *Die Italischen Gutshöfe nach den Schriften Catos und Varros* (dissertation) Cologne.

Dolci, D. (1959). *Poverty in Sicily* translated by P. D. Cummins, MacGibbon and Kee, London (first published as *Inchiesta a Palermo*, Einaudi, Turin, 1956).

Dominiguez, Ortiz, A. (1974). Las rentas episcopales de la Corona de Aragon en el Siglo XVIII In *Agricultura, Comercio Colonial y Crecimiento Economico en la Espana Contemporanea* (J. Nadal and G. Tortella, eds.), Barcelona.

D'Onofrio, C. (1970). *Il Tevere e Roma*. Ugo Bozzi, Rome.

Drew, K. (1973). *The Lombard Laws*. University of Pennsylvania Press, Philadelphia.

Duby, G. (1958). Techniques et rendements agricoles dans les Alpes du Sud en 1338. *Annales du Midi* **LXX,** 403–413.

Duby, G. (1968). *Rural Economy and Country Life in the Medieval West.* Translated by C. Postan. Arnold, London.

Dugrand, R. (1963a). *Villes et Campagnes en Bas-Languedoc.* Presses Universitaires de France, Paris.

Dugrand, R. (1963b). La garrigue montpelliéraine. *Bulletin de la Société Languedocienne de Géographie* **34,** 1–266.

Dumont, R. (1957). *Types of Rural Economy.* Methuen, London.

Duncan-Jones, R. (1974). *The Economy of the Roman Empire.* Cambridge University Press, Cambridge.

Duran I Sanpere, A. (1973). *Barcelona I la Seva Historia* 3 vols. Curial, Barcelona.

Durrieu, P. (1886–1887). Les Archives Angevines de Naples: étude sur les registres du Roi Charles I. *Ecole Française d'Athènes,* Paris, 46 and 51 (2 vols.)

Egidi, P. (1917). *Codice Diplomatici di Sareceni di Lucera 1285–1343* Naples.

Egidi, P. (1920) Ricerche intorno alla popolazione dell'Italia meridionale nelle fine del secolo XIII e principe del XIV. *Miscellanea di Studi Storica di G. Sforza,* Lucca.

Emberger, L. (1930). La végétation de la région Méditerranéenne. *Revue Générale Botanique* **32,** 461–662 and 705–721

Emelyanov, E. M. and Shimkus, K. M. (1972). Suspended matter in the Mediterranean Sea. In *The Mediterranean Sea* (D. J. Stanley, ed.), pp. 417–439. Dowden, Hutchinson and Ross, Stroudsbury.

Enequist, G. (1959). Geographical Changes of Rural Settlement in Northwestern Sweden since 1523. *Uppsala Universitets arrsskrift* 8 Uppsala.

Escalon de Fonton, M. (1969). Les séquences sédimento—climatiques du Midi méditerranéen du Würm à l'Holocene. *Bulletin du Musée d'Anthropologie Préhistorique de Monaco* **14,** 125–185.

Estyn Evans, E. (1940). Transhumance in Europe. *Geography* **25,** 172–180.

Evans, J. D. (1972). *Land Snails in Archaeology.* Seminar Press, London and New York.

Evans-Pritchard, E. E. (1940). *The Nuer.* Clarendon Press, Oxford.

Evoli, Fr. (1931). L'economia agraria delle provincie meridionale durante la feudalità. *Archivio Storico per la Calabria e la Lucania* n.s. I, 175–223.

Eyssette, A. (1884–1888). *Histoire Administrative de Beaucaire depuis le XIII siècle jusqu'à la Révolution Aubane,* Beaucaire, 2 vols.

Fabrège, F. (1894–1911). *Histoire de Maguelonne.* Paris, 3 vols.

Fairbridge, R. W. (1961). Eustatic changes in sea level. *Physics and Chemistry of the Earth* **4,** 99–185.

Fara, G. F. (1580). *Geografia della Sardegna* (P. Secchi, ed.). Quattromori, Sassari, 1975.

Fasoli, G. (1959). *Introduzione allo Studio del Feudalismo Italiano* Riccardo Patron, Bologna.

Fernandez, J. G. (1965). Campos abiertos y campos cercados en Castilla la Vieja. *Annales, Economies, Sociétés Civilisations* **20,** 692–718.

Ferrarini, E. and Padula, M. (1969). Indagini sui pollini fossili di alcune localita della Calabria (Sila piccola e Serra) con osservazioni sulla vegetazione attuale. *Giornale Botanico Italiano* 103.6.597–636.

Février, P. A. (1977). Towns in the western Mediterranean. In *European Towns: their Archaeology and Early History* (M. W. Barley, ed.), pp. 315–342. Academic Press, London and New York.

Firbas, F. (1931). Contribution à l'histoire post-glaciaire des forêts des Cévennes méridionales S.I.G.M.A. (*Station Internationale Géobotanique Méditerranéenne et Alpine*) Montpellier, 15.

Firth, R. (1967). Themes in economic anthropology: a general comment. *In Themes in Economic Anthropology* (R. Frith, ed.) A.S.A. Monographs, Tavistock, London and New York.

Fiumi, E. (1962). La populazione del territorio Volterrano sangimignanese ed il problema demografico dell'età communale. In *Studi in Onore di Amintone Fanfani* Milan, 249–290.

Flahault, Ch. (1937). La distribution géographique de la végétation dans la région Méditerranéene française *Encyclopédie Biologique XVIII.* Lechevalier, Paris.

Flemming, N. C. (1968) Holocene earth movements and eustatic sea level change in the Peloponnese *Nature* **217,** 1031–1032.

Flemming, N. C. (1969). Archaeological evidence for eustatic change of sea level and earth movements in the Western Mediterranean during the last 2000 years. *The Geological Society of America*, Special Paper No 109.

Flemming, N. C. (1972). *Cities in the Sea.* New English Library, London.

Fontavella Gonzalez, V. (1949). La evolucion de los cultivos en las huertas levantinas de Espana. *Congrès International de Géographie*, Lisbon Comptes-rendus Tome 3, Section 4, 286–306.

Fontavella, V. (1951). La transhumancia y la evolucion gañaderolana en la provincia de Valencia *Estudios Geograficos* **12,** 773–806.

Fontavella, V. (1952). *La Huerta de Gandia* C.S.I.C. Zaragonza.

Food and Agriculture Organisation (1953). *Water Laws in Italy.* UNESCO, Rome.

Forbes, R. J. (1964). *Studies in Ancient Technology* Vols VIII and IX (2nd edition of *Metallurgy in Antiquity*, 1950). Brill, Leiden.

Franciosa, L. (1951). La transumanza nell'Appennino centro-meridionale *Memorie di Geografia Economica* Vol. IV. Naples.

Frank, A. H. E. (1969). Pollen stratigraphy of the lake of Vico (central Italy). *Palaeogeography, Palaeoclimate, Palaeoecology* **6,** 67–85.

Frank, T. (1933–1940). *An Economic Survey of Ancient Rome* Vol. I Rome and Italy of the Republic, Vol. V Rome and Italy of the Empire. John Hopkins Press, Baltimore.

Franklin, S. H. (1969). *The European Peasantry*. Methuen, London.

Fraser, D. (1968). *Village Planning in the Primitive World*. Studio Vista, London.

Freises, A. and Montjardin, R. (1974–1975). Le gisement Cardial de l'Ile de Corrège à Port-Leucate (Aude). *Bulletin de la Société d'Etudes Scientifiques de Sète et sa Région* **VI–VII**, 1–5.

Gagnière, S., Lanfranchi, F. de, Miskovsky, J-C., Prost, M. and Renault-Miskovsky, J. (1969). L'abri d'Araguina-Sennola à Bonifacio (Corse). *Bulletin de la Société Préhistorique Française* **66**, Etudes et Travaux Fasc. I, 376–388.

Galanti, G. M. (1788–1790). *Nuovo Descrizione Storica e Geografica delle Due Sicile* (2nd edition). Naples, 4 vols. in 2.

Galtier, G. (1958). *La Côte Sableuse du Golfe du Lion*. Université de Paris, Faculté des Lettres, Paris.

Galtier, G. (1960). *Le Vignoble du Languedoc Méditerranéen et du Roussillon*. Causse, Graille et Castelnau, Montpellier, 3 vols.

Garcia y Bellido, A., Torres Balbos, L., Cervera, L., Chueca, F. and Bidagor, P. (1968). *Resumen Historico del Urbanism en España*. (2nd edition) Instituto de Estudios de Administracion Local, Madrid.

Garcia de Cortazar, J. A. (1973). *La epoca medieval*. Alianza, Madrid.

Gautier-Dalché, J. (1962). Le domaine du monastère de Santo Toribo de Liébana: formation, structures et mode d'exploitation. *Annuario de Estudios Medievales* **II**, 63–117.

Gay, J. (1904). L'Italie Méridionale et l'Empire Byzantin 867–1071. *Ecole Française d'Athènes*, Paris, 2 vols.

Gemelli, F. (1776). Rifiorimento della Sardegna proposito nel miglioramento di sua agricoltura, Turin.

Gennaro, G. de (1970). Le 'difese' in Puglia e Lucania tra sei e settecento: note di storia agraria. *Economia e Storia* **17**, 17–41.

George, P. (1935). *La Région du Bas-Rhône*. Baillière, Paris.

Gèze, B. (1947). Paléosols et sols dûs à l'évolution actuelle. *Annales de l'Ecole Nationale d'Agriculture*, Montpellier, XXVII, 1–25.

Gil Crespo, A. (1975). El openfield hispanico y su transformacion por la concentration parcelaria. *I Paesaggi Rurali Europei* Atti del Convegno Internazionale Perugia 1973, 249–261.

Gilles, I. (1896–1897). *Le Pays d'Arles*. Paris, 2 vols.

Giovanni, G. de (1848). *Difesa del popolo Romano sull'abbandono della Campagna Roma*. Puccinelli, Rome.

Glick, T. F. (1970). *Irrigation and Society in Medieval Valencia*. Harvard University Press, Cambridge, Mass.

Goethe, J. W. von (1962). *Italian Journey 1786–1788*. Translated and edited by W. H. Auden and E. Meyer, Collins, London.

Gortoni, M. (1950). Gli studi sui terrazzi fluviale e marini d'Italia dal 1938–1948. *Bollettino delle Societa Geografica Italiana* **84**, 298–322.

Goudie, A. (1973). *Duricrusts in Tropical and Sub-tropical Landscapes*. Oxford Research Studies in Geography, Clarendon Press, Oxford.

Gozalvez Perez, V. (1974). La *centuriatio* de Ilici. In *Estudios Sobre Centuriaciones Romana en España*, pp. 101–113. Universidad Autonoma de Madrid, Madrid.

Grendi, E. (1970). Genova alla meta'del Cinquecento: una politica del grano? *Quaderni Storici* **13**, 106–160.

Grenier, A. (1905). La transhumance des troupeaux en Italie et son rôle dans l'histoire romaine. *Mélanges d'Archéologie et d'Histoire*, XXV, pp. 293–328. Paris and Rome.

Grenier, A. (1931–1958). *Manuel d'Archéologie Gallo-Romaine*. Picard, Paris, 3 vols.

Grimal, J. and Pauzes, B. (1974–1975). Un fond de cabane à poterie cardiale dans la plaine de l'Hérault. *Bulletin de la Société d'Etudes Scientifiques de Sète et sa Région* **VI–VII**, 7–22.

Grimal, P. (1964). *In Search of Ancient Italy* translated by P. D. Cummins (A la Recherche de l'Italie Antique, Paris, 1961). Evans , London.

Grimal, P. (1969). *Les Jardins Romains*. Presses Universitaires de France, Paris.

Grohmann, A. (1969). Un Registro della Cancelleria di Alfonso I d'Aragona Re di Napoli (1451–1453). *Economia e Storia* **16**, 7–26.

Grosjean, R. (1966). *La Corse avant l'Histoire*. Keincksieck, Paris.

Guido, M. (1963). *Sardinia*. Thames and Hudson, London.

Guilaine, J. (1976a). *Premiers Bergers et Paysans de l'Occident Méditerranéen*. Mouton, Paris.

Guilaine, J. (1976b). Problèmes relatifs à la Néolithisation de la Cerdagne *Cypsela* Diputacion Provincial de Gerona, Servicio de Investigaciones Arqueologicas, Gerona 31–33.

Guilaine, J. (ed.) (1976). *La Préhistoire Française II: Les Civilisations Néolithiques et Protohistoriques de la France*. Published on the occasion of the IX Congrès de l'Union Internationale des Sciences Préhistoriques et Protohistoriques, Nice, 1976.

Guilaine, J. and Roudil, J-L. (1976). Les civilisations Néolithiques en Languedoc. *La Préhistoire Française* (J. Guilaine, ed.) C.N.R.S. Paris II, 267–278.

Guillot Valls, D. (1974). Importacion Valenciana de Cereales Mediante el sistema de "Ayudas" en el segunda cuarto del siglo XV *Estudis, 2*, pp. 35–59. Universidad de Valencia, Valencia.

Guillou, A. (1966). Notes sur la société dans le Katépanat d'Italie au XI ème siècle. *Mélanges d'Archéologie et d'Historie* **78,** 439–465.

Gutkind, E. A. (1967). *Urban Development in Southern Europe: Spain and Portugal.* International History of City Development, III, Free Press, New York; Collier-Macmillan, London.

Gutkind, E. A. (1969). *Urban Development in Southern Europe: Italy and Greece.* International History of City Development, IV, Free Press, New York; Collier-Macmillan, London.

Hackett, L. W. (1937). *Malaria in Europe: An Ecological Study.* Macmillan, Cambridge.

Hagget, P. (1965). *Locational Analysis in Human Geography.* Arnold, London.

Hale, J. R. (ed.) (1956) *The Italian Journal of Samuel Rogers.* Faber and Faber, London.

Hallam, B. R., Warren, S. E. and Renfrew, C. (1976) Obsidian in the western Mediterranean: characterisation by neutron activation analysis and optical emission spectroscopy. *Proceedings of the Prehistoric Society* **42,** 85–110.

Hamilton, E. J. (1936). *Money, Prices and Wages in Valencia, Aragon and Navarre 1351–1500.* Harvard University Press, Cambridge, Mass.

Hamlin, F. R. (1959). *Le suffixe -acum dans la toponymie de l'Hérault. Contribution à l'étude des noms de lieu du Languedoc.* Ph.D. thesis, University of Birmingham. Cyclostyled by Centre Regional de Documentation Pédagogique.

Harant, H. and Jarray, D. (1960–1963). *Guide du Naturaliste dans le Midi de la France.* Delachaux and Niestlé, Neuchâtel, 2 vols.

Hasluck, M. (1954). *The Unwritten Law in Albania.* Cambridge University Press, Cambridge.

Haudricourt, A. G. and Delamarre, M. J. L. (1955). *L'Homme et la Charrue à travers le Monde.* Gallimard, Paris.

Havinden, M. A. (1974). Lime as a means of agricultural improvement: the Devon example. In *Rural Change and Urban Growth 1500 to 1800* (C. W. Chalkin and M. A. Havinden, eds), pp. 104–134. Essays in English Regional History in Honour of W. G. Hoskins. Longman, London.

Hemardinquer, J. J. (1973). Les débuts du maïs en Méditerranée (premiere aperçu). *Histoire Economique du Monde Méditerranéen 1450–1650,* I, 227–244. Mélanges en l'Honneur de Fernand Braudel. Privat, Paris, 2 vols.

Herlihy, D. (1958a). *Pisa in the Early Renaissance. A Study of Urban Growth.* Yale University Press, New Haven.

✓Herlihy, D. (1958b). The agrarian revolution in southern France and Italy 801–1150. *Speculum* **33,** 23–41.

Herlihy, D. (1965). Population, plague and social change in rural Pistoia. *Economic History Review* **18,** 225–244.

Herlihy, D. (1967). *Medieval and Renaissance Pistoia. The Social History of an Italian Town 1200–1430*. Yale University Press, New Haven and London.

Higgs, E. S. (ed.) (1975). *Palaeoeconomy*. Papers in Economic Prehistory, Vol. II. Cambridge University Press, Cambridge.

Higgs, E. S. and Jarman, M. R. (1969). The origins of agriculture: a reconsideration. *Antiquity* **43**, 31–41.

Higgs, E. S. and Vita-Finzi, C. (1970). Prehistoric economies in the Mount Carmel area of Palestine: site catchment analysis. *Proceedings of the Prehistoric Society* **26**, 1–37.

Higgs, E. S. and Vita-Finzi, C. (1972). Prehistoric economies: a territorial approach. In *Papers in Economic Prehistory* (E. S. Higgs, ed.) pp. 27–36. Cambridge University Press, Cambridge.

Higgs, E. S., Vita-Finzi, C., Harris, D. R. and Fagg, A. E. (1967). The climate, environment and industries of Stone Age Greece, part III. *Proceedings of the Prehistoric Society* **33**, 1–29.

Hillgarth, J. N. (1976). *The Spanish Kingdoms* I 1250–1410. Clarendon Press, Oxford.

Hiorns, F. R. (1956). *Town Building in History*. Harrap, London.

Hodgkin, T. (1896). *Italy and her Invaders 600–744* Vol. VI The Lombard Kingdom. Clarendon Press, Oxford, 9 vols.

Holloway, R. R. *et al.* (1975). Buccino: the Early Bronze Age village of Tufariella. *Journal of Field Archaeology* **2**, 11–81.

Hoskins, W. G. (1963). *Provincial England*. Macmillan, London.

Houston, J. M. (1949). *The Social Geography of the Huerta of Valencia* (unpublished). D. Phil. thesis, University of Oxford.

Houston, J. M. (1959). Land use and society in the plain of Valencia. In *Geographical Essays in Memory of A. G. Ogilvie* (R. Miller and J. Wreford Watson, eds.), pp. 166–194. Nelson, Edinburgh.

Houston, J. M. (1964). *The Western Mediterranean World*. Longmans, London.

Huillard-Brèholles, J. L. A. (1844). *Recherches sur les Monuments et l'Histoire des Normands et de la Maison de Suabe dans l'Italie méridionale*, Paris.

Huillard-Brèholles, J. L. A. (1852–1861). *Historia Diplomatica Frederici Secundi*, Paris, 12 vols.

Hyde, J. K. (1973). *Society and Politics in Medieval Italy*. Macmillan, London.

Imamuddin, S. M. (1965). *Some aspects of the socio-economic and cultural history of Muslim Spain 711–1492* A.D. E. J. Brill, Leidon.

Isnard, H. (1973). *Pays et Paysages Méditerranéens*. Presses Universitaires de France, Paris.

Isserlin, B. S. J. (1971). New light on the 'cothon' at Motya. *Antiquity* **XLV**, 179, 178–186.

Jackson, F. H. (1906). *The Shores of the Adriatic*. John Murray, London, 2 vols.

Jarman, H. (1976). Early crop agriculture in Europe. In *Origine de L'Elevage et de la Domestication* Papers of Colloquium XX, IX Congrès, pp. 116–144. Union Internationale des Sciences Préhistoriques et Protohistoriques, Nice.

Jarman, M. R. (1972). The territorial model for archaeology: a behavioural and geographical approach. In *Models in Archaeology* (D. L. Clarke, ed.), pp. 705–734. Methuen, London.

Jarman, M. R. and Webley, D. (1975). Settlement and land use in Capitanata, Italy. In *Palaeoeconomy: Papers in Economic Prehistory* (E. S. Higgs, ed.), Vol. II, pp. 177–221. Cambridge University Press, Cambridge.

Jarman, M. R., Vita-Finzi, C. and Higgs, E. S. (1972). Site catchment analysis in archaeology. In *Man, Settlement and Urbanism* (P. J. Ucko, G. W. Dimbleby, and R. Tringham, eds), pp. 61–66. Duckworths, London.

Jehasse, J. and L. (1973). La Nécropole Préromaine d'Aléria. *Gallia,* Supplément No. 25, C.N.R.S., Paris.

Jelgersma, S. (1966). Sea level changes during the last 10 000 years. *Proceedings of the International Symposium on World Climate from 8000* B.C. *to 0* B.C., pp. 54–71. Royal Meteorological Society, London.

Jones, A. H. M. (1953). Census records of the later Roman Empire. *Journal of Roman Studies,* **XLIII** 49–64.

Jones, A. H. M. (1964). *The Later Roman Empire 284–602.* Blackwell, Oxford, 3 vols.

Jones, A. H. M. (1974). *The Roman Economy* (P. A. Brunt, ed.) Blackwell, Oxford.

Jones, P. J. (1955). An Italian estate 900–1200. *Economic History Review*, 2nd Ser., **7**, 18–32.

Jones, P. J. (1966). L'Italia agraria nell'alto Mediaevo: problemi di cronologia e di continuita. In *Agricoltura e Mondo Rurale in Occidente nell'Alto Mediaevo,* Settimane di Studio del Centro Italiano di Studi Sull'alto mediaevo XIII, 57–92, Centro Italiano etc., Spoleto.

Jones, P. J. (1966b). Italy. In *The Agrarian Life of the Middle Ages* (M. M. Postan, ed.), Cambridge Economic History, Vol. I, pp. 340–341. Cambridge University Press, Cambridge (2nd edition).

Jones, P. J. (1968). From manor to mezzadria: a Tuscan case-study in the medieval origins of modern agrarian society. In *Florentine Studies: Politics and Society in Renaissance Italy* (N. Rubinstein, ed.) pp. 193–241. Faber and Faber, London.

Jones, W. H. S. (1907). *Maleria: A Neglected Factor in the History of Greece and Rome.* Macmillan, Cambridge.

Judson, S. (1963a). Erosion and deposition of Italian stream valleys during historic time. *Science* **140**, 898–899.

Judson, S. (1963b). Stream changes during historic time in east-central Sicily. *American Journal of Archaeology* **67**, 287–289.

Kantorowicz, E. H. (1931). *Frederick the Second 1194–1250*. Constable, London.

Karman, Y. (1964). Land use survey in Mediterranean countries: cartographical suggestions. *Land Use in Semi-Arid Mediterranean Climates* (L. D. Stamp, ed.) Arid Zone Research XXVI, pp. 159–165. U.N.E.S.C.O.

Kayser, B. (1961). *Recherches sur les sols et l'érosion en Italie méridionale: Lucanie.* SEDES, Paris.

Kenny, M. (1961). *A Spanish Tapestry*. Cohen and West, London.

King, P. D. (1972). *Law and Society in the Visigothic Kingdom*. Cambridge University Press, Cambridge.

✓King, R. (1973). Poverty and banditry. *The Geographical Magazine* **XLVI,** 127–132.

Kirkby, M. J. (1969). Infiltration, through flow and overland flow *and* Erosion by water on hillslopes. In *Water, Earth and Man* (R. J. Chorley, ed.) pp. 215–238. Methuen, London.

Klapisch-Zuber, C. and Day, J. (1965). *Villages désertés et histoire economique XI au XVIII siècles.* Troisième conférence internationale des historiens de l'économie, Munich, pp. 419–459.

Kleffens, E. N. (1968). *Hispanic Law until the end of the Middle Ages*. Edinburgh University Press, Edinburgh.

Klein, J. (1920). *The Mesta: a study in Spanish economic history 1275–1836*. Harvard University Press, Cambridge, Mass.

Koeningsberger, H. (1951). *The Government of Sicily under Philip II of Spain.* Staples, London and New York.

Kruit, C. (1955). *Sediments of the Rhone Delta: Grain-size and micro-fauna*. Mouton, Gravenhage.

Kuhnholtz-Lordat, G. (1945). La *silva*, les *saltus* et l'*ager* de Garrigue. *Annales de l'Ecole Nationale d'Agriculture, Montpellier, XXVI*, f.IV.

Kuhnholtz-Lordat, G. (1952). *Le Tapis végétal dans ses rapports avec les phénomènes actuels de surface en Basse-Provence.* Encyclopédie Biogéographique et Ecologique IX, Lechevalier, Paris.

Kuhnholtz-Lordat, G. (1958). L'Ecran Vert. *Mémoires du Museum National d'Histoire Naturelle* n.s. B. Botanique, IX, Paris (revised edition of *La Terre Incendiée*, Maison Carrée, Nimes, 1938).

Labadessa, R. (1932). *Il Tavoliere di Puglia*. Pinciana, Roma.

La Force, J. C. (1965). *The Development of the Spanish Textile Industry 1750–1800*. University of California Press, Berkeley.

Lamb, H. H. (1966). *The changing climate: selected papers* Methuen, London.

Lamb, H. H. (1977). *Climate: Past, Present and Future*, Vol. 2 Climatic History and the Future, Methuen, London.

La Marmora, A. de (1839–1860). *Voyage en Sardaigne, ou description statistique et politique de cette île* (2nd edition) Paris and Turin, 3 vols.

Lanciani, R. (1897). *The Ruins and Excavations of Ancient Rome*. Macmillan, London.

Lanfranchi, F. de, and Weiss, M-C. (1972). Le Néolithique ancien de l'abri d'Araguina-Sennola (Bonifacio, Corse). *Bulletin de la Société Préhistorique Française* **69**, Etudes et Travaux, fasc. I, 376–388.

Lapeyre, H. (1959). *Géographie de L'Espagne Morisque*, S.E.V.P.E.N., Paris.

Larner, J. (1965). *The Lords of Romagna*. Macmillan, London.

Laville, H. and Renault-Miskovsky, J. (eds) (1977). *Approche écologique de l'Homme fossile*. Bulletin de l'Association Française pour l'Etude du Quaternaire. Supplement no 47.

Leciejewicz, L. and Tabaczynska, E. (eds) (1969/1970) Commento archeologico ai reperti naturali, antichi e medioevali scoperti a Torcello (1961–1962). *Memorie di Biografia Adriatica* **8**, 89–105.

Lefebvre, Th. (1933). *Les Modes de Vie dans les Pyrénées Atlantiques* Colin, Paris.

Le Gall, J. C. (1953). *Le Tibre dans l'Antiquité* Presses Universitaires de France, Paris.

Le Lannou, M. (1941). *Pâtres et Paysons de la Sardaigne*. Arrault, Tours.

Lennard, R. (1959). *Rural England 1086–1135*. Clarendon Press, Oxford.

Lenthéric, C. (1876). *Les Villes Mortes du Golfe de Lyon*. Plon, Paris.

Lenthéric, C. (1878). *La Grèce et l'Orient en Provence*. Paris.

Lenthéric, C. (1895). *The Riviera Ancient and Modern*, translated by C. West. Unwin, London.

Leon, R. (1969). *Sobre el puerto fenico de Malaga*. Malaga.

Léonard, E. G. (1954). *Les Angevins de Naples*. Presses Universitaires de France, Paris.

Le Roy Ladurie, E. (1957). Sur Montpellier et sa campagne au XVI et XVII siècles. *Annales, Economies, Sociétés, Civilisations* **12**, 223–230.

Le Roy Ladurie, E. (1966). *Les Paysans de Languedoc* S.E.V.P.E.N. Paris 2 vols. Abridged edition translated by J. Day and published as *The Peasants of Languedoc* by University of Illinois Press, Urbana-Chicago-London, 1974.

Le Roy Ladurie, E. (1972). *Times of Feast, Times of Famine: a history of climate since the year 1000*. Translated by B. Bray. Allen and Unwin, London.

Le Roy Ladurie, E. (1975). *Montaillou, village occitan de 1294 à 1324*. Gallimard, Paris.

Levi, C. (1948). *Christ Stopped at Eboli*. Translated by F. Frenaye. Cassell, London.

Lévi-Provençal, E. (1950–1953). *Histoire de l'Espagne Musulmane* (2nd edition). Maisonneuve, Paris and Brill, Leiden, 3 vols.

Lewis, P. R. and Jones, G. B. D. (1970). Roman gold-mining in north-west Spain. *Journal of Roman Studies* **LX**, 169–185.

Lilliu, G. (1963). *La Civiltà dei Sardi*, E.R.I., Turin.

Lilliu, G. (1967). Prima dei nuraghi *and* Al tempo dei nuraghi. In *La Societa in Sardegna nei Secoli* E.R.I., Turin, 7–18.

Lison-Tolosana, C. (1966). *Belmonte de los Caballeros. A Sociological Study of a Spanish Town.* Oxford University Press, Oxford.

Livet, R. (1962). *Habitat Rural et Structures Agraires en Basse-Provence.* Orphys, Gap.

Llop-Catela, M. (1974). Importacion de trigo por "ayuda" en Valencia 1450–1472. *Estudis*, Universidad de Valencia, **2**, 61–95.

Lloris, M. B. (1972). Los grabados rupestres de Bedolina (Val Camonico) *Bollettino del Centre Camuno di Studi Preistorici*, Brescia, VIII, 121–158.

Loddo-Canepa, F. (1952). Note sulle condizione economiche degli abitanti di Cagliari del Secoli XI al XIV, *Studi Sardi* anno 10/11, 228–336.

Lognon, A. (1920). *Noms de Lieu de France.* Paris, 2 vols.

Longano, F. (1790). *Viaggio dell'Abate Longano per la Capitanata.* Napoli.

Longworth, P. (1974). *The Rise and Fall of Venice.* Constable, London.

Lopez, R. S. (1945). Silk industry in the Byzantine Empire. *Speculum* XX, 1–42.

Lopez, R. S. (1953). The origin of the merino sheep. *Jewish Social Studies: Joshua Starr Memorial*, New York, Vol. 5, 161–168.

Lopez, S. R. and Raymond, I. W. (eds) (1955). *Medieval Trade in the Mediterranean World (illustrative documents).* Oxford University Press, London.

Lopez Gomez, A. (1957). Evolucion agraria de la Plana de Castellon. *Estudios Geograficas* XVIII, 309–360.

Lösch, A. (1967). *The Economics of Location.* J. Wiley, New York.

Louis, M. (1937). Le village anhistorique de la Liquière de Calvisson. *Cahiers d'Histoire et d'Archéologie*, Nimes, XII, 3–38.

Louis, M. (1948). *Préhistoire du Languedoc Méditerranéen et du Roussillon.* Nîmes.

Louis, M., Peyrolle, D. and Arnal, J. (1947). Les fonds de cabanes énéolithiques de Fontbouisse. *Gallia Préhistorique*, V, Fasc. II.

Louis, M. and Taffnel, O. and J. (1955). *Le Premiere Age du Fer Languedocien.* Institut d'Etudes Ligures, Bordighera-Montpellier, 3 vols.

Luzzato, G. (1950). Le vicende del Porto. *In* Il Porti di Venezia (L. Candida) *Memoria di Geografia Economica* Naples 11, 7–46.

Luzzato, G. (1961). *An Economic History of Italy.* Translated by P. J. Jones. Routledge and Kegan Paul, London.

Mackay, A. (1977). *Spain in the Middle Ages. From Frontier to Empire 1000–1500.* Macmillan, London.

Mackendrick, P. (1971). *Roman France.* Bell, London.

Mack-Smith, D. (1965). *The Latifundia in Modern Sicilian History.* Italian Lecture, British Academy, read 1965, *Proceedings of the British Academy* **LV,** 85–124.

Mack-Smith, D. (1969). *A History of Sicily.* Chatto and Windus, London, 2 vols.

Maffre- (1871–1872). Etablissements agricoles du Midi sous la domination Romaine. *Bulletin de la Société d'Archéologie de Béziers* **VI,** 193ff.

Magistris, L. F. (1930). Lo stato attuale della conoscenza della distribuzione della malaria nell'Italia meridionale. *Atti dell'XI Congresso Geografico Italiano*, Naples, III, 40–51.

Mahiques, J. Carmarena (1966). *Padron demografico-economico del Reino de Valencia ? 1735* Estudios y Materiales para la Historia de Valencia I, Universidad de Valencia, Valencia.

Malefakis, E. (1970). *Agrarian Reform and Peasant Revolution in Spain: Origins of the Civil War*. Yale University Press, New Haven.

Mallett, M. and Whitehouse, D. (1967). Castel Porciano: an abandoned medieval village of the Roman Campagna. *Papers of the British School at Rome* **XXXV**, 113–146.

Mandrou, R. (1961). Théorie ou hypothese de travail? *Annales, Economies, Sociétés, Civilisations* **16**, 965–971.

Mannoni, T. and Poleggi, E. (1977). The condition and study of historic town centres in North Italy. In *European Towns: their archaeology and early history* (M. W. Barley, ed.), pp. 219–241. Academic Press, London and New York.

Manzoni, A. (1872). *I Promessi Sposi*.

Maraspina, A. L. (1968). *Study of an Italian Village* Centre de Sciences Sociales d'Athènes. Mouton, Paris.

Marcelin, P. (1946–1960). Sur les terres rouges. *Bulletin de la Société d'Etudes de Sciences Naturelles de Nîmes*, 67–71.

Marques, M. A. and Julia, R. (1977). Caractéristiques lithostrati-graphiques des embouchures des fleuves du N. E. de l'Espagne (du Llobregat aux Pyrénnées). In *Approche Ecologique de l'Homme Fossile* (H. Laville and J. Renault-Miskovsky, eds), pp. 187–196, Bulletin de L'Association Française pour l'Etude du Quaternaire, Supplement 47, Paris.

Marres, P. (1935). *Les Grandes Causses*. Aurrault, Tours, 2 vols.

Marres, P. (1962). Les garrigues languedociennes: le milieu et l'homme *Actes du 86ème Congrès National des Sociétés Savantes, Montpellier, 1961*, 201–216.

Martinez Perona J-V. (1975). Carta arqueologica de Pedralba y Bugarra (Valencia) *Archivio de Preistorica Levantina* **XIV**, 169–192.

Masson, G. (1973). *Frederick II of Hohenstaufen: a life*. Secker and Warburg, London.

May, J. M. (1961). The ecology of malaria. In *Studies in Disease Ecology*, 1961–229, Studies in Medical Geography 2. Hafner, New York.

Mazzolani, L. Storoni (1970). *The Idea of the City in Roman Thought: from walled city to spiritual commonwealth*. Translated by S. O'Donnell. Hollis and Carter, London.

McNeill, W. H. (1977). *Plagues and Peoples*. Blackwell, Oxford.

Meiggs, R. (1973). *Roman Ostia*. (2nd edition) Clarendon Press, Oxford.

Mellars, P. (1976). Fire ecology, animal populations and man: a study of some ecological relationships in prehistory. *Proceedings of the Prehistoric Society* **42**, 15–45.

Meloni, G. (1972). Sull'alleanza veneto-aragonese all'epoca di Pietro il Cerimonioso. *Medioevo eta'Moderna: Saggi in onove del Prof. Alberto Boscolo*, pp. 111–117. Sarda Fossataro, Cagliari.

Meloni, G. (1975). *La Sardegna Romana*. Chiorilla, Sassari.

Meloni, P. (1967). Dalla conquista romana alla fine della Republica *and* Da Augusto all'invasione vandalica. In *La Società in Sardegna nei Secoli* E.R.I. Turin, 71–98.

Mertens, J. E. (1969). *Alba Fucens: rapports et études*. Centre Belge de Recherches Archéologiques en Italie Centrale et Méridionale, Brussels, 2 vols.

Mertens, J. E. (1976). Ordona: rapports et études. *Etudes de Philologie, d'Archéologie et d'Histoire oennes* **XVI**, 7–32.

Meyerhoff, H. A. (1967). Geologic factors affecting the search for Sybaris. In *The Search for Sybaris* 1960–1965 (F. G. Rainey and C. M. Lerici, eds), Vol. I, pp. 250–311. Lerici, Rome, 2 vols.

Mickwith, G. (1941). Italy. In *The Agrarian Life of the Middle Ages* (1st edition) Cambridge Economic History (J. H. Clapham and E. Power, eds), Vol. I, pp. 323–343. Cambridge University Press, Cambridge.

Milanese, M. (1976). Genova, scavo di strutture portuali medievali. *Notiziario di Archeologia Medievale* **18**, 42–43. Centro Ligure per la Storia della Ceramica, Genoa.

✓Miller, K. (ed.) (1962). *Die Peutingez Tafel*. Brockhous, Stuttgart.

Mira, J. F. (1971). Mariage et famille dans une communauté rurale du Pays de Valence (Espagne). *Etudes Rurales* 41–44, 105–119.

Molina, F. V. (1972). *El Valle de Lecrin*. C.S.I.C. Granada.

Molinari, V. (1880. *Trattato Completo di Agricoltura Practica*. Angelis Naples.

Mols, R. (1954–1956). *Introduction à la démographie historique des villes d'Europe du Xmiu XVIII Siècles*. Louvain, 3 vols.

Mondolfo, U. G. (1967). Agricoltura e pastorizia in Sardegna nel tramonte del feudalismo. In *Il Feudalismo in Sardegna* (A. Boscolo, ed.), pp. 431–455, Sarda Fossataro, Cagliari; first published in *Rivista Italiana di Sociologia*, Rome 1904, Vol. VIII, Fasc.IV.

Montarlot, G. (1960). Concentrations calcaires dans le département de l'Hérault. *Bulletin de la Société Languedocienne de Géographie* **XXXI**, 71–78.

Monti, G. M. (1939). *Per la Storia dei Borboni Napoli e dei patrioti meridionali* R. Deputazione di Storia Patria per la Puglie, Documenti e Monografie, Vol. 22, Trani.

Montjardin, R. (1970). Problèmes du Chasséen à la lumière des fouilles d'Escanin. In *Les Civilisations Néolithiques du Midi de la France*. Actes du colloque de Narbonne, 33–35, Laborato ie de Préhistoire et de Palethnologie, Carcassonne.

More, R. J. (1969). Water and crops. In *Water, Earth and Man* (R. J. Chorley, ed.), pp. 197–208. Methuen, London.

Moreno, D. (1973). La colonizzazione dei "Boschi d'Ovada" nei secoli XVI–XVII *Quaderni Storici* 24, fasc. III, 977–1016.

Moreno, D. and Maestri, S. de (1975). Casa rurale e cultura materiale nella colonizzazione dell'Appennino genoese tra XVI e XVII secolo. In *I Paesaggi Rurali Europei* Atti del Convegno Internazione Perugia 1975, 389–407.

Morgan, M. A. (1969). Overland flow and man. In *Water, Earth and Man* (R. J. Chorley ed.), pp. 239–258. Methuen, London.

Morgan, W. B. and Munton, R. J. C. (1971). *Agricultural Geography*. Methuen, London.

Mori, A. (1950). Le Saline della Sardegna. *Memorie di Geografia Economica*, Naples, III.

Mörner, N.-A. (1971). Eustatic and climatic oscillations. *Arctic and Alpine Research* 3.2.167–171.

Morrison, I. A. (1976). Comparative stratigraphy and radiocarbon chronology of Holocene marine changes on the western seaboard of Europe. In *Geoarchaeology: Earth science and the past* (D. A. Davidson and M. L. Shackley, eds), pp. 159–174. Duckworth, London.

Morton, H. V. (1964). *A Traveller in Italy*. Methuen, London.

Motzo, R. (1947). *Il Compasso di Navigare*. Cagliari.

Mosso, V. (1957). *Architettura Domestica in Sardegna*. Zattera, Cagliari.

Muciaccia, F. (1906). *Il Libro Rosso della Citta di Monopoli*. Documenti e Monografie, Societa de Storia Patria per la Puglia, IV, Bari.

Mumford, L. (1961). *The City in History*. Secker and Warburg, London.

Musto, D. (1964). *La Region Dogana della Mena delle Pecore di Puglia*, Quaderni della Rassegna degli Archivio di Stato, 28, Rome.

Nahal, I. (1962). *Le Pin d'Alep*. Annales de l'Ecole Nationale des Eaux et Forêts, monograph XIX. Ecole Nationale des Eaux et Forêts, Nancy.

Nef, J. U. (1952). Mining and metallurgy in medieval civilisation. In *Trade and Industry in the Middle Ages*. Cambridge Economic History II (M. M. Postan and E. E. Rich, eds), pp. 429–492. Cambridge University Press, Cambridge.

Nelli, R. (1958). *Le Languedoc et le Comté de Foix, le Roussillon* (2nd edition). Gallimard, Paris.

Nicolini, I. (1965). *Codice Diplomatico sui Rapporti Veneto-Napoletane durante il regno di Carlo d'Angio*. Regesta Chartarum Italiae 36, Rome.

Nougier, L. R. (1959). *Géographie Humaine Préhistorique*. Gallimard, Paris.

Oldham, R. D. (1925). The portolan maps of the Rhone Delta. *Geographical Journal* **65,** 403–428.

Oldham, R. D. (1970). Historic changes of level in the delta of the Rhone. *Quarterly Journal of the Geological Society of London* **86,** 63–93.

Orange, A, and Amalbert, A. (1924). *Les Merinos d'Arles*, Antibes.

Origo, I. (1957). *The Merchant of Prato*. Jonathan Cape, London.

Orwin, C. S. and Orwin, C. S. (1967). *The Open Fields* (3rd edition) Clarendon Press, Oxford.

Osheim, D. J. (1977). *An Italian Lordship: the bishopric of Lucca in the late Middle Ages*. Centre for Medieval and Renaissance Studies, University of California, Los Angeles.

Ostrogovsky, G. (1956). *History of the Byzantine State*. Translated from the 2nd edition by J. M. Hussey. Blackwell, Oxford.

Ottman, F. (1958). Les formations Pliocènes et Quaternaires sur le littoral Corse. *Mémoires de la Société Géologique de France*, n.s. XXXVIII, 15, Mémoire 84.

Pais, E. (1923). *Storia della Sardegna e della Corsica duvo il Dominio Romano*. Rome, 2 vols.

Pannoux, P. and C. (1953). Préhistoire et climat dans la région des Matelles (Hérault). *Cahiers Ligures de Préhistoire et d'Archéologie* **2,** 14, 121.

Papon, J. P. (1777–1786). *Histoire Générale de Provence*. 4 vols.

Pardo, L. (1942). *La Albufera de Valencia*. Instituto Forestal de Investigaciones v Experiencas, Madrid, Anno XIII, No. 24.

Paris, P. (1910). *Promenades Archéologiques en Espagne*, Paris.

Parr, C. (ed.) (1952). *The Theodosian Code*. Princeton University Press, Princeton.

Partner, P. (1967). Notes on the lands of the Roman church in the early Middle Ages. *Papers of the British School at Rome* **XXXV,** 68–78.

Partner, P. (1972). *The Lands of St. Peter*. Eyre-Methuen, London.

Paulet, M. (1959). Les plantes aromatiques des garrigues languedociennes. *Annales de la Société d'Horticulture et l'Histoire Naturelle de l'Hérault* Année **98,** 89–115.

Pecora, A. (1960). Manfredonia e il suo territorio. *Rivista Geografica Italiana* **67,** 237–267.

Perez, J. A. (1975). Los yacimientos prehistoricos de la albufera de Anna (Valencia). *XIII Congresso National de Arqueologia*, 191–196.

Perez, J. T. (1958). El poblamiento antiguo de la Huerta de Murcia *Estudios Geograficos* (Madrid) **73,** 465–486.

Peri, I. (1962). Grigenti, porto di sale e del grano. In *Studi in Onone di A. Fanfani* **I,** 529–617, Giuffre, Milan.

Perry, D. T. (1967). Economy, landscape and society in La Castagniccia (Corsica) since the late eighteenth century. *Transactions of the Institute of British Geographers* **41,** 209–221.

Pesche, G. (1957). *Nora, Guida agli Scavi*. Cocco, Cagliari.

Pesche, G. (1960). *Sardegna Punica*. Sarda Fossataro, Cagliari.

✓Phillips, P. (1975). *Early Farmers of West Mediterranean Europe*. Hutchinson, London.

Piggot, S. (1965). *Ancient Europe*. Edinburgh University Press, Edinburgh.

Pinna, M. (1969). Le variazioni del clima in epoca storica e i loro effetti sulla vita e le attività umane. Un tentivo di sintesi. *Bollettino della Società Geografica Italiana* **X,** 198–275.

Pinot, J. P. (1974). *Le Précontinent Breton.* Impram, Lannion.

Pirazzoli, P. A. (1973). *Inondations et niveaux marins à Venise.* Mémoires du Laboratoire de Géomorphologie de l'Ecole Pratique des Hautes Etudes, 22, Dinard.

Pirazzoli, P. A. (1976a). *Les Variations du Niveau Marin dépuis 2000 ans.* Mémoires du Laboratoire de Géomorphologie de l'Ecole Pratique des Hautes Etudes, 30, Dinard.

Pirazzoli, P. A. (1976b). Sea level variation in the north-eastern Mediterranean during Roman times. *Science* **194,** 519–521.

Pitt-Rivers, J. A. (1954). *The People of the Sierra.* Weidenfeld and Nicolson, London.

Planchais, N., Renault-Miskovsky, J. and Vernet, J. L. (1977). Les facteurs d'évolution de la végétation dans le Sud-Est de la France—côte à moyenne montagne—depuis le Tardi-glaciaire, d'après l'analyse pollinique et les charbons de bois. In *Approche Ecologique de l'Homme Fossile* (H. Laville and J. Renault-Miskovsky, eds), pp. 323–328. Bulletin de l'Association Française pour l'Etude du Quaternaire, Supplement 47, Paris.

Platter, F. and Th. (1892). *Félix et Thomas Platter à Montpellier 1552–1559–1595–1599* Société des Bibliophiles de Montpellier 1892; in English published as *The Journal of a Younger Brother, the life of Thomas Platter as a medical student in Montpellier at the close of the sixteenth century.* Translated by S. Jennet, Muller, London (1963).

Polunin, O. and Huxley, A. (1965). *Flowers of the Mediterranean.* Chatto and Windus, London.

Poppe, D. (1966). Saint-Christol à l'époque Medieval. *Cahiers du Centre d'études des Societés Mediterranéennes* **I,** 7–33, Aix-en-Provence.

Porzio, C. (1595–1597). Relazione del Regno di Napoli al Marchese di Mondescia, Vicere di Napoli tra il 1577 ed il 1575. In *La Congiura de Baroni del Regno di Napoli contra il re Ferdinando Primo* etc. (E. Pontiere, ed.). Esl. Naples 1958.

Potter, T. W. (1976a). *A Faliscan Town in Southern Etruria: Excavations at Narce 1966–71.* British School at Rome, London.

Potter, T. W. (1976b). Valleys and settlement: some new evidence. *World Archaeology* **8,** 2, 207–219.

Pounds, N. J. G. (1974). *An Economic History of Medieval Europe.* Longman, London.

Powell, J. M. (1971). *The Liber Augustalis.* Syracuse University Press, New York.

Powell, S. C. (1964). *Puritan Village: the formation of a New England town.* Wesleyan University Press, Middletown.

Prades, H. (1973). *Les Terramares Melgoriens.* Groupe Archéologique Painlévé, Montpellier.

Prades, H. *et al.* (1967). La colonisation antique des rivages lagunaires du Languedoc. *Rivista di Studi Liguri* **33**, 110–130.

Previté-Orton, C. W. (1926). The Italian cities till *c.*1200. In *Contest of Empire and Papacy* Cambridge Medieval History V, pp. 208–241. Cambridge University Press, Cambridge (reprinted 1968).

Puglisi, S. M. (1959). *La Civiltà Appenninica: Origine delle communità pastorali in Italia.* Florence.

Pullé, G. (1915). La pastorizia nella Campagna Romana. *Rivista Geograpaliana* **22**, 490–501.

Putzulu, E. (1967). Il periodo aragones. In *La Società in Sardegna nei Secoli* E.R.I. Turin, 139–162.

Puxeddu, C. (1975). La Romanizzazione. In *Diocesi di Ales-Usellus-Terralba: aspettie valori.* Sarda Fossataro, Cagliari, 165–220.

Quaini, M. (1973). *Per la storia del paesaggio agrario in Liguria.* Camera di commercio industria, Savona.

Rainey, F. G. and Lerici, C. M. (1967). *The Search for Sybaris 1960–65.* Lerici, Rome, 2 vols.

Randsborg, K. (1975). Social dimensions of Early Neolithic Denmark. *Proceedings of the Prehistoric Society* **41**, 105–118.

Raper, R. A. (1977). The analysis of the urban structure of Pompeii: a sociological examination of land-use (semi-micro). In *Spatial Archaeology* (D. L. Clarke, ed.), pp. 189–221. Academic Press, London and New York.

Rasmussen, H. (1969). Grain harvest and threshing in Calabria. *Tools and Tillage* **I**, (2), 93–104.

Rausell, Boizas, H. (1974). Importacion de cereales mediante "ajudes" en la Valencia del primer cuarto del siglo XV, *Estudis* Universidad de Valencia **2**, 13–34.

Rausell, Boizas, H., Guillot Valls, D., Llop Catela, M. and Belenguer Cebria, V. E. (1974). Movimento secular de las importaciones trigueras del siglo XV mediante las "ayudas de la cuidad de Valencia". *Estudis* Universidad de Valencia, **2**, 5–95.

Ravis-Giordani, G. (1974). Typologie et répartition micro-régionale des araires Corse. *Etudes Corses* **3**, 43–73.

Reale Academia delle Scienze e delle Belle Lettere di Napoli (1784). *Istoria de 'Fenomeni del tremoto avvenuto nelle Calabria, e nel Valdemone nell'anno 1783*, Naples.

Reclus, E. *The Earth and its Inhabitants* (E. G. Ravenstein, ed.). Appleton, New York (undated), 2 vols.

Reille, M. (1975). *Contribution pollenanalytique à l'histoire tardiglaciaire et holocène de la végétation de la montagne corse.* em'Etat University of Aix—Marseille, 2 vols.

Reille, M. (1976). Histoire de la végétation de la montagne corse depuis le Tardiglaciaire. In *La Préhistoire Française* I, C.N.R.S. Paris.

Renault-Miskovsky, J. (1971). Analyse pollinique des sédiments post-glaciaires de l'abri de Chateauneuf-les-Martigues (Bouches-Rhone) *Bulletin de l'Association Française pour l'Etude du Quaternaire* I 33–46.

Renouard, Y. (1935–1936). Une éxpédition de céréales des Pouilles en Arménie par les Bardi pour le compte de Benoît XII. *Mélanges d'Archéologie et d'Histoire* 52–53, 287–329.

Renucci, J. (1974). *Corse Traditionnelle et Corse Nouvelle.* Audin, Lyon.

Ripoll Perello, E. (1973). *Ampurias: Itinerary Guide.* Diputacion Provincial de Barcelona, Barcelona.

Riquet, R. (1976). L'Anthropoligie protohistorique francaise. In *La Préhistoire Française* II (J. Guilaine, ed.), pp. 135–152. CNRS Paris.

Roth, A. and Conges, G. (1976). Un dépôtoir à l'étang de Diane. *Sites Préhistoriques et protohistoriques de l'Ile de Corse* (J. Jehasse and R. Grosjean, eds) 119–1–3, Livret-guide de l'excursion, Union Internationale des Sciences Préhistoriques et Protohistoriques, IXème Congrès, à Nice.

Rother, K. (1968). Die Albaner in Suditalien *Mitteilungen der Österreichischen Geographischen Gesellschaft* Band 110, Heft I, 1–20.

Rossello Verger, V. M. (1972). Los rios Jucar y Turia en la genesis de la Albufera de Valencia *Saitabi*, Revista de la Faculdad de Filosofia y Letras, University of Valencia, XXII, 129–147.

Rossello, Verger, V. M. (1975). El medio geografico-geologico dels Estanys de Almenara y su habitat arqueologico. *Cuadernos de Prehistoria y Arqueologia Castellones*, 2, 14–21. Diputacion Provinciale de Castellon de la Plana, Departmento de Arqueologia.

RosselloVerger, V. M. (1976). Evolution récente de l'Albufera de Valencia et de ses environs. *Méditerranée* **4**, 19–30.

Rostovtzeff, M. I. (1957). *The Social and Economic History of the Roman Empire* (revised by P. M. Fraser). Clarendon Press, Oxford, 2 vols.

Rostow, W. W. (1975). *How it all Began: origins of the modern economy.* Methuen, London.

Roudil, J. L. (1972). *L'Age du Bronze en Languedoc Oriental* Mémoires de la Société Préhistorique Française, 10, Lkinckseich, Paris.

Roudil, J. L. and Canet, J. (1977). Les villages en pierres sèches du Languedoc oriental. In *Approche Ecologique de l'Homme Fossile* (H. Laville and J. Renault-Miskovsky, eds), pp. 371–382. Bulletin de l'Association Française pour l'Etude du Quaternaire, 47, Paris.

Roux, I. and Leroi-Gourhan, A. (1964). Les défrichements de la période Atlantique. *Bulletin de la Société Préhistorique Française* **LXI**, 309–315.

P

Rouquette, P. (1913). *La Transhumance des Troupeaux en Provence et en Bas-Languedoc.* Thèse de Droit, University of Montpellier, Firman and Moutane, Montpellier.

Rovira I Port, J. (1976). El neolitic a la Cerdanya i Alta vall del Serge. *Cypsela,* Diputacion Provincial de Gerona, Servicio de Investigaciones Arqueologicas, 39–48.

Rovira I Port, J. (1976). Eneolithic i edat del bronze a la Cerdanya i Alta Vall del Segre. *ibid,* 61–68.

Russell, J. C. (1958). Late ancient and medieval population. *Transactions of the American Philosophical Society Philadelphia* **43,** No. 3.

Russell, J. C. (1972). *Medieval Regions and their Cities.* David and Charles, Newton Abbot.

Russell, R. J. (1942). Geomorphology of the Rhone Delta. *Annals of the Association of American Geographers* **32** (2) 149–254.

Russi, V. (1967). ''Casalenovum'' *Notiziario Storico-Archeologico* Centro di Studi, San Severo, 3–13.

Russi, V. (1972). Insediamenti medievali in territorio di San Severo (Foggia). *Notiziario Storico-Archeologico* Centro di Studi, San Severo, 3–21.

Russi, V. (1976). Nuove scoperti in Capitanata. *Notiziario di Archeologia Medievale,* Centro Li gure per la Storia della Ceramica, Genoa.

Rykmert, J. (1976). *The Idea of a Town: The Anthropology of Urban Form in Rome, Italy and the Ancient World.* Faber, London.

Sahlins, M. (1965). On the sociology of primitive exchange. In *The Relevance of Models for Social Anthropology* (M. Banton, ed.), Vol. I, pp. 139–236. A.S.A. Monographs, Tavistock, London.

Salmon, E. T. (1969). *Roman Colonisation under the Republic.* Thames and Hudson, London.

Salmon, N. (1964). *La Campagne de Nouvelle Castille à la fin du XVI siècle d'après les Relaciones topograficas.* S.E.V.P.E.N. Paris.

Sanchez-Albornoz, C. (1963). The frontier and Castilian liberties. In *The New World Looks at its History* (A. R. Lewis and T. F. McGann, eds). Austin 25–46.

Sarfatti, G. (1953). Considerazione e ricerche botaniche sui pascoli del Tavoliere di Foggia. *Annali della Facoltà di Agraria,* University of Bari, VII, 1–28.

Savory, H. N. (1968). *Spain and Portugal: the prehistory of the Iberian peninsula.* Thames and Hudson, London.

Schlicher von Bath, B. H. (1963). *The Agrarian History of Western Europe 500–1850.* Arnold, London.

Schmiedt, G. (1964). *Contribution of photo interpretation to the reconstruction of the geographic-topographic situation of ancient ports in Italy.* Paper for the 10th Congress of International Photogrammetry, Lisbon; Istituto Geografico Militare, Florence.

Schmiedt, G. (1965). Antichi porti d'Italia *L'Universo* XLV (2), 224–274.

Sclaffert, T. (1959). *Cultures en Haute-Provence: déboisements et pâturages au Moyen Age.* S.E.V.P.E.N., Paris.

Segret, M. and Riu, M. (1969). Una villa señorial Catalana en el siglo XV: Sant Llorenç de Morunys. *Annuario de Estudios Medievales* **6,** 345–379.

Ségui, E. (1946). La guerre aux chèvres sous l'Ancien Régime. *Cahiers d'Histoire et d'Archéologie* Nîmes, 11–21.

Semple, E. C. (1932). *The Geography of the Mediterranean Region. Its Relation to Ancient History.* Constable, London.

Sherwin White, A. N. (1966). A synoptic view of Republican Italy (review of Hannibal's Legacy, A. Toynbee 1965). *The Oxford Magazine* 447–448.

Shneidman, J. (1970). *The Rise of the Aragonese-Catalan Empire 1200–1350.* University Press, New York, 2 vols.

Small, A. (ed.) (1977). *Monte Irsi, Southern Italy: the Canadian excavations in the Iron Age and Roman sites 1971–1972.* Supplementary Series 20, British Archaeological Reports, Oxford.

Smith, R. S. (1966). Spain: agricultural and pastoral pursuits. In *The Agrarian Life of the Middle Ages.* (2nd edition), Cambridge Economic History (M. Postan ed.) Vol. I. Cambridge University Press, Cambridge.

Soboul, A. (1958). *La Campagne Montpelliéraine à la fin de l'Ancien Régime.* Thesis, University of Paris, Presses Universitaires de France, Paris.

Sorgia, G. (1967). Il periodo spagnola. In *La Società in Sardegna nei Secoli,* 163–180, E. R. I. Turin.

Sorgia, G. (1972). Note sui provvedimenti a favore dell'agricoltura Sarda nella seconda meta del secoli XVI. In *Medievo eta'Moderna: Saggi in Onore del Prof. Alberto Boscolo,* 149–170, Sarda Fossatara, Cagliari.

Sorre, M. (1913). *Les Pyrénées Méditerranéennes.* Colin, Paris.

Spano, B., (1954). La pesca di stagno in Sardegna. *Bollettino della Societa Geografica Italiana* **41,** 462–496.

Spano, B. and Pinna, M. (1956). *Le Spiagge della Sardegna.* Centro di studi per la Geografia Fisica, University of Bologna, Bologna.

Spola, V. (1953). Documenti del secolo XV relativi alla Dogana di Foggia. *Archivio Storico Pagliese* **VI,** 130–182.

Stanley, D. J. (ed.) (1972). *The Mediterranean Sea. A Natural Sedimentation Laboratory.* Dowden, Hutchinson and Ross, Stroudsbury.

Stevens, C. E. (1966). Agriculture and rural life in the Later Roman Empire. In *The Agrarian Life of the Middle Ages* (2nd edition). Cambridge Economic History, (M. M. Postan ed.), Vol. I, pp. 92–124. Cambridge University Press, Cambridge.

Stiesdal, H. (1962). Three deserted medieval villages in the Roman Campagna. *Analecta Romana* **ii,** 63–100.

432 REFERENCES

Stoddard, D. R. (1969). World erosion and sedimentation. In *Water, Earth and Man* (R. J. Chorley, ed.), pp. 43–66. Methuen, London.

Sunyer, J. C. (1963). El molino de Armentera. *Anales del Instituto d'Estudios Ampurdanes*, Figueras, 113–122.

Swinburne, H. (1779). *Travels through Spain in the years 1775 and 1776 etc.* London.

Swinburne, H. (1783–1785). *Travels in the two Sicilies in the years 1777, 1778, 1779 and 1780.* Elmsly, London, 2 vols.

Swinburne, H. (1787). *Travels through Spain . . . The second edition; to which is added, a Journey from Bayonne to Marseilles.* Elmsly, London, 2 vols.

Symons, L. (1968). *Agricultural Geography.* Bell, London.

Tangheroni, M. (1972). Su un contrasto tra feudatari in Sardegna nei primissimi tempi della dominazione aragonese. In *Medioevo Eta'Moderna Saggi in Onore del Prof. Alberto Boscolo*, pp. 85–100. Sarda Fossatara, Cagliari.

Tardieu (1860). *La Commune d'Arles et le droit d'Esplèche.* Arles.

Tarradell, M. and Sanchis i Guarner M. (1975). *Historia del Pais Valencia*, Part I Preistoria i Antiguitat (M. Tarradell). Part II Epoca Musulmana (M. Sanchis i Guarner) Barcelona (2nd edition).

Tchou, Y. (1948). Etudes écologiques et phytosociologiques sur les forêts riveraines du Bas-Languedoc. *Vegetatio* I, 217–257.

Temple, P. (1936). La préhistoire du département de l'Aveyron. *Cahiers d'Histoire et d'Archéologie*, Nimes.

Tennant, R. (1885). *Sardinia and its Resources.* Stanford, London and Spithöver, Rome.

Termier, H. and Termier, G. (1961). *La Trame Géologique de l'Histoire.* Masson, Paris.

Terresu Asole, A. (1960). Osservazioni preliminari sull'insediamento costiero nel Lazio. *Bollettino della Societa Geografica Italiana* IX (1) 401–445.

Terresu Asole, A. (1974). L'insediamento umano medioevale e i centri abbandonati tra il secolo XIV ed il secolo XVII. *Atlante della Sardegna* Supplement to fac. II, Rome.

Ters, M. (1977). Le déplacement de la ligne de rivage, au cours de l'Holocène, le long de la cote atlantique française. In *Approche Ecologique de l'Homme Fossile* (H. Laville and J. Renault-Miskovsky, eds), pp. 179–182. Bulletin de l'Association Francaise pour l'Etude du Quanternaire, Supplement 47, Paris.

Thiel, J. H. (1954). *A History of Roman Sea-power before the Second Punic War.* North-Holland, Amsterdam.

Thirsk, J. (1964). The common fields. *Past and Present* 29, 3–25.

Thom, R. (1969). Topological models in biology. *Topology* 8, 313–335.

Thom, R. (1975). *Structural Stability and Morphogenesis.* Reading, Mass., 1–11.

Thomas, E. (1865). *Dictionnaire Topographique du Département de l'Hérault*. Dictionnaire Topographique de la France, VI.

Thornes, J. (1974). Devastation in Almeria. *The Geographical Magazine* **XLVI** (7), 337–343.

Tinè, S. (1975). La Cività Neolitica del Tavoliere. *Civiltà Preistoriche e Protostoriche della Daunia*. Atti del Colloquio Internazionale Foggia 1973, 99–111, Florence.

Tinè, S. and Tinè, F. (1969). In *La Magna Grecia e Roma nell'eta arcaica* 233–241, Atti dell-Ottavo Convegno di Studi sulla Magna Grecia, Taranto, Naples.

Tomassetti, G. (1910–1926). *La Campagna Romana: antica, medioevo, moderna* Rome, 4 vols.

Touring Club Italiano (1958). *La Flora*. Conosci l'Italia, II, Milan.

Townsend, J. (1791). *Journey through Spain in the years 1786–1787*. C. Dilly, London, 3 vols.

Toynbee, A. (1965). *Hannibal's Legacy: the Hannibalic War's Effects on Roman Life*. Oxford University Press, London, 2 vols.

Tramonte, R. (1949). *Irrigazione in Puglia*. Conferenze avolte nella Facolta d'Agraria e d'Ingegneria, University of Bari, Bari.

Trinchera, F. (1865). *Syllabus Graecorum Membranorum*. Naples.

Trump, D. H. (1966). *Central and Southern Italy before Rome*. Thames and Hudson, London.

U.A.M. (1974). *Estudios sobre centuriaciones Romanos en Espana*. Universidad Autonoma de Madrid, Cantoblanco.

Ucko, P. J., Tringham R., and Dimbleby, G. W. (1972). *Man, Settlement and Urbanism*. Proceedings of a meeting of the Research Seminar on Archaeology and Related Subjects, Duckworth, London.

Van Cleve, T. C. (1972). *The Emperor Frederick II of Hohenstaufen*. Clarendon Press, Oxford.

Vaquer, J. (1976). Gisements néolithiques en Cerdagne. *Cypsela* 36–38, Dipatacion Provincale de Gerona, Servicio de Investigaciones Arqueologicas, Gerona.

Vardobasso, S. (1939). L'industria mineraria in Sardegna. In *Sardegna Romana* (A. Taramelli *et al.*, eds.), Vol. II, pp. 19–38. Istituto di Studi Romani, Rome.

Vaudour, J. (1972). Chronique de pédologie méditerranéenne. *Méditerranée* **9,** 117–127.

Vaudour, J. (1975). Encroûtements, croûtes et carapaces calcaires dans la région de Madrid. *Méditerranée* **2,** 39–59.

Verga, G. (1883). *Novelle Rusticane* translated by D. H. Lawrence as *Little Novels of Sicily*. Blackwell, Oxford, 1925.

Vicens-Vives, J. (1969). *An Economic History of Spain*. Princeton University Press, Princeton, N.J.

Vicens-Vives, J. (1961). *Historia de España* y America Vicens-Vives, Barcelona, 5 vols.

Vidal de la Blache, P. and Gallois, L. (eds) (1934). Italie. In *Géographie Universelle* VII, Méditerranée, Péninsules Mediterranéennes. Colin , Paris.

Vilar, P. (1967). L'exploitation agricole d'une propriété dans l'horta de Tarraga. In *Homenaje a Jaime Vicens-Vives* Vol. II, 761–783.

Vita-Finzi, C. (1966). The new Elysian fields. *American Journal of Archaeology* **70,** 175–178.

Vita-Finzi, C. (1969). *The Mediterranean valleys: Geological changes in historical time*. Cambridge University Press, Cambridge.

Vita-Finzi, C. (1972). Supply of fluvial sediment to the Mediterranean during the last 20,000 years. In *The Mediterranean Sea* (D. J. Stanley, (ed.), pp. 43–46. Dowden, Hutchinson and Ross, Stroudsbury.

Wace, A. J. B. and Thompson, M. S. (1914). *Nomads of the Balkans*. Methuen, London (reprinted 1972).

Wagstaff, J. M. (1976). *Aspects of Land Use in Melos: a report on a project financed by the Social Sciences Research Council and the Frederick Soddy Trust*. Department of Geography, University of Southampton.

Wagstaff, M. (1978). Settlement patterns and Catastrophe theory. *Transactions of the Institute of British Geographers* **3,** 165–178.

Ward Perkins, J. (1961). Veii. The historical topography of the ancient city. *Papers of the British School at Rome* **XXIX,** 1–123.

Ward Perkins, J. (1962). Etruscan towns, Roman roads and medieval villages: the historical geography of southern Etruria. *The Geographical Journal* **128,** 389–405.

Ward Perkins, J. (1964). Landscape and history in central Italy. *Second J. L. Myres Memorial Lecture*. Blackwell, Oxford.

Ward Perkins, J. (1970). Monterosi in the Etruscan and Roman periods. In *Ianula: an account of the history and development of the Lago di Monterosi, Latium, Italy* (G. E. Hutchinson, ed.) pp. 10–12. Transactions of the American Philosophical Society, LX(4).

Ward Perkins, J. (1972). Central authority and patterns of rural settlement. In *Man, Settlement and Urbanism* (Ucko, P. J. *et al*, eds), pp. 867–882. Duckworth, London.

Ward Perkins, J. (1974). *Cities of ancient Greece and Italy: Planning in Classical Antiquity*. Braziller, New York.

Whitaker, J. I. S. (1921). *Motya: a Phoenician colony in Sicily*. Bell, London.

White, K. D. (1963). Wheat farming in Roman times. *Antiquity* **37,** 208–212.

White, K. D. (1965). The productivity of labour in Roman agriculture *Antiquity* **39,** 102–107.

White, K. D. (1967a). Latifundia: a critical review of the evidence. *Bulletin of the Institute of Classical Studies of the University of London* **XIV,** 62–79.

White, K. D. (1967b). *Agricultural Implements of the Roman World*. Cambridge University Press, Cambridge.

White, K. D. (1970). *Roman Farming*. Thames and Hudson, London.

Whitehouse, D. (1970). Excavations at Satriano: a deserted medieval settlement in Basilicata. *Papers of the British School at Rome* **XXV**, 189–219.

Whitehouse, D. (1973). Sedi medievali nella Campagna Romana: la "domusculta" e il villaggio fortificato *Quaderni Storici* **24**, 861–876.

Whitehouse, R. (1968a). The early Neolithic of southern Italy. *Antiquity* **42**, 188–193.

Whitehouse, R. (1968b). Settlement and economy in southern Italy in the neothermal period. *Proceedings of the Prehistoric Society* **34**, 332–367.

Whitehouse, R. (1974). Prehistoric settlement on the Tavoliere, Italy: a comment. *Proceedings of the Prehistoric Society* **40**, 203.

Whitehouse, R. (1978). Italian prehistory, carbon 14 and the tree-ring calibration. In *Papers in Italian Archaeology I: The Lancaster Seminar* (H. M. Blake, T. W. Potter and D. B. Whitehouse, eds), pp. 71–91. British Archaeological Reports, Supplementary Series 41.

Whittlesey, D. (1936). Major agricultural regions of the earth *Annals of the Association of American Geographers* **26**, 199–240.

Willey, G. R. (1973). Man, Settlement and Urbanism: a review. *Antiquity* **XLVII**, 269–279.

Wolf, E. R. (1966). *Peasants*. Prentice-Hall, Englewood Cliffs, N.J.

Wolff, P. (1951). Trois études de démographie médiévale en France méridionale *Studi in Onore di Amando Sapori* **I**, 493–503, Milan.

Young, D. (1886). *Rome in Winter and the Tuscan Hills in Summer: A contribution to the climate of Italy*. K. Lewis, London.

Zeeman, E. C. (1976). Catastrophe Theory. *Scientific American* **234** (4), 65–83.

Index

Figures in *italics* refer to pages with illustrations

Languedoc, 23, 64, 84, 283, 285, 299,
312, 364, 366, 387
agriculture, 208–209, 216, 249
charcoal burning, 303–304
estates, 99, 108, 136
Etats, 225
house-types, 47, 55, 57
population, 8, 13, 107, 295
prehistoric settlement, 286, 287,
290, 269
settlement, 59, 40
Lansargues, 285, *289*, 290, 341–352,
343, *350*, 378, 384, 391
Latifundia, 51, 98–104, 249, 395, *see
also* Estates
Latium, 212, 339
Lattes (*Lattara*), 136–137, 342, 364,
378–382, *380*, *381*, 383
Le Vigan, 299
Lébous, 71
Leon, 36, 92
Lesina
Count of, 118
Lago di, 388
Les Matelles, 40, 304
Leucate, lagoon, 289–290
Lez, river, 137, 347, 378–282 *passim*
Liber Focorum, *see* Pistoia
Liguria, 59, 112, 183, 208, 210, *211*,
390
Little Ice Age, 314, 321, 353, 358
Livestock, 25, 30, 47, 55, 68, 98, 132,
223, 226, 230, 231, 234, 246,
254, 265, 266, 296–297, 316,
397 n.4, *see also* Animals
farms, farming, *11*, *54*, 55, 192,
228
Locatione, *247*, 248
Locust, plagues, 203
Lodève, 107
Lombards, 52, 112
Lombardy, 112, 179, 207, 209, 386

Los Millares, 71
Lucania, 100, 101, 161, 166, 278, 283
Lucca, *132*, 134, 311
Lucera, 43, 66, 142, *143*
Saracen colony, 119–120, 229, 241
Lunel, *289*, 342

M
Madrid, 35, 118, 135
Mailhacian, culture, 283, 342, 343,
347–351 *passim*, 384
Maize, 136, 206, 207, 208–209
Malaga, 330
Malaria, 59, 107, 191, 207, 384–388
Mallorca, 145
Malpaga, 117
Manfredonia, 329, 390
Bay of, 336, 355, 358
Manors, manorialization, 77, 88, 111
Mantua, 52
Manure, manuring, 58, 81, 131, 197,
213, 219, 224, 226, 236, 294
Marana di Lupara, *356*, 357
Marche, 267
Maremma, 138, 305, 339, 385
Market gardening, Roman, 140–142
passim
Markets, 22, 26, 82, 140
Marsala (Lilibeum), 361
Marseilles (*Massilia*), 121, 195, 209,
225, 296, 330, 360–361, *360*,
362, 364–365, 366, 375–378,
376, *377*, *379*, *380*
Marsh, marshland, 107, 289, 290,
308, 342, 354–356 *passim*,
375, 384–388 *passim*
Marsillargues, 107
Mas, 52, 55–56, 58, 85, 115, *see also*
Settlement
Mas d'Azil, 194, 285, 287
Masseria, 39, 52, *54*, 58, 59, 115, 225,
248, *see also* Settlement